SOAS Studies on South Asia: Understandings and Perspectives

The Concept of Race in South Asia

SOAS Studies on South Asia

Terence J. Byres, ed., *The State and Development Planning in India*
Terence J. Byres, ed., *The State, Development Planning and Liberalisation in India*
Indira Chowdhury, *The Frail Hero and Virile History: Gender and the Politics of Culture in Colonial Bengal*
Nigel Crook, *India's Industrial Cities: Essays in Economy and Demography*
Dagmar Engels, *Beyond Purdah? Women in Bengal, 1890-1930*
Michael Hutt, ed., *Nepal in the Nineties*
Sudipta Kaviraj, *The Unhappy Consciousness: Bankim Chandra Chattopadhyay and the Formation of Nationalist Discourse in India*
William Radice, *Swami Vivekananda and the Modernization of Hinduism*
Peter Robb, ed., *Dalit Movements and the Meanings of Labour in India*
Peter Robb, ed., *Rural India: Land, Power and Society under British Rule*
Peter Robb, ed., *Society and Ideology: Essays in South Asian History*
Ujjwal K. Singh, *Political Prisoners in India*
Burton Stein and Sanjay Subrahmanyam, eds., *Institutions and Economic Change in South Asia*

SOAS Studies on South Asia: Understandings and Perspectives

Peter Robb, ed., *Meanings of Agriculture: Essays in South Asian History and Economics*
Nigel Crook, ed., *Transmission of Knowledge in South Asia: Essays on Education, Religion and Politics*
C. J. Fuller, *Caste Today*
Michael Anderson and Sumit Guha, eds., *Changing Concepts of Rights Justice in South Asia*
Daud Ali ed., *Invoking the Past: The Uses of History in South Asia* (forthcoming)

SOAS South Asian Texts Series

Christopher Shackle and Javed Majeed, *Hali's Musaddas: The Ebb and Flow of Islam*
Michael Hutt, *Modern Literary Nepali: An Introduction*

SOAS Studies on South Asia
Understandings and Perspectives Series

The Concept of Race in South Asia

edited by

Peter Robb

OXFORD
UNIVERSITY PRESS

OXFORD
UNIVERSITY PRESS

Oxford University Press is a department of the University of Oxford.
It furthers the University's objective of excellence in research, scholarship,
and education by publishing worldwide. Oxford is a registered trademark of
Oxford University Press in the UK and in certain other countries

Published in India by
Oxford University Press
YMCA Library Building, 1 Jai Singh Road, New Delhi 110001, India

First Edition published in 1995
Oxford India Paperbacks 1997
Sixth impression 2015

ISBN-13: 978-0-19-564268-1
ISBN-10: 0-19-564268-6

CRC prepared in the Centre of South Asia Studies
SOAS, University of London

SOUTH ASIA: UNDERSTANDINGS AND PERSPECTIVES
GENERAL EDITOR'S INTRODUCTION

The present volume forms part of a project sponsored by the School of Oriental and African Studies, University of London, and initiated during my tenure as chairman of the SOAS Centre of South Asian Studies. It involves many members and associates of the Centre. The intention is to take a number of important terms or concepts, and to discuss each one's different meanings. In each case a volume will be prepared comprising a critical introduction to sum up and reflect upon the state of our knowledge of this concept, plus a number of illustrative essays containing their own analysis, which may or may not agree with that of the introduction. The essays are also intended to be fairly detailed and empirical in emphasis, so as to stand in regard to the introduction in something of the relationship of evidence to interpretation. The project is directed both at specific problems and at a number of fundamental debates on the nature of discourse; and yet it is not intended primarily to generate new theory but rather to make its contribution by approaching questions from a new direction.

Part of the dissatisfaction which lies behind the project is with Eurocentric terminology. This is not because we deny the possibility of there being any universal terms, nor because we think all knowledge produced by Europeans essentially the same and equally corrupted by power. It is because we are impressed by the need to avoid all essentialism, and by the importance, both intellectually and in practical situations, of an appreciation of difference. It is because we are uncertain how larger categories may properly be constructed. Similar concerns are expressed in various ways in many disciplines, and constitute a crisis of interpretation.

We want to start with detailed and concrete studies. Part of our question is: what is it that constitutes 'South Asian' perceptions? We do not think there is—that is, that anyone can provide—an adequate answer to this question as a whole. Moreover we do not intend our work to be merely comparative, especially not between South Asia and

Europe as if the latter were a yardstick. Though we will investigate the question, we are not at all sure that there *are* peculiarly South Asian perceptions, as a type, and we are as interested in differences within the region and over time as in discrepancies between the terminology of our disciplines and that of its subjects. On this basis, we think it worthwhile, with regard to concepts in frequent and often uncritical use, to examine the different meanings they have, and then reflect upon the differences. The exercise can be substantive rather than terminological. We question whether the 'virtual reality' of our studies bears any close relation to the complexities of its subjects. We think we can get closer, provided we work with small components. We do so not to be restricted to them out of context, but to use them to focus on larger issues.

Peter Robb
School of Oriental and African Studies, London

PREFACE

India always played a part in the European imagining of race, but has not been much considered in the scholarly literature of the present generation; nor, recently, have concepts of race figured very prominently in South Asian studies. This volume constitutes one of the first attempts to raise the question comparatively and over a long time-span with regard to South Asia. It seeks to open up an important new field of inquiry.

The volume arose from a suggestion by Michael Dwyer, which fitted with an upsurge of interest in this topic, and with my invitation to Kenneth Ballhatchet to deliver the 1992 Annual Lecture of the Centre of South Asian Studies at the School of Oriental and African Studies (SOAS) in London. The volume includes the text of that lecture, though it was never delivered, sadly, because of the illness of Professor Ballhatchet. Nor was he able to revise the essay; but I have included it as it stood because, though concerned with problems of historiography and not directly about race, it raises some of the underlying issues in an important and interesting way.

The remainder of the volume comprises a selection of papers from a SOAS workshop held in London in December 1992 plus some specially-commissioned essays. My introduction attempts an extended survey of the subject as discussed here. There are nine other papers of differing scope. Some cover specific aspects quite briefly, but others, especially Susan Bayly's essay, range widely over a broad field. There are three major themes: 'race' elements in 'traditional' South Asian thinking (Brockington on Sanskrit epics; Hellmann-Rajanayagam on Tamil identity; Rogers on Sri Lanka), the nature of Western racial ideas as applied to South Asia (Bates on anthropometry, Bayly on caste, Caplan on 'martial' Gurkhas), and modern South Asian responses to race theory (Chowdhury-Sengupta on Bengal nationalists, Majeed on Iqbal, Jaffrelot on Hindu ideologists). Several of the papers touch on more than one of these themes.

I am grateful to the many participants and helpers at the original workshop, to the SOAS Research Committee for financial assistance, and to Janet Marks in the Centre of South Asian Studies, for the preparation of the camera-ready copy. Transliteration, citation and other conventions have not been standardised between papers from different disciplines.

P.G.R., London, 1995

I am sorry to have to record the death of Professor K.A. Ballhatchet after this volume went to print, in March 1995.

LIST OF CONTRIBUTORS

Kenneth Ballhatchet	Department of History, SOAS (Professor Emeritus)
Susan Bayly	Christ's College, University of Cambridge
Crispin Bates	Department of History, University of Edinburgh
John Brockington	Department of Sanskrit, University of Edinburgh
Lionel Caplan	Department of Anthropology, SOAS
Indira Chowdhury-Sengupta	Department of English, University of Jadavpur
Dagmar Hellman-Rajanayagam	South Asia Institute, University of Heidelberg
Christophe Jaffrelot	Centre d'Etudes et de Recherches Internationales, Fondation Nationale des Sciences Politiques, Paris
Javed Majeed	Department of the Languages and Cultures of South Asia, SOAS
Peter Robb	Department of History, SOAS
John Rogers	University of Harvard, and Center of South Asian and Indian Ocean Studies, Tufts University

CONTENTS

Chapter 1

SOUTH ASIA AND THE CONCEPT OF RACE

Peter Robb

The title of this book belonged to a workshop held in SOAS in December 1992. It asked whether there were South Asian concepts of race, or whether, as initially seemed likely and often has been argued, 'race' became an issue in the subcontinent only under Western influence after the eighteenth century. This was not a question about all prejudice or all interpretations of the Other. It was an investigation of one form of prejudice, or of the influences upon some of the terms in which the Other could be described. The issues examined included South Asian equivalents of the idea of race, the nature of Western concepts as applied to India during colonial rule, and the origin and type of more recent variants. The papers could be seen as engaging generally with a large and growing body of writing on such issues, embracing studies of the person, identity, civil society, ethnicity, and nationalism.[1]

According to our working definition, the concept of 'race' included any essentialising of groups of people which held them to display inherent, heritable, persistent or predictive characteristics, and which thus had a biological or quasi-biological basis.[2] Difficulties of definition arise because (quite apart from semantic shifts over time) there

[1] Particularly relevant are studies of identity and history, for example H.L. Seneviratne, ed., *Identity, Consciousness and the Past* (special issue of *Social Analysis*, 25; Adelaide, 1989), and Frank Dikötter, *The Discourse of Race in Modern China* (London, 1992) which argues that parts of the historical experience of the Chinese predisposed them to perceive the world after Western expansion in terms of race. Writing this essay, I am indebted to suggestions made, on a draft, by Avril Powell, and by Dikötter, and to ideas expressed by some of those recently participating in SOAS seminars: Susan Bayly, André Béteille, Vasudha Dalmia, Andrew Grout, Kenneth Jones, Dermot Killingley, Pragati Mohapatra, William Pinch, Tapan Raychaudhuri, Glyn Richards, Raymond B. Williams, and many others. See also note 65 below.

[2] Compare Ruth Benedict: racism is the doctrine that 'one ethnic group is destined to congenital superiority'; quoted by John Solomos, *Race and Racism in Britain* (second ed., London, 1993), p.17.

may be different kinds of race theory, reflecting various understandings of biology, history or societies. Ambiguities arise too because categorisation is by definition essentialising, but all essentialising of people is not equally 'racist'. In constructing, say, the type 'table', one has to privilege certain essential features over others which are less or not 'table'; one values, as tables, some sub-sets of 'table' or 'almost table' more than others. The idea of race is a form of this process applied to humans. Although of course humans constitute a single category, plainly we cannot ignore sub-sets, as they exist in politics, culture or sociology. These overlap and over time are eclectic, but at any one point are recognisable, sometimes even objective in terms of power, geography, economy and ideology. This does not mean that we have agreed and satisfactory ways of defining difference. The more complex the organism the more abstract the defining features, and the greater the need for subjective interventions. Racism occurs when characteristics are assumed from generalisations and are not verifiable. Its crucial measures include the degrees of mutability or plurality admitted to exist within categories, and the arbitrariness of their outer limits. But, above all, racism implies a *ranking* according to the biological origins and features already mentioned.

In the nineteenth century specifically racist theories, by this definition, became commonplace in the sense of being almost unwitting as a mode of explanation, held as axiomatic by people who regarded themselves as enlightened, and who were not, in a general sense, particularly prejudiced or irrational. These theories were distinguishable from other Western views of non-Western societies, but joined them in casting a shadow over wide areas of understanding. It was sometimes complete and explicit, and at other times indistinct but nonetheless influential. The theories were, in form, quasi-scientific in that they sought to explain the observable, and did so by means of social analysis or, frequently, empirical physical observations.[3] As particular histories and

[3] Anthropometrical methods of 'establishing' racial identities and groups—which persisted in the mainstream of anthropological writing well into this century—are described by Bates in his essay below. See also Bayly in this volume for discussion of phrenology, cranology and nineteenth-century ethnography. She traces race theory also to linguistic and cultural categorisations of

causations were advanced to account for differences between 'races', individual characteristics were assumed to be, beyond a certain point, extrinsic, shared and immutable. And boundaries that racism created, eugenics would police. Mixtures of category (arguably a source of vigour) came to be regarded as dangerous, feeble or ridiculous—as with 'mulattos', Babus or Company-style art, all of which 'bastard' forms were thought necessarily inferior to their 'purer' equivalents. History too was yoked to this cause, as a *single* progress—in Britain reflected in Whig theories of national superiority, in celebrations of high culture, and in fashionable medievalisms of literature, art and architecture. (The role of *Ivanhoe* as *ur*-race text is well-known.)[4] Indeed purity—of blood, habits and motivation—became a gauge for virtue and legitimacy, even though (as we shall see) it was not crucial to race theory. So too propriety, honour, honesty and duty were all companions of race, either swelling its importance or redefined by it. Part of the tenacity of race theories, as of nationalism and fascism, was explained by this mixture of highmindedness, biological determinism, bigotry, and suppositions of superiority or inferiority in science, technology, military skill, governance and culture.

One precondition for this situation was that qualities were thought to be given rather than achieved, and that perfectability should be expected in terms of linear evolution. Whereas cyclical theories supposed that innovation was necessary to a momentum which went both up and down, the belief in progress implied that only consistency would maintain improvement. Darwinism added a theory of how acquired charac-

---

the eighteenth century. For a resumé of the contributions to European racism of Enlightenment and later thinkers in the new anthropology—Voltaire, Buffon, Hume, Kant, Fichte, Paul Broca—see Léon Poliakov, 'Racism from the enlightenment to the age of imperialism', in Robert Ross, ed., *Racism and Colonialiism. Essays on ideology and social structure* (The Hague, 1982), pp.55-64.

[4] Note that 'Four generations had not sufficed to blend the hostile blood of the Normans and the Anglo-Saxons', those 'great national distinctions'; how blood was associated with 'that independence that was so dear to every English bosom' and with 'rich grassy glades', evocations of ideal landscape; but also, in the end, that the marriage of Rowena and Wilfrid was 'a pledge of future peace and harmony betwixt two races' (a unity of the 'English' similar to that of the 'British' which was in prospect in Scott's own day): Sir Walter Scott, *Ivanhoe* (Melrose edition), pp.1-3 and 388-90.

teristics might be thus inherited, and how a human hierarchy could emerge so as to reflect objectively superior or inferior qualities. The suggestion is not that racism depended on Darwinian theories, but that they provided a helpful gloss and terminology.[5] There are examples of 'racism' well before Darwin: for example, when Lord Hastings referred to the Hindus as beings 'nearly limited to mere animal functions, and even in them indifferent', or Charles Grant to the 'people of Hindostan' as 'a race of men lamentably degenerate and base', or James Mill, in what Stokes aptly called his 'astonishing arraignment', to the 'hideously' low place on the 'scale of civilization' of Indian and Chinese society, to vices, to people 'dissembling, treacherous, mendacious'.[6]

[5] That social evolutionism preceded Darwin has been pointed out by Claude Lévi-Strauss, 'Race and history', in Leo Kuper, ed., *Race, Science and Society* (Paris and London, 1975). In his essay below Bates links Darwin's contribution not only to evolutionism but to a large extension of the supposed duration of mankind's existence. Earlier, both change over time and an extended timespan had been proposed by Buffon in his *Histoire naturelle*; what made his view distinct from later ones was its universalism: insistence on nature's (and time's) 'infinite gradation', and that not all differences were necessarily functional.

[6] See *The Private Journal of the Marquess of Hastings*, vol. 1 (London, 1858), p.32; Charles Grant, 'Observations on the state of society among the Asiatic subjects of Great Britain...' (1797; published as a parliamentary paper in 1813 and 1832) in Mss.Eur.E.93, Oriental and India Office Collections, British Library, London (hereafter OIOC); and Eric Stokes, *The English Utilitarians and India* (Oxford, 1959), esp. pp.24, 29-35 and 47-58. See also the verdict of Macaulay, quoted below by Chowdhury-Sengupta, for its citation of both inherent and environmental short-comings of Indians. But one should contrast this with, say, John Malcolm's *Sketch of the Political History of India...* (London, 1811), which argued that, while assessing his 'Indian prejudices', his English readers would 'do well to recollect that there are also English prejudices: and that those, who never saw a country so distant, and so unlike every thing in Europe, as in India, must acknowledge at least one great inferiority in such discussions' (p.vi). Malcolm also remarked that the 'English Government in India...has been founded in a spirit of attention and respect to the usages and religion of the different tribes in India; nor can it ever be maintained upon any other principles' (p.468)—that is, that there were differences between races, to be respected. He added that the 'advance of the natives of India in every branch of useful knowledge, will be exactly proportionate to the means and examples which we afford them' (pp.475-6)—that is, though Europe had something to offer India, the potential of different races was equal. For convenient accounts of earlier European ambivalence towards India see O.P. Kejariwal, *The Asiatic Society of Bengal and the Discovery of India's Past, 1784-1838* (Delhi, 1988), ch.1; or P.J. Marshall, ed., *The British Discovery of Hinduism in the Eighteenth Century* (Cambridge, 1970), introduction.

But all these archetypical insults drew *inter alia* on the idea of categorising according to innate characteristics, whereby the fashion of Linnæus met with earlier doctrines of nature. India was supposed to be backward and stagnating, either for inherent reasons or for ineluctable ones such as climate. With Darwin, the old dichotomies of civilised/barbarian and cultivated/savage took on new resonances. Evolution, like history, like fiction, provided a moral.

These concepts of race, as is well known, did not apply only to anthropological or ethno-linguistic analyses, but infected whole realms of perception and policy, particularly in the middle and later decades of the nineteenth century. By such reasoning, for example, the Indigo Commission of 1860 was able, gratuitously, to refer to 'well-known defects of the national character of the Bengali; ...his cunning, ...indolence, ...procrastination, and...proneness to concealment'.[7] By the end of the nineteenth century, as in G.W. Steevens' bizarre and repugnant attacks, to which Chowdhury-Sengupta refers in this volume, the denigration clearly implied that by their *appearance* shall they be judged. Even the historian Seeley, discussed in the same paper, though offering an encomium on the intellectual and literary talents of the 'Hindu', bewailed the lack of progress achieved by 'Aryans' in India.[8] These attitudes did not require the term 'race', but that was the word around which they were to gather. The term already had at least three distinct meanings—genus, species or variety; a tribe or nation of people of common stock; and a great division of mankind—and here was another: race as a congeries of attributes.[9]

[7] Report of the Indigo Commission of 1861, reprinted in S.D. Punekar and R. Varickayil, eds, *Labour Movement in India. Documents 1850-1890*, vol. 1 (New Delhi, 1989), p.27. This was a clear echo of Mill's *History*, one which persisted despite the running commentary of qualifications and refutation supplied in footnotes by H.H. Wilson in the edition of 1858 with which the Commission would have been familiar.

[8] As will be shown below, this might be traced *inter alia* to Gobineau.

[9] The O.E.D. dates for the first three definitions are 1596 or 1605, 1600, and 1774 in that order. For 'race' as a 'distinct ethnical group' it proposes 1842. Though as ever it is plain that Shakespeare is acutely interested in confusions of category, it may be significant that Shylock refers to his 'nation' and his 'tribe', and that his daughter, Jessica, after 'escaping' disguised as a boy, can become, by conversion, and through the love of a Christian, a 'Gentile, and no Jew'. In

The very specificity of the ideas of race, and their interdependence with other developments, imply that they arose in a particular place and time. In Europe was fostered that oppression of one people by another which was justified by ideal constructions of nation and race.[10] In Europe were found scientific methods and discoveries, including those of categorisation itself—arguments about the subjectivity of perception, as in Comte, and hence of the varieties and relativities of human experience and knowledge; a belief in progress; and avowedly 'modern' means of recognising and maintaining identified communities. Moreover, in nineteenth-century India, similarly, it was European rule that brought improving communications through print and travel; there was a heightened awareness of the Other through greater contact with Europeans and their culture; there were new ideas of the 'rational', the 'scientific' and the 'modern'; there were reconstructions of the Indian past, and historical categorisations of regions, languages and people. In religion and ethical debate such ideas could take on a 'Reformation' character.[11] It is instructive too how often different or opposed theories

---

Merchant of Venice the term 'race' is reserved for horses (Act V, i: 74) and then is half a pun. See also the paper by Hellmann-Rajanayagam in this volume. For a broader discussion see M. Banton, *The Idea of Race* (London, 1977), which argues, however, that the 'student of race relations must not limit himself to the participants' conception of what was racial' (p.2).

[10] See Ross, *Racism*: 'racist ideologies clearly in part derived from the experience of Europeans in colonising and exploiting the overseas world' (p.2); in the same volume (pp.33-54), Ernst van de Boogaart, 'Colour prejudice and the yardstick of civility: the initial Dutch confrontation with black African, 1590-1635', argues that Dutch racism resulted from slavery—contrary to Winthrop D. Jordan, *White over Black: American attitudes to the Negro, 1550-1812*, who thought racism preceded and endorsed slavery. My suggestion is not that Europe alone invented oppression; but see Paul Gilroy, *The Black Atlantic. Modernity and double consciousness* (London, 1993), for arguments linking British racism to central and not peripheral elements of Western thought—to an illusion of a single national culture (of which a single 'black' culture is now an equally essentialist mirror-image), and to a rationalising and would-be civilising vision which justified colonialism. Of course the reified images were and are real enough in the sense of being fervently believed, immanent and instrumental.

[11] Thus assertions that there was nothing equivalent to traditional Protestantism in Hinduism, carry their own refutation in the very use of the term 'Hinduism'; see N.S. Bose, 'Swami Vivekananda and the challenge to Hinduism', paper given at SOAS, 27 November 1993. Vivekananda, by asserting that 'Hindu'

and administrative expedients of British rule in India depended on explanations of India's perceived precolonial failures: on its supposed lack of private property and individual rights, of social interests or political institutions, of 'normal' moral and economic development.

In these circumstances racial concepts might provide an appropriate, even an inevitable, vocabulary; indeed specific theories of race were available and being applied to India, families of ideas circulating around notions of taxonomy and evolution, in forms both universal and relativist. In this environment, even labels that were ahistorical, externally imposed and arbitrary, could become indigenised, not only recognised by but, ironically, vital to those to whom they were applied. As a consequence, alternative views might be subverted or corralled, as with the Islamic idea of a community not of birth but of belief: this, like its Christian counterparts, would prove relatively susceptible to the onslaught of pragmatic and opportunist racialism and nationalism.

Was this what was happening when race prejudice was evident in Indians? Was it learnt behaviour to notice skin colour, as in typical Indian marriage advertisements even today, or when an Indian general could describe himself (in 1978) as looking 'like a nigger minstrel minus his banjo', or when Cornelia Sorabji's niece refused to walk in public with her no doubt fractionally darker-skinned relatives? Was it borrowed racism when even Gandhi, writing in praise of Zulus, could still call them 'innocent children of nature', timid and 'not used to hard work'?[12] Or was all this merely a continuation of age-old Indian atti-

---

originally meant all the people living east of the Indus, actually prepares the ground, unwittingly, as in his view of Hindu spirituality, for later national and fundamentalist arguments about the essential character of Indians or Hindus. See also Jaffrelot's paper below.

[12] *General J.N. Chaudhuri—an autobiography as narrated to B.K. Narayan* (New Delhi, 1978), p.17; Cornelia Sorabji, 22 July 1891, Mss.Eur.F. 165/4, OIOC; M.K. Gandhi, *Satyagraha in South Africa* (Ahmedabad, 1928), pp.8-21. I am indebted for the first two of these references to Shompa Lahiri. For a more recent Parsi views, drawn to my attention by Frank Dikötter, see Sapur Faredun Desai, *Parsis and Eugenics* (Bombay, 1940), or H.R. Bana arguing that sexual intercourse with a non-Parsi male would defile 'our noble blood' and injure, mix and change a Parsi girls 'original racial traits'; quoted in J. Hinnells, 'Parsi attitudes to religious pluralism' in Harold Coward, ed., *Indian Attitudes and Religious Pluralism* (Albany, 1987). In Gandhi's case it is interesting that, while recognising that both 'dark' and 'brown' races were suffering from a

tudes which happened to coincide with race theories? Was Indian racial prejudice encouraged by tendencies in pre-existing, non-European modes and explanations of identity? To some degree or other the answer to all these questions is bound to be 'yes', and any special prominence of race theories must be attributed to a conjuncture of various forces. More particularly, then, was an idea of race already a commonplace in Indian thinking before it was articulated in Western terms?

There were indigenous categorisations in which physical characteristics played a part, though it is not clear how far biology can be considered to have been *essential*. Skin colour was significant—so many of the mythic heroes and heroines are fair, like Siva coloured by the moon, and the villains are, like the Fury of Brahmanicide in *Mahabharata*, not only deformed and hairy but 'dark and tawny'. Yet colour was not unambiguously related to merit or status.[13] Again, there were clear and early representations of hierarchy and of separate tasks within the moral order, and of its defence at the expense of the individual; and, at least in later periods (if not certainly in *Ramayana* or other epics), such differences, the *varna*, were intrinsic in the sense of being created *ab initio*, and perpetuated through sexual relations and birth.[14] Brockington argues in this book that distinctions, originally principally of language,

'colour bar' (p.87), he centred his South African campaigns (except for a few Chinese) wholly around 'Indians'—though from all regions and classes, Hindu and Muslim. Without very clear ideas, he was seeking to establish a national identity, mainly, as in 'Hind Swaraj', on the basis of culture and geography. As we shall see, as soon as these criteria are generalised (for example in attacking a more materialistic West), they may lend themselves to race-like essentialisms.

[13] See Wendy O'Flaherty, tr., *Hindu Myths* (Harmondsworth, 1975), p.87, and particularly pp. 252-61, an excerpt from the *Skanda Purana*, with its complex play on blackness, moonlight, snow, ash, gold, blue-lotus colour, and on virtue, ascetism and desire. Below, the ambiguity about colour values is also mentioned by Hellmann-Rajanayagam, and discussed with regard to varna by Bayly.

[14] J.L. Brockington, *Righteous Rama. The evolution of an epic* (Delhi, 1985), for example p.170; note the execution of a Sudra by the benevolent Rama (p.130). In this context (which, with untouchability, he discusses in general), it is difficult to share Washbrook's confidence that the racism inherent in varna was seldom expressed (in conflict) except in towns and times of social breakdown; D.A. Washbrook, 'Ethnicity and racialism in colonial Indian society' in Ross, *Racism*, pp.145 ff.

became the basis of quasi-racial discrimination and stereotyping. Initially varna seemed clear and important, but then more ambiguous and incidental, before finally hardening into hierarchy. Distinct peoples were also identified in *Mahabharata* and *Ramayana,* some regarded as 'foreign', and some later explained as resulting from inter-varna unions. By these and other means the status of certain groups seems to have been lowered over time. Jaffrelot may seem to disagree, for he argues that the fluid assimilations of vedic thinking militated against race theory, but he too suspects that assimilation was no longer so easy by about the ninth century. Moreover he adheres to a Dumontian view of the centrality of hierarchy, so that his understanding of *jati* is as species, or, we might say, effectively 'race'. Hellmann-Rajanayagam, in this volume, also puts the case that a term for 'race', in its present meaning, did not exist in Tamil, but that nonetheless there was an early concept of 'Tamil-ness', and later a Tamil tradition guarded by the Vellalars in concert with the Brahmans. Arguably then material and intellectual conditions existed in which South Asian ideas of race could have emerged. There were long and ancient encounters between distinct groups and peoples, and there was also a rough but growing congruence between linguistic and political divisions.

However it is not clear that these categories were wholly biological. We may think that the *mleccha* was racially stigmatised as was the 'barbarian' elsewhere; or we may agree with Hellmann-Rajanayagam, who discusses the point at a lexicographical level with regard to Tamils, that it was possible for a people to distinguish themselves from others, here in terms of *inam* or jati, without developing a concept of 'race'. (On the other hand she also stresses the longevity of certain notions—a focus upon land, and upon chastity and purity of behaviour, blood and language—which seem to have expressed similar senses of self at different times.) Again, we may think that 'racial' elements were present unequivocally in regard to 'untouchability', of which the core is the *exclusion* of certain groups from the community. It seems plain that, though in India untouchability and indeed other concepts of Otherness were pre-eminently matters of the body, yet they were concerned more fundamentally with conduct than with physical characteristics. On the other hand, in many European theories of race too the alleged cultural and moral differences assumed greater importance than the physical ones. In Indian tradition and practice there is perhaps something of the same tension, conflation or ambiguity between ritual and actual status, as exists, in the West, between 'gentleness' of birth and 'gentleness' of character or appearance.

For Brahmanical ideas generally, one might postulate a kind of balance sheet of similarities and distinctions in comparison with a concept of race. For example, the idea of 'jati' does not seem racial when it evokes the oneness of creation, as in transmigration and social interdependence; but perhaps it *is* racial in its definition of essential, hierarchical, distinctive characteristics and roles (*dharma*), which are 'inherited' (even if cyclical in theoretical underpinning). Jati may be racial too in emphasising purity, and fearing miscegenation, factors which at least imply a biological origin for identity and Otherness.[15] Moreover, jati is arguably racial to the extent that distinct 'essences' are invented, as if to avert attention from physical and intellectual similarities, and that hierarchies are subject to occasional examples of permitted inversion or of assimilation by the disadvantaged.

II

Let us now trace these arguments in more detail. Race theory, now discredited, in the nineteenth century took its place, for some people, among proper investigations and orderings of knowledge. It follows that there are strong arguments that racial thinking is peculiarly European in origin, derived over the last 200 years from elements in European history and ideas, as well as from Europe's contacts with other peoples. Its closest cousin, of course, is nationalism.[16] This common ground of race theory, scientific method and the modern state is an important theme to be considered (and in particular it is the starting-point

[15] Compare 'lineage', 'blood', 'breeding' and so on in the vocabulary of social class or indeed of anthropology; and see also the discussion of jati as race or species (drawn to my attention by Christophe Jaffrelot) in G. Herrenschmitt, *Les meilleurs dieux sont hindous* (Paris, 1982). However, Hellmann-Rajanayagam, below, assumes that jati was quite distinct in meaning from race, though possibly translated as such.

[16] See Banton, *Race*, pp.13-26.

for Bates' essay in this volume). It is especially useful, for purposes of analysis, to separate out intellectual from other factors, not least in our case of India because ideas and attitudes were often more readily transmitted than social or political conditions; they were produced under the influence of circumstance and experiences but also had a life and history independent of them.[17] This introduction will discuss the subject initially in three preliminary aspects: the intellectual revolution and a possible universal race theory, the specific features of European attitudes during the nineteenth century, and the characteristics of race studies more recently.

The partitioning of humankind into races, and the attribution of essential qualities to each race, have their origin in a very broad intellectual tendency. Race theory is a part of the larger process and reflects its conceptual anomalies. This may help explain its popularity. Race-thinking sought to define fields of expertise, to characterise on the basis of dominant features, and at the same time to explain difference, especially by methods which related cause and effect, or functions to origins.[18] Thus, because this volume is about race, it is also about definitions. In the first essay, as well as introducing some specific topics (comprehension of and attitudes to the Other; the 'golden age' and other devices of national legitimation), Ballhatchet raises the question very generally—he tackles 'race' in the older sense of 'category'. He reminds us of the difficulties of definition. In all, though the tendency of the modern era has been for the divisions of knowledge to grow, yet there are no clear principles whereby subdivision occurs; there can be schisms and re-formations. These confusions still beget the imbecilities of race theory.

[17] The importance of non-intellectual factors is not at all denied. For a brief discussion of the role of class in the formation and popularising of Victorian theories of race, see D.A. Lorimer, *Colour, Class and the Victorians* (London 1978), ch.10.

[18] It is even implicit below, in Bayly's account (though not in Bates') that 'scientific' racism, through its empiricism, could (and did, as with Broca and anthropometry) sow the seeds of its own refutation. As will be argued shortly, it is significant in the history of race theory that scientific knowledge, including that of history or sociology, progresses cumulatively, through correction of errors—to a greater degree than does artistic, moral or religious achievement.

Ballhatchet's solution is a modification of the principles of Linnæus, not (as discussed by Bates in this volume) with reference to his hierarchical categorisation of human races, but with regard to the basis of his system of classification.[19] Ballhatchet starts with the *selection of significant features*—for example categorising slavery on the basis of its being involuntary, or feudalism as a decentralised political system focused on land. Whether this solves the problem of categories is uncertain, and Ballhatchet is aware of the difficulty of deciding which features should be considered essential, and hence where to set the boundaries of particular terms. The chosen criteria may be insufficient: Ballhatchet notes, for example, that slaves differ very markedly in privileges and life-style, just as 'landowners', though legally identical, vary enormously in wealth. On the other hand, any one criterion may be too general—for example, in the case of slavery, because *all* employment is in some degree involuntary. I understand Ballhatchet's proposition to be that we cannot avoid generalisation at some level, and that it should be on the basis of objective though flexible criteria. Functions change—as, we might add, do viewpoints—but at any place or time one can define categories according to function, and essential criteria in terms of means whereby the functions are performed.

This is not a re-introduction of Weberian 'ideal types', because it is avowedly morphological. One point it seems to be making is the apparently obvious but frequently overlooked one that categories should be determined by the questions being asked, so that, for example, we describe agrarian structure in legal terms for some purposes, but, in other cases, according to economic classes or indigenous social divisions. Ballhatchet's is therefore a partly teleological approach, which selects relevant features from an external, analytical perspective. The historian looks back and reshapes the past according what it is he is trying to explain. As an addition or corrective, Ballhatchet seems to add

[19] The importance of Linnæan principles of categorisation may be judged in comparison with the view of Buffon in *Histoire naturelle*: considering Linnæan distinctions artificial, Buffon argued that nature was a continuous whole, divided only for convenience by man's observations and purposes. Buffon may be compared in turn with the thirteenth-century 'Nasirean Ethics', described below by Majeed.

a category-centred method, whereby the appropriateness and content of defining features are assessed on the basis of their internal significance and function. This is akin to the historical test of interpretations by their presumed intelligibility to people in the period being studied, and arguably also to the German concept of 'Wesen' as described in this volume by Hellmann-Rajanayagam, who most closely takes up Ballhatchet's position. In such typology the 'slave', say, would be identified by the key characteristics which constructed slavery in a given society. The first, teleological strategy allows us to propose categories which extend comparatively over time and space; the other suggests categories that are *sui generis*. In practice, we adopt mixtures of both, a bipolar approach which does not show whether indigenous terms are to be preferred to general ones, or how we cope with the way the meaning of categories may change over time, but which does provide a series of checks on assumptions that terminology is unproblematic.

Alive to these considerations, we may return to the concept of race. It will become plain that Ballhatchet's essay reveals aspects of the nature of the problem rather than providing a solution which will necessarily be adopted in these essays. If there is common ground in our studies of race, it is found perhaps in a tendency to question essentialist categorisations and rational binary oppositions. By comparison Ballhatchet's argumentation is more typically 'modern'. It might be contrasted with the Indian concept of *advaita*, the point of which is to insist not on internal uniformities, or on spiritual and physical entities, but on universal unity.[20] Thus there are two opposing positions that pitch idealism against relativism: either form is merely *maya* (illusion), or form defines content. To put it in Cartesian terms, the material either does or does not exist independently of the spiritual.[21] The anti-racist argument that all humans are essentially the

[20] Scientific progress, being cumulative (see above), does advance at different rates in different conditions. Dualism was powerfully boosted in the nineteenth century as borders changed between spiritual/material, divine/temporal, past/present, self/other, public/private, teacher/pupil, text/tradition, and so on. But scientific progress is also universally, definingly human. Hence in relating rationalism here to race theory, I am not saying that *advaita* is always typical of 'Indian' thought, and dualism of 'Western'.

[21] In qualifying current essentialist categories in this book, we are using em-

same is analogous to the doctrine of *advaita*.[22] Racism, however, is in an important sense dualist.[23] Though race theory seeks to be comprehensive, ranking all humankind, and though it may seem to endorse the interdependence of the material and the spiritual, yet it postulates essences which exist only as separate entities, not universally. They represent, despite their moral judgments, predominantly the material determined by the material, unredeemed by the spiritual or universal. The effect is seen in phrenology, sexual myths or colour prejudice. Perhaps the race-metaphor appealed because rational thought in the West is also (or rather was) almost completely dualist and materialist.

The suggestion, in short, is that European racism was not only a reaction to Europe's historical experience, but also an outcrop of its general intellectual history. We find, at the least, that the methods of analysis which Ballhatchet suggests for historians are interestingly

---

pirical methods to question dualism and rationalism *as descriptions of all phenomena*. This not to abandon Descartes and historical method, as means for the determination of knowledge—discussed and advocated by Ballhatchet—and certainly not in comparison with racist, ideological or religious historiographies which 'prove' only what is already known (that is, believed, by faith).

[22] For an apparently contrary argument see Washbrook, 'Ethnicity', pp.151-2 and 158: he argues that when McKim Marriott and Ronald Inden proposed a monistic view of Indian society, they implied that caste had 'ethnic' elements (he seems to mean 'racialist', by his own definitions, pp.143-5). The point is that monist belief in a nature/society continuum paralleled 'assumptions which underlay Social Darwinism and...eugenicist thought' (presumably the equation of physical with moral character). One may view things thus, but the binary elements of racial hierarchy seem to me more significant—also indicating how racism, pre-eminently a theory of the group, co-exists with individualism (a problem considered but not resolved by Washbrook).

[23] See Louis Dumont's discussion, *Homo Hierarchicus* (Chicago, 1970), pp.239-58 (originally an article in *Cahiers internationaux de sociologie* XXIX, 1960, and reprinted as 'Caste, "racism" and stratification' in John Stone, *Race, Ethnicity and Social Change*, North Scituate, Mass., 1977, pp.299-316). Noting that we espouse liberalism but ascribe physical characteristic to groups, and then equate the physical with the moral, Dumont considers racism traceable to dualistic religion and philosophy. He quotes (ibid., p.312) Gunnar Myrdal, in *An American Dilemma. The Negro problem and modern democracy* (London [1944]), p.89, who also speculated that racial inequality may have been a strange fruit of the Enlightenment: his argument, which others have criticised as a smokescreen for class exploitation, was that race theory was a way out of the idea of equality. My argument will go beyond this instrumentalism and its more material variations, so as to locate racism also in developments of thought.

paralleled by those adopted in regard to race. Both formed part of an intellectual revolution—ultimately the Baconian reformation of knowledge. Theologically, revelation had been regarded as producing order out of chaos (the very task now allocated to science). Already this encouraged a teleological reading of history (though of course the pre-revelation disorder could be real). The mode of understanding was authoritarian: a tradition which, without being unchanging, restricted the mechanisms for change. For example, in India the priest or the guru was a disseminator of information but also an instrument of change, as his role was constantly to define (to re-make) tradition. As with the authority of an institutional structure, a church, this allowed adaptation without indiscipline. Race theory was an attack, on pseudo-rationalist grounds, upon this view of knowledge. An example, offered by Bayly in this volume, was the savaging of Brahmans and gurus by William Ward and other evangelicals. In doing this—at one level (dangerous to their own position as Christians)—they were challenging ways in which culture and knowledge were transmitted. A racist belief in 'blood' ruled out the need for—or rendered pointless—any human or indeed spiritual agency (Brahmanic or otherwise). At the same time, paradoxically, the same advocates celebrated independence in mind and action.

In modern scientific thought, similarly, one can trace attempts to reconcile the divine and the material, theory and empiricism; but the most profound trend has been a desire to construct general laws, whether of the natural world or in ideas, and to discover 'truth' on the basis of reason (rather than revelation and obedience). And only in the modern age, in the shift from supernatural to empirical explanations, has it been so acutely felt that universal laws needed to be tested against particular examples. Hence, paradoxically the ever more detailed search for universals has led to subdivisions of knowledge, so that the growth in public or standard understandings has come to depend increasingly upon reasoning within closed systems; private judgments create spheres of study that are public yet restricted; the process parallels the categorisation discussed by Ballhatchet. As with knowledge and divisions of disciplines, so with geographical space divided into regions: each of them became the preserve of experts whose *raison d'être* and scientific credibility depended upon separation and distinctiveness. This was the case for, say, Indian geology, separated out from natural history,[24] as it was for Indian sociology, as distinguished from the study of humankind in all its activities. Sets of knowledge were bundled together, each presided over by experts, who were fashioned by training and reason; the accretion of such expertise produced a canon of fundamentals and methods. As with Ballhatchet's categories, standardisation permitted information to be disseminated, but always there was a tension between the value of such knowledge-in-use, and the mystique and prestige of ownership, of control over knowledge—this is well illustrated in what are now jealously-guarded fiefdoms of medicine or law.

The suggestion is not that European thought is monolithic. Indeed, there are several problems with what one may call binary universalist explanations: some of them may be considered by looking at the alternatives to the kinds of intellectual development which, it is suggested, helped breed racism. Of course, even within European universalism, one should not ignore the many alternative, liberal traditions, which lean, in the sphere of politics for example, towards equity and democracy. And there have also been many reactions against modern tendencies to regulate spheres of knowledge; they include relativism and postmodernism. The former in particular has played its part in discrediting race theory, without, however, having driven it out. I will mention just one example, Claude Lévi-Strauss, who, concluding that any view of difference is bound to be an illusion at some level, chided the race theorists for their false evolutionism. He meant not only that the lesson from Darwin was inappropriate because culture and artefacts are developed and replicated, not evolved genetically; but also that our very concept of progress is subjective: all societies may seek improvement and maximisation, and those which appear to us stationary may merely be

[24] Andrew Grout, 'Geology and India, 1775-1805', *South Asia Research* 10, 1 (1990), pp.1-18. Grout's full-length account should be available in 1995. See also Bayly's paper in this volume, for 'practical geology'. None of this should be read as implying that there *are* such divisions as 'Indian geology' on analytical rather than practical grounds, any more that we should accept that there is, in the same sense, an Indian history, or utter polarisation in historical forces as between, say, metropolitan and peripheral or colonial and nationalist.

progressing along a different road, according to a different set of priorities.

This was a spirited and impressive parry. If it did not win the day, it was because the entrenched fiefdoms are still fairly secure. Perhaps the reasons for this are threefold: intellectual, empirical and utilitarian. First, the desire to find, as it were, autarkic, self-contained explanations remains strong. Lévi-Strauss's approach tends to dissolve the usual understandings of difference, and to make expected categories irrelevant: for example he would attribute the rapidity of Western progress not to those many indigenous features which have long been proposed, but to exploration, empire and better communications, to the end of Europe's isolation and to its raids upon the rest of the world: the causes were not intrinsic but due to new opportunities to learn from others. This fits extremely well with many new and desirable developments in the study of non-Western societies in particular.[25] But it also raises the second question: whether this relativist approach conforms with change in recent times. We need not deny the salience of different societies, to wonder if there was not something rather different, and more linear, about the world during the centuries of European dominance. Cultural development may be backward-looking and hence cyclical, but the scientific and technological revolutions are generally cumulative. The first may produce societies in which, despite diversity, one generation lived and thought recognisably as its predecessors did; in other words only limited changes were possible. But advanced technology produces rapid and sudden changes in life-style, politics, economy, values and ideas, within a single generation. It produces a specific kind of progress, a kind of sustained and accelerating crisis. (It is not irreversible, and the current ecological threats may be foreshadowing the next dominant world order, one in which change is deliberately slowed.) Applying this to the question of race, we might think that Lévi-Strauss's argument leads in the end to a universalist theory, whereas the still-prevailing habits of analysis

[25] Of course there have been and are parallel views of European expansion from the periphery, and no doubt knowledge advances very often because of factors brought in from beyond the established borders of explanation.

encourage us to locate the theory in nineteenth-century Europe.

In a third element, we encounter the utility of race theory. Lévi-Strauss attacked the habitual determinism of our interpretations on the ground that technologically similar societies are not necessarily culturally similar. (In fact it might now be said that technologically-advanced societies *are* culturally similar in some senses, and tending to become more so in others.) He proposed a paradox: plurality and borrowings seem critical to progress, but, though diversity is normal, societies or belief systems tend to identify themselves as the norm, so as to imply superiority over others. Lévi-Strauss called this attitude 'barbaric'—that is, typical of isolated tribes—but it seems a *necessary* element, appearing with more or less sophistry in the construction of all societies, and perhaps originating in the individual psychology.[26] Moreover schemes of universal brotherhood mostly attempt to extend this 'normal' community rather than to give equal value to diversity; they are limited indeed by the ability to comprehend difference. Hellmann-Rajanayagam notes that universalism usually means one's own type standing for all; it is never complete, but allows for extensions to cover once-excluded groups.[27] Thus concepts of race, like kin, might be said to be designed to establish the borders of supportive or egalitarian behaviour: while brotherhood might be a universal value, it is given boundaries by defining those outside as not potentially kin or even as not human. Mixing race up with nation is explained by the sense that both are serving similar purposes in defining the group of 'affines'.

An account of intellectual connections has suggested an approach which this essay promised to explore: that race theory was specific, but that it can be compared with other theories of difference. Our second preliminary question thus concerns the developing attitudes to race in nineteenth-century Europe. It is to be hoped that in future renewed

[26] Lévi-Strauss, 'Race and History', especially pp.101-3.

[27] Whether that is a liberal or totalitarian process depends on the nature of the categorisation; Jaffrelot in this volume makes a similar point with regard to the alleged ability of Hinduism to assimilate, and we will see below that the *type* nonetheless remained *one* in the would-be incorporations of his ideologues, whose categories are never plural.

attention will be paid to the links between the development of such race theories and European perceptions of India, especially in the eighteenth century, not so much with regard to the precursors discussed in this volume by Bates, as in respect of such commentators as John Zephaniah Holwell, Alexander Dow, Johann Herder, and William Jones, who can be regarded as trying to place India in the universal scheme of things, paralleling the efforts of Jesuits to understand its religion, or of Pierre Sonnerat in respect of natural history, or of Jean Sylvain Bailly and Joseph de Lisle with regard to astronomy. Here space does not permit a comprehensive survey, and (except with regard to this Indian connection) existing studies render it unnecessary. We need only to remind ourselves of common features in European thinking on race. The Comte de Gobineau will serve us as an example.

As suggested in the opening sentence of his *Essai sur l'inégalité des races humaines*, his subject was the rise and decay of civilisations. Writing with apocalyptic vision after the events of 1848 (and of France's preceding half-century), he suggested that the modern generation was the first to recognise that all societies and cultures were bound to perish. The reason was not error (fanaticism, indolence, false religion, bad government and so on) but systematic human degeneration, caused by the admixture of inferior with superior strains of mankind. Gobineau did not claim that every European was superior to any member of another race (he thought that a vulgar fallacy, and criticised European intolerance), but he insisted on the general superiority of 'Aryans' as a group. In line with the principles of 'modern' social analysis, though not of truly scientific method, he argued that generic characteristics superseded or took priority over the individual case, and also that these general features survived and were immutable even when variously mixed in particular individuals. Thus from a hermeneutic principle, a concept of generalisation bearing a family resemblance to that proposed in this volume by Ballhatchet, he developed a theory of history through inheritance. The latter, again repeating the dilemmas of categorisation, seemed to be non-genetic in that constituent strains, though somehow surviving as essenses, also mixed to produce each new generation.[28]

The argument implied that essential types had been formed long ago, and had reached their optimum level in the past. So convinced was Gobineau of the advantage of antiquity that he argued that, 'Au point de vue des arts, notre infériorité vis-à-vis de l'Inde est marquée, tout autant qu'en face de l'Égypte, de la Grèce et de l'Amerique': modern Europe had nothing to compare in grandeur or beauty with the ancient arts of these lands. (By contrast, nowadays in India, 'le brahmanisme est en décadence complète; ses grands hommes ont disparu'.)[29] It may be noted here that the standards of measurement were æsthetic, technical, moral and cultural, but all of them were attributed to the effect of 'blood'; moreover 'il y a une série de gradations par laquelle les peuples qui ne sont pas du sang des blancs approchent de la beauté, mais ne l'atteignent pas'—such permanent superiority of 'Aryans' and their achievements logically depended upon the denial of any *continuing* instrumentality for culture or education. Accordingly, Gobineau's explanation of the declinc in standards began from the premise that humankind was one, as required by religion and universalist doctrines. But he went on to conclude also that there were hierarchies of races, each with defining features. There were masculine and feminine peoples, he wrote. Alternatively, in the immense tapestry woven by history, man's 'deux variétés inférieures' (the black and yellow races) might be said to be made of cotton and wool, and the second-rank whites of silk, but the Aryan group, 'faisant circuler ses filets plus minces à travers les

[28] The assumption was that inheritance ('blood') was infinitely divisible and miscible. See L.C. Dunn, 'Race and biology' in Leo Kuper, ed., *Race, Science and Society* (Paris and London, 1975). In a curious sense Gobineau's essenses foreshadowed what Mendel would show in 1865, that inheritance depended on 'discrete elementary particles', that is genes; but (like Darwin) Gobineau also seems to have thought that each *individual* was an amalgam (made of one blood rather than of discrete elements); later the hoped-for purification of eugenics also required the older theory to be true. Banton, *Race*, ch.5, points out that various versions of social Darwinism also held out a prospect that races could improve by racial selection.

[29] As will be clear from Chowdhury-Sengupta below, Gobineau was here repeating both the Orientalist praise for ancient 'Hindu' past, and the Evangelical and Utilitarian contempt for the Indian present. More generally, on the respective means and rates of progress in arts and sciences, see note 18 above.

générations ennoblies, applique à surface, en éblouissant chef-d'oeuvre, ses arabesques d'argent et d'or'.

This fanciful and heart-quickening stuff probably sufficed to convince many of its readers. Certainly it strikes many chords with other pessimistic writings which also believed in limits on the possibility of improvement for non-European peoples—a feature characteristic of polygenist race theories of the mid nineteenth century. Gobineau too needed to establish principles on which mankind could be subdivided. Inequality, he thought, was basic and ancient, everywhere to be found—interestingly he referred not only to aristocracy and primogeniture but also (without of course drawing relativist conclusions) to man's natural antipathy and feelings of superiority towards strangers. All political theories took account of inequality, he claimed, except the most recent, whose adherents accepted it in practice while denying it in principle. The differences between races were physical and intellectual, and did not depend on present religion, institutions or environment; rather they were inherited from primitive man and primordial conditions. For that reason there could be no lasting spread of civilisation, and no fundamental improvement through the actions of men—none for example (as others hoped) from British influence over India. This was not a doctrine of the Creation, the Fall and original sin (which hitherto had supported monogenist, and hence social or environmental race theories), but it was close enough to it. To sum up: because man, 'étant nouvellement créé, présentait des formes encore incertaines', racial essenses were fixed very early (arguably by the luck of environment), and then passed down unchanged; this resulted in physical and intellectual differences between races, which, however, were bound to mingle and hence (despite the beauty to be perceived in individuals of mixed race) to decline over time.[30] In short Gobineau encompassed

[30] Le Comte de Gobineau, *Essai sur l'inégalité des races humaines* (4th ed.; 1st ed. Paris, 1854); for the quotations, see especially vol. I, pp.33, 35-7, 44, 73-5, 99-105, 143-4, 153-7, 446, and vol. II, p.539. See Poliakov, 'Racism', suggesting that Gobineau was a scapegoat, while Ernest Renon, though also racist, remains a 'leading figure of French thought'. Since Gobineau, aesthetics has been a continual theme of racism and eugenics, not just in Nazism but (under the influence of E.A. Hooton at Harvard and W.H. Sheldon at Columbia) in American college 'posture' photographs, which continued from the

different trends of race theory. He allowed creationists and environmentalists their moment, when humankind was still one species, a fact of genetics which, however, for Gobineau ensured man's long-term decline through interbreeding under modern conditions. But by also insisting on racial essenses he came down in favour of the 'scientific' racism of mid- and late Victorian thought, built on supposed discoveries by the growing sub-divisions of science or pseudo-science such as linguistics, phrenology, palæontology, evolution and anthropology. Just this compromise, entrenching racism and making it seem respectable, was offered by Darwin and his concept of the mutability of species, which (incidentally) provided a new explanation of difference, of the 'failures' of pre-colonial India, and of the 'savagery' of most of the world before European conquest.[31]

Many variations of such ideas arose, but the basic elements are there in Gobineau: history, inherited difference, essential categories, the material and æsthetic as sign or progenitor of the moral and intellectual. Further discussion of such theories, with particular reference to anthropometry, will be found in Bates' essay below. Gobineau, like others of his time, sought to explain origins and functions, reconciling the divine with the material, revelation with observation, on the basis of his individual judgment, his willingness to interpret data. Gobineau's was an argument set against theories of progress, and also against a related egalitarianism—and owed much to the fact that these ideas also were powerful and ascendant in nineteenth-century Europe. (It is interesting, given those who consider Western thought *imbued* with racism, or indeed 'Orientalism', that such attitudes of mind should have been constructed in part as a reply to the stronger showing by liberal, democratic traditions.) Gobineau's pessimism set him apart from believers in progress such as Marx with his belief in an 'eternal law of history' whereby inferior civilisations must give way to superior,[32] or from the social evolutionists who, even before bolstered in their

---

1880s until as late as the 1960s. The association of appearance with merit, beauty with virtue, remains fundamental to much art and almost all fashion.

[31] See Lorimer, *Colour, Class*, ch.7.

[32] Karl Marx, 'The future results of British rule in India', *New York Daily Tribune*, 8 August 1853, reprinted in Stone, *Race*.

theories by Darwin, considered that natural selection would allow races to improve themselves.[33] On the other hand, even many theorists of more optimistic view treated race in much the same terms as Gobineau. They might, for example, welcome mixtures of races, as did Gustav Klemm, Carl Gustavus Carus or Victor Courtet de l'Isle, but they did so on the reasoning, the counterpart to Gobineau's, that a more active type might raise up an inferior.[34] They argued over the relative importance of innate characteristics and social or institutional conditions, whether there were many principles of ranking or just one, whether intellectual and moral features affected or merely reflected socio-economic conditions (Weber versus Marx), but they all agreed that a hierarchy of races existed, demonstrable in the varied behaviour and capacities attributable to race. Weber, in a way that often foreshadows recent, even postmodernist suggestions, was acutely aware of the cultural origins of concepts as well as of the influence of ideas upon behaviour: he considered racial aversions to be social in nature and origin, and denied that common polity, language or blood were necessary to the identification of nations. But he too proposed a 'community of sentiment' which could be reinforced by historical memory, culture (especially language), state organisation, and race.[35] Though Weber's is not a racist doctrine, yet it seems that Gobineau's (which certainly is)

[33] See Banton, *Race*, ch.5. Gobineau is not consistent, but his view seems to have been that selective breeding would do no more than delay the inevitable decline.

[34] See Banton, *Race*, pp.38-44, including the quotation (p.39) from Hermann Blome, *Der Rassengedanke in der deutschen Romantik und seine Grundlegen im 18 Jahrhundert* (Munchen and Berlin, 1943), pp.254-5. Gobineau insisted of course that races pursue their separate destinies, so as to avoid further degeneration of the 'white' blood-stock. Compare Robert Knox who believed 'hybrid' races to be ultimately infertile, presumably by analogy with the mule; on Knox and 'hybridisation' see also Bayly's essay below. But see also her reference to Topinard and the benefits of mixing essential racial characteristics. Similarly the optimistic ending of *Ivanhoe* endorses the advantages of shared (though still unblended) characteristics between races—though only within limits, between Saxons and Normans, as may be judged from Scott's denouement for the Jewish Rebecca. See also note 28 above: the inherited essences and their influence rather than purity of blood was the crucial element of race theory.

[35] Max Weber, *Essays in Sociology* (tr. and ed. H.H. Gerth and C.W. Mills), quoted in Stone, *Race*, pp.18-24.

should be understood as a version of the same idea of causation; and even Gobineau's extreme and selective determinism is also to be found elsewhere. His prior causes ruled out most of the explanations beloved by his contemporaries—he mocked the suggestion that institutional factors, say, or climate could account for different levels of average achievement between races, and rejected relativist cultural judgments of the levels of civilisations.[36] But his search for rational causes lay within the same intellectual universe which they too inhabited: the idea that everything, including physical appearance and aptitudes, had both causes and effects, and the related notion that organisms, including man, were discrete forms capable of being explained, in effect, as mechanical systems.

It is clear that the race theories applied in India belonged to this same family. There may be an echo of Gobineau's belief in primal superiority and determinism, for example, in what Caplan tells us, in this volume, of the association of 'masculinity' with hills, hardship and even a lack of 'civilisation', and of 'feminity' with plains, easy living, literacy, and the fact of having been conquered. Similar but much earlier instances are noted in her paper below by Bayly, namely Forbes' characterisations of Rajputs, and by commentators who wrote before the new ethnographic emphasis upon caste. (The point has a long pedigree, and might also be traced to David Hume.)[37] Chowdhury-Sengupta reports instances of such arguments in Bengal. Gobineau would certainly have been in tune with another of the ideas Caplan reports: that

[36] De Tocqueville wrote to Gobineau stressing the determinism of his theories, and arguing that it could not be proved that any innate tendencies are insuperable. See John Stone, 'Race relations and the sociological tradition' in Stone, *Race*, p.65.

[37] David Hume, *An Enquiry concerning the Principles of Morals* and *A Dialogue* (1777, ed. by L.A. Selby-Bigge; ed. C.B. Macpherson, Harmondsworth, 1981), for example pp.255 and 333-8, on Homeric ethics, appropriate values, the utility and influence of custom, and absolute principles. Another element, mentioned by Bayly, is the Aryan conquest-myth devised by Sir William Jones. For a Bengali example of environmental determinism see the preface to *Karnel Suresh Bishvas*; quoted by Chowdhury-Sengupta. On the gender issue (her main subject) she cites the Bengalis' use of Tod and his accounts of Rajput history as an instance relevant to the construction of an 'Indian' identity and past.

the martial races of Nepal were supposedly reduced in quality by migration, presumably because of intermarriage.[38]

What of our third matter, race studies more recently? Notably, of course, they examine racism rather than apply race as an explanation of other subjects. The specificity of race theories—whether or not there is 'merely one form taken from a primordial ethnocentricism'—[39] has been a favourite problem for race studies since Gobineau, though the Indian case, originally so prominent, is apparently no longer familiar to the mainstream of scholarship. However there has not been any very powerful theory to replace those of nineteenth-century Europe. This may be one reason why prejudice and atavism remain so crudely prevalent, almost in the language of Gobineau, resisting the blandishments of liberalism, plurality and harmony. Moreover, even those who have studied race from a wholly sceptical perspective have not always escaped their own essentialisms;[40] and essentialism about race has always been one of the *defences* against racism, achieving artificial solidarities among Jews, Afro-Americans, British migrant communities, and (as we shall see) colonial Indians. One focus of study has been on race *relations*—empirical accounts of attitudes and behaviour, especially in the United States and latterly, to some extent by imitation, in Britain. The focus has tended to reinforce the notion that racism is 'normally' European, a view which has been assisted rather than qualified by attempts to study racism as a part of other concepts of identity and social practice within particular groups.

A second subject has been the origin of prejudice; this too suggests a potential for more general interpretations, but it is interesting that sev-

[38] See the discussion of 'feeble' racial mixtures above.

[39] David Mason, 'Controversies and continuities in race and ethnic relations theory', in John Rex and Mason, eds., *Theories of Race and Ethnic Relations* (Cambridge, 1986), p.5.

[40] Peter Watson, for example, while arguing against a 'good guys' versus 'bad guys' approach, considered it a 'pretty obvious fact that blacks could never have a white frame of reference'; Watson, ed., *Psychology and Race* (Harmondsworth, 1973), p.16. Other examples abound. In Britain, for example, the racist notion of innate characteristics has encouraged adoption agencies to insist on placing (even partially) 'black' babies only with 'black' adoptive parents, a strategy also supported apparently by an assumption that racial prejudice cannot be eradicated and is best faced by social apartheid.

eral important theories have stressed the effect of 'plural' societies, and particularly the influence of socio-economic differences, again implying that race theories were the product of colonialism, slavery and migration.[41] One of the scholarly approaches has been 'rational-choice theory', explaining social phenomena in terms of individual choices, conscious and unconscious, writ large; but it is difficult to see how even this can rule out an independent impact whereby society and ideology confine the choices individuals can make or even imagine.[42] Thus all these theories tend to assume both that race theories are produced as a consequence of difference (for example, the arguments of Robert Park), *and* that they are mostly or effectively European.[43]

Rational-choice theory certainly deals in aggregates (the sum of individual choices) but does so in a fashion which Michael Banton concedes to be akin to the sociology of Durkheim (as in suicide, personal choices collectively produce patterns) or to the structural-functionalism of Talcott Parsons: it explains social action in terms of the common

[41] Washbrook's is the strongest statement of this with regard to India ('Ethnicity'); he suggests that racism had no force or utility without class. For a view of racism as a 'culturally sanctioned, rational response to struggles over scarce resources', see David T. Wellmann, *Portraits of White Racism* (Cambridge, 1977). See also D. van Arkel, 'Racism in Europe', in Ross, *Racism*, pp.11-31, arguing that anti-Semitism arose not only among dominant exploiters, but among those *suffering* from social change, as a form of social protest. For a stress on migration, and the supposed creativity of the marginal, see R.E. Park, 'Human migration and the marginal man', *American Journal of Sociology* 33 (1928), pp.881-93, quoted by Jack Mann, 'Status; the marginal reaction—mixed bloods and Jews', in Watson, *Psychology*, pp.213-23. Migration or conflict theories, even Mann's despite his stressing multiple identities and *experienced* conflict, still depend upon essentialising racial or other human categories. For clearer examples of the persistence of elements of race thinking, in concepts replacing race or tribe, see Bates' essay below.

[42] Michael Hechter, with Banton an exponent of rational-choice theory, indirectly admits as much in his discussion of 'preference formation' and institutional and environmental contraints (which, note, may be 'real' or perceived); 'Rational choice theory and the study of race and ethnic relations', in Rex and Mason, *Theories*, pp.273-8. However, Banton, on this point seems to consider only those impediments to choice which are narrowly sociological—the actual contraints which make the costs of some courses of action outweigh their benefits; Michael Banton, *Racial and Ethnic Competition* (Cambridge, 1983), pp.107-8. I have in mind also subliminal and ideational constraints.

[43] See Mason, 'Controversies and continuties' in ibid.

pattern of individual preferences in a given society.[44] This describes a mechanism for producing racism, but otherwise does not seem to have great exegetical force: the 'common pattern' and the 'given society' take us back to the normative instruments for producing racism, such as biology, psychology, or social institutions.[45] They take us back as far as Gobineau, or to the special culpability of Europe. Europe and 'white' racism are in the frame also when Banton argues that competition was the 'critical process shaping patterns of racial and ethnic relations',[46] and in the many other attempts which have been made to associate ethnocentricism with power. And, though, generally, these explanations have not regarded ideas as independent variables, nowadays, even in the intellectual sphere, it has seemed possible to trace racism to the 'power' of discourse, to the extension of 'rational' explanations to societies outside the ring of those in Europe where modes of 'rationality' were devised, and especially to societies once thought primitive or irrational. This same process, turning in upon itself, has led to the interpretation of identities as necessarily rational, constructed and calculated.[47] The subject of this essay and of this book, by contrast, is the extent to which a European focus does or does not provide a sufficient account of race theory.

III

We have considered three arguments for a European origin for racism: the links (persisting despite alternatives) between race theory and broad intellectual currents, the specific contributions of figures such as Gobineau to the content of race theory, and the findings of more recent students of race. We will now turn to India, again in three aspects: nationality, religious identity, and caste. (A comparative test is also included, in Rogers' paper on Sri Lanka.)

[44] See Banton, *Racial and Ethnic Competition*, pp.107-8.

[45] See ibid., pp.82-4, for John Dollard's linking of racism and aggression; see also Watson, *Psychology,* for example James Ritchie, 'Culture, personality and prejudice', pp.311-29, an attempt to co-opt anti-racism to the cause of permissive child-rearing by blaming racism on authoritarian fathers!

[46] Banton, *Racial and Ethnic Competition*, p.12.

[47] For a discussion of the objective bases of intergroup prejudice, see Henri Tajfel, 'The roots of prejudice: cognitive aspects', in Watson, *Psychology.*

The first, an obvious but problematic arena for race theory, was a product of the construction of India as a nation. In so far as this succeeded, it is the clearest instance of Indian race theory as a borrowing from the West and through colonial rule.[48] A new idea of the nation occurred (as we shall see) among Indians who wholly rejected the West and favoured, for example, a separate Hindu or Muslim identity. It developed as well among admirers of the West who found there standards of politics, ethics, education, and professional or scientific knowledge, from conviction as well as from self-interest, for they too did not submerge their own distinct identities; indeed their sense of themselves as Indians and of Indian values and interests was often enhanced by their Western encounters and by new public connections

[48] Parallel accounts could be provided of regional 'nationalities', of Muslim and Sikh identities and of various 'tribal' movements. Religious identities fell somewhere between the nation and the sect, and will be discussed later in this section, with reference to Hindus. For Muslims, see the brief discussion by Majeeb below. The only previous overview of which I am aware is Washbrook, 'Ethnicity'. From an avowed Marxist viewpoint—'only by virtue of the fact that ethnic movements...are related to class issues...can they be...instruments of control' (p.181)—it considers 'ethnicity' (territorial identity) and 'racism' (ascriptive hierarchy) to have been inherent in India but to have developed in modern times, not so much out of primordial loyalties (though caste and religion proved more important than language, *pace* E. Gellner in *Thought and Change*, London, 1964), nor out of political utility (there being insufficient modernisation for social mobilisation à la Deutsch), but rather, in the main, *first* from changes in the class structure (though it is not clear why 'ethnicity' should have been the mode of such identities, unless it be on grounds of 'æsthetic' appeal as Washbrook rather curiously proposes, p.177, or by accident—the argument in effect offered by Washbrook and since elaborated by Partha Chatterjee with regard to East Bengal, where class and religious differences appeared to coincide), and *secondly* from the colonial state's corporatism (in the sense of P. Schmitter) which encouraged groups to organise and compete, and which in colonial times and since expected identities and social stratification on a quasi-racial basis of religion and caste, theories internalised by Indians; the indigenous basis of such identities was implied by the fact that 'modern' elements (anyway not uniformly to be found in the colonial state and economy) were least strong in the most popular movements; there were also strong tendencies towards wider 'national' unity, so that 'ethnic' or 'racial' identities were most extreme among those with least power in the class structure (an odd claim in view of the high-caste origins of Hindu chauvinist parties), a situation likely to continue so long as capitalism disrupts society without bringing countervailing benefits for all.

and institutions forged in the colonial era.[49]

As a background and explanation of this, several strands may be discerned also in European views of India: they co-existed and overlapped, even when mutually inconsistent, though they gained in prominence at different times. One possible reference point is the parallel development of theories of race, though the colonial rulers can also be said to have been building an idea of India or a series of Indias. European observers began with their own maps, and with texts explained by pandits. The social model was varna-based and Brahmanical. This was usefully simple, especially in the eighteenth century when, to understand and to pacify India at the moment of conquest, the British needed order above all. However, though India was strange to them, and measured within a distinct realm comparable with that of 'Europe' as defined from the sixteenth century onwards (again by mapping and cultural, historical criteria),[50] at first the British image of it was contrapuntal rather than alien, being qualified by recognition of 'Indo-European' features in language and even religion (note the Unitarians and the search for vedic monotheism): part of this was that readiness already noted to admire the ancient world of India as of Europe, admiration which contributed to the idea of a golden age, and to the authority assumed for original forms and texts, which influenced Hindu reformers and nationalists. And then, as the nineteenth century continued, as Evangelical, romantic and Utilitarian influence grew, and as British rule became more established, then difference was emphasised. In particular, Brahmanical tyranny was condemned. The British began their long quest to find supporters beyond the ranks of possibly

[49] Tapan Raychaudhuri, *Europe Reconsidered. Perceptions of the West in nineteenth century Bengal* (Delhi, 1988), rightly describes the critical reassessments of the West by Bhudev, Bankim and Vivekananda; but even these figures and later nationalists, Gandhians, Communists and fundamentalists partook ambivalently of aspects of Western forms of organisation, propaganda and reasoning. On the other hand Westernisers, social reformers and allies of British cultural and political norms, from Rammohan to Naoroji, Gokhale or Jawaharlal Nehru, also identified themselves as counterposed to and partly critical of Europe.

[50] See John Hale, *The Civilisation of Europe in the Renaissance* (London, 1993), especially ch. 1 and pp.15-27. The reference is to Europe as opposed to a fractured Christendom.

untrustworthy elites. On most (not all) occasions the Indian order was compared unfavourably with European values and institutions. Yet still, under the continuing influence of universalist Enlightenment thinking, a common view was that India was not essentially debased but had fallen off from the standards of a presumed better age. In short India was improvable. Such was the preferred justification of imperial expansion in the nineteenth century: material and administrative change would 'civilise'—that is, create—India.

Evolutionary ideas were added. In mid-century Henry Maine saw India as being at an earlier stage of development than Europe, which meant that British institutions were necessary to good government.[51] However it also implied that they should be introduced with care and appropriate modifications. (In this volume, Bates discusses such evolutionary thought in some detail.) Clearly, behind British rule and its attitude to Indians, and indeed behind thinking on many issues much more recently, there lay a key dichotomy or tension: between universalism (the idea of one preferred law, ethics, knowledge, functions, method) and essentialism or relativism (the emphasis on distinct, culturally-appropriate rules and behaviour). Comparative history and anthropology, as in Maine, represented one of the ways of trying to reconcile the two approaches. Accordingly, in India by the later nineteenth century the administrators had discovered complexity and contradiction (jati rather than varna). While they continued to underestimate the long and persistent history of dissent (especially against caste), at the same time they emphasised features of India which they regarded as preventing political or social unity. Though there was 'Indianness' (made up of pervasive characteristics), there were also great divisions between 'tribes', between caste/outcaste, Hindu/Muslim, urban/rural and advanced/loyal. Hence—a lesson drawn also from the 1857 uprisings

[51] For an example of Maine's influence on Indians, see the children's book discussed by Chowdhury-Sengupta: in describing the 'Aryan' invasions it suggested a past still present—'primitive' Santhals or Kols (like Amazonian Indians or Australian Aboriginals in popular parlance to this day) were 'survivals' from earlier societies, preserved in the midst of others which had evolved to various degrees. Maine's influence is discussed similarly by Bates below.

and from later religious or agrarian disturbances—social authority, including caste hierarchy, was a necessary bulwark against anarchy. Another functional explanation appeared: caste and social difference had originated to preserve the race purity of the Aryans and were necessary to keep the 'primitive' (irrational and volatile) Indians under control. Hierarchy, including princely houses and a largely-invented aristocracy, could be seen as maintaining stability and defining Hinduism and, very often, Indianness: traditional elites preserved a degree of consensus between distinct social groups. British conservatives took this view, anxious to avoid the dangers of rapid social change. Many officials became pessimistic about improvement. They argued that India's problems were interrelated: one aspect could not be improved without all the others. A possible implication was that India's inferiority was intrinsic, permanent and racial, so that British institutions could not be successfully transferred at all. This was an argument to oppose decolonisation,[52] but again it was defining a category, 'India'.

At this time, of course, by the last quarter of the nineteenth century and the early decades of the twentieth, race theories were used to account for difference and to define identity. Race became, gradually, a necessary concomitant of Indianness, though first it was discovered in regional or religious guises. For example, as shown several times in this book, when the term Aryan, meaning Indo-European, came to be widely used by Indians in the nineteenth and twentieth centuries, a racial element developed also, in reaction, in the arguments of those who opposed it: thus the pseudo-history of Dravidian nationalism tells of an original people, probably morally and culturally superior, but subjugated by Aryan invaders.[53] Folk qualities and identities were

[52] I have discussed this in Peter G. Robb, *The Evolution of British Policy towards Indian Politics* (New Delhi, 1992).

[53] In addition to Hellmann-Rajanayagam in this volume, for Dravidian identity see Robert Caldwell on the Tinnevelly Shanars (1849) or his *Comparative Grammar* (1856), as discussed by Dirks, 'Caste and race in Southern India'; see note 65 below. There are of course many similar instances of European constructions placed upon history for other regions and peoples of India. Nandini Gooptu has shown similar beliefs among the appropriately self-named Adi-Hindus, 'Caste, deprivation and politics: the untouchables in UP towns in the

regarded as primordial—that is, original but still extant—and purity of inheritance came to be important. Gradually the word 'Indian' came to imply 'race', even before it clearly meant 'nation'.

These race theories had currency during the rise of the nation-state, and therefore race had to fuse with nationality. Majeed makes the point that a broader arena for the discussion of ideas of race was found in the concept of citizenship. In South Africa around the turn of the twentieth century, in later re-drawings of the maps of eastern Europe, or in the evolution of the British Commonwealth, race and citizenship have colluded or collided. The South African case helped forge a single Indian identity (by race and citizenship), with more lasting consequences in India than in Africa. Chowdhury-Sengupta too describes an evolution in Bengal of ideas of the 'nation' as distinct from country of residence, and of 'Hindu' as a racial (Aryan) identity (though one that was, as in other cases, cultural rather than biological).

We must distinguish here between borrowings, reactions to 'modernity', and longer-term trends. Chowdhury-Sengupta's nationalists were clearly reacting to what they then regarded as a denigration of Bengali character as effeminate,[54] in European accounts, but they were also choosing among aspects of their own tradition. In his paper here on the Gurkhas, Caplan mentions briefly how, less ambivalently perhaps, the 'martial' stereotype was taken up by Gurkhas themselves, partly for expediency and partly as an item of conviction. Majeed, in his paper for this volume, discusses the antecedents of race theory with regard to Muhammad Iqbal. He takes the process of reaction and synthesis as his

---

early twentieth century', in P. Robb (ed.), *Dalit Movements and the Meanings of Labour in India* (Delhi, 1993).

[54] The same stereotype might be used positively, either with reference to the supposed moral and spiritual qualities of women and hence Indians (as by Vivekananda and Gandhi), or by redefining the attributes of women. Chowdhury-Sengupta's discussion of Bankimchandra and others shows how the exercise depended on essentialist assumptions about physical traits, even while it provided a counterweight to accusations of 'effeminacy'. Bengalis also proposed indigenous qualities and values, such as *nyaya* and *dharma*, but otherwise accepted the language and mind-set of Western racism even as they contested it. Of course the notions of male and female in all this were themselves stereotypes; by contrast see, in the same paper, *shakti*, heroines and mother-images.

main subject, as does Jaffrelot. The paper in this volume by Rogers, and indeed the case of Sri Lanka, presents this same problem of interpretation in what is perhaps its most acute form. Though Rogers asks explicitly whether race theories were imported or added to indigenous, developing categorisations, he is analysing a situation with external influences over a very long period, from India, from various European intruders—a situation which reinforces our sense of the eclectic nature of cultures.[55] He thinks there were, in the seventeenth and eighteenth centuries (in the midst of such influences), clear identities of a racial or quasi-racial character—ideas of type defined by inheritance and role—but that there were also other identities of different kinds. Rogers goes on to suggest that what happened in the nineteenth century under British influence was the emergence of new, preponderant concepts, a coalescing of larger ethnic categories, which may be traced to Victorian ideas of race. In this case a 'racial' Sinhalese identity came to be associated with Buddhism, even though the latter's univeralist character was also admitted.

Unity of race, territory and belief was seen as a source of strength—an argument much applied by Indians including Hindu chauvinists, possibly in reaction to European jibes about the weakness, irrationality and femininity of Asian peoples.[56] Certainly such ideas seem to have

[55] We are used to regarding Sri Lanka as a separate entity, but this is clearly recent at least in the sense of its being juxtaposed to a single 'India'; and it is distinctly hard to say what is internal and external to it, especially as far as India is concerned. When Vivekananda reached Colombo in 1896 he regarded it as part of the soil of India; L.M. Singhvi, 'Swami Vivekananda—India to Europe and the United States of America', talk given at the Nehru Centre, London, 4 December 1993.

[56] Of course Indians hardly needed Europeans to teach them concepts which glorified strength, but interesting questions are raised about this which I am not equipped to discuss. The idea of *shakti* (potent force) is certainly female, in parallel with fertility or mother goddesses, but it may also be seen as the worldly arm of a detached and hence superior male. Thus the dichotomy seems different but somewhat adjacent to that in European thought between feminine and masculine qualities, and between feminine and female. There are some interesting parallels here between different nationalist cults of the body and of physical fitness, even homoeroticism, which emerged in conjunction with essentialist fantasies of race, for example among European fascists or the R.S.S. in India.

been particularly appealing not only to peoples congratulating themselves on their dominance and wishing it to be permanent (the British, the French), but also to peoples with experience of conditions of disunity or temporary weakness (Germans, Italians, Indians): for the latter, the strength gained from unity was stressed as a remedy for a decentralised polity, a paucity of imperial possessions, or a colonial yoke. In such settings, demagogues readily embraced doctrines of racial regeneration and race-nationalism, and played upon fears of 'miscegenation' and the scapegoating of 'aliens'. That strength and unity are still regarded as *solutions* is seen in the determined stands against the Balkanisation of independent India, and in resentment at the difficulties of German reunification.

The legitimacy of national self-rule depends upon the construction of the whole nation (elites and subordinates) as the self; the fear of military invasion is akin to (and often conflated with) that of miscegenation. Such ideas were important during imperial expansion (that is, the subjugation of other subordinates by the elite West), and when India, Japan or other countries sought to beat Europe on its own terms of political power, science and economic development, rather than, as with Vivekananda or Gandhi, by changing the terms of the argument. Characteristic forms of the former response were nationalism, industrialisation and militarism; the latter was typified by the essentialist dichotomy of spiritual East and material West. However, in reactions at both these extremes, and between them, the categories, reasoning and view of history all seem eminently Western in inspiration. One can go further and argue that the construction of Indianness *by the colonial rulers*, for all its self-serving distortions and fictions, was to some extent powered by the same assumptions as the nationalist constructions in Europe. Hence it could be adopted in large part by Indians who were themselves engaged in the 'making of the nation' of India.[57]

[57] Cohn and Dirks say as much when talking of 'social technologies of knowledge' which could constitute a modern state: 'Beyond the fringe: the nation-state, colonialism and the technologies of power', *Journal of Historical Sociology* 1, 2 (June, 1988); also quoted by Ghosh, 'Sir Herbert Hope Risley and the colonial construction of caste in India'; see note 65 below. An interesting topic for further investigation is how far colonial definitions of India—in boundaries,

Gradually the unsuitable elements were dropped (for example the early Congressites' qualified endorsement of Britain's so-called civilising mission, and of the need for it), though many painful legacies remain, such as essentialisations of Hinduism, Tamil-ness and so on. Equally, some useful aspects were taken up, such as Gandhi's (and some present-day scholars') romanticising of the pre-capitalist Indian village community, or the 'non-Brahman' adoption of the many anti-Brahman sentiments expressed by Europeans throughout the nineteenth century. Echoing current debates, in the first example institutions such as caste and myth could be presented as a mutually-supportive social cement, partaking of a single essense and culture. However, in the second case, elites could appear in tyrannical conspiracy against the majority, the same argument that was applied (not only by the British) against high-caste Western-educated nationalists.

A special instance of this problem, and another colonial legacy, was the notion of the racial groups within India, which we have already encountered in the so-called Aryan/non-Aryan divide. Bates in particular illustrates here the fervour with which such racial identities were pursued in the late nineteenth and early twentieth centuries. Similar assumptions are still evident in much subsequent anthropological work, with the same preference, popularised by Risley (as Bates shows), for physical over cultural and linguistic determinants; one might cite the

peoples, institutions, role and jurisdiction of the state, and so on—did in fact establish the India which now exists, and how far that was either contested by or reliant upon parameters of Indian origin. One limit on the change—and perhaps an explanation of the co-existence of a politico-territorial 'Indian' identity and of cultural-religious-racial communities—is on the one hand the fit between the realm of British supremacy and the region of South Asia, and on the other hand the misfit between British provinces or districts and 'traditional' Indian sub-units of language, religion and culture. Washbrook's 'Ethnicity', p.173, suggests something similar; it is well-illustrated by letters from Sir Ashley Eden, for example to Northbrook, 19 November 1880, enclosed with Eden to Ripon, 14 January 1881, in B.M. Add. Mss. 43592, arguing for the 'non-Bihari' character of many Bihari districts, and for the quintessential 'Bihari'-ness of the seven districts of the old Patna Division. The Lower Provinces of Bengal, before 1912, were notably diverse, but so were the Presidencies of Madras and Bombay. Independent India has not resisted either the formation of new, arguably more homogeneous states or the bifurcation of districts.

rash of studies of the hill peoples of northeast India which appeared under the auspices of the Assam government in the 1920s. These represent forces of division which remain strong. But, working against them, there was first the test of the market-place or the classroom (the frequent difficulty of distinguishing castes and tribes casually as physical types, noted by J.C. Nesfield in 1885, and quoted here by Bates). Secondly, there was also a powerful influence from the activities of the state as it tried to define sovereignty, national subjects and a civil society in India. These efforts created a space for an Indian identity which could be described in terms of race. If there were an *Indian* race, then the contests and imperfections of category would disappear into the shadows as internal affairs, fraternal squabbles: such arguments are still used today.

A second arena for race theory was in the construction of religious identities. We will here briefly consider Hindus, but there are significant parallels with Muslims some of which may be traced in Majeed's paper below. (There is an important story still to be told—unfortunately it is not covered in this volume—about Muslim atttitudes to 'race' in India from the Sultanate period, not only with regard to Hindus, but in respect of immigrant and convert Muslims.) In the Hindu case, there were at least two distinct if intertwined strands: very broadly speaking they were communities of belief structured according to mainly Western principles, and communities of practice advancing a supposedly indigenous tradition. Nonetheless, though there had always been religious debate in India, both these nineteenth-century positions developed largely in response to Western influences, theological, intellectual and material. They revolved around at least three rival forms of revelation—divine (original and textual), continuous (tradition and practice) and scientific (findings of investigation and conclusions from reason). The challenge represented by the West was far wider than that from ideologies, but ideas did focus it narrowly. European missionaries, for example, fronted an attack on what they defined as the Hindu religion—meaning, significantly, the religion of the Hindus. The distinctive features of the attack were disgust at some Hindu practices and images as unworthy of representing the divine, and a judgment that belief and cultures could be ranked by rational principles according to levels of progress. Missionaries supported a particular, æsthetic view of the divine, matching the race-theory expectation that there would be physical confirmations of moral character in humans. God was supremely moral and hence beautiful, just as sin, of course, was ugly. Similarly, monotheism was advanced and rational, as Christianity was civilised and universal, while idolatry and fetishism indicated barbarity. Hindu replies to assaults made on this basis claimed equivalence for Hinduism *using similar criteria*: they measured its standing according to authority, history and reason. They would construct Hinduism as a world religion expressed in its believers' understandings of doctrine, symbols and ritual. Thus, in an ironic echo of the pretensions of both Christianity and Islam, Vivekananda argued that there was truth in all religions, but that Hindu traditions were its fount, their superiority demonstrated in their eclecticism.[58]

In his attempt to reform Hinduism, Rammohan Roy had earlier invoked scriptural authority, but also called for judgments on the credibility of religious arguments and practices. He advocated the primacy of the original text (and one of the great divides, not for the first time, was then opened up according to the standing accorded to later traditions, the Puranas and Tantras rather than the Vedas). In asserting the supremacy of the original form, Rammohan was borrowing from theories of decay and corruption (from the Fall, as we saw in Gobineau, from ideas of innocence, or the golden age), and from quasi-juristic concepts of precedence. He also drew of course on the work of Western Orientalists in establishing the historicity of the texts he favoured.

The prestige of the written form was not new in India, but it was enormously reinforced by being at the core of the innovations introduced by the British in India. Indeed, given the vigour of the Western

[58] In writing the paragraphs which follow, I have been influenced by Vasudha Dalmia, 'The modernity of tradition: Hariscandra of Banaras and the defence of *Hindu dharma*', paper read at SOAS on 26 November 1993, and by her references to James Kennedy, *Christianity and the Religions of India* (1879), Rammohan Roy, 'A second defence of the monothestic system of the Vedas...' (1817), Dayananda Saraswati, *Light of Truth* (1883) and Hariscandra, ed., *Kavivacansudha* 7, 44 (10 July 1876) and 8, 22 (2 April 1877) and *Bharatendu granthavali* III (ed. Brajatnadas; Banaras, 1954).

influence in that and other spheres, it is unsurprising that other religious reformers in India should have adopted similar criteria to those of Rammohan: Dayananda Saraswati, for example, also cited vedic authority, condemned polytheism and image-worship, and advocated a religious truth that was pervasive and transparent in the believers. However, reliance on the text reduced the authority and flexibility of tradition by opening the 'original' to scrutiny; hence the need for a substitute certainty, which some found in reason. Like the Christian theologists, Rammohan claimed historical legitimacy both by virtue of divine revelation *and* through reason: here was the familiar Protestant or reformers' paradox, between the supreme authority of the text and the need for interpretation, and between the desire for a single inherited truth and for the exercise of individual judgment. For his rationality Rammohan depended upon theories of progress and modernity. Reason was both moral (judging good and evil) and æsthetic (rejecting the obscenities of theft, anger, luxury, and so on). Reason was also self-evident, a system amenable to common sense, and consistent, like mathematics, within its own rules. On this basis both text and reason were then marshalled against historical practice; custom was thought inferior to texts precisely because it was contingent and fluid.

By contrast, Indians had long shown great respect also to alternative authorities expressed in oral tradition, social custom and enactment (festivals, dance, drama, images, architecture and so on). In the nineteenth century, these remained far more important in India than in Europe, for all the latter's nationalist attempts to recover folk traditions. Hence Rammohan's approach to religious authority was contested within India, though still on its own Western-influenced terms, with Western history and argumentation. Hariscandra of Banaras, for example, developed an argument querying the provenance of the vedic texts as revelation; if they contained commentary, he asked, why should later traditions *and practices* be invalid? He also pointed out the risk of abandoning the living authority of tradition, such as was implied in a modern reliance on reason and the individual conscience—that is, something quite different from what happened in devotional *bhakti* or with a sadhu when the individual will was submitted to a guru or the divine order.

The danger of relying on individual reason, of course, was that religion would altogether be undermined; the dilemma was already contained in the paradoxes faced by Rammohan; recognition of the problem, I suspect, had been one reason for the emphasis on beauty and morality in Victorian Christianity. For Hariscandra the preferred alternative to will and reason was faith. The divine was not only pure and beautiful but accessible by love alone. God was a being out of this world: hence intellectual arguments about him were arrogant and irrelevant; they merely obscured the devotion of the believer. However this too turned the focus on the individual: what mattered was his fervour and purity rather than the form of the worship intended to assist him. According to this line of thought, espoused by Hariscandra, heterodox views were rejected, not because they were historically or rationally unsound, but because they did not accord with the one faith. The fact of faith's being preferred to reason, was likely to lead to the privileging of one set of beliefs over others—towards schism and fundamentalism. It led to new forms of authority, those of the doctrine and the sect; it may be that such re-organisations of religion were particularly valuable at times of actual and intellectual uncertainty (such as pre-Christian Rome, eighteenth-century Arabia, or nineteenth-century India). Sectarianism developed in Europe and India and elsewhere in the nineteenth century, and has gone on spreading, for example in the doctrine of Hindutva, as a counterweight but also a parallel to the humanist and scientific revolution.

All these religious movements borrowed from the West *and* reworked strands of Hindu tradition; perhaps religions can only reform themselves by breaking and re-forming aspects of their institutions and authority. Though the content of the movements and their resonances for the people were of course largely indigenous, the terms of debate and the goals were very often exogenous, introduced mainly from Britain, even for those reacting against the West.[59] Both Rammohan Roy

[59] This is not a hegemonic argument: the most frequent reaction to Western influence was probably indifference, and the influence was modified by India; but this does not mean that effects were not felt.

and the recent advocates of Hindutva were responding to repeated changes in the understanding of knowledge and truth, in the face of an assertive Christian and/or scientific method. They sought to describe a set of beliefs which (as was the assumption) in turn would define them. The proposed changes all had reference to identity. They implied a delineation (and proselytising extensions) of group boundaries, resting upon a reflectiveness about self, in terms of discovering or constructing identity from a choice among elements. The nineteenth century was a period of broader identities and more standardised forms in India, as has widely been recognised. In new contexts new rationalisations developed: essential categories defined by history, rights and rivalries. These flowed into the idea of large bodies of people with similar characteristics, what is sometimes called *qawm* or community, as in the Punjab—that is, into nation, or race.[60] They provided for schools of thought as to the means whereby similarities were achieved and enforced. How were individuals to acquire the markers of identity, it was asked? Were teachers bearers of culture or trainers of the power to reason; was education to be a spiritual, psychological or material quest? Were some faiths more appropriate to some people, as belonging and sympathetic to them? The need to establish categories and doctrinal parameters brought the religious debate into line with a whole range of other inquiries; it made available to it powerful doctrines, including that of race. After all race theory was so often an indistinguishable part of those prevailing, commonplace explanations. Those who thought religion mattered, thought that it helped define and defend identity. We have noticed that, in dividing up humankind according to supposedly typical criteria, race theory was following the diktat of broader concepts of categorisation. Similarly and very readily the re-creation of Hinduism or Sikhism or Islam in India also became the construction of a religion which would typify a people. Vivekananda's great coup (like that of the Theosophists before him) was in inverting Western racism into a kind of race pride in being Hindu. Thus those who defended 'Hindu traditions' so vehemently against Western intrusion accepted the methodology with which its debates were conducted, and the same

[60] On this and alternative terms, see also Majeed's paper below.

criteria of revelation, history and reason.[61]

In her paper below, Bayly only hints at the internalising and adaptation of race theory by Indians, but she has treated the question fully elsewhere.[62] She has shown how an indigenous critique of caste developed during British rule, and how the redefinition of 'Hindu' was part of the creation of 'nationality' in India, from emergent Hindu kingdoms of the eighteenth century to the anti-colonial movements of the twentieth. In distinctive confrontation with Muslims and Westernisers, 'Hinduism' became a 'national' faith, spread beyond belief and worship to create identity. Such Hindu-ness was raised in esteem, according to universal standards, and its hierarchy and values were reinforced, in a time of modernisation and individualism. It was employed in this role because it was available and, more than that, from pressing need. Another route for the creation of nations was the establishment of civil society: we may note the work of uplift in behaviour, as directed towards 'criminal tribes' and all violators of social norms. But this too may perhaps be regarded as an attempt to define a community in terms of common characteristics. Also among available models of organisation and identity was that of the church—hence *shuddhi* or temple-entry

[61] It is significant that this is seldom admitted even today. Of course one should not forget the important and more familiar role attributed to European racism in encouraging Indian reactions; for a short account see J.R. McLane, *Indian Nationalism and the Early Congress* (Princeton, 1970, especially pp.21-2, 37-45 and 249. However, denying 'ethnicity' (apparently meaning the divisions between Hindus and Muslims, or Brahmans and non-Brahmans) was a common determinant of political allegiance (p.9, though see also pp.271-2 and 322-3), McLane does not use the term 'race' to discuss, say, cow protection (see Dayananda's assertion that the 'race' was degenerating for want of dairy products, p.286), or Lajpat Rai's plea for 'unity and strength as a religious nationality' (p.336), or Hindu martial revivalists and extremists (for example, Damodar Chapekar's attack on a reformist wedding procession, p.357). On *quam* see its usage by Saiyid Ahmad Khan, in P. Hardy, *The Muslims of British India* (Cambridge, 1972), pp.136-7; as Avril Powell has pointed out to me, this raises the yet-unresolved question of what terms were employed (or rather of what exactly the terms meant), in languages other than English, for 'race', 'creed', 'nation' and so on: how far did meanings evolve in different languages *in parallel*, from the influence of general ideas on connotations and concepts?

[62] See below, note 65, and Susan Bayly, 'Hindu "modernizers" and the "public" arena: indigenous critiques of caste in colonial India' (presented at SOAS, 26 November 1993).

campaigns. However Bayly sees this too in terms of race theory, as stressing the 'survival' of the fittest (those most able to proselytise and organise). Hence it was race that was the central theme.[63] Colonial rule, partly from its own propaganda, came to be regarded by many Indian intellectuals as a *moral* crisis: conquest proved India's spiritual as well as material faults. Self-rule was needed, it was said, not only to prevent political and economic exploitation, and to help express a national identity, but also, as Gandhi so keenly advocated, to discipline people, remove the causes of failure, and promote the regeneration of individuals and communities.[64]

IV

Both nationalism and religious reform or revival thus contained elements of race theory, and of the wider intellectual revolution to which it belonged. Religion also drew strongly upon Indian antecedents and preferences, but re-interpreted them within the same field of concepts and priorities. Broadly speaking, however, caste is the most likely candidate for the location of an Indian theory of race—one which is not derivative to the same extent as the race-elements of nationality or sectarianism.[65] The matter is complicated by the variety of meanings given

[63] Ibid. On the basis of their shared thought and borrowings, Bayly argues that Hindu sects were not protestant reformers facing a definite Hindu orthodoxy. Nonetheless the model of the church as an organisation of believers was certainly present.

[64] In this connection, Vivekananda and Dayananda are discussed by Jaffrelot for stressing socio-cultural rather than racial problems. However Bayly's account, and to some extent that of Chowdhury-Sengupta, qualify this, and suggest a greater currency for biological explanations of India's 'decline' and 'subjection'.

[65] An early discussion of this question is André Béteille, 'Race, caste and ethnic identity' in Kuper, *Race*, pp.211-33. He was prepared to regard caste as 'a system of ethnic groups... integrated within a hierarchical order' (p.224) but noted that many kinds of difference 'are at times expressed in a racial idiom' (p.228). I am not here concerned with analytical issues or with the physical investigations which might serve to elucidate, for example, how old and consistent were endogamous groups, which are sub-castes (divisions of previously united castes) and which caste-clusters (combinations of historically separate but comparable jati), and so on. I am more concerned with ideological similarities between caste and race theory. Even for a sociologist the analysis of caste in these terms would be difficult, and for a historian it may be unwise.

to 'caste', the ways it has changed, the extent to which Western theories of race were grafted on to it, and the many debates and uncertainties which currently surround it. The issue is not whether there are 'race theories' in India today. Clearly there are; and they are Indian in the sense of being peculiar to the subcontinent, albeit combining Western with indigenous influences. (This is, after all, the only sense in which the category 'Indian' exists, as a compound identity at a point of time—unless we endorse the historical essentialisms of race theory itself.) The debate concerns the nature of this mix and its origins, in particular whether there were long-standing Indian theories of race which preceded and merged with imported ones. These are in one sense the same questions as are raised about caste. Successive Western interpretations were adopted in some measure by Indians: they quickly became part of indigenous knowledge, and now can probably never be expunged, reinforced as they are by socio-economic and political trends worldwide. But did they also grow out of pre-existing 'Indian' practices and ideologies? Washbrook suggests that 'Colonialism in South Asia had a set of "indigenous" origins as well—...[namely] South Asia's own history of capitalist development'. (Anjan Ghosh calls this blaming the victims, which is, however, a reaction not an argument.)[66] A

However, I have hit upon the expedient of basing a discussion around one snapshot of current ideas. In 1993 I organised a conference at SOAS on 'Caste Today' (with Chris Fuller as convenor). Revised papers will be published in a volume edited by Fuller. What follows are some reflections on this event. It will refer also to Declan Quigley, *The Interpretation of Caste* (Oxford, 1993). References to the Caste Today workshop are shown as 'CT'; participants, to whom I am indebted for their contributions, include André Béteille, Robert Deliège, Nick Dirks, Frank Fanselow, Chris Fuller, Anjan Ghosh, Tony Good, John Harriss, Raymond Jamous, M.A. Kalam, Karin Kapadia, Helen Lambert, Adrian Mayer, Johnny Parry, P. Radhakrishnan, Gloria Raheja, Marie-Louise Reiniche, Burton Stein, Sylvia Vatuk, and David Washbrook. After drafting this discussion I also had the last-minute benefit of a strong empirical and theoretical piece, partly on just this topic, in Bayly, 'Modernizers'. I have benefited from this work when revising this essay, but also have been encouraged by it insofar as it fortified me in my original approach and conclusions. I expect Bayly's forthcoming volume in the *New Cambridge History of India* will also help future discussions.

[66] D.A. Washbrook, 'Progress and problems: South Asian economic and social history c.1720-1860', *Modern Asian Studies* 22, 1 (1988), pp. 57-96; and 'Ethnicity'; also Ghosh, 'Risley', and discussion, CT.

similar approach to the analysis of identities in India, provides our question here: how far caste is a form of race theory, or race a caste-like ideology. Western race theory added a potency and finality to the arguments about identity, whether 'Indian' or sectional. Was this because the theory was hegemonic, or because it fitted like a virus on the host cell, caste? Our discussion will look first at the caste/race equation in the nineteenth century, and secondly at what may be said of the longer-term or intrinsic nature of caste as a type of race theory.

Hellmann-Rajanayagam shows how, in the south, caste difference became one of ethnicity, partly to promote unity, once 'Dravidians' were discovered in the nineteenth century. Even though, later, 'Periyar' (the 'great one', E.V. Ramaswami Naicker) would argue that Tamil the language should be distinguished from Dravidian the race, the effect was to present the Tamils as people who had been subjected by Brahmans and others on racial grounds. Similarly Indian social reformers turned to caste. According to Bayly,[67] the would-be nationalists might interpret it as divisive, or as a basis for regeneration or national solidarity, or as a means of upward group mobility and social reform; in race terms, this meant caste either contradicted the true 'Aryan' spirit, or it expressed that spirit (despite current corruptions and excesses) by creating a unity out of diversity, and embodying a distinct moral order. During controversies, caste became, for some (Europeans and Indians), a national signifier, an embodiment of Hindu values, a matter of norms: castes were interdependent moral communities which together comprised races, and the races composed the nation. Even those opposed to caste used it as a reference point, for example in food-sharing ceremonies or inter-caste marriages, changes which sought to create a greater caste of Hindu or sectarian identity, rather than to combine on a entirely new basis—often they retained notions of a gradation of purity.[68] Race theory also affected the attitude to 'untouchables' and 'tribals': the question was whether such difference resulted from 'real' history (the

[67] Bayly, 'Modernizers'.

[68] It seems likely that the character of these debates was influenced by the attention paid to them by outsiders (the subject of Bayly's paper in this volume). A caste debate took place in Sri Lanka as well, as Rogers shows, but it was muted; the colonial rulers' interest in it was also slight.

tasks performed by such people) or from biology, or from both.[69] A change in the modern era was that *advaita* plus modern humanism might imply that the pariah could develop into the Brahman, not by re-birth but by self-improvement within a single life; equally his low status might seem to have resulted from current and not prior misdeeds and impurities.

The major theme of Bayly's paper in the present volume is the colonial application of race theory to the analysis of caste, or rather the analysis of caste as a species of race theory, in so far as it developed in India as part of a wider intellectual world and as a possible motivator for Indian reformers. Bayly makes the point that nineteenth-century race theories were not confined to colonial settings or colonial ethnographers, though in other senses they were no doubt heightened—as the hierarchy of civilisations was justified—by conquest and empire. Her subject is the concept of race as purveyed in texts produced by official ethnographers; her comprehensive coverage makes it unnecessary to dwell on that subject now. She is explicitly not concerned on this occasion with underlying social or economic structures, or the colonial impact upon them; nor, directly, with the issues raised by Bates in his essay: the selfish utility of caste-ist and racist categorisations. But the interpretations produced by British ethnographers are certainly germane to these questions. One concern is with the extent to which there was an interplay between Western and Indian ideologies of caste—neither of them monolithic or unchanging. Even from Bayly's account it is plain that different strains of thought shared a central notion that racial essences resulted in patterns of behaviour and character, including, for example, love of liberty and truthfulness.

A second, fundamental concern is the contradiction in approach illustrated in this volume by Bayly and Bates. It takes us to the heart of the arguments of this introduction: why it was important to to relate one form of racism to a Western intellectual tradition, to 'scientific' method, and why it is equally important to consider the traces of race theories in other traditions as well. Here the form of the question is: did

[69] For an Indian eugenicist, B.N. Bhajekar, taking a line generally opposed by social reformers, see Bayly, 'Modernizers', pp.37-8.

colonial ethnographers pursue 'real' as opposed to 'pseudo'-science? Bates' perspective, unlike Bayly's, is not only that nineteenth-century popular opinion and policy ignored less essentialist views, such as Ibbetson's, but also that most colonial investigations (as by Risley or Grierson) were wholly and equally arbitrary and deductive in their methodology. However, even from Bates' examples, it might be argued that (for all their admitted absurdities) in part such investigators did employ 'scientific' method, for they were avowedly seeking objective measures—of anthropometry or language—to explain observed, but immeasurable, cultural phenomena. There is a danger in not recognising this. It is that interpretation of these sources, the refutation of 'Orientalism' or racism, may itself also be determined by an extraneous, 'politically-correct' standard. What unacceptable essentialisms deny, the particularity of different groups, needs to be admitted as much when its forms are 'evil' or 'bizarre' as when they are 'good' or 'normal' and 'human'. The defence of the worth of the individual, ultimately against all categorisation, depends on *management* of that age-old tension, discussed already in connection with Ballhatchet's paper, between the universal and the particular—as also, indeed, of that which Plato observed between the necessary and the good. Thus it is that this introduction has suggested that the power of European race theories lay partly in the extent to which they were based on actual measurement and observation, and that it will go on to argue that an effective defence against racism needs to take into account that pedigree (and its more recent manifestations).

We may pursue this matter by asking why the model of race was so prominent in the contest over caste. An earlier issue is whether caste itself was taking new form. We need to consider this because, as said, the difficulty is not in showing that race theory was grafted on to developments in caste, but in considering if caste may be regarded as a type of race theory. A possibility to be considered is that caste was being 'invented' under colonial influence during the heyday of race theory. In some senses this is the question: did caste exist? The first need, therefore, is to disentangle the evidence as it appeared in colonial records. It is interesting that, according to Rogers, the Dutch, for example, should have intervened when in Ceylon to try to increase the numbers of the cinnamon-peeler caste (Salagama) by labelling as Salagama all children of Salagama fathers: the implication is that the barriers between castes were not strong (if there were many unions between Salagama men and the women of other castes), and that the borders of castes could be influenced by re-definition, but also that caste passed through the generations and affected occupation. This kind of ambiguity has increased the significance of the colonial perceptions of caste. Two conclusions have tended to be reached about colonial special-pleading and its legacy: first, that they present wholly unacceptable views *a priori*, and secondly that they created a false image. Finally, in regard to caste, the definition matters so that we can be sure that we are not merely talking of systems of inequality in general.

There are two main interpretations. One, associated with Dumont, and centred on varna, regards caste not only as hierarchical but as religious, concerned with a persistent belief system. This view (represented here indirectly by Jaffrelot) is linked by its opponents to the colonial perceptions of unchanging caste, and sometimes criticised by means of an exposure of colonial misdemeanours. The other interpretation, drawing on ideas from Chicago, and emphasising jati, considers caste to be fluid because expressive of interdependence, a matter of political and material relations defined by kinship, service and duty. This understanding is influenced by the examination of both present-day and pre-colonial evidence on caste. It suggests that the kind of caste described by Dumont was a creation of the colonial era.[70] Partly endorsing this

[70] See Ronald Inden, *Imagining India* (Oxford, 1990), and also the discussion of Dumont and Chicago sociologists in Washbrook, 'Ethnicity'. The latter is somewhat vitiated not so much by its economic determinism as by all-embracing definitions which rather dissolve the problem addressed in the present essay: Washbrook repeatedly conflates territorial and ascriptive identities, and suggests it does not matter if 'race' is thought biological, cultural, sociological (in nineteenth-century terms) or religious (pp.143-5). However (pp.145 ff.) Washbrook does provide a useful summary and consideration, on one hand of the 'holistic' view of Dumont (with its value consensus, precluding race theory), noting *inter alia* the ability of Rajputs (unlike some south Indian groups where economic status did not affect caste standing or customs) to incorporate, and define the life-style of, other dominant groups; and, on the

latter view, Declan Quigley has recently proposed a concentric model of caste, focused on the king or dominant caste, in contrast with the linear hierarchy of what he claims to be Dumont's single-factor explanation.[71]

Quigley also considers and somewhat qualifies the Chicago conclusions, including those of Dirks. If I understand it correctly, Dirks' argument, developing the alternative to Dumont, is that indigenous race (or caste) theories did not define nineteenth-century Indian identity, because the views of society which became predominant under colonial rule were not universal at earlier times.[72] He cites the relatively low status of Brahmans in some areas. As will be seen from Bayly's and Bates' essays, with their references to Denzil Ibbetson's attacks on the orthodoxy of colonial theories of caste, these points by Dirks reveal that the current debate is, in part, a replay of nineteenth-century disagreements. We need to consider several questions in assessing Dirks' arguments, or for that matter Ibbetson's. Are they sufficient? If caste and other social features were fluid and indeterminate, were they generally so? Was there no norm? Dirks and others have talked of the invention of caste; and of course caste has changed over the last two or three hundred years: orthodoxies, and harder and broader divisions, as well as variations and contestations, have probably increased. But surely the colonial construction used material to hand—texts and customs? For example, the fact that Brahmans were not always and everywhere regarded as higher or ritually more pure than other castes does not show that there was no effective category 'Brahman' and no norm of Brahman superiority.

Dirks' second, related argument is that the constructions of caste and race in fact differed from actual practices which they then obscured. It may be, for example, that nowadays (as discussed here by Hellmann-Rajanayagam) in popular perception Tamil Brahmans have effectively been excluded from a quasi-racial identity, 'Tamil'. Part of

---

other hand, of Dumont's critics, citing evidence of 'Hindu' consciousness and symbols, the connection of caste-status to biological substances, and the inclusion of non-'Hindu' elements, not least the Islamic.

[71] Quigley, *Interpretation of Caste*, especially the conclusion.

[72] Dirks, 'Caste and race in Southern India', CT.

the explanation, according to Dirks and others, is that Sanskritic, textual orthodoxies were fashioned under colonial influence and made it seem that the south Indian Brahmans' many affiliations with tutelary deities and cults, and with the lower and rural classes, were inappropriate or (for the Brahmans) demeaning. In general, British assumptions and growing orthodoxy ruled certain practices to be impossible or unnatural—for example, Muslim participation in Hindu festivals. This sense of the inappropriate, so the argument goes, may have been imposed by the Europeans in advance of Indian pressure. Exclusivity was not invented in colonial times, but it spread then, and is spreading still. It was a matter of new ideology and not traditional practice.[73]

The argument against Dumont is partly that his model is too static and one-dimensional. It is partly that it is too caste-centred. Criticisms of the first kind are now very widely accepted. But it is more difficult to find agreement on how far we should repudiate the centrality of caste hierarchy. If one pursues the view of Dumont, one tends to find that the public sphere of life withers in favour of the ritual: hence the allegations about India's political and social segmentation. These have been shown to be misleading. Yet the view of *homo hierarchicus* should not be dismissed out of hand, at a more abstract level. It explains caste as the ultimate 'private' attribute, a denial of the 'public' —that is, an attribute which found its place (and, according to Adrian Mayer, still finds it) most strongly in behaviour internal to itself, in the *kachha* rather than *pakka* spheres: in so far as it dictated public matters it did so because of their private importance.[74] How far, therefore, did caste or caste-like hierarchies influence social conduct? For such influence the *same* hierarchical system would not have had to prevail universally; comparable features could have constantly reappeared. As it affects agricultural production for example, caste may be described as

[73] Clever people like to debate whether there is any difference between the two; but we should have no difficulty in distinguishing between, say, the idea of how Brahmans should behave and the fact of how Brahmans did behave.

[74] Mayer, 'Caste in an Indian village: change and continuity: 1954-92', CT. His point is about the loosening of caste restrictions in Ramkheri over commensality on public occasions serving *pakka* (oil-cooked) food, but not, at least ostensibly, for private sharing of *kachha* (water-cooked) food. In actual practice of course there is a good deal of variety, contingency and rationalisation.

an expression of relations which are specific between particular households, as well as between recognised 'types'. This does not mean that no general sets are identified as well, but that their spheres of relevance are quite narrow.[75] For example, being recognised as Muslim would not necessarily prevent one from being also a part of service or other relations within a village, or of sharing in local rituals and beliefs. (Here a difference between town and country, localised and metropolitan norms may be noted.) Does this allow localisms and variants generally to subscribe to caste-like ideas of hierarchy?

In detail the idea of endless replications making up Indian society has been questioned, alongside the waning popularity of village studies. But does anyone believe that there are no common denominators peculiar to this culture? Nowadays we are more aware than Dumont of the long history of protest against the domination of particular castes, and even of dissent from the idea of caste hierarchy itself. But were there alternative ideologies of equal power and influence? In answering these questions we address the crucial issue, which remains how far South Asia has distinctive social norms, and whether they may be described in caste-hierarchical terms. The contrary view, as in some students of colonial and anthropological discourse such as Ronald Inden, seems to be that, at base, significant human characteristics are universal, if not North American. While very much of such work is salutary and rightly influential, it retains therefore an element within it which might unkindly be called neo-Orientalist.[76]

We need to reach a conclusion on this debate before we can decide about South Asian concepts of race. No doubt the decision will be that universal tendencies to identify the Other were mixed in with particular characteristics in which caste ideas played a part. But we will wish to

[75] This is akin to the debate on rational-choice theory mentioned above.

[76] Mechanistic explanations on the basis of essential characteristics may indeed be criticised from the viewpoint of a 'complex and shifting' human agency; and it is demonstrable that peoples and cultures interact and change. Yet can there be 'human' agency on the basis, as it were, of some universal individualism (the theory of the American constitution, or of the Enlightenment) and quite independent of distinct sets of prevailing or collective characteristics? If not, then those changing 'essences' may have some instrumentality after all. See Inden, *Imagining India*, pp.2-3 and *passim*.

establish the nature and weight of these different influences. Our attention must be directed to the interpretation not only of present-day anthropological findings, but also, and more acutely for present purposes, of nineteenth-century ethnography. It is important to consider how we may interpret the record and the alternative modes of identity which it supposedly ignored.

A problem of the invention-of-caste argument is that it supposes a massive influence on the part of the colonial power. It also assumes a close relation between the ideas and the effects of policy. Finally, with a sociological scrupulousness which would put any historian out of business, it seems to find evidence discredited if it contains preconceptions or mistaken interpretations. Yet, as Bayly demonstrates in this volume, a chance for assessing nineteenth-century views of caste *is* provided in the extensive records of social practices, customary sayings and myths of origin collected by British officials.[77] We notice that one idea was that custom was a realm of un-reason and an abrogation of individual will—it affected everyone, but dominated the 'savage' who knew no other law—[78] and we will want to criticise the official ethnographers who saw this as peculiar to more primitive societies, and who regarded custom (and speech, in the form of proverbs and folklore) as thus *determining* Indian behaviour. But we may think they were also right—and from present-day perspectives, even 'modern'—in suggesting that vocabulary and sayings illustrate habits of mind and likely limits of action. Elsewhere I have made the self-evident argument that people whose language recognises a huge variety of soils, or types of ploughing, and whose proverbs associate certain activities with particular seasons, will be able or even predisposed to make practical distinctions between those soils and ploughings, and to conduct activities at the times appointed.[79] By this same argument, if recorded sayings

[77] As suggested above, Bates seems to represent the opposite position, in this volume, in his unwillingness to credit nineteenth-century accounts of 'tribes' whenever they reported unpalatable customs.

[78] R.C. Temple, *Anthropology as a Practical Science* (London, 1914), quoted by Gloria Raheja, 'Proverbial wisdom: language, caste and colonial rule in Northern India', CT.

[79] See P. Robb, 'Peasants' choices? Indian agriculture and the limits of commercialisation in nineteenth-century Bihar', *Economic History Review* XLV, 1

habitually use the metaphor of caste, and associate behaviour or characteristics with castes, then it is surely perverse not to hypothesise that caste was a prevailing mode of thought among Indians. One does not have to accept particular interpretations or imagine that European compilations of Indian sayings were complete or representative. The principle—that sayings will give some insights into attitude—remains unaffected by short-comings in the record, or in the motives behind its collection, or in changes in circumstance. Those are all matters for interpretation. And fortunately, despite some recent arguments, even the official sources are neither monolithic nor consistent: in addition to accidents of the record, there were many strong personal or policy motives which led officials to promote different views of India. By investigating the collectors we can identify and to an extent allow for the bias in the sample.[80]

The ubiquity of caste might be a distortion of the record, the product of mistaken essentialism by the British, or attributable to the influence of Brahman texts and informants, an influence necessitated by European assumptions about the means of rational inquiry. It might be an innovation of the nineteenth century; Washbrook has proposed that the view of status propagated by scribal and trading groups became more widely accepted (in comparison with those of warriors) at just the same time as scribal and trading castes rose under the colonial state.[81] But it might also have been central to indigenous perceptions. Its centrality does seem to be supported by much other evidence. This is the argument, in this volume, of Hellmann-Rajanayagam when she suggests that the status and role of the Vellalars 'predestined them to claim the status of Tamils *par excellence*'.[82] The view of the great colonial offi-

(1992), especially pp.114-16.

[80] Raheja (CT) makes a notable start. However, despite (or because of) her credentials as an ethnographer who attempts to let us hear her subjects' voices, she seems reluctant to discern South Asian perceptions in evidence which she regards as skewed by colonial observers. Thus current worries about the construction of discourse inhibit the full use of sources. To an historian the bias of past records does not form an insuperable obstacle to interpretation, any more than do the assumptions and priorities of present-day social scientists.

[81] Discussion, CT; see also Washbrook, 'Ethnicity'.

[82] She also cites one authority claiming Vellalar status was open to any who

cial and ethnographer, Denzil Ibbetson, discussed here by Bates and by Bayly, was rather different. It was that caste was a perpetuation through religious sanctions of a primitive link between inheritance and occupation. Ibbetson perceived the fluidity and contingency of caste in practice in the Punjab (as other observers did, Rogers tells us, in Sri Lanka). For colonial observers as for indigenous ideologues, various voices and sources were available, and only some were taken up. As a close and long-term observer, Ibbetson used race, according to Bayly, merely as a figure of speech, despite his occasional lapses into such stereotypes as 'fanatical' Pathans or 'truthful' Baluchis (and, I would add, 'peasant' and 'agricultural castes', terms of great import for colonial legislation and policy in Punjab and beyond—even perhaps into Africa). It seems that Ibbetson believed in race, but not in the existence of any 'pure' races: his tribes are all mixtures; and for him status reflected behaviour and behaviour determined status, and not vice versa.

The reassessment of the value of colonial observations can work two ways: there may also be an analogy with the interest taken by British Indian officials in peasant society in the later nineteenth century, which was not only because it fitted the current agenda of the rulers, but also because peasant societies had been observed and described by individuals who were then rising to prominence. That is, the utility of views explains their profile but not necessarily their origin. The same point might be—in a sense has been—[83] made about the *raiyatwari* model of society. It derived from preconceptions *and* from observation: distortions arose through the suppression of other evidence and the hypotheses they supported. The assumptions and the choice of evidence can both be seen as processes.

The issue of caste among Muslims is another notable test-case. Though there are exceptions—and certainly one must not assume that

conformed with appropriate customs and occupations. But this is not entirely compatible with the idea of Vellalar as archetypical Tamil, and it may be that openness was a nineteenth- or twentieth-century device of incorporation, akin to others whereby communities or castes or caste-clusters sought to extend their boundaries and increase their numbers, by pseudo-history, modern associations, census returns, political claims and so on.

[83] Burton Stein, *Thomas Munro. The origins of the colonial state and his vision of empire* (Delhi. 1989).

all differentiation in India is caste-like—[84] yet there can be no doubt that many Muslim groups were identified by themselves and others as castes, either because they were regarded as one of the local jati comprising the people of a locality, or because they shared caste names and caste practices, including endogamy. (This mixed use of 'caste' must affect our definition of the term.) Some Muslim jati are apparently subsets of multi-religion castes, sharing the same clan names, and so on. There may or may not be myths of conversion to explain the situation, and the connections may be vague. For example, according to Raymond Jamous, the Meo claim to affiliate to the Rajput *gotra* but in ways known only to their Brahman genealogists.[85] The idea now current in certain Hindu circles, of Muslims having inherited caste from before conversion, presumes a prior and improbable substantialisation of caste. But in general the parallels and congruences between local 'Hindu' norms and those of Muslims as a group, or of groups within Muslims, do seem to be more than a mirroring of modes of behaviour and labels of identity, and more than an extension of notoriously vague and permeable identities such as that of 'Rajput'. They represent further evidence of a shared norm of categorisation, overlapping and co-existing with religious divisions. They show, in common with other factors, including practices railed against by orthodox religious teachers, how far all local peoples partook of a local culture. The same point might be made about occupational or educational categories, and even in assessing the alleged retreat of caste in modern and urban settings.

Anthropologists seem to get answers referring to caste-like divisions when they ask for descriptions of the types of people in a village. Even without a detailed enumeration of the considerations involved, the commonsense conclusion is that these are quite different kinds of answer from the ones that would be obtained if the same question were asked in a neighbourhood in France or a town in America. The difference does not lie in the questions, and to some degree it seems just the same kind of difference observed by those colonial ethnographers. It persists

[84] See Fanselow, 'The case against caste among Indian Muslims', CT; the point was repeatedly made during the workshop.

[85] Jamous, 'The Meo as Rajput caste and as Muslim community', CT.

even though many other criteria of ranking may also be present and—albeit often in particular forms or with specific resonance—used by respondents in India as in the West: criteria of locality, levels of wealth, education, influence and so on.

Alternative modes of identity provide one of the main arguments against regarding caste as a prevailing social metaphor. Caste borders and relative standing have probably always been ambiguous.[86] When one hears of recent relaxations of caste rules, one has to remember a long history (and indeed, in myth, a pre-history) of misalliances and exceptions and adaptations, and much more variation of practice than of ideology. Differentiation also exists within castes: inside kin-groups, by individual action, for social and economic needs, or as a result of family cycles. Moreover, there have always been non-caste affiliations. Ethnographers, preoccupied with marriage as a crucial moment of self-identification and the ultimate expression of the private function of caste, have played down the other occasions on which different kinds of identity may be felt; and yet, over the long term, there have been many providers other than caste of conceptual maps: kinship, religion, polity, gender, locality, occupation, class and race all offered their own possibilities. There were distinct 'tribes'. There were networks of settlements interconnected by marriage, trade and commerce, or government—places which had specialities and reputations. There were duties according to sex, age, marital status, power, and so on. On occasions some were more important than caste; many cut across it. Presumably more alternatives are available today than in the past, with the expansion of the nation-state, of public life, of education and the trained professions, of trades unions. Alternative criteria may increasingly be determining standing among the Indian middle classes, even (it has been suggested), in a distinctly neo-colonialist echo, as a device for

[86] Rogers makes the same point about caste in Sri Lanka in this volume. Washbrook, 'Ethnicity', suggests that claims for equality crept in under Western influence, and that previous disputes had been only about hierarchy. I doubt that the distinction means much: equality-claims (even when written by Thomas Jefferson) and hierarchy-disputes both usually involve a selective demand for high status or upward mobility. The distinctiveness of South Asia is surely its greater inhibition both of *individual* mobility and of change in the status-indicators.

distinguishing themselves from the 'backward', caste-ridden poor.[87] There are signs too of the 'backward' voting together in elections in the hope of improving their lot through new solidarity.

On the other hand, these alternatives do not seem always to have had, in India, at least until recently, their own articulated ideologies. Their co-existence with caste might indeed be argued to strengthen rather than to weaken the case for caste as a long-prevailing mode of identity. Even elaborate social geographies of place, or subtle distinctions of family, borrowed and contributed to the discourse of caste, so that caste was a key or persistent element in many of these other identities. Its only rival as a metaphor seems to be kinship—*bhaiachara* ties, for example, or *rakhi* ceremonies, or alliances expressed in 'fictive' family relationships.[88] But then Indian kinship is scarcely separable from caste. For this reason, we can see caste as normative and persistent. The colonial period certainly changed it, but did not invent it: the observable grouping of various co-existing identities under its ægis did not begin under British rule, and the supposedly current processes of disaggregation are not a reversion to the pre-colonial past. And, though it cannot be denied that the changes of the nineteenth century re-defined caste, yet they did not create its centrality, but rather were shaped by it. As caste elites grew in rivalry with each other, they had the option of improving their position by substantialising and mobilising a caste (or a caste-like community—one thinks of Parsis or Syrian Christians). Caste-groupings provided a vehicle for the understanding and advancement of identity. As a result, though the advent of Western law, especially of property and contract, tended to replace private with public (that is, general and externally-defined) arrangements, yet the process was gradual and is not yet complete. Western orthodoxies were imposed on the public sphere, but the private aspects remained (as in all societies). Indeed they adapted, for example in the evolution of public versions of caste. One reason why caste survives is that, though it was stretched and its formal restrictions apparently loosened, yet its broader

[87] The suggestion was André Béteille's, at CT.

[88] Helen Lambert has written of alliances and cross-caste connections expressed in the last of these terms; CT.

institutionalising and wider role strengthened its ability to define boundaries and enforce or restrict conduct.

The question is not whether caste was the only but if it was a characteristic marker of identity: how important was it as a way of identifying self and deciding on appropriate behaviour? Was local culture a caste culture? In particular, how far were references to one's own standing explicable only with regard to the system as a whole—that is, to caste as a series of kin-sets? We do not need to be concerned, when considering the role of the idea of caste, about the means whereby caste sanctions were enforced, or the uses to which caste allegiances were put.[89] We conclude that, after all, there is something rather special about caste and its role in Indian society. It seems to be defined by an attempt to promote a holistic view on the basis of endogamous units, extending at least notionally beyond the household or immediate kin. Marriage is certainly important, more so than interdining, because it measures endogamy. And the endogamous sets do always have the potential of being ranked; despite Quigley's concentric model, there is rivalry between adjacent jatis which are not in a service or ritual relationship with each other. On the other hand we do not need to adhere to any one criterion of caste-ranking—occupation, pollution, pedigree or so on. Caste is not in a simple sense a system of stratification, as class is. It is an ideal status system, self-generating in that it produces behaviour and attitudes which can only be explained in its own terms. It is influenced but not determined by power or wealth, and though often expressed in terms of purity is not necessarily a ranking by degrees of pollution. A lot of confusion about caste is caused by a search for external explanations, in the way that material factors may be said to explain class.

[89] I have in mind, for example, André Béteille's idea (CT) that the family rather than the subcaste is now regulating marriage unions—a development one might expect with the growth of broader units of identity—and also the well-known suggestions that caste changed over this century because castes were used as vote-banks (though the political significance of caste-allegiances is certainly not new); however, one should not take this argument too far. For example, any caste sanctions which are applied only by the household (rather than in the household as a reaction to societal norms) are clearly so weakened as no longer to be caste-based at all, except as a kind of echo (or, in the simile applied by Adrian Mayer, as the smile of the Cheshire cat).

Caste is explained only by caste.

On such a definition, it seems that caste is to be equated with race in so far as it is varna (particularly in respect of purity and pollution) and also, because of endogamy, when it means jati. This was argued in the nineteenth century by those who applied race theories to caste and also to ethnicities of language. The view of Risley is the most often quoted (as in this volume by Bates), namely that caste originated in racial characteristics (physical and cultural), that caste barriers were equivalent to racial ones, and caste antipathies akin to racial. Even his critics have found it difficult to escape his assumptions: Ghurye, for example, in arguing that any 'real' racial element in caste had long been 'lost', thereby conceded a reality for racial distinctions that they do not have.[90] Upward mobility too has been associated with inventions of history of a racial kind, among Adi-Hindus and Mahars for example.[91] Caste and race came together too, as already noted, in the south, where a supposed divide between Brahmans and Sudras produced a non-Brahman, Dravidian identity. A similar tendency was apparent in Maharashtra with the organisation of the majority non-Brahmans.[92] In Bengal, however, where the same point was made about pre-colonial caste configuration, the tendency of the bhadralok (recorded here by Chowdhury-Sengupta) was to enthuse over Rajput or Maratha heroes and heroines, thus embracing Indianness as well as Bengali and Hindu identity; under Bharat Mata, they sought a brother- and sister-hood

[90] G.S. Ghurye, *Caste and Race in India* (London, 1932); also discussed by Dirks in CT. This was first pointed out by André Béteille, 'Race, caste and ethnic identity', in Kuper, *Race*, pp.219-20. On Risley see also the discussion by Chowdhury-Sengupta, and Sekhar Bandyopadhyay, *Caste, Politics and the Raj. Bengal 1872-1937* (Calcutta, 1990).

[91] See Gooptu, 'Caste, deprivation and politics'. For a discussion of the relation of *dalit* origin-myths first to race theory, but subsequently (by Ambedkar, arguably in reaction against fascist racism) to a Buddhist/Brahman struggle from Mauryan to Gupta times (and supposedly reflected in *Manusmrti* and *Bhagavad Gita*), see Philip Constable, 'From Bhakti to Buddhism: early dalit literature and ideology, 1888-1956' (unpublished PhD dissertation, London, SOAS, 1993), chs. 5 and 6. Hellmann-Rajanayagam also records the reversal of the model, when Dravidians were argued to have been more civilised than Aryans.

[92] See Rosalind O'Hanlon, *Caste, Conflict and Ideology. Mahatma Jotirao Phule and low caste protest in nineteenth-century western India* (Cambridge, 1985).

within all these putative communities. The reasons may have been the presence of a Muslim majority in some areas, the long colonial influence, the size of the intelligentsia, and its continuing rural links (despite its urban preponderance) through landowning, service to zamindars, and contact with natal villages. But, even in Bengal, there was quasi-racial opposition, for example from Muslims, Oriyas, Biharis, Namasudras and Santhals.[93]

Race was chosen to label such identities because it was available. Similarly caste was adopted by Europeans and Indians as a defining principle. But caste is different from other other forms of identity, as is race, by being theoretically non-elective, collective and immutable. Each caste or race is defined as a component of the whole, and as a mutually exclusive set (hybrids being anomalous). Many other kinds of identities—including in some contexts the nation—are avowedly of the opposite view: they are open, even prosyletising. Castes and races are too, in practice; the fluctuating boundaries of castes, as of 'Europeans' or 'blacks', are well documented. But the long-recognised difference remains, between an identity attained through qualifications or employment, and one avowedly inherited and intrinsic. Nationality, with its possibility of 'naturalisation', falls somewhere in the middle. And whatever colonial interventions did to the practice of caste in India, it cannot be said that they invented its ideology. One interpretation of the

[93] See for example Bandyopadhyay, *Caste*. For Tamil Nad, it has been suggested by Washbrook and Dirks (CT) that the divide and hence claims of Dravidian identity were exaggerated by the decline of the old order, first under Muslim rule and later under the British, which detached the Tamil Brahmans from the population at large. This is ingenious, and suggests that one difference with Bengal may have been the zamindari system, producing overarching regulation but a local weakness of the state: as a result the elites (who employed the intelligentsia to a greater degree even than the colonial administration) had their roles limited but were encouraged to seek legitimacy and influence through political, charitable and religious works. More generally, see D.A. Washbrook, 'The development of caste organisation in south India, 1880 to 1925', in C.J. Baker and Washbrook, *South India. Political institutions and political change, 1880-1940* (Delhi, 1975), on the development of broader caste identities, the weakness of caste for establishing supralocal links for castes other than those already having them, and the role of new occupations, of economic change, and especially of the state in encouraging caste organisations and caste politics.

nineteenth-century changes is that, rather than an imposition of race theory upon jati, there was a coalescing between relatively new European and somewhat older Indian theories of identity and status.

One way the comparison caste/race is posed by the papers in this volume is in terms of the openness of caste identities. There is no doubt that Indian traditions were eclectic—all traditions are—and to an extent fluid. Hellmann-Rajanayagam regards the category Brahman as exclusive, but the status of Vellalar as occupational; a similar point by Denzil Ibbetson is recorded by Bayly and Bates with regard to Rajputs and Jats; Jaffrelot considers that a 'xenological' tradition of incorporation, as well as the current needs for unity and adherents, prevented Hindu ideologues from adopting a genetic or eugenic concept of identity, for all their fascist sympathies in the 1930s and 1940s. Jaffrelot would propose this as a limit to the influence of biological race theories. It is interesting however that, even when status is applied more or less freely, according to behaviour and role rather than inheritance, the content of the categories seems to remain remarkably consistent and uniform in each case. Those who gained a particular label, whether 'Vellalar', 'Rajput', 'Jat' or 'Hindu', did so by adhering to a set of attitudes, work and customs: none of these identities was plural in any one instance, or at least not in those incidents of social interaction which were considered essential. It was perhaps for that reason (and because of the importance of marriage customs) that there was a strong tendency for status to be inherited. In Jaffrelot's example, though there were some flirtations with universalism, the project was primarily to create a greater Hindu identity based on territory, culture and sentiment; this involved denying a separate identity to such as 'tribals', 'Dravidians', 'untouchables' and most Indian Muslims. Jaffrelot has a chilling phrase for the 'traditional' attitude to *mlecchas*: they were 'required to integrate'. In this century the equivalent imperative was (and is) not a liberal offer of citizenship but the construction of a nation essentialised around a single identity. As a twin impulse of inclusion and exclusion, it was, it might be argued, akin to race theory in its mode of categorisation as well as its purpose, methods and effect. Such a Hindu 'race' might be open to converts, but only on the basis of conformity to some 'race' ideal: the prospectus is to be contrasted with that of plural nationality or multiple identities, and compared with that of fundamentalist religion. The double-think is aptly summed up in a pamphlet of 1940, quoted by Jaffrelot, which called on Muslims to re-name themselves Kshatriyas and to '*begin to act like Kshatriyas*' without '*in any way* going against the important teaching of the Holy Prophet' (emphasis added). Jaffrelot calls this a racism of assimilation rather than extermination: that is to say, the required deaths are cultural rather than physical.

From the discussion here of prevailing modes of identity in India, we may conclude, in so far as caste is concerned, that its race-like essentialism was not—or not only—a nineteenth-century borrowing. Race 'science' never went uncontested, not least by Indian nationalists; nor was caste undisputed. Nonetheless, together they provided a powerful, even unconscious orthodoxy in India as elsewhere. People always have multiple identities and means of defining self, but not all are equally salient at all times. Race forecloses some options, and caste, so often a metaphor as well as a stereotype, does so too.

V

Two challenges now present themselves to scholars of race theory and practice. The first is the existence of racial ideas and prejudices outside Europe and among non-Europeans. The second is that presented by new discoveries in genetics. The first of these points, with regard to South Asia, is the subject of this volume; but the second is also worth a brief comment even here. It has two aspects: the relation between inheritance and progress, and the origin of difference. First, we find that, whereas social Darwinists held that higher attributes might be concentrated in particular races, through evolution (that is, successful genes produced civilisation), modern geneticists might now hold the diametrically opposite view, that the effect of society and science has been to halt the march of human evolution (despite the reduced isolation of particular agnate groups), by restricting the impact of genetic mutations, and by protecting the weak so as to prevent 'natural selection'. This new argument might seem to connect civilisation with peculiarly 'un-smart' genes, or even to be a belated vindication of Gobineau's pessimism. The usual riposte is to show empirically, in reaction to an age when market survivors deny the existence of society, that there is utility in unselfish conduct. But the paradox is really just a salutary warning against excessive functionalism: the nature of social development is no subject for ideology.

On the origin of difference, there is a Weberian consensus in antipathy to racism that, although divergences may occur through geographical or genetic separation, social and political factors have the most powerful impact upon human development. 'Race, *of course*,' claims Dikötter, 'is a cultural construct with no relationship to objective reality'.[94] Race prejudice 'is a cultural acquisition which...finds no justification in biology', says L.C. Dunn.[95] Lévi-Strauss denies that biological races have any special traits, or rather he considers that they may differ in aptitudes, and 'intellectually, in æsthetics and society', but not biologically or in 'absolute value'. He does not want to attach an 'intellectual or moral significance' to skin colour.[96] Even more cautiously, though it is still not certain that the argument quite sees off racism, Max Gluckmann has argued that 'biogenetic differences are negligible ...when compared with the effects of historical contacts, of health and

[94] Dikötter, *Discourse of Race* (emphasis added). He means the linking of physical and cultural differences, but it is a matter of debate how far cultural constructs can ignore 'objective' reality.

[95] L.C. Dunn, 'Race and biology' in Leo Kuper, ed., *Race, Science and Society* (Paris and London, 1975), p.66. This is also the view of N.P. Dubinin, 'Race and contemporary genetics', loc.cit. Michael Leiris, 'Race and culture', loc.cit., denies that there are any innate racial aversions; this may well be true, but there are surely innate aversions and a tendency to form into groups.

[96] Lévi-Strauss, 'Race and History', p.95. M.G. Smith has argued for the objective existence of races alongside folk constructions of 'race'; 'Pluralism, race and ethnicity in selected African countries' in John Rex and David Mason, eds., *Theories of Race and Ethnic Relations* (Cambridge, 1986), pp.187-225. Mason, 'Controversies and continuities in race and ethnic relations theory' (loc.cit.), objects that both are ideologically constructed; but there *are* demonstrable marriage and gene pools caused by geography and marriage customs. For a much stronger liberal position, indistinguishable in the end from a theological belief in the soul, see Michael Leiris, 'Race and culture', p.146: 'psychological traits cannot be transmitted direct as part of the heredity', because heredity affects only physical characteristics.

nutrition, of economic situation, of culture and education, and so on'.[97]

Some of these now seem rather dangerous arguments. There is obviously no question of any discrete physical trait such as skin colour causing intellectual or moral differences, but a range of genetic characteristics may well do so. We know that genetic differences are greater within than between what we call races, and suspect that complex characterictics must depend upon a whole range of genes. But present research *is* tracing particular features to particular genes, and defining biological groups ever more precisely. The concrete existence of genetic distinctions—long recognised in blood types for example, but now being located in more detail—thus poses a challenge to some refutations of race theory.[98] So-called racial differences are the compounded effects of individual traits derived from mutations: this means that each 'race' represents a clustering of characteristics, though of course not uniformity or a monopoly of those features. As skin colour and other physical features are clustered in this way, and as individuals have different aptitudes, the way is open for the assertion that intellectual and other abilities are clustered too. The argument against this was first that moral and mental qualities were really spiritual in character, a suggestion which is merely the mirror-image of the phrenological certainty that they were *determined* by physical features. Secondly—and this is perhaps just the same argument—it was said that the origins of aptitudes were so diffused and complex, and humankind so very similar and intermixed genetically, that concentrations in particular groups were extremely unlikely if not impossible. It was said therefore that all human races are, in biological terms, 'on the same level'.[99]

[97] Max Gluckman, 'New dimensions of change, conflict and settlement', in Kuper, *Race*, pp.319-40. He goes on to say that were there such genetic differences not only would they be negligible but they should not be used as a basis for discrimination (p.321). It does not seem that he intended the second proposition to depend on the first; rather it was an absolute—'our values demand' it.

[98] See Stone, *Race*, p.45, quoting John Rex, *Race and Racialism* (London, 1970). See also Dunn, 'Race and biology'.

[99] Dubinin, 'Race'. According to David Mason, despite the biological origin of phenotypical difference, intellectual and moral qualities are 'complexly and polygenetically determined' so that they should not be assumed to 'vary simultaneously along a single scale'; Mason, 'Controversies and continuities'.

Aspects of these conclusions, however, are matters of preference and not proof. Class, custom and geography mean that human genes are *not* freely and randomly mixed through reproduction. After recent genetics perhaps we should no longer refute race theory on the proposition that all races are identical. Though its investigations raise ethical issues, and though single genes seem most unlikely to bear responsibility for complex outcomes, yet science will probably discover more and more genetic characteristics that may enable people to be constituted in groups or categories. Some groupings will have policy implications, for example for preventative medicine. Claims will certainly be made that some such categories correspond to 'races' or 'classes'. These will be based on a reification of genes as 'causes', repeating what happened with 'race' under the influence of rational, empirical method.[100] The claims can hardly be prevented, and, even if they could, there

---

But, though broad characteristics by definition may have many origins, one cannot be confident which traits will remain broad, as geneticists analyse genes ever more precisely. An early and hotly-contested response to this possible challenge was made by Pierre van den Berghe (see 'Ethnicity and the sociobiology debate', in Rex and Mason, *Theories,* pp.246-63; and also *The Ethnic Phenomenon*, New York, 1981)—a Darwinian socio-biology which traces ethnicity back though kinship and nepotism to the selfish (self-perpetuating) gene, but which, despite the author's denials, seems reductionist, in that we have to suppose that the behaviour of the individual and of the 'race' are identically sustained.

[100] The argument here is that, although genetic variations within so-called 'races' are as great or greater, and are far more numerous (notably among Africans), than between any two individuals of 'different' race, this fact will not prevent clusters of genetic characteristics from being identified, defining various biological groups according to different crtieria. Though these groups and criteria are very unlikely wholly to coincide with what are now called 'races', their existence may feed or help rationalise racial prejudices—particularly as there must be at least a chance either that new genetic 'races' may be identified in future, or that some groupings of specific features will coincide, concentrating certain abilities along with discrete physical characteristics. It cannot be ruled out that a genetic basis will be found for some popular opinions—say, that certain Indian peoples tend to be good at mathematics or some Africans at sprinting, and so on. (Bearing out these predictions, after this essay was written and before it finally went to press, newspapers filled with controversies generated by Charles Murray's *The Bell Curve: intelligence and class structure in American life*, and by other research yet again claiming or seeking to link a class of people, though genes, with intelligence and behaviour; generally, and despite the warnings of geneticists, a re-emphasis on physical inheritance over environment will not only influence child-rearing and social policy,

are great intellectual and political dangers in outlawing certain kinds of inquiry, dangers which probably always outweigh the risks from uncomfortable answers. What should be the response then, to some future inquirer who argues that there are genetic explanations for an attribute of a certain 'race', and who thus, once again, gives a 'scientific' gloss to habits of prejudice or a 'scientific' cover for yet more horrors of racism? As material explanations of human conduct extend their scope, we may still insist that genes influence rather than determine complex attributes, and thus that no set of genetic characteristics will in fact be confined within the boundaries of other sets (associating, say, intellectual abilities with skin colour). But it will be prudent to base opposition to racism also on, first, a reassertion of the importance of learning and environment as human determinants (reinforced by research on early development of the brain, as well as by explanations of human progress), and, second, on arguments from morals and social policy: that it is intellectually dishonest to draw conclusions about groups, and thus individuals, beyond the range of the common, proven features which define the group, that measurements of ability and character are nearly always culturally subjective,[101] and that all humans have value and should be treated equitably. Ironically, these are also strong arguments against positive discrimination on the basis of 'race'.

These considerations are not irrelevant to the discussions of this book. Of course race theory had above all that effect of both obscuring and inventing difference, which is unavoidable in any system of generalisation. But we need to distinguish between its theory and practice, a point at issue when we try to assess the degree of observation contained

---

but also fuel class and race prejudice.)

[101] This is the refutation usually and properly made to the work of A.R. Jensen or Hans Eysenek. See Otto Lineberg, 'Race and psychology', in Kuper, *Race*, pp.173-207. However, *on its own*, a stress on the effect of cultural, educational and social differences in producing misleading scores in tests is no real answer to racism. To some degree it applies to all qualitative assessments (not least university examinations) and argues that the fault lies in the attempt to assess; and it risks merely locating the supposed inferiority of low-scoring 'races' in some other characteristic, which, in reality, may be even less amenable to change than test scores.

in the colonial view of caste. Caplan's discussion of 'martial race' theory and the Gurkhas asks whether, by cultural and physical aptitudes, some groups *were* more fit than others for military service—a question also implicit in Chowdhury-Sengupta's references to the 'slight physique' of Bengalis. Caplan's Gurkhas had fighting qualities which were, he says, 'discovered' in the early nineteenth century (on the battle field), and more detailed preferences—including the later bias in favour of 'country-based' recruits—also arose from 'personal observations' and on pragmatic grounds; there were striking regional patterns of recruitment for armies other than those of British India.[102] The theory was that environment and biology created particular aptitudes. Of course this was a prior hypothesis which affected what people saw, and led to policies based on deductive reasoning. But the theory was also a rationalisation *ex post facto*. In the case of the Gurkhas, it was policy-considerations which led to the preference for the heavily-recruited Magars and Gurungs over members of similar tribal groups from comparable environments. There may equally have been practical reasons why 'line boys' (the sons of soldiers brought up with the regiments) were not so malleable or sturdy, and why, given political and other considerations, European officers should have been preferred regardless of any racial stereotypes. It is evident, to reinforce this point, that re-classifications occurred quite readily, when convenient, dragging biological theory along behind them.[103] In short—and this was one of the lessons of our discussion of colonial ethnography and of caste—we must describe race theory as a self-serving intellectual habit, rooted in

[102] Note the Bhojpuri region, useful for the Bengal army and the Calcutta police, but also for Mughal recruiters; Dirk Kolff, *Naukar, Rajput and Sepoy ....1450-1850* (Cambridge, 1990). In his paper to the SOAS 'Race' workshop, Clive Dewey stressed such practical as well as stereotypical aptitudes. This does not mean of course that such 'race' differences are *biological* in origin. Indian movements for, say, meat-eating or physical training demonstrated both an acceptance of the stereotypes *and* a belief that remedies were available.

[103] Caplan gives examples. Another is the Indianisation of the Indian Civil Service after 1920. On the 'appropriateness' of Europeans, note (in a correspondence among advocates of Indianisation) H.J.S. Cotton to Lord Ripon, 6 June 1883, B.M. Add.Mss.43618: 'Our present system of administration was designed by foreigners for foreigners and we must be prepared to make modifications in it when the natives of the country take our place.'

relations of power and exploitation, but this does not mean that there were no actual differences or conditions which also helped explain its deployment in practice. Such practice shows on one hand adjustments to fit facts, and on the other a residual gullibility (blindness to contrary data) derived from faith in a revealed system of knowledge.

Racial and caste thinking are both clearly ideological, firstly because each may be regarded as a *response*: among a host of functional explanations are suggestions that caste was created by the circumstances of Aryan settlement, in reaction to political and Islamic challenges, or during colonial rule; and there are arguments that trace social Darwinism ultimately to Christian encounters with Islam, or to European expansion and imperialism. Both racial and caste thinking are ideological secondly because they extend beyond the demonstrable, to 'see' falsely and to provide pseudo-rational expositions of discrimination. Both do not reflect the observed so much as project the observer. They are not unique in this, however. To greater or lesser degrees all 'knowledge' has the same quality. Thus, as Ballhatchet reminded us, history, like science, does not simply reveal what is already there; it is an activity of creation as well as discovery. However inchoate and open-ended the processes of research, history, when written, is a matter of demonstration and not experiment. Yet this does not mean that history is less readily distinguished from myth or fiction, than science is from magic or astrology. Scientific exposition too is creative and demonstrative, while history is tied to actuality by its reliance on contemporary witness, and particularly by the discipline of remaining within the limits of what such witness either did or conceivably could have articulated. History's descriptions and explanations are invented, but not imaginary. One can apply the same arguments to 'race', theories of which often try to enlist both history and science. All categories are artificial in that some generalisation and selection are needed to establish boundaries; there is a large area for self-deception and mystification in human categorisations; the 'community' will always be more or less imaginary in Benedict Anderson's sense of extending beyond actual contact.[104] But it

[104] Benedict Anderson, *Imagined Communities. Reflections on the Origin and Spread of Nationalism* (revised ed., London and New York, 1991).

cannot extend beyond experience, 'real' and shared, if only at an ideological level. In short categories must have some relationship to actuality; there are elements of *observed* difference in theories of race, and all societies are bound to have some theory of difference—meaning a theory of race at least in the earlier sense of type or species.

Conversely, races as commonly defined, are of course frequently *not* co-extensive with cultures; in this book both Chowdhury-Sengupta and Jaffrelot in particular reflect on this. But race theory assumes a correspondence, as does much of the colonial discourse on caste. Hindu nationalists insist on it too, thereby constructing Hindus as a race. Our inquiry has been, partly, into the origin and extent of such common cultural themes. Thus we show how race and caste theory, while resting only lightly on reality, also influenced it. Just as an articulated race theory had its purpose in helping Europeans interpret the unknowable that was India, so it contained an obvious challenge for those it identified as losers, and a convenient rhetoric for their political leaders and for nationalists. As a commonplace the idea of race became a metaphor, helping define perceptions, even when the language of race was not directly employed. Thus, in Rees' *The Real India,*[105] diversity is fully recognised but India's history is taken to have been one and continuous from the stone age, its 'centripetal force' to have been Brahmanism since the seventh century, and its peoples always to have shown a preference for speculation over practical deductions. Hence: 'All Indian questions are caste questions.' Rees was not otherwise 'racist' with regard to what he called the 'real' India; he produced an encomium for traditional Hindu values and customs, including child marriage, and noted among other things that 'caste rules...are the most reasonable in the world, elastic where they cannot be kept, and rigid when they can'. But harsh conclusions also follow, in his account: the dubious benefits of self-government were not for Indians, not just

[105] J.D. Rees, *The Real India* (London, 1908). Rees was an M.P. and onetime additional (legislative) member of the Governor-General's Council, and official translator for the Madras government. Some of the attitudes to India typified by his book, among others, are discussed in Robb, *Evolution*, and also in P.G. Robb, 'Muslim identity and separatism in India', *Bulletin of the School of Oriental and African Studies* LIV, 1 (1991), pp.114-19.

because of their lack of education 'in the English sense', but because, with the spread of education, the 'caste and race spirit seems to increase'. For example, because they were effeminate in their marked and emotional Hinduism, with their licentious rites, instances of polygamy and other social deformities, the Bengalis in particular had no claim to be a nation. Their cry of 'Bande Mataram' was not to India the Motherland but to Kali the Mother; it was 'an appeal to the lower instincts and ideals of Hindooism in its most demoralising aspects'.[106]

This was not exactly, or at least not only, a race theory, but it would hardly have been conceived without the half-conscious racism prevailing among many of Rees' predecessors and contemporaries. Some of these attitudes have gone underground into twentieth-century thinking which prides itself on having escaped such 'medievalisms'. The influence was felt by Indians. In his *Discovery*, Jawaharlal Nehru, scourge of 'medievalism', identified India as an emotional unity, which, though he was 'almost alien', was 'in his blood'. The metaphor of race may have been unconscious, but it formed a consistent theory. Amidst the constant changes of India, across its diverse history, geography and cultures, there existed, according to Jawaharlal, a mystical core; it was 'of Hindustan, Bharata, the old Sanskrit name derived from the mythical founder of the race'. Despite the different 'racial stocks' (which possibly had 'common strands running through them'), a 'long cultural background and a common outlook on life' had developed 'a spirit that is peculiar to it...and impressed on all its children'.[107]

The relativist sympathy of such as Rees—in the mode of Denzil Ibbetson, for example—characteristically denied Indians Western-style political ambitions; and there was indeed a need, initially eschewed by the Indian National Congress, for these goals to be linked to the concerns of the people at large. Nehru's direct or subliminal references to race, his defining of an identity impressed on children through the

[106] Rees, *Real India*, pp.1, 175, 179, 180, 265, 270, 273 and 282.

[107] Nehru, *The Discovery of India* (London, 1947), pp.38-9. Compare this with Chailley, for whom race implied Aryans, Dravidians and so on, but caste depended on purity of blood (Joseph Chailley, tr. W. Meyer, *Administrative Problems of British India*, London, 1910, pp.49-50), or with Atul Chandra Chatterjee's little guide, *The New India* (London, 1948).

blood-line, was precisely the kind of device which would bring atavistic sentiments and 'modern' nationalism into the same camp. Like many of the utterances of Gandhi, they helped mobilise self-awareness in the cause of independence. But it is a curious testimony to the way that prevailing theories determine and move the middle ground of discourse, that Nehru's strivings for national identity should so closely have resembled those of V.D. Savarkar, as quoted by Jaffrelot. Given this example of racial theories in a high-minded liberal secularist, there should be no surprise at the re-cyclings of prejudice for political advantage which continue at the present day. The commonplace nowadays is that India is defined by sacred geography and ancient pilgrimage, by *Upanishads, Sastras, Mahabharata* and *Ramayana*, by race and culture, as well as by colonial borders and international law; the difficulty is that that has been considered axiomatic and, until recently, relatively unproblematic.

The purpose of talking at the one time about racism, parallel kinds of prejudice, and observable difference, was to open a space for the specific assessment of ways identity is formed and utilised. We have considered cases when race theory was a response to observation, a mis-diagnosis from empirical data, and when it was merely a prior categorisation on the basis of typical qualities, what has been called here 'quasi-biological' generalisation. The first possibility took us on to the assessment of colonial observations of India, and the second to definitions of race theory which might have a wide applicability in South Asia. As indicated by Javed Majeed in his paper, and explored fully by Bayly, we are not proposing a single theory of race, but rather a series of typologies with common features.

The issue of race in South Asia offered four possibilities. The first was that there were indigenous race theories, developing on a line more or less distinct from that in Europe. This seemed to be ruled out, in the end, by the extent to which the ideology of race shared in wide-ranging but specific intellectual trends. The second was that race theories were really to be found only in the West and occurred in India by imitation. This too seemed largely at variance with the facts. The third was that Indians adopted elements of Western race theory and applied them for their own purposes—for example, to help define caste, to raise the status of underprivileged groups, or to present Hinduism as a single and superior religion, or as a prevailing regional identity (all of which may in fact be regarded as aspects of a single argument). This was more convincing, and easy to illustrate. It implied perhaps that the salience of race was a reflection, not just of currently available terms of discourse, but of the rate of social change: while rejecting the usual impression of past stability giving way to present dynamism, we might still recognise that change is not constant and equal, and that from the later nineteenth century the pace, variety and range greatly increased in India. Thus the reification of India by means of intellectual as well as socio-economic and political developments was an important preparation which allowed race theory to be applied to India. Finally, the fourth possibility was that Indian race theories, though constructed with some elements from ideas which developed in the West, and with some of the same arguments about history and rationality, in fact represented a particular and new type—a part-Western package with an Indian content; a response to very many influences of which Western theories and intellectual developments constituted but a part. This fourth option is of course merely an extension of the third, distinguished by a judgment on the extent to which it is possible to separate form and function. It depended on a reassessment of the first point, finding that there *were* elements of race theory in some institutions, notably caste, other than those 'inserted' by European observers and ethnographers.

Of course, the hierarchies of caste operate on a different basis from post-Darwinian hierarchies of race. If caste is nonetheless regarded as containing aspects of race, does this make that term too broad, by attaching it to a quite different order of belief and perception? Or does it reveal common elements in different cultures? The argument *against* a universality of race theories is, more generally, that concepts, whether expressed in texts or in practice, must rest upon two variables: material conditions—such as occupations, technical culture, power-relations, communications—and intellectual environment, including language, socio-religious ideas, and information; and that the variables will change at different speeds and in different directions. Moreover, as a whole they are more or less interdependent, to the extent that ideas follow function and function follows ideas. Comparably, words, which also shape events, develop so as to match activities and experience, though also partly as a result of fashion and borrowing. It follows that there will be parallels between race theories or racism, and other ideologies of difference—for example, with regard to sexual distinctions—but also that alternative concepts will arise in particular contexts, which in turn will affect how far the concepts have a basis in fact. Theories of race, inevitable in complex societies, will take on the colour of other understandings, and display, in common with those other theories, varied degrees of perversion at different times and places. In short, it was a particular concept of race and not race theory as such that resulted from other Western ideas and preoccupations in nineteenth-century India. Put another way, 'race' is a more general notion to which certain accretions of nineteenth-century Europe were added. Late imperial doctrines of race, and some variants of caste-ism, were particular instances of malignancy.

At this point Majeed's exposition of the antecedents and contradictions of Iqbal's thinking on identity repays study. Majeed offers us early Islamic theories akin to race, and also Western race theory, both combated by Iqbal in favour of a non-racial pan-Islamic community. But Majeed also illustrates the race elements in nationalism and religious identity, in new Middle East states, for India and for Indian Muslims. The result is a complex mixture in which counter-arguments to race theories blend with their unconscious assimilation. This is compatible with Jaffrelot's interpretation of the extent to which Hindu nationalists restricted their borrowings from Western biological racism, and instead were more influenced by a legacy of so-called 'Hindu xenology', a racism of ritual rather than genetic purity.

Even in a context of 'imagined' identities,[108] it is quite difficult to tease out the ways and extent to which South Asian experience is *sui generis*. But it seems that it too contributed to the particular, nineteenth- and twentieth-century idea of race in India, from its own race-like theories. How might we construct a theory which would account for

[108] Anderson, *Imagined Communities*.

these in terms of historical processes parallel to those elsewhere? Analytically we might postulate a difference between identities contained within and subordinate to a hegemonic community and culture (as of Christendom), and identities which compete as potentially separate entities. The presumption in the first is that all identity is open, shared or universal, and its constituents equal if only in their inferiority to the central authority; there is a kind of admitted plurality, and the identity is of humankind, at least as perceived or in potential. In the second case, however, each identity is thought to be bounded, fixed and arranged in a hierarchy. Historically, therefore, it sometimes seems as if there has been a progression from the first condition to the second, in accordance with developing individualism, modernisation and nationalism. The change is paralleled by the intellectual move towards rational categories and causation. Perhaps at the point at which a greater community ceases to be expanding, encompassing and plausibly universal, and has to see itself as one aspect of a divided world, then it begins to splinter into distinct and closed (though still of course heterogeneous) fragments. Comparisons may be instructive here between Christendom or Islam or the Chinese Middle Kingdom on the one hand, and the development of nation-states and nationalities on the other:[109] whatever their similarities as ideological type, the forms religious community, dynastic realm and nation (or its cousin 'race') clearly occupy quite different situations. The last of the three usually seems the most exclusive and confining. Perhaps, on the other hand, paradoxically, religions and dynasties, though producing greater communities, depended on a restricted possession of the tools and opportunities of high or shared culture, while the narrow 'nation' resulted from their diffusion.

Though it should not be taken that identities are expressed and transmitted only in speech, writing and printing—there are always also ceremony, ritual, the seasonal rhythm, landscape, art, economic roles, technology—yet language may provide a useful metaphor for the arguments just advanced. In the one case, there is a classical language

[109] Plural unions such as Yugoslavia or Soviet Russia, however, may also lean towards the first category, and for the same reasons; at their break-up narrower 'nations' have appeared and fought together.

(Greek, Latin, Sanskrit, Pali, Arabic, Persian, Mandarin and so on)[110] as the repository and arbiter of tradition. It is shared putatively by all within its orbit, though in practice interpreted by specialists (priests, Brahmans, scribes),[111] access to whose ranks may be more or less closely regulated, more or less closed by birth or rank. Against these classical or (within their sphere) universal languages, the 'vernaculars' have lower status and specific functions. But then the vernaculars also may develop so as to be both high and low, to take on a full range of attributes and tasks, and thus to compete amongst themselves, defining their boundaries and relative standing. They acquire histories; they take on a definite form and create a new standard—vocabulary, orthography—in which each is sovereign unto itself. Some are imperialist, as was English over Welsh, or French over Breton, or Bengali over Oriya, Assamese and Maithili. (It is hardly new to appreciate the importance of power and political institutions for the outcome of such struggles.)[112]

Changes certainly were visible in South Asia, with the evolution of regional languages, the perceived hardening of their boundaries, their acquisition of formal and literary aspects: they too are both 'imagined' and constructed. If a chronology or progression is implied by all this, then its character would seem to reinforce the idea that race categories emerged with the decline of universal and the rise of national identities, that is, in the 'modern' era—but, in South Asia, not only from outside. The difficulty, for general theories based upon this model, is that no two classical 'empires', and no two vernacular 'nations', are really the

[110] And arguably Russian; see note 109.

[111] Or Communists; see note 110.

[112] See, for example, Suniti Kumar Chatterji, *The Origin and Development of the Bengali Language* (London, 1970; first published 1926), especially vol.1, pp.91-149. Note (p.100) how Magahi had been 'one of the least fortunate' among languages: for the 'land of Magadha [southern Bihar] was one of the most prosperous parts..., and its people...formed the most powerful nation', but 'with the fall of the Mauryas' its importance waned, and by the fourth century A.D. it had become 'jungly, and...sparsely populated'. Compare p.81: vernacular writing in Bengal began during the sway of the Pala dynasty from c.740, and by 'the middle of the 10th century the Bengali language may be said to have become distinctive'; and 'Bengal, which so long formed more or less an appendage of Magadha, seems to have distinctly broken way...about 1100, with the elevation [to power there] of the Senas'.

same in their content or the kinds of relationship and identities which they permit. The Brahmanical world-view no doubt was in some senses as hegemonic and universalist as the Christian, but it was never a single system of belief: its 'decay' and the 'rise' of regional languages took particular forms, in part because of variant conditions (for example under colonialism), and in part because of differing reactions to agents of change, such as the printing press or education.[113]

On the one hand there seems to have been sufficient similarity in the processes of change and the building of identities, in two different civilisations, to ensure at least that European race theories could successfully be grafted, in India, on to the idea of the nation, its religion, history and society. India appears to have twin, overlapping or complementary legacies: nineteenth-century racism from the West, and the ancient prejudices, in the Hindu case, of caste and Brahmanism. The common trends imply a coalescence. We may be able to propose, in some cases, similar conclusions from parallel experiences, in the way that Dikötter remarks on the Chinese equation of (their) civilisation with humanity, of skin colour with moral character, of foreigners with demons—in short, of typologies just like many of those in Europe and arising not from mimicry but from separate responses to comparable needs and experiences.[114] On the other hand, the story is also of rival and contradictory tendencies, in European as in Indian thought and practice. There were internal as well as external contests between rival paradigms, non-racial and well as racist.[115] Moreover, race theory is false categorisation (the yoking-together of much that is dissimilar on

[113] I owe this point, which awaits elaboration and verification, to discussion with Pragati Mohapatra, and to her studies of linguistic identity among Oriyas, the remarkable story of how over one or two generations what some supposed to be a backward dialect of Bengali became recognised as a distinct language. Of course the story does not begin so recently. In India it can be traced back hundreds of years to the rise of vernacular languages, including localised, even folksy adaptations of 'classical' texts, and to identifications of place as cultural and historical constructs as well as regional polities.

[114] Dikötter, *Discourse of Race*, pp.1-60.

[115] Compare Peter van der Veer, *Religious Nationalism. Hindus and Muslims in India* (Berkeley, 1994), which was received too late to be discussed in this essay, but which provides an important, well-considered overview, not least in stressing the contested and contextual nature of religious and national identities.

the basis of a little that is more or less the same); the same fallacy is repeated whenever binary distinctions are applied to complex forms or to conditions dependant upon context. By these arguments race theories in different places were neither identical nor inevitable. The borrowings in India under colonial rule, and for that matter in the opposite direction, from India, suggest the existence of distinct race theories and of other social forms. From plurality, we draw some hope and comfort. But India's twin legacies, and those elsewhere, bound up with 'modern' thought and statehood, are thus characteristic of this era, and may never work through their potential for bloodshed and hatred.

Chapter 2

THE LANGUAGE OF HISTORIANS AND THE MORPHOLOGY OF HISTORY*

Kenneth Ballhatchet

Words change in meaning as they move through time and space. But historians use the same words in ancient and in modern history, in Western, in Asian and in African history. They also use similar types of explanation. Do unchanging concepts and models lurk behind the vocabulary of historians? Is there a morphology of historiography, or even more important, of history itself? Such questions are given urgency by the growth of comparative historical studies, in which Giorgio Borsa has been such a distinguished pioneer.[1]

History as a discipline has no agreed vocabulary, unlike economics, geography, sociology, or for that matter literary criticism. We can find the explanation in the history of historical writing. The modern discipline began with political history, where historians found the terms they needed in the sources—government, policy, legislation, and so on.[2] Economic history, on the other hand, took its terms from economics, and they were usually defined with rigour. The problem of terminology only became explicit in social history. Social history did not contain most of its terms within its sources, and there was no general agreement about the meaning of terms in sociology. In social history, in Giorgio Borsa's words, 'the historian makes more or less conscious use of categories, ideal types, analytical models elaborated from sociology'.[3] There is the difficulty: 'more or less conscious'. Even political histo-

* Centre for South Asian Studies Annual Lecture 1992.

[1] This is based on my lecture 'Il vocabolario e la morfologia della storia' at the University of Pavia in December 1989, on the occasion of Professor Giorgio Borsa's retirement.

[2] The origins of historiography may lie in genealogy or mythology, but this does not affect the argument.

[3] 'Lo storico fa un uso più o meno consapevole di categorie, tipi ideali, modelli analitici elaborati dalla sociologia', G. Borsa, *Introduzione alla Storia* (Firenze, 1980), p. 48.

rians took their terminology from the sources without troubling over much about definition. So the language of most historical writing hovers uneasily 'between everyday speech and scientific terminology', in Pietro Rossi's phrase.[4]

Should historians use the same terminology whatever the period? Robert Lauffer once suggested that it was anachronistic and misleading to use the word 'slave' when speaking of society in ancient Greece.[5] The word was associated not only with medieval Slav war captives but also with negro slaves in the ante-bellum South of the United States, who suffered from racial prejudice. A slave in Ancient Greece or Rome, on the other hand, never had to contend with such difficulties, and some slaves lived in comfort and were entrusted with responsibility. Instead of using the word 'slave' in histories of ancient Greece or Rome, one solution would be to use the terminology of the time—*doulos* or *servus*. Another solution would be to use the word 'serf'. But in a symposium about the problems of general statements in historical explanation, Finley argued in this connection that 'serf' was as imprecise a term as 'slave'.[6] In short, '*traduttore, traditore*!' On the other hand, if using the terminology of the time avoids the problems of translation, it also impedes comparative studies. However, there remains a fundamental characteristic of slavery, whether in ancient Greece or ante-bellum America—the fact that it is involuntary. This must be the essence of a generally applicable definition.

Should historians use the same terminology whatever the region?

[4] P. Rossi, 'Die Sprache des Historikers zwischen Umgangsprache und Wissenchaftssprache', *XVe Congrès international des sciences historiques, Rapports* I (Bucharest, 1980), pp.440-7.

[5] 'Das Wort Sklave, esclave, schiavo, das aus dem Mittelalter stammt und ursprünglich der Kriegsgefangenen Slaven aus Osteuropa bezeichnete, laßt sich nur in anachronistischer, also misverständlicher Bedeutung auf die Antike übertragen. Es erinnert anßerdem an die Negersklaverei in Nordamerika und in den Kolonialgebeten während der letzen Jahrhunderte was seine historische Übertragbarkeit auf antike Verhältnisse weiter erschwert, Der antike "Sklave" ist ein ganz anderer gesellschaftlicher Typus'; R. Laugger, 'Die Sklaverei in der griechen-römischem Welt', Eleventh International Congress of Historical Sciences, Uppsala, 1960.

[6] M.T. Finley, 'Generalizations in Ancient History', in L. Gottschalk (ed.), *Generalization in the Writing of History* (Chicago, 1963).

What has come to be the accepted solution in India historiography was reiterated by a group of American historians fascinated by the differences which they perceived in rights over land in India as compared with the Western world: therefore they used Indian terminology.[7] But is it realistic to suppose a precision and uniformity of meaning in terms used over such a vast region as the Indian subcontinent and over a substantial period of time? *Zamindar*, the word for a landholder in Bengal, is usually taken to denote a large landholder, since most of the zamindars in Bengal were substantial men. But in East Bengal there were people called 'zamindar' who were very poor men, cultivating the soil with their own hands. Nevertheless, a vast mythology of revenue history developed, in which zamindari settlements of the type concluded by the British government with the great landholders of Bengal, were contrasted with *raiyatwari* settlements of the type that the British concluded with small cultivators in South India. The word *raiyat* was often translated as 'peasant', and many raiyats resembled peasants. But there were also in South India some people called 'raiyat' who were rich farmers, cultivating large estates with low-caste labourers. Ignoring such troublesome inconsistencies, historians have written multitudes of volumes about *zamindari* and *raiyatwari* land settlements as if they were opposite extremes. Using the language of a region solves few problems.

Although many historians shrink from theory, some have devoted much energy to refuting the notion that feudalism could exist anywhere but in medieval Europe, perhaps to demonstrate their respectability as opponents of Marxism. In the nineteenth century historians were moved by other emotions. When James Tod, one of the British East India Company's enthusiastic officers, wrote admiringly of the *Annals and Antiquities of Rajasthan*, he was intrigued by Hallam's analysis of feudal institutions in medieval Europe,[8] and he readily found feudalism among the Rajputs.[9] The first volume of his epic appeared in 1829, but

[7] R.E. Frykenberg (ed.), *Land Control and Social Structure in Indian History* (Madison, 1969).

[8] *View of the State of Europe during the Middle Ages* (London, 1818).

[9] James Tod, *Annals and Antiquities of Rajasthan* (first published in two volumes; republished in three, edited by W. Crooke, London, 1920; reprinted

in a less romantic age half a century later, the civil servant, Alfred Lyall, accused him of confusing tribal and feudal structures.[10] In the age of imperialism, 'tribe' was a concept conveying primitive if not pejorative overtones. Lyall's criticisms were later elaborated, if not acknowledged, by William Crooke, another official, who emphasised that feudalism was European, and that the Rajputs had the 'defects' of 'most Orientals'.[11] Historians with no love for the British Empire followed suit, often using the term 'clan' instead of 'tribe': there might be tribes in Africa, but there were clans in more enlightened countries—Scotland, for example. As late as 1956 Daniel Thorner agreed that there could have been no feudalism in India.[12] However, three decades before this, a new theory had gained acceptance within the secretive bureaucracy, suited to the needs of the British raj in its last decades. Indian rulers were no longer feared or suspected: they were regarded as useful allies against nationalism, and their usefulness could be increased if they had the power to enforce land reforms in spite of the opposition of their nobles. C.U. Wills, a retired British official employed by the ruler of the important Rajput state of Jaipur, studied the archives and declared that there was no historical basis for any feudal limitations on his power. Historiography needs to be extricated from the preoccupations of bureaucrats.[13]

Delhi, 1971).

[10] A.C. Lyall, 'The Rajput states of India', *Asiatic Studies* i (London, 1907).

[11] Crooke, introduction to Tod's *Annals*, pp.xxxviii-xxxix.

[12] D. Thorner, 'Feudalism in India', in R. Coulborn (ed.), *Feudalism in History* (Princeton, 1956); compare E. Leach, S.N. Mukherjee and J. Ward (eds.), *Feudalism: Comparative studies* (Sydney, 1985).

[13] Wills's theories have been brought to light and analysed by Robert W. Stern, *The Cat and the Lion: Jaipur state in the British raj* (Leiden, 1881). Histories sponsored by the establishment tend to proceed from assumptions suited to its purposes. In the 1930s the *Oxford History of England* ignored the Immigration Act of 1905, devised to check Jewish immigration, which was the basis for subsequent legislation designed to check other immigration, although R.C.K. Ensor, the author of the relevant volume, went into considerable detail about other social policies which cast a more favourable light on Britain. Also in the 1930s the *Cambridge History of India* portrayed British policies as having many beneficial consequences. But by the 1980s criticism of the evil consequences of imperialism was much more widespread, and the *New Cambridge History of India*, at least in the volumes so far published, stressed that the British government was powerless to effect fundamental changes, whether

Tod was not unique. In the second half of the nineteenth century the English diplomat, Algernon Mitford, wrote admiringly of the feudal customs he had seen in Japan.[14] And when in the twentieth century Marc Bloch turned from medieval Europe to Japan he concluded that feudalism had indeed existed there. He found striking resemblances to European feudalism in the history of pre-modern Japan.[15] There were murmurs of indignation among various English scholars at the suggestion that an Asian country could have had such a European-style institution as feudalism. In the *Economic History Review* an Oxford historian praised R.S. Lopez for confining his analysis to Europe: 'Japanese and other outlandish feudalisms are sent home where they belong'.[16] So much for scholars like Bloch. But even Bloch assumed that his model must be European. Feudalism could be said to have existed in Japan only if it resembled the European model. And it is true that the concept itself is of European origin, juristic in the seventeenth century if pejorative in the eighteenth.[17] However, if one disengages the concept from the purely European sense of a system of landholding in return for military service, one can define it to suit both Europe and Asia: for example, to treat as feudal a situation in which political power is decentralised and associated with rights over land.

Can one devise an historical vocabulary in terms of structure, function and process, applicable to all periods and regions? Weber formulated his celebrated ideal types to answer specific theoretical needs. Can we identify historical forms, like Weber's ideal types in that they are the abstractions we need for historical analysis, but unlike them in that they are neither limited to particular theories nor to specific regions or

---

for good or evil.

[14] Toshio Yokohama, *Japan in the Victorian Mind. A study of stereotyped images of a nation, 1850-80* (London, 1987), p.96.

[15] M. Bloch (ed. M.M. Postan), *Feudal Society* (London, 1965).

[16] P.J. Jones, *Economic History Review* 2nd series, XVI, 2 (December 1962), pp.375-6.

[17] J.Q.C. Mackrell, *The Attack on 'Feudalism' in Eighteenth-Century France* (London, 1973). Compare Fernand Braudel, with reference to what has become, but was perhaps not originally intended to be, a pejorative term, *l'histoire événementielle*: 'Les philosophes nous diraient, sans doute, que c'est vider le mot d'une grosse partie de son sens', in 'La longue durée', republished from *Annales* in *Recits sur l'histoire* (Paris, 1969), p.45.

periods? This will involve identifying the minimal characteristics needed for historical analysis. It will involve emptying historical terms of some of the meanings and associations they have acquired through the years.[18] The result will be a morphology of history, based on the logic of historical explanation. This is quite a different enterprise from the attempt of Hayden White to identify deep structures of a rhetorical type in historiography.[19] Nor is this the occasion to speculate in a Braudelian manner between those of long, medium and short duration, nor to reify the past.

We need not postulate the existence of an historical reality somewhere in some Platonic world, could we but grasp it. Some historians seem ready to term an idea or a practice 'essentially Hindu' or to deny such a status to other ideas or practices. Other historians will ask whether Christians in some Asian or African country in some period other than the present were 'really Christian', though until recently such a question has rarely been asked in relation to European countries. However, an historian of Tarantism in Europe now tells us that it is possible to distinguish between what is Christian and what is 'authentically pagan'.[20] This seems to involve the historian's agreement with definitions of Christianity formulated by a particular ecclesiastical authority. Menocchio thought himself a Christian while his inquisitors thought him a heretic. Why should the historian side with the inquisitors?[21] Apart from the difficulty of adopting elite definitions, to which Dominique Julia has drawn attention,[22] such procedures ignore the

[18] I am in sympathy with the general insight of Dominick LaCapra into historiography as 'a "dialogical" exchange both with the past and with others enquiring into it', provided that this does not imply a reification of the past; Dominick LaCapra, *History and Criticism* (Ithaca, 1985).

[19] Hayden White, *Metahistory* (Baltimore, 1978).

[20] Ernesto de Martino, *La terre du remords* (Paris, 1966).

[21] Carlo Ginsberg, *Il formaggio e i vermi. Il cosmo di un mugnaio del' 1500* (Torino, 1976). Compare Roger Cartier, 'Intellectual history or sociocultural history? The French trajectories', in Dominick LaCapra and Steven L. Kaplan (eds.), *Modern European Intellectual History. Reappraisals and new perspectives* (Ithaca, 1982).

[22] Dominique Julia, 'La Religion—histoire religieuse', in Jacques le Goff and Pierre Nora (eds.), *Faire de l'histoire.* II, *Nouvelles approches* (Paris, 1974), pp.184-224.

historical fact that Christianity itself was from its earliest days an eclectic religion. In what period, and with what right, can the historian pronounce that it ceased to be so?

Bernard Lewis often warns us against thinking of Islam in Christian terms.[23] We should not speak of Muslim 'sects' or 'heresies' since Islam has no pope to define orthodoxy and heresy. Here we have a similar difficulty. From the Protestant Reformation onwards large numbers of Christians rejected papal authority: henceforth Christianity was on a par with Islam in this matter. What of Hindus? Until Mahatma Gandhi argued the contrary, the Brahmans' view—indeed the view of high castes generally—was that untouchables were not Hindus. So whose viewpoint does the historian adopt? With a minimal definition such confusions should disappear. We could term Christians those who thought themselves to be such, and Muslims likewise. Perhaps Hindus also? But until the second half of the nineteenth century the category 'Hindu' seems to have been used only by Westerners, and those regarded by Westerners as Hindus seem to have thought of themselves essentially as members of a particular caste, and as included or not within the three twice-born classes. There was a pejorative name for those outside the system—*mleccha*. An alternative is to look at behaviour. Hindus are those accepted as such through the caste system, Muslims are those who go to the mosque for Friday prayers, Christians are those who go to church on Sundays. These are minimal definitions. This is not of course to say that historiography necessarily ignores self-image. Nor is it to suggest that morphology has no place in the history of religion, still less in the comparative history of religions. One thinks at once of attitudes to women, money, life after death.

Function is a term used by most historians, even those whose acquaintance with systems theory is rudimentary or non-existent. Religion has been seen as serving the hegemonic purposes of the dominant classes in a society, inculcating the virtue of submission. Alternatively there has been some analysis of religion's cognitive affinities with the assumptions behind the dominant socio-economic system, whether caste or capitalism, again with functionalist implications. But if one is

[23] B. Lewis, *Islam in History* (London, 1973), pp.217-36.

to include functionalist terminology one must distinguish between overt and latent functions—for example support of the throne on the one hand, or of elite hegemony on the other.

John Elster has recently criticised the tendency to assume that identifying the function of X is to provide an historical explanation for the existence of X.[24] But while it may not explain the existence of X in the sense of the origin of X, it may explain the persistence of X. And the function of X may itself change in time. The British monarchy persists although it has lost its power: the political elite consider that it has other functions that justify its cost—especially the encouragement of patriotic and hegemonic attitudes. The office of Mughal emperor persisted into the nineteenth century, although powerless: both British and Indian governments valued his legitimisation of their power.

If with every minute, with every second, the past leaves us for ever, and all we have are the statements of historians who try to make sense of the traces which it leaves, out task is to analyse their language or potential language and identify the morphology behind it. Historiography may therefore be the key to history. This means an analysis not only of the language which has actually been used by historians but also of that which could logically be used. To criticise such analysis as ignoring the uniqueness of historical reality would be to fall into the trap which Alphonse Dupront has called that 'obstinate historical *pointillisme*' which 'treats the fact as a separate and singular reality, isolable and existing in itself'.[25]

As an example of historical morphology we may consider the ways in which an historian can think of government finance, whether premodern or modern. These can be seen as structural forms. There are clearly three possible methods of satisfying a government's demands: in kind, in labour services, or in cash—cash being taken to include taxes, tariffs and borrowing. These forms can be identified *a priori*, by

[24] John Elster, *Psychologie politique* (*Veyne, Zinoviev, Tocqueville*) (Paris, 1990), p.52.

[25] 'Un pointillisme historique obstiné traite le fair comme realité separée, singulière, isolable, existant en soi', A. Dupront, 'Langage et histoire', *XIIIe Congrès international des sciences historiques, Rapports* I (Moscow, 1970), p.23.

considering the logic of the historical situation. There is no question of postulating a progression from one to another, as if cash were the inevitable conclusion of some historical process. In fact, military conscription has been a form of labour service in the nineteenth and twentieth centuries. Several years after the end of the Second World War, the Labour government in Britain continued to enforce industrial conscription, until it lost a series of by-elections. In devising the morphology of history we do not propose some overarching theoretical explanation. Nor do we rule it out of court.

Similarly, one can identify patterns of change in time, or forms of historical process. In cultural interraction there seem to be five possibilities. At the extremes there are the possibilities of the rejection of all inputs or of the acceptance of all. There were examples of total rejection during the mutiny and rebellion in India in 1857. Some local dignitaries not only opposed British rule as foreign but also as encouraging crime and immorality: they wanted a return to the torture and mutilation of criminals. This is not to ignore such matters as the use of Western rifles by the mutineers. The *sakoku* policy of closing Japan against foreign contact is another example. To cite *sakoku* as a case of cultural rejection is not to ignore the controversy over the reasons for the policy—whether it was a reaction to foreign intrusion or an aspect of the establishment of Tokugawa authority. Our aim is a vocabulary of history that does not imply specific explanations for specific events or processes.

An example of total acceptance can be found in Calcutta in the 1820s: a group of Western-educated high-caste Bengalis nicknamed 'Young Bengal' even took to eating beef and drinking wine, not to speak of wearing Western clothes. In addition to these extremes there are two types of compromise—that of selective acceptance and that of concealed acceptance. As an example of selective acceptance one may think of the Japanese slogan—'Western technology but our own values'. Nor need it be merely a matter of technology. The Dharma Sabha was founded to oppose the prohibition of widow-burning in Bengal in 1828, but after this campaign failed the organisation continued in existence to advise how far one could preserve Hindu values, and especially one's caste in the environment of a modern city like Calcutta: amongst its leading members were some of the strongest advocates of Western education through the English language, and in its meetings use was made of Western bureaucratic procedures, with an agenda, minutes, a secretary, a treasurer and so on. Another example of selective acceptance can be found in the Indian National Congress. From its foundation in 1885 onwards it followed Western-style procedure in its meetings and used Western slogans such as 'No taxation without representation' to which the British seemed susceptible. But it also made use of caste and specifically Hindu motifs when addressing Indian electorates.

For an example of the strategy of concealed acceptance one can look again to India in the second half of the nineteenth century. Dayananda Saraswati, who founded the Arya Samaj, another Hindu society dedicated to religious reform, argued that ancient India had known the technological achievements, such as steamshipping, of which the West was so proud, but had since forgotten them. Some recent scholars have misunderstood this strategy and have spoken of the modernity of Indian tradition. Finally there is the possibility of accepting an input and then transforming it: obvious examples are Third World newspapers and films. But to adopt a terminology based on a morphology of acceptance and rejection need not exclude the possibility of superimposing another, for example one based on notions of cognitive affinity. Here one may have recourse to dichotomies. A crude but nonetheless intriguing question is raised by the emergence of Darwinism in the context of an overarching ideology of progress through competition, with the fittest surviving through an unplanned struggle, as compared with Lysenkoism in the context of an ideology of progress through purposeful striving.

Michael Postan used to satirise the historians' tendency to use the rise of the middle classes as an explanation for everything from the growth of towns to the French Revolution: the middle classes always seemed to be rising but never to be getting anywhere. Recently their rise has been extended to Rome in the age of Cicero and Japan in the Tokugawa era. B.B. Misra began his history of *The Indian Middle*

Classes in a characteristically forthright manner: 'The term middle class is much used and since most of us, without the aid of specialist, understand what we mean when we use it in our everyday conversation, I am not attempting a meticulous definition'.[26] Instead he provided a detailed list of categories which he thought constituted the Indian middle classes, among whom he included 'peasant proprietors'. This exhaustive, not to say exhausting, book was published under the highest political, if not intellectual, auspices—those of the Royal Institute of International Affairs. Only a few decades after 1947 it was reassuring to British politicians and diplomats to think that independent India was not so independent as to reject the three-class model of England. But could one identity three classes in a society with thousands of castes?

Misra was not the only historian to be confused. Many scholars have used a three-class model. Aristotle looked at the amount of wealth: there were the rich, the poor and the people in between. Adam Smith looked at the origins of wealth and found three social 'orders' based respectively on rent, trade and manual labour. Looking at power, Machiavelli thought that a city-state contained only 40 or 50 who held it. In the modern state there are more, but their number is limited. We have arrived at the idea of an elite. Mosca thought of an elite with power, Pareto of one with and another without it. Dahrendorf writes of holders of power, among whom are the capitalists, bridging the separation between economics and politics.[27] So indeed did Marx. Notwithstanding the ambiguities that a variety of critics have emphasised, he usually seems to have thought of three classes—bourgeoisie, proletariat and in the middle the petty bourgeoisie. Yet he studied in England, where it was customary to speak of the aristocracy, the middle classes and the working class. Can one ignore the class consciousness inherent in a society?[28] If not, one may postulate many more classes.

[26] B.B. Misra, *The Indian Middle Classes. their growth in modern times* (London, 1961), pp.12-13.

[27] R. Dahrendorf, *Class and Class Conflict in an Industrial Society* (London, 1959).

[28] And false consciousness, in the sense of a misunderstanding of 'real' class interests? This is clearly excluded insofar as it implies that there is an historical 'reality' that can somehow be grasped by ratiocination, meditation or intuition.

R.S. Neale found five in nineteenth-century England.[29] It follows that an historical vocabulary should include both economic class and class in the sense of status group (*Stand*). Similarly there are two types of elite to be distinguished.

Though one may criticise the uncritical way in which historians have applied the three-class model to India, one must admit that there was some basis for it in contemporary sources. In nineteenth-century Bengal the term *madyabhitto* indicated those of middling wealth, and in Calcutta the Western-educated spoke of themselves, and have since been described, as the *bhadralok*, the respectable people. Here was a similar distinction between economic class and class as a status group. Using English, the Western-educated of Calcutta spoke of themselves as the middle class. A recent English historian has written also of 'nobility' and 'gentry' in eighteenth-century India, but without disentangling these words from their English associations.[30] On the other hand, the term caste was occasionally applied, of course in a pejorative sense, to European countries. In the era of the French Revolution, Marie-Joseph Chénier wrote of 'this terrible struggle between the rights of the people and the privileges of two insolent castes', in other words the *noblesse* and the clergy.[31]

Can one think of class and caste as gradations of different rigidity along the continuum of social stratification? Not in Louis Dumont's view. He thought the Indian caste system unique because of the agreement between social and spiritual stratification—a Hindu notion. According to Dumont, the superiority of the Brahmans was recognised by all.[32] However, though in the present century many persons of low caste have rejected this superiority, yet caste remains strong. Apart from this, in Sri Lanka one finds a caste system without the notion of

[29] R.S. Neale, *Class and Ideology in the Nineteenth Century* (London, 1972). Compare G. Himmelfarb, *The New History and the Old* (Cambridge, Mass., 1987). pp.47-69.

[30] C.A. Bayly, *Indian Society and the Making of the British Empire* (*The New Cambridge History of India*, II, 1, Cambridge, 1988), passim.

[31] '...[C]ette lutte terrible entre les droits du peuple et les privilèges de deux castes insolentes', in J. Cellard, *Ah! ça ira ça ira... Ces mots que nous devons à la Révolution* (Paris, 1989).

[32] L. Dumont, *Homo Hierarchicus* (Paris, 1966).

an agreement between social and spiritual status but with the other characteristics of the Indian system. It seems to be the mortal sin of specialists to postulate that the society and even the period of their specialisation is unique. A minimal definition of caste applicable both to India and to Sri Lanka would be a system of social stratification based on the prohibition of marriage outside caste.[33]

Recently the Dutch historian, André Wink, criticised all historians of pre-nineteenth-century India on the ground that they thought they saw states with modern Augustinian-style sovereignty.[34] Analogous criticisms of historians of medieval England were once made by such scholars as Maitland and McIlwain. According to Wink there were merely rulers who ruled by means of alliances with personages of local power and influence. they ruled by division. Wink thought that this technique was a Muslim one, and he used for it the Arabic word *fitna*. In fact it is not the case that all historians of pre-modern India except Wink have misunderstood the methods and nature of Indian polities. Nor is it true that Indian, or Muslim, governments were unique. The difference may rather be between personal and impersonal governments, and this has become an essential dichotomy in the vocabulary of historians. Rather than a term chosen for its associations (in this case, Muslim), a term divested of associations, whether cultural or chronological, would have facilitated comparative analysis. It would also have avoided the Euro-centric danger of studying other periods and cultures as Other, with the implication that they can have little or nothing in common with the periods and cultural forms of Western history.

There have in fact been considerable changes through the years in the writing of political history. First came the epic and the chronicle. Then came narrative history which is essentially a paraphrase of such sources with inconsistencies eliminated; and then the beginnings of modern historiography based on 'original sources'—in other words the records left by governments in action. The historian examined treaties, laws, speeches, minutes and despatches. Memoirs were also considered but

[33] Within this type we then create a sub-type restricted to Hindu India in terms of *varna* and *jati*.

[34] A. Wink, *Land and Sovereignty in India* (Cambridge, 1986).

assigned a lesser validity. The reasons for policies were then found in the statements of politicians and administrators. These were accepted as a sufficient explanation if they were not contradicted by the statements of others. If there were contradictions the historian tried to reconcile them. The basic forms of this type of analysis are relatively simple: conquest, expansion, defensible frontiers, dynastic alliances, the balance of power, and so on. The abstract form of such theses is that the formulation of a policy is its explanation.

A further dimension was added to the analysis of political history by economics, especially Marxist theory, by elite theory, and by psychoanalysis, especially Freudian theory. Explanations were found below the surface of policy formulation. Politicians were in search of profit, patronage and prestige as they jostled each other along the corridors of power. Their words were merely a camouflage for these covert motives and impulses. So were the despatches of ambassadors and the minutes of bureaucrats. Officials on an Indian frontier might send alarmist reports about French threats early in the nineteenth century or Russian threats later, but their underlying concern was for the expansionist policies which would bring them advancement up the ladders of the official hierarchy. So it was with the army officers who prepared for the wars that would bring them promotion. 'The Great Game in Central Asia' was a favourite term for Anglo-Russian rivalries. This gave substance to Schumpeter's notion of the atavistic nature of imperialism—officials playing in adult life the games first learnt as schoolboys.[35] The case is similar with the analysis of formal and informal empires. The explanations are found below the surface, and the overt statements of politicians are discounted. An adequate terminology for political historiography depends on the identification of its morphology along these various lines.

There have been similar transformations in the historiography of nationalisms. At first historians accepted with little question the versions found in the speeches and writings of nationalists themselves, who were portrayed as challenging the oppressive and exploitative

[35] J.A. Schumpeter, *Imperialism and Social Classes* (Cambridge, Mass., 1951).

nature of foreign rule, sometimes as appealing to the values of their oppressors. Again the formulation of a policy or of a party programme was its explanation. Later there were attempts to identify stages in the development of nationalisms. There was the primary nationalism of an uncomprehending reaction against foreigners and the secondary nationalism that followed a period of collaboration with foreign rule. Alternatively there have been explanations of nationalism as a phenomenon manipulated by politicians in search of power, influence and profit: it was a self-interested response to imperialism. Imperialism in turn was seen in search of local support, distributing benefits to collaborators. As the available benefits came to disappoint the growing number of recipients, collaborators became competitors. This type of explanation was first associated with the Cambridge historians, Gallagher and Robinson, and it has been refined by some of their pupils. Its obvious limitation was in its focus—the leaders. Their hold over their followers was then explained in terms of patron-client relationships or of the activities of 'power-brokers' at various levels. Still this was limited in that, by definition, the benefits available became so tenuous as to be invisible the larger the number of followers involved. Alternatively there were studies of the cultural content of various nationalist movements, coupled with analyses of the subconscious appeal of specific myths and symbols. In terms of morphology one can identify the myth of a Golden Age followed by decline as the result of luxury and corruption or as a result of foreign incursion through conquest or immigration. And in symbols we may distinguish between religious, cultural, social and psychological references.

But the terminology used in the history of nationalisms is now in grave need of repair. Take the example of India. Indian historians slid imperceptibly from the 'nationalist' movement to the 'national' movement. The word 'national' not only conveyed approval but implied that those who did not support the movement were not members of the Indian 'nation'. Another slide was from the 'national' movement to the 'freedom' movement. Freedom was an even more respectable goal, and 'freedom fighters' were much more respectable than terrorists. One senior scholar still claims, as if it were evidence of patriotic merit, that as a member of the Indian freedom movement he was once prosecuted for trying to burn a policeman alive. The term 'freedom movement' not only covers a multitude of sins but ignores the fact that for decades independence was not a goal of the nationalist leaders, still less of their followers, who to the end were moved by other emotions beyond or beneath the goal of independence of foreign rule. Their nature was revealed not only in the course of unrest stimulated by the slackening of colonial authority but by the continuing communal, caste and tribal violence in various countries of the Third World after independence.

Some of the most basic terms of political history now seem obsolescent, if not obsolete. The classical typology of monarchy, aristocracy and democracy now seems naive, though it is still used in various undergraduate courses, on the history of 'political philosophy', which proceed on the assumption that the explanation of political obedience is to be found in Aristotle or Locke rather than in Freud or Gramsci. Most historians now seem to think in terms of political mechanisms, in Elster's language.[36] One basic distinction seems to be between personal power on the one hand and bureaucratic power on the other. Another distinction lies in terms of the distance between the political and administrative elite and other social groups. What of periodisation? The traditional three periods—ancient, medieval and modern—were coming to seem awkward before the awareness of Asia made them seem parochial. In India attempts had in fact been made to use them by treating the period of Muslim invasion and conquest as medieval compared with a previous era of 'classical' Hindu culture and a modern period of nationalism and technological change. The pejorative implications of medievalism satisfied the assumptions of opponents of Islam, and the progressive implications of the notion of modernity were attractive to the patriotic. In fact there was a certain similarity between the admiration felt by many Hindus for a golden age of Hindu civilisation and the admiration felt by many Europeans for ancient Greece and Rome. Elsewhere there seemed to be no justification for three periods. The alternative distinction between the modern and the pre-modern derives some support from the magnitude of the changes

[36] Elster, *Psychologie politique*, passim.

experienced throughout the world from the nineteenth century onwards, associated with fundamental changes in attitudes, however superficial some of these changes may have been in certain countries. One may note the attention paid by historians of various countries to attitudes to legitimation, to education and to differences of generation and gender.

Legitimation is another fundamental pattern. In the logic of the historical situation there seem to be four possible forms: religious, traditional, moral or pragmatic. Structures and processes are justified either as favoured by God, or as following in the footsteps of one's ancestors, or as morally right, or in terms of results. the last seems a generally accepted characteristic of modernity. The history of education is also related to ideas of modernity in that it presents two forms—one the continuation of past knowledge, the other its replacement by fresh discoveries. The former emphasises memory, and is characteristic of pre-modern cultures: the most esteemed scholars, the most revered pandits, are those with the longest memories. The latter is associated with modernity, with the assumption that the higher learning involves not so much the transmission of past knowledge, but rather its reinterpretation, still more its supersession: the most esteemed scholars are not so much those with the longest memories but those with the greatest originality. The former reinforces respect for age, the latter admiration for youth. So one may distinguish as fundamental two types of attitude to knowledge.

The historiography of gender has not yet developed sufficiently to enable one to identify forms clearly. But some initial comments can be made. Gender is so far generally understood by historians as female, and attitudes to women are seen either as an aspect of power relationships or in terms of economic class. An alternative level of analysis can be seen in the history of religions: woman seen as a temptation to man. But at a deeper level one can detect the fear of woman as a threat to man—to his sexual, intellectual, economic or spiritual potential.

At this stage we come to attitudes towards the Other(s). Otherness, alterity, may be seen negatively, as evil, or neutrally, as indifferent, or positively, as good or beneficent. In the history of Christian attitudes tc other religions we perceive first the notion that other religions are evil, inspired by the Devil. Secondly, they come to be seen merely as human—as indifferent, containing good and evil, rational and irrational, but defective, lacking the truths of Christianity. Thirdly, they are seen as positive, as God's way of leading men to Christianity—as preparations for the Gospel. This was the approach recommended in the early Church by Tertullian, but it was abandoned later. We see it again among Protestant missionaries in the second half of the nineteenth century, and it was later ratified by the World Conference of Protestant missionaries at Edinburgh in 1910. Among Roman Catholics we find it again, for example, among scholars like Robin Zaehner in the 1950s, and later ratified by the Second Vatican Council.

Similar forms can be perceived in Western attitudes to Asia. First, the positive: *ex oriente lux*, especially in the eighteenth century. The Jesuits for their purposes, the *philosophes* for theirs, found much to admire in China. Voltaire's praise gradually turned to India, and he was joined by various British scholars towards the end of the eighteenth century. Admiration for Indian wisdom took root in Germany, encouraged by the Romantic movement. In Britain it wilted, and attitudes to Indian culture took either of the other possibilities we have already noted in Christian attitudes to other religions. Either it was despised as inefficient, or it was detested as evil. Similar patterns can be perceived again in Indian attitudes to Britain, or more broadly in Asian attitudes to the West, seeing it as progressive, exploitative, or purely evil. Identifying basic forms in this way offers the possibility of avoiding the dilemma of exclusive interpretations.

Recent historical writing on South Asia presents us with a warning. The phrase 'Subaltern Studies' has been used as a synonym for working-class history by British and Indian historians who claim to be influenced by Gramsci, although in some cases his influence is virtually impossible to detect. When Gramsci told historians to study the attitudes of *le classi subalterne*, he was using the term in its Italian meaning—the working classes. In England, on the other hand, the word 'subaltern' is customarily used for a junior officer, especially in the old British Indian army. Indeed, many of the articles published in the series of volumes entitled *Subaltern Studies* have in fact dealt with small-town or village sub-elites. Hence the confusion still rests at the basis of the series. Worse, some contributors to the series write of 'subalterns' as if this term were synonymous with lower classes.

Other scholars have been asking Gramscian-type questions, with sociologists in the lead. In England, Basil Berstein has analysed the ways in which patterns of speech differentiate the upper from the lower classes. In France, Pierre Bourdieu has asked how upper-class and lower-class styles of speech are shaped by the educational system.[37] Comparative historical research in this difficult field should be facilitated by an agreed vocabulary and the formulation of potential forms. Clearly, change is more readily perceptible in certain societies in certain periods—for example the growing use of the polite form *lei* in speaking to servants in Italy from the Fascist era onwards, or of *ap* rather than *tum* in urban India from the 1960s.[38]

The historical study of broader questions on a comparative basis may similarly be facilitated. A recurrent dichotomy is between the images of the city and of the countryside—the one or the other being seen as offering the better life, whether criterion be one of aesthetic culture, moral virtue or physical health. Correlations between such changing attitudes and a context of socio-economic change immediately suggest themselves for testing on a comparative basis. Still broader is the problem of attitudes to material wealth. There is, for example, the description of ownership in a direct manner in the languages of Western Europe: 'I have', 'ich habe', 'j'ai', '[io] ho'. In contrast, we find an indirect manner of speech in Russian—*у меня*—and in Asian languages, suggesting a negative attitude towards material wealth. Changing speech patterns in Japan may be crucial here.[39]

It might be argued that any attempt to identify a universal vocabulary for historiography or a morphology of history is doomed to failure in

[37] Pierre Bourdieu and Jean-Claude Passeron, *La Reproduction. Éléments pour une théorie du système d'enseignement* (Paris, 1970).

[38] For example, the English preoccupation with social distance. Until the 1950s English working-class characters were usually portrayed humorously in the theatre and cinema, for example as late as 1946 in the 'serious' film *Brief Encounter*.

[39] This particular question was first asked by Victor Kiernan.

that the formulation of concepts must rest on a theoretical basis.[40] But it is the lack of any theoretical basis that bedevils historiography. What is now suggested is not merely the making explicit of the terminology of historians but also the morphology at the root of historical analysis. The more abstract and the less exclusive our morphology the more readily our vocabulary can be disentangled from contemporary assumptions.

[40] Compare an analogous argument in Peter L. Berger and Hansfried Kellner, *Sociology Reinterpreted* (Harmondsworth, 1982), p.47ff.

Chapter 3

CONCEPTS OF RACE IN THE MAHĀBHĀRATA AND RĀMĀYAṆA

John Brockington

The concept of race carries with it, it seems inevitably, ideas of racial superiority, of the innate superiority of one group over another or others. It was therefore only natural—especially in the colonial period—that the strongly hierarchical nature of Hindu society should be seen as having a racial basis and that its origins should be traced back to the arrival of fair-skinned Āryans, who subjugated a darker indigenous population, the Dasyus. Another form of the latter term, *dāsa*, became later the word for a slave (just as that word is derived from Slav), suggesting that a definite element of racial superiority was involved; this is reinforced by the use in the oldest text, the *Ṛgveda*, of the term *varṇa*, meaning 'colour, complexion', to distinguish the Āryan *varṇa* from the *dāsa varṇa*. Although expressed in these terms, it seems clear that the distinction was in fact primarily one of language, with the Sanskrit-speaking Āryans setting themselves apart from speakers of other languages, and secondarily one of culture, while considerations of political or ritual status and economic power even at this period tended to alter the picture.

However, by the period of the *Brāhmaṇas*, spanning the first half of the first millenium B.C., this binary distinction had been superseded by the structuring of society into a four-class system (designated by the same term, *varṇa*, but now probably in another of its senses, 'description' or 'arrangement'), in which social and especially occupational distinctions were more important. The earliest presentation of this scheme, in one of the latest hymns of the *Ṛgveda* (the *Puruṣasūkta*, RV 10.90), both ranks and implicitly assigns types of occupation to the four *varṇas* by making the brāhmans emerge from the head or mouth of the cosmic man, the kṣatriyas from his arms, the vaiśyas from his thighs and the śūdras from his feet; this scheme was to remain a favourite paradigm in later Hindu thought.

The two great Sanskrit epics, the *Mahābhārata* and the *Rāmāyaṇa*, are the main repositories of information about the next, post-Vedic stages of Indian culture, but the sheer wealth of data and more particularly the length of time over which the epics grew to their present shape—usually reckoned as being from the fourth century B.C. to the fourth century A.D.—mean that the material is often at first sight confusing.[1] The clearest picture of the authors' or compilers' attitudes towards the *varṇas* and other features that we may broadly for the present term racial concepts comes in their later, more didactic parts, belonging probably to the second to fourth centuries A.D.; these are particularly the twelfth and thirteenth books of the *Mahābhārata* and the first and last books of the *Rāmāyaṇa* (books 1 and 7). It is convenient, therefore, to begin with this evidence, even though it is the latest.

At several points in the *Śāntiparvan,* the twelfth book of the *Mahābhārata*, the origin of the four *varṇas* is deal with. At 12.74.4-8, in answer to a question, the wind-God Vāyu declares that the personal deity, Īśvara, created the four *varṇas* (as in the *Puruṣasūkta*)[2] and assigned to the brāhmans, as their duty, protection of *dharma,* to the kṣatriyas protection of the people, to the vaiśyas support of the [first] three *varṇas* by wealth, and to the śūdras service of the others (Vāyu then elaborates on these ideas in the next few verses, gradually shifting to the duties of a king). A conversation between the two ancient sages Bhṛgu and Bharadvāja is recorded in 12.181, where Bhṛgu first declares that Brahmā Prajāpati, the creator deity, emitted all creation—the gods

[1] All references to the *Mahābhārata* and *Rāmāyaṇa* are to their Critical Editions, published at Poona and Baroda respectively. Some general information on this subect may be found in Aloka Parasher, *Mlecchas in Early India: a study in attitudes towards outsiders up to AD 600* (New Delhi 1991), and Ram Sharan Sharma, *Śūdras in Ancient India* (Delhi 1958).

[2] Similarly, in another theistic adaptation of the *Puruṣasūkta*, at 12.200.31-33 Bhīṣma, who is the overall narrator of Books 12-13, declares that Kṛṣṇa created a hundred individuals of each of the four named classes from the various parts of his body and placed Dhātṛ ('the orderer', a form of Prajāpati, the creator deity) as their superintendent.

and other divine beings, brāhmans, kṣatriyas, vaiśyas, śūdras and other sorts of men or beings—and assigns a colour to each *varṇa* (white, red, yellow and black respectively), but then, when Bharadvāja objects to this that there is an intermixture of colours (*varṇasaṃkara*, also 'confusion of classes') in all classes and variation of colour in many species, Bhṛgu moves on to give a more symbolic or psychological explanation of the four colours: originally Brahmā created just brāhmans but those who were short-tempered and violent left their *varṇa*, turned red and became kṣatriyas, those who took to cattle-rearing and agriculture turned yellow and became vaiśyas, and those who in their delusion took to injury and untruth turned black and became śūdras (12.181.10-13); those who diverged still further from the proper norms and did not recognise them became Piśācas, Rākṣasas, Pretas ('ghosts') and various sorts of Mlecchas ('foreigners, barbarians').[3]

In a still more elaborately worked out passage, at 12.285.4-9, the *Puruṣasūkta* model of the origin of the four castes is followed by a scheme for the origin of what are usually termed the 'mixed castes' by both hypogamy and hypergamy, including Ambaṣṭhas, Ugras and Niṣādas (on whom I shall have more to say below). As Horst Brinkhaus has convincingly shown,[4] this represents the second stage in the development of the theory of *varṇasaṃkara*, 'confusion of classes'. The first phase, when only the offspring of *pratiloma* ('against the [lie of the] hair', hypogamous) unions are counted as 'mixed castes', is seen in the *Mahābhārata* in 13.48.4-29 and 13.49.7-11,[5] whereas by the second stage, as in Mbh.12.285.4-9, some of the *anuloma* (hypergamous) offspring are included. This theory, found in its most developed form in

[3] The irrelevance of skin colour to *varṇa* classification is also suggested by the fact that several of the main characters in the *Mahābhārata* are said at one point or another to have a dark complexion—not just Kṛṣṇa (for whom there may well be particular reasons) but also Draupadī (also called Kṛṣṇā 'the dark woman'), Arjuna and Nakula.

[4] *Die Altindischen Mischkastensysteme* (Wiesbaden, 1978); on this passage, see pp.102-9 (especially 107-8). 'Confusion of castes' is also mentioned as a sign of disorder or anarchy at Mbh.3.177.26-27, 6.23.41-43 (BhG 1.41-43) and 12.49.61.

[5] On these two passages, see Brinkhaus, pp.24-9 and 71-4. Brinkhaus also treats Mbh.13.44.10-12 and 47.4+7 on pp.52-4.

the *dharmaśāstras*, clearly does carry overtones of superiority by birth in its emphasis on miscegenation.

Elsewhere in the *Mahābhārata*, two single verses recapitulate the *Puruṣasūkta* scheme of the origin of the four classes (3.187.13 and 8.23.32), while three passages indicate their duties or their qualities (5.29.20-24, 6.40.41-44/BhG 18.41-44, 10.3.18-20). The first of these in fact seems relatively late, in view of its more elaborate metre and its use of the term *cāturvarṇya*, 'the four-caste system'.[6] Nevertheless, their relative brevity and simplicity is in marked contrast to the passages just examined from the twelfth and thirteenth books.[7]

In the *Rāmāyaṇa* references to the four *varṇas* are almost all incidental, indicating that little significance was attached to the topic.[8] On one occasion, however, in a cosmogonic discourse the *Puruṣasūkta* scheme for the origin of the four *varṇas* is given (3.13.29-30) and on another Nārada bewails the decline of *dharma* in successive *yugas* as the other *varṇas* usurp the privileges of brāhmans (7.65.8-26). There is no reference as such to 'confusion of castes', although it is implicit in some episodes included in later portions.

The main exception to this general pattern occurs in the late first book, where the lengthy Viśvāmitra episode (Rām. 1.31-64) centres on the antagonism between the brāhman Vasiṣṭha and the kṣatriya Viśvāmitra. On the surface this story points to the separateness and mutual distinctiveness of the *varṇas* but its ramifications give a slightly different picture when looked at with attention. The main focus of the quarrel is Vasiṣṭha's wonder-cow. When Viśvāmitra resorts to force in

[6] The use of such a derivative term obviously follows at some interval the development of the system itself. The word also occurs for example at Mbh.3.177.18a, 6.26.13a (=BhG 4.13a), 8.23.33b and 12.181.6a, *Harivaṃśa* 31.94c and 96c, and *Rāmāyaṇa* 1.1.75c, 24.15c, 5.33.11b, 6.113.29c and 7.65.14d.

[7] In addition to the four passages mentioned in the text and footnote 2, book 12 also includes, for example, a purely incidental mention of the four *varṇas* at 12.314.45c. Thus, the frequency of mention is also striking.

[8] They are found at 1.1.75, 79, 6.16-17, 12.12, 17cd, 24.15, 25.5, 2.15.11, 76.30b, 98.57, 5.33.11, 6.113.29, 7.65.8-26 and 67.10. Further details on the *varṇas* and society in the *Rāmāyaṇa* may be found in my *Righteous Rāma* (Delhi, 1985), pp.153-8. The word *varṇa* is much commoner in the *Rāmāyaṇa* in the general sense of colour or complexion than in the sense of a social group.

his attempt to seize her, she aids Vasiṣṭha by creating hundreds of foreign warriors: Pahlavas, Śakas, Yavanas, Kāmbojas, Mlecchas, Hāritas and Kirātas (1.53.18-54.3). The equivalent *Mahābhārata* passage has an even longer list of warlike groups (1.165.35-37): Pahlavas, Śabaras, Śakas, Yavanas, Puṇḍras, Kirātas, Dramiḍas, Siṃhalas, Barbaras, Daradas and Mlecchas, collectively summed up as Mlecchas (foreigners/barbarians). Quite apart from providing an approximate dating for this passage, mention of the Pahlavas, Śakas and Yavanas (the Parthian, Scythian and Greek rulers who were politically significant in the Northwest around the beginning of the Christian era) is interesting because their role in this context is to defend brahmanical values; this accords with the fact that they were ranked in the lawbooks as 'degenerate kṣatriyas' in recognition of their status as rulers.[9] Elsewhere in the *Mahābhārata* a Yavana ruler attends Yudhiṣṭhira's court (2.4.22b), and Yavanas are regarded as 'knowing everything' (8.30.80a); at a later stage, however, their unorthodoxy is emphasised when Bhīṣma lists them among kṣatriya *jātis* which have fallen into untouchability through disregard of brāhmans (13.33.19-21b and 35.17-18).[10]

Before we explore further these lists of peoples, the outcome of the quarrel between Vasiṣṭha and Viśvāmitra deserves notice. Viśvāmitra's hundred sons and the rest of his army are destroyed by these magically produced forces, so Viśvāmitra abdicates in favour of his one surviving son and goes off to perform austerities. Brahmā in due course grants him recognition as a royal seer (*rājarṣi*) but this does not satisfy him and he sets about accumulating still greater ascetic powers; eventually, after

[9] Since these foreign groups had acquired political power, it was necessary in some way to incorporate them into the structure of society and so the term 'degenerate kṣatriya' (*vrātyakṣatriya*) gained currency to designate them. It was held that they were originally kṣatriyas whose loss of status was due to non-performance of rituals or disregard of the brāhmans (cf. *Manu* 10.43-45). It is also of interest to note that one late version of the Agnikula legend, accounting for the origin of the premier Rājput dynasties of the Parihāras, Cauhāns, Solaṅkis and Pawārs, integrates it with the story of Vasiṣṭha's wonder-cow, thus implicitly equating these Rājput dynasties with the Yavanas and other foreigners.

[10] Other references to Yavanas occur at Mbh 1.80-26b, 2.47.12c, 3.13.29b, 48.20d, 7.97.13d, 12.65.13a, *Harivaṃśa* 85.18b, Rām.1.53.20d, 21b, 54.3a, 4.42.11a.

he has challenged the gods by elevating Triśaṅku bodily to heaven and threatening to create another Indra, he is granted the status of brāhman and has his ultimate ambition fulfilled when he is addressed as *brahmarṣi* by Vasiṣṭha. He has achieved the theoretically impossible, at least by later standards: as an individual he has changed his *varṇa* status. This is underlined in the didactic portions of the *Mahābhārata* where Yudhiṣṭhira asks whether a kṣatriya, vaiśya or śūdra can gain the status of a brāhman (13.28.2-3) and Bhīṣma's reply is to narrate the story of Mataṅga (13.28.4-30.16). Mataṅga was brought up as a brāhman but one day his true status as a caṇḍāla,[11] because of his mother's adultery with one, is betrayed by his conduct; he spends the rest of his life in austerities in a vain attempt to gain brāhmanhood and finally settles for the power to move at will in the sky. Thus, by the latest stages of the *Mahābhārata*—from perhaps the second century A.D.—the *varṇa* system has become completely rigid and the exclusivity is absolute.

To return now to those lists of peoples or tribes, their heterogeneity is one of the most obvious features. For example the *Mahābhārata* list (1.165.35-37) contains not only the invading groups in the Northwest (the Pahlavas, Śakas and Yavanas, to which the *Rāmāyaṇa* adds the Kāmbojas) but also the Tamils of South India (Dramiḍas, given as Dramiḷas at 13.33.20a), Sinhalese and several tribal peoples (Śabaras, Kirātas and Daradas), as well as two general terms for foreigners: Mlecchas and Barbaras. Yet the real point is that, though impure in various ways, these groups are acting in support of brāhman values—co-operation rather than exclusion is the rationale for their mention. This is in fact even clearer in some other similar lists in the *Mahābhārata*, the purpose of which seems to be to include everyone as a participant in the action. At 2.23-29, as a preliminary to Yudhiṣṭhira's celebration of the *rājasūya* ritual, the five Pāṇḍava brothers set out on the conquest of the world and one of the twins, Nakula, is recorded as defeating among

[11] The term caṇḍāla, with its overtones of strong contempt for untouchables, is not in fact very frequent in the epics; the main passages in which the term is used are at Mbh 12.139.41ff and 13.48.28-33 and Rām.1.57-58. The only other occurrence of the term in the text of the *Rāmāyaṇa* is at 3.54.18d

others the Śibis, Trigartas, Ambaṣṭhas and Mālavas, the Śūdras and Ābhīras, the Harahūṇas and all the rulers of the west (2.29.6-11). To the *rājasūya* itself came not only Mlecchas (2.31.10a), who as foreigners should have been totally excluded from such rituals, but also the Tamils and Sinhalese again and many individually named kings. Just before the start of the war, the narrator Saṃjaya recites to the blind Dhṛtarāṣṭra a list of all the participants on both sides (6.10.37-74), which includes Māhiṣakas (45b and 57c), Ābhīras (45d and 66a), Śūdras (46a and 66a), Pahlavas (46b), Śabaras (46c), Kirātas (49c, 55c and 67d), Śakas and Niṣādas (50a), Barbaras (55c), Tamils and Keralans (57a), Mlecchas (63c), the Mleccha *jātis* of the Yavanas and Kāmbojas (64ab), Hūṇas (64d) and Daradas (66a). Although clearly much expanded, these lists are linked to the main plot of the epic, unlike the various lists in the twelfth and thirteenth books: a list of all mankind at 12.65.13-14 (which places Yavanas, Kirātas, Gāndhāras, Cīnas, Śabaras, Barbaras, Śakas, Tuṣāras, Kahvas, Pahlavas, Andhras, Madrakas, Oḍras, Pulindas, Ramaṭhas, Kācas and Mlecchas alongside brāhmans, kṣatriyas, vaiśyas and śūdras), a listing of first southern and then northern peoples at 12.200.38-41, and the two lists of lapsed kṣatriyas already mentioned (13.33.19-21 and 35.17-18).

Several of the groups in the earlier lists are later regarded as the results of 'confusion of classes' but here figure as independent cultural groups. Most strikingly of all, Śūdras and Ābhīras are mentioned together—obviously as tribal peoples—not only in the second list (Mbh.6.10.66a) but also on other occasions (Mbh.2.29.9a and 3.186.30d). The probably related name of the Kṣudrakas is similarly linked with the Mālavas at Mbh.2.48.14d, in a list of those peoples from different regions who brought tribute to the *rājasūya*, a list which also includes Ambaṣṭhas (14a, also 2.29.6c) and Kirātas, (8d and 10a), here clearly seen as groups with some prestige, by contrast with their treatment in Mbh.12.285.4-9 above. The Kirātas are in fact mentioned a number of times in the older parts of the *Mahābhārata* as a group evidently respected for their martial prowess.[12] In the same way the

[12] Other mentions include 1.165.36a, 2.4.21b, 22a (where their king Sumanas attends Yudhiṣṭhira's court), 13.19a, 3.48.20d, 6.10.49c, 55c, 67d, 12.65.13a

Māhiṣakas, originally participants in the action (Mbh 6.10.45b, 57c, 8.30.45a), are later classed as 'lapsed kṣatriyas' (Mbh 13.33.20c) and are probably to be identified with the Māhiṣyas whom later legal texts classify as the offspring of a kṣatriya man and a vaiśya woman.[13] In a relatively late part of the *Rāmāyaṇa* they are listed among the peoples of the south (4.40.11b) and so presumably were then still an independent group.

The list of participants in the *Mahābhārata* war includes the Niṣādas (6.10.50a) and elsewhere their king Ekalavya is recorded as a noted opponent of Kṛṣṇa (5.47.71), while they are also named in the list of Sahadeva's conquests (2.28.5a, 44c). These examples suggest that they were accorded some respect in the earliest stages of the epic but before long they are a clearly despised group. Already in Mbh 3.130.4 the river Sarasvatī is said to disappear to avoid being seen by Niṣādas (at the place later well known as Vinaśana) and in the twelfth book the sages churn the right thigh of the wicked king Vena's corpse and produce the deformed and ugly Niṣāda, from whom originate the cruel Niṣādas and other Mlecchas who live in the Vindhyas (12.59.101-3); they are still an independent group but their status is low. An equivalent progression is seen in the *Rāmāyaṇa*, where in the core of the work the Niṣādas are shown as allies and more or less equals of the people of Ayodhyā. Their chief, Guha, welcomes Rāma warmly when Rāma's party reach the Gaṅgā (2.44.9-12), referring to his traditional friendship with his father, and offers him food, which is refused not because of caste barriers but on grounds of Rāma's ascetic vows; later on, Guha prepares food for Rāma's brother, Bharata (2.78.9). However, in the late first book of the *Rāmāyaṇa* the Niṣādas are definitely despised, as is graphically shown by the well-known story of Vālmīki witnessing the Niṣāda hunter killing the *krauñca* bird (1.2.9-14) and also by Viśvāmitra cursing Vasiṣṭha's son to such status (1.58.21).

Other groups, such as the Śabaras, seem at all stages to have been

---

and 13.35.18a (where they are classed as 'lapsed kṣatriyas'). In the *Rāmāyaṇa* they are located in the eastern direction (4.39.26a) and also mentioned at 1.54.3d.

[13] Cf. *Yājñavalkyasmṛti* 1.91-94, and *Gautamadharmasūtra* 4.18-21.

regarded as separate tribes or peoples and in such instances what changes is simply the esteem in which they are held, the earliest references suggesting their significance as potential foes and implicitly their rough equality with Āryan society, and later references stressing what are seen as their cultural deviations and so relegating them to a low status. Broadly speaking, it is the same process that is visible with the Niṣādas, later seen as a despised occupational group of hunters as much as a tribal society, and with the Ambaṣṭhas and Māhiṣakas, later reduced to the status of 'mixed castes'. Such groups were seen originally as outsiders, as culturally and probably racially distinct, but it was their interaction, however limited, with Āryan society which interested the early poets of the epics—no doubt because it most interested their kṣatriya audience—and ideas of racial superiority seem absent.

Although the attendance of Mlecchas ('foreigners', more generally 'outsiders') at Yudhiṣṭhira's *rājasūya* is perhaps the most striking example of their participation in the action of the *Mahābhārata*, it is noticeable that they are included in the various lists alongside other tribes or peoples who were regarded much less as outsiders, and that the term is not uncommon in the *Mahābhārata*.[14] The word tended to denote any non-Sanskrit-speaking outsider but it is interesting to note that internal distinctions, Mleccha *jātis*, were recognised (6.10.64b), Mleccha teachers are mentioned (*mlecchācāryāḥ*, Mbh 12.4.8c) and Yudhiṣṭhira asks why Mlecchas also engage in fasting (13.109.1b), so they were not simply regarded as some undifferentiated 'other'. Indeed, it is noticeable that many early references are to their fighting on one side or the other in the great war (5.22.21c, 158.20d, 9.1.26c, 2.18a, 36c) or being conquered by one or other of the Pāṇḍava heroes

[14] It occurs at Mbh.1.62.5a, 79.13d, 80.26d, 135.6b, 165.36c, 202.8d, 2.27.23c, 28.44b, 29.15b, 31.10a, 47.12b, 3.48.19c, 61.2d, 186.29a, 188.29a, 37a, 45a, 52a, 70a, 93d, 5.22.21c, 49.26b, 158.20d, 6.10.12c, 63c, 64b, 13.15b, 41.103a, 7.25.17b, 68.42a, 44e, 69.0d, 87.37c, 95.36b, 69.23b, 8.27.91c, 30.70ab, 80c, 51.19c, 9.1.26c, 2.18a, 36c, 12.4.8c, 59.103d, 65.14b, 162.68d, 181.18b, 13.109.1b, 112.108b, 14.72.24c, 83.30b (and Rām.1.54.3c, 2.3.9a and 4.42.10a, also *Harivaṃśa* 85.18c), whereas Barbara, perhaps deriving from the Greek βαρβαρος, is rather less common, occurring at Mbh.1.165.36b, 2.29.15c, 3.48.19c, 6.10.55c, 7.95.13b, 38d, 12.65.13b, 200.40d and 13.35.17d (and in Rām. only as variant readings at 1.54.2d and 4.42.12b).

(2.27.23c, 28.44b, 29.15b, 5.49.26b), while the extent of the Pāṇḍava dynasty's power is indicated by saying that it ruled over the four quarters of the world up to or including the Mlecchas and the forest tribes (1.62.5). The extent of their presence is also indicated by the assertion that Āryans and Mlecchas alike drink water from the various rivers of Bhāratavarṣa (6.10.12). The most intriguing reference is to Vidura speaking to Yudhiṣṭhira in Mleccha language (*mlecchavācā* 1.135.6b) when he wants to keep something secret. If we take this at face value, it suggests that political or economic considerations had encouraged them to learn the language; however, it must be borne in mind that in the core of the epics narrative considerations may well be more important than didactic ones.

However, in the long run, the Mlecchas' disregard for brahmanical values led to their being despised and we see this in later didactic parts of the *Mahābhārata*. Mārkaṇḍeya predicts that at the end of this degenerate age many Mleccha, Yavana, Śaka, Śūdra and Ābhīra kings will rule (3.186.29-30) and the whole world will become Mleccha (here clearly used in a pejorative sense, 'barbarian', 3.188.29, 37, 45, 52, 70), while Bṛhaspati declares that evil-doers are reborn as Mlecchas (13.112.108). The culmination of this trend is then seen in Mārkaṇḍeya's prediction that Kalki Viṣṇuyaśas will arise and root out all the Mlecchas (3.188.89-93), as well as in passages so late that they are excluded from the text of the *Mahābhārata*, when praise of Viṣṇu's *avatāras* includes Kalkin who will destroy the Mlecchas (12 App.6.39-40 and App.7.19-20). By this stage racial overtones are clearly apparent.

More integral to the plot of the epics than the lists of participants in the warfare, from which many of the references so far have come, are the activities of the main characters themselves. In the *Rāmāyaṇa*, for example, it is interesting to compare two episodes involving low-caste ascetics. In the story of an ascetic youth killed by Daśaratha (2.57-58), the youth's birth from a vaiśya father and a śūdra mother (2.57.37) in no way disqualifies him from practising asceticism, but for Daśaratha to kill him, even accidentally, is so serious a fault that it accounts for Daśaratha's present misfortune in having to exile Rāma. In the last book, on the other hand, for a śūdra to practise asceticism brings disaster on society, and it is necessary and indeed praiseworthy for Rāma to execute the culprit, Śambūka (7.67, cf.7.65). The increase in rigidity of the *varṇa* system is quite remarkable.

In the *Mahābhārata*, in contrast to the condemnation of 'confusion of castes' in the didactic portions, there are significant characters participating in the action who are the offspring of mixed marriages or who marry wives who clearly are not of the same *varṇa*. The term *karaṇa* (later denoting the offspring of a kṣatriya man and a vaiśya woman) is used incidentally and, it seems, purely factually of Yuyutsu, the son of Dhṛtarāṣṭra and a vaiśya woman (1.57.99d and 107.36d), who fought on the side of the Pāṇḍavas, and of Vidura, the wise adviser, who was fathered by Vyāsa on a slavegirl substituted for Queen Ambikā (1.102.23 and 107.1) and is considered the brother of Dhṛtarāṣṭra and Pāṇḍu. Vidura in particular is accorded much respect by the other characters for his wisdom. Besides Draupadī, the five Pāṇḍava brothers also marry other wives, some of whom come from tribal peoples (1.90.83-87), and have liaisons with women from still more unusual backgrounds. Bhīma has a son Ghaṭotkaca by the rākṣasī Hiḍimbā (Mbh.1.139-143) and Arjuna has a son Irāvān by Ulūpī, the daughter of a Nāga king (1.206.8-34); in both instances the son is brought up by his mother but later fights on the side of the Pāṇḍavas in the great battle. This type of motif is not unusual in other heroic literatures and another example in the *Mahābhārata* is that Babhruvāhana, Arjuna's son by Citrāṅgadā, daughter of King Citravāhana, becomes Citravāhana's heir (1.207.14-23 and 209.23-24). In all of these we no doubt see kṣatriya readiness to enter into any union which was politically desirable or which took the individual's fancy, in contrast to the legalism of the brāhmans expressed in the elaborate classification of 'mixed castes' together with abhorrence of the unions held to produce them.

It was to the advantage of the kṣatriyas as the rulers to make alliances and so to convert the potentially hostile 'other' into an ally. Their aim was not in the main to manufacture artificial divisions but even if necessary to gloss over real ones. Perhaps the most extraordinary statement about the Mlecchas and others in the *Mahābhārata* is contained in a genealogical part of the first book, where the story of

Yayāti and his five sons is given. Incidentally, King Yayāti has two sons by his wife Devayānī, who is the daughter of the brāhman Śukra (thus strictly a *pratiloma* union), and three by her servant Śarmiṣṭhā, daughter of King Vṛṣaparvan. Within this passage the narrator tells the Pāṇḍavas' great-grandson: 'From Yadu were born the Yādavas, Turvasu's sons are the Yavanas, Druhyu's sons are the Bhojas, while Anu's are the Mleccha *jātis*. From Puru comes the Paurava dynasty in which you were born, O king' (1.80.26-27). So the foreigners are no longer completely unrelated.

This last example illustrates clearly the flexibility of approach typical of much of the older epic material, in which the dictates of realpolitik took precedence over abstract theorising for the poets. The interests of the epic poets' masters, the ruling class, were best served by such realism. While, therefore, we can find in some of the statements about the *varṇas* and about the distinctiveness of various groups of outsiders (whether those who may loosely be termed tribal groups or foreigners as such), attitudes which seem to reflect certain concepts of racial distinctiveness, in general the pattern in the earlier period was one where outsiders of all sorts are distinguished more by divergence of culture and language. However, these distinctions were recognised not so much as a means of excluding such groups but rather as a preliminary to their absorption within the Āryan political and cultural framework. In that process of incorporation, as the evidence of later stages of the epics shows, many groups were assigned a relatively low status as a result of their way of life or occupation. Earlier, though, such groups seem to have been rated primarily on their warlike capabilities and accorded respect in relation to them. By the end of the epics' growth, and more particularly in other literature, groups which had previously been treated as roughly equals of the Āryans are subject to the sort of discrimination that is a concomitant of racialist attitudes.

Chapter 4

IS THERE A TAMIL 'RACE'?[1]

Dagmar Hellman-Rajanayagam

Preliminaries

'No, she is not pretty, she is dark', was the stock answer of most of my Indian friends whenever I happened to mention that I thought my *ayah* one of the most beautiful women I had ever met. I can hear an outraged howl of 'racism' going up. But is it? Or is it a different concept of beauty which we are uncomfortable with because notions of 'dark', 'ugly' and 'racism' have in fact often been linked in European thinking? Is there a concept equivalent to our concept of 'race' in South India? That is what I want to explore philologically and historically in this article, that grew out of the SOAS workshop on the concept of race in South Asia. The 'multi-cultural' composition of the workshop prevented a single and simple understanding of 'race' from the start. Especially the 'orderly' Germans found it difficult to comprehend the fluidity and also the unselfconscious use of the English concept in contrast to the rather more strictly defined and delimited German *Rasse* which today is often used with audible quotation marks. If our own understandings varied so widely, how would it then be possible to talk of a 'South Asian concept of race'?

'Race' in European languages is a comparatively recent term, and its etymology is not at all clear. Some authors[2] derive it from the Arabic

[1] Many colleagues have helped me with discussions and comments in this article. I want to acknowledge specially the help of Professor Kothandaraman with translation and interpretation of relevant *Caṅkam* stanzas and clarifying perceptions of ethnicity and caste. D.A.A.D. and D.F.G. helped with research grants without which I could not have completed this study.

[2] Immanuel Geiss, *Geschichte des Rassismus* (Frankfurt, 1988,) p.16; similarly David Theo Goldberg, 'The semantics of race', *Ethnic and Racial Studies* 15, 4, (1992), p.545, who then describes the different applications of 'race'. See E.J. Hobsbawm, *Nations and Nationalism since 1780. Programme, myth, reality* (Cambridge, 1992), p.65, for the rendering of 'race' as 'ethnicity' which in German usage is impossible and shows the vast differences in lexical meaning.

'*as*, denoting a family or lineage, a natural kind, also a high breed of horse, a term which gained currency in Southern Europe in the thirteenth century and in the rest of Europe in the sixteenth and seventeenth centuries.[3] 'Race' in English covers a multitude of meanings, that could and did comprise at one time or other such varied concepts as ethnicity, tribe, clan, caste, nationality, religion and so on. The German term *Rasse* hardly corresponds to this. It is defined in a more narrowly biological sense—that is, it proceeds strictly from real or assumed physical differences between people. From these in turn mental and intellectual differences were also deduced. Most often the distinguishing feature was skin colour. Yet in addition, it has also relied on head, nose and eye shapes and so on to postulate varying numbers (mostly five) of *Rassen*. The broad and purportedly 'scientific' classification according to skin colour was complicated by the theory of a linkage between language and *Rasse* and accompanying value judgments. When the Indo-Aryan family of languages was discovered, race theoreticians had to tie themselves into intellectual knots to preserve 'white supremacy'. The attempt to define a physical 'semitic race' in Nazi ideology and its ghastly consequences led the whole concept of *Rasse* to crash completely, and discredited physical anthropology in Germany for decades. These were some of the difficulties confronting me in the attempt to find out about 'race' in a South Indian context. It was made more tricky, since ostensibly equivalent translations exist which 'confirm' that the concept existed. These translations, however, and the accompanying perceptions, have been fractured and influenced by European perceptions, and whether the 'direct' translations do really express the same meaning is highly doubtful.

If the term itself is so young in Europe, how can we presume to talk about such a concept in (ancient) South Asia? Would that *not* be another instance of Orientalism, where we displace our categories onto people whom we construct in our own image but as inferior? Ronald Inden has demonstrated how India was defined as the 'Other' for nine-

[3] If this derivation is correct, then traces of it are still to be seen in German usage, where 'rasse' can also denote a breed of animal, etc.

teenth-century British and German scholars who looked less to what India 'really was', as to what they thought it was.[4] These scholars not only conflated caste, religion, and race, but also postulated a racial dichotomy between higher Aryan and inferior Dravidian races, which were stratified into castes which then took on racial characteristics.[5] This was less to do with India itself, than with European perceptions. The need of the rulers to legitimate their rule entailed the need to construct superior and inferior races. And the superior race of India was perceived as coming from outside India and being 'Aryan', a race which had to conquer a primitive, inferior, savage and tribal Dravidian substratum, which eventually engulfed and debased the invaders. They never explained, however, how it was that these inferior, effeminate, weak Dravidians eventually engulfed the 'superior' Aryans, and put their own stamp on them. Moreover, the perception of the Dravidians as inferior hardly changed with the discovery of the Indus civilisation and its Dravidian origin. When the diehards could no longer deny the evidence (for example, of the great empires in the south), they found a new twist: a settled, agricultural civilisation suddenly was deemed stagnant, and the pastoral, nomadic, hunting culture of the early Aryans was termed dynamic and progressive.[6]

I go a long way with Inden in this evaluation, but I think his view falls short when applied to German perceptions. Inden's critique of 'essentialism'—the attempt to locate the one defining characteristic of a people, a group, or an institution outside itself, in some 'essence'—while valid for British perceptions in the nineteenth century, falls flat when he applies it to German theory. Essence is, as I assume, the English translation of the German *Wesen* and, while this embodies the meaning of 'essence', it is at the same time far less narrow. It denotes not only the reduction to an essence—something you can distil and then put in a jar to look at, preferably preserved in spirit, thus simplifying and rigidifying it—but also at the same time an inner core of being, one or more basic and important features. In contrast to 'essence' this

[4] Ronald Inden, *Imagining India* (London, 1990), p.40.
[5] Ibid., p.118-19 and passim.
[6] Ibid., p.141.

Wesen pervades a person or a group; it is not outside and beyond them, and it makes them recognisable in more than one characteristic. *Wesen* is not reducible to one single feature, nor is it rigidified and immutable. As Herder described it, *Wesen* does rely on certain basic features, but is at the same time open to change, to acceptance, rejection and manipulation. In the famous words of Goethe: '*Was Du ererbt von deinen Vätern hast, erwirb'es, um es zu besitzen*'.[7] Thus, even if we assume that *Wesen* is inherent or inherited, this *Wesen* will be neither active or valid, unless we make it so and in the process change it. *Wesen* is not, like essence, fate, but involves active participation and choice. Therefore, even if we say for argument's sake that the *Wesen* of India is caste (not that I agree with this statement), it means saying something rather different from saying that the 'essence' of India is caste. This, if nothing else, shows us the danger of arguing a case not from originals, but from (bad) translations, something Inden explicitly does and plausibly justifies.[8] While his explanation holds good for Anglo-Saxon scholars who knew only these translations and argued on that basis, to criticise Hegel on the basis of misunderstood English renderings misses the point. There are enough aspects on which Hegel is open to criticism (and, alas, to misunderstanding) in the German version, but his conception of *Wesen* is not one of them.

This seemingly leads us away from the question of race among the

[7] 'What you have inherited from your fathers, acquire it in order to possess it.'

[8] Ibid., pp.43; 667ff.; 85. While the bulk of academics assumed the equation of caste and race, missionaries in the field like Karl Graul were much less convinced of this: he explicitly argues the intermixture of 'Aryans' and 'original' tribes from Brahmans down to low castes, because only in this way can he explain the wide range of Aryan 'civilising influence' among the Tamils. Karl Graul, *Reise nach Ostindien über Palästina und Egypten von Juli 1849 bis April 1853*. Vierter Theil: *Der Süden Ostindiens und Ceylon* (first published Leipzig, 1855), pp.151-52; 171 ff. His description, especially of temple Brahmans, is anything but flattering, and he describes the Paraiyars as an untouchable, but respectable and respected caste; ibid., pp.157-61 and 189 ff. Incidentally, Graul never used the term '*Rasse*' to denote Aryans and 'Dravidians'. He seems here to have followed the German classicists and Herder (another Protestant theologian) who rejected the term '*Rasse*' to denote human beings, and assumed the basic equality of all mankind on the basis of the Bible. Compare Geiss, *Geschichte des Rassismus*, p.206.

Tamils. Its importance will, however, become clear soon. If we talk about looking for essences, that is what 'race' does. The assumptions of race look for the one definite feature that distinguishes one from another unchangeably for all times. We might more profitably proceed from another angle, leaving out the ambiguous term. The phenomenon we are studying is that of distinguishing, classifying and stratifying people or groups of people according to some visible or perceived criteria, and this is certainly universal. What we can find and explore are perceptions of similarity and difference. How are differences seen and what are the determining ones, the ones that make the 'others' different from 'us'? Where do in-group differences turn into borders towards out-groups?

Iṉam

The accepted equivalent for 'race' in Tamil is 'iṉam'. We find it as such today in numerous contexts: for example, the Tamil militant group EROS some years ago brought out a pamphlet *Iṉaveṟippiṭikkul Īḻat Tamiḻ Iṉam* [9] translatable as 'The Sri Lankan Tamil race in the grip of racism. We have here another popular term, *iṉaveṟi* (race hatred, meaning racism). Both appear in the latest Tamil dictionary published by Cre-A. Race, however, is only the third meaning of the word and appears as synonymous with ethnic group and community.[10] As examples of usage *Tamiḻ iṉam* and *Āriya īṉam* are cited. The primary meaning is given as 'type' or 'superclass', and the fourth and fifth meanings are 'item' and 'identity' respectively. The fourth meaning is used in newspaper language to denote, for example, a series, a class or a budgetary head.[11] The term is widely used and seems to have somewhat explosive power. In the last ten years it has found its way into academic studies which trace the term back to classical literature and in some cases seem to project present-day conceptions, uses and meanings onto the *Caṅkam* age thereby claiming Tamil nationalism and consciousness from time immemorial. Kiruṣṇaṉ, for example, seems to argue, in his study on the meaning of *iṉam* in Tamil

[9] EROS pamphlet ([Madras or London], 1981).
[10] *Kriyāviṉ taṟkālat Tamiḻ akarāti* (Madras, 1992), p.120.
[11] *Tiṉamaṉi*, 19 March 1993.

literature,[12] for a quite early usage of *iṉam* as similar to 'race', though he states that this usage was not based on physical differences. His study contains a wealth of well-researched material on the usage and meaning of *iṉam* and is to my knowledge one of the first of its kind.

'Race' seems, however, to be a comparatively late meaning of the term. This is suggested by the fact that this meaning occurs for the first time in the Tamil Lexicon published from 1926-36. A stanza from the Kantapurāṇam, a comparatively late text, is quoted for *iṉam* as race. Other meanings are 'clan', with 'tribe' as the second meaning along with the usual 'class, group, division, kin, species, sort, flock, herd', but also 'comrades, associates, brotherhood, fellowship, society, companion', and 'assorted items' and 'individual'.[13] We also find a range of composita ranging from *iṉañcaṉam* (kith and kin) to *iṉamāṟṟal* (conversion of one kind of currency to another). However, the important dictionaries of the nineteenth century—Winslow, published in 1862, and Fabricius, first printed in 1779 and republished several times until 1933—do not list 'race' as one of the meanings of *iṉam*: we find the usual 'kindred, relationship, class, sort, company, flock, herd, individual' and 'equality' in the sense of 'sameness'.[14] Winslow also lists *iṉam* in the meaning of 'caste', and all give *iṉavaḻi* as 'descent from the same line'. *Iṉam* as 'race' therefore seems to have been a development of the early twentieth century.

All occurrences in the *Caṅkam* literature use *iṉam* in the sense of 'flock, herd, kind, sort', mainly for animals like birds, bees, deer, monkeys and so on.[15] One instance refers to humans in connection with *iṉam* where it is used in the sense of 'one's own kind, friends'.[16] Apart from a classificatory term for living or natural beings, it also merely

[12] Pa. Kiruṣṇaṉ, *Tamiḻ nūlkaḷil Tamiḻ moḻi, Tamiḻ iṉam, Tamiḻ nāṭu,* (Madras, 1984).

[13] *Tamil Lexicon* (Madras, reprint 1982).

[14] J.P. Fabricius's *Tamil and English Dictionary*, based on Johann Philip Fabricius's *Malabar-English Dictionary* (Tranquebar, 1799; repr. Tranquebar, 1972), p.95; Winslow's *A Comprehensive Tamil and English Dictionary* (Madras, 1862; repr. Delhi, 1979), p.115.

[15] *Puṟam* 13, 15, 138, 157; *Kuṟuntokai* 221, 235, 252, 285, 301,5 ('many bells').

[16] *Kuṟuntokai* 336,2; also *Tirukkuṟaḷ* (Kuṟaḷ) 453, 568 and *Naṉṉūl* 91.

denotes a plural, a group of similar animate or inanimate things; and it can easily be rendered as 'kind', 'hood', or the German *heit.* In this sense it is used in the grammars *Tolkāppiyam* and Naṉṉūl and in mediaeval literature.[17] This emphasis on *iṉam* denoting 'sameness' is important, because the perception is quite different from Western methods of classification: the latter highlight differences to separate things into categories, sameness is incidental. *Iṉam*, on the contrary, denotes the similarity and sameness in things. This is significant for present-day usage of the term. In the epics the term occurs rarely and then in the same meaning. A change occurs in the devotional and later the puranic literature of the Middle Ages. Now the meaning approximates 'race' for the first time, though 'clan', 'lineage', or 'tribe' might be a better rendering. Iṉam, while still being used in a classificatory way, is now applied to distinguish groups of living beings of different kinds, such as the Tīvar *iṉam* the Irakṣacar *iṉam* or the Maṉitar *Iṉam*.[18] This approaches present-day usage of the term, but the criteria of definition and distinction in these cases do not yet seem to be biological. It is not *iṉaṅkaḷ* of humans that are compared according to physical differences, but living beings distinguished by varying grades of power. Though Kiruṣṇaṉ detects 'ethnic consciousness' in this literature, he does not give any instances of *iṉam* being used in this sense.[19]

In the nineteenth century the picture changes radically. It was the high noon of British rule in India and of racial theories in Europe. Dictionaries of Indian languages were compiled, and both European and Tamil scholars endeavoured to find equivalent native translations for European concepts. Strangely, however, it now gets rather difficult to pin down occurrences and usages of *iṉam* particularly in the meaning of 'race' or related terms. In Tamil texts of this time *iṉam* is hard to find except in the writings of Maṟai Malai Aṭikaḷ from the late nineteenth and early twentieth centuries. A straight translation of 'race'

[17] *Naṉṉūl* 358; also *Tiruvāymoḻi* 9,3,5. A similar meaning we find in a Jaffna paper of the 1930s: *nāṅkaḷ iṉattavarkaḷ* (people such as we), *Īḻakēcari*, 11 December 1938.

[18] Kantapurāṇam, *Akkiṉimukam* 203. The terms mean gods, demons and humans respectively.

[19] Kiruṣṇaṉ, *Tamiḻ nūlkaḷil,* p.145-7.

as *iṉam* and vice versa is nearly impossible to establish. The point, however, is not whether *iṉam* denotes 'race' or 'kind' in these or earlier times. Rather the question should be asked: why it was *iṉam* that was chosen to denote the English term 'race' in preference to *kulam, kuṭumpam, kuṭi*, and other related words? That is the really interesting feature. One reason would have been the classificatory but also residual nature of *iṉam*. It could denote all kinds of differences and similarities, not just biological ones, and it was not loaded in other directions as were such terms as *cāti, kulam,* and *kuṭi*

Still, in English texts and translations of the time 'race' jumps at us from every other page! The 'Native Newspaper Reports', established in 1874, have 'race' in all sorts of contexts. The difficulty is that it is virtually impossible to match these translations with the Tamil originals which are inaccessible or destroyed. We can therefore not really find the original terms for 'race'. But the few instances where I had access to Tamil papers of the time I formed the strong suspicion that what the English translated as 'race' might have been rendered as *cāti* (jāti) in Tamil. Apart from European and Indian races, we find the Muslim 'race', the Hindu 'race', and even the Vellalar and Paraiyar 'race'. In Tamil articles 'race' and 'nation' were both rendered as *cāti.*[20] What this provides is less a picture of the Tamil concept of the term than of what the British thought the Tamils thought.

Tamil and Tamils

The exploration of *iṉam* apparently does not help us much to understand who and what a 'Tamil' is or was; the two did simply not go together. We do not encounter the Tamiḻ *iṉam* until the twentieth century has considerably progressed, but the fact is that we do encounter it in an explosive way in both Tamil Nadu and Sri Lanka. Even today usage of the term remains confusing. Alongside the modern rendering as ethnicity, we find now also some strange and surprising new composita, such as *Nāṭṭiṉam* for 'nation' and *Iṉamaiyak koḷkai* for 'ethno-

[20] *Ñaṉa Vinōtiṉi*, April and August 1890. It might be interesting to note here that in Sinhalese the terms for nation and caste are very similar: *jatika* and *jati*; and race is also rendered as *jatika*.

centrism'.[21] How did the two combine? To understand that we should now consider what was meant by 'Tamil': who was a Tamil and how was he defined? Even if there was no concept of race, the Tamils did differentiate between themselves and others; they knew who they were. However, the basis and the terms for this distinction were not considered in terms of *iṉam*.[22]

The question of who was a Tamil and how was he defined sounds simple. The answer, however, is extremely complicated. In the *Caṅkam* literature, which is nowadays perceived as the fount and origin of Tamil identity,[23] Tamils as a people or a group do not appear at all. We find Tamil mentioned for the language, we find the 'Three Kingdoms' of Tamiḻakam where *muttamiḻ* (threefold Tamil) was flourishing (*muttamiḻ vēntar*), and we find Tamil warriors or Tamil elders, but no Tamils.[24] The *Tirukkuṟaḷ*, a collection of ethical aphorisms, mentions neither Tamil nor Tamils.[25] Why then, do we assign the term Tamil to all these people and this society? And how do we distinguish them from non-Tamils, whoever *they* were?

The difficulty we encounter here is one not unfamiliar to historians: for the authors of the classical songs it was self-evident who and what was a Tamil, or, to put it better, who they were, whom they sang for, and who belonged to them. They did not need to be defined. Yet authors writing after the event had to give a name to the society they were talking about, and they applied the term 'Tamils', as by that time it had become the name for the speakers of the language: they had to determine for us what characterised the Tamils of the classical age as

[21] From *nāṭu* meaning country, and *iṉam*, probably in contradistinction to the Sanskrit-derived term *tĭcam*, often denoting the whole of the supposed Indian nation. Both terms are used in Kiruṣṇaṉ,*Tamiḻ nūlkaḷil*, p.1.

[22] Ibid., p.86.

[23] Ibid., p.166: 'Even the basis for the language, ethnic and nationals consciousness in Tamilnadu of the 20th century was established there [in *Caṅkam* literature]'.

[24] Kamil V. Zvelebil, *Companion Studies to the History of Tamil Literature* (Leiden, 1992), p.x. For the wide range of composita using *tamiḻ* in old and medieval literature and the origin of the word itself, see ibid., pp.xi-xvii; see also Kiruṣṇaṉ, *Tamiḻ nūlkaḷil*, p.65.

[25] Ibid., p.124.

Tamils. However, to my knowledge, only Zvelebil, Kailasapathy and Kiruṣṇan̲ begin to question this unselfconscious use and try to define Tamils of the classical age in their own terms.[26] Our view of 'the Tamils' and 'Tamil society' might well be challenged by the fact of the constant internecine fighting we hear about and by the absence of the term itself.

There is, however, one thing that is reasonably certain (and does not change very much over a considerable time), and that is the geographical area that constitutes the Tamilland or Tamiḻakam. Its borders are clearly defined in the *Tolkāppiyam*—as 'where the three kings rule', and 'the beautiful world where Tamil is spoken from Venkatam in the North to Kanyakumari in the South'.[27] We then have references to chieftains, professional groups, different classes of people: bards, dancers, warriors, cultivators, and so on. At the top, ultimately, are the three kings of Tamiḻakam, the Colas, Ceras, Pandyas, mythical figures or tropes of literature or both, who represented the Tamiḻakam. The concept of Tamiḻakam, therefore, does not seem to have had any notion of a nation state or a unitary state under one ruler tied to it, but it is seen as a geographical unit of one language, if not of one people. The other important motif in this regard is that of the five landscapes into which the Tamiḻakam was 'literally' divided. The three kings and the five landscapes belong together even if they are fighting each other most of the time, and in a way that sets them apart from, for example, the Yavanas or the Vaṭavars.[28] The people living in Tamiḻakam and speaking Tamil are, in the later literature, clearly named as Tamils. But were they all 'Tamils' in the *Caṅkam* age? Kailasapathy questions the

[26] Ibid.; also K. Kailasapathy, *Tamil Heroic Poetry* (London, 1968; Zvelebil, *Companion Studies*, and *The Smile of Murugan* (Leiden, 1973) and his two vols. on *Tamil Literature* (Wiesbaden, 1974 and Leiden/Köln, 1975). George L. Hart III, *The Poems of Ancient Tamil. Their milieu and their Sanskrit counterparts* (Berkeley, 1975), does not address the problem at all.

[27] *Tolkāppiyam Poruḷatikāram* 331; and Pan̲ampāran̲ār, *Tolkāppiyam Pāyiram.*

[28] On these two motifs and *Caṅkam* literature in general see Zvelebil, *The Smile of Murukan*; A.K. Ramanujan, *The Interior Landscape* (Bloomington, 1969), and *Poems of Love and War. From the eight anthologies and the ten long poems of classical Tamil* (Delhi, 1985).

assumption, while Kiruṣṇaṉ supports it.[29] Let us look at this problem in a bit more detail.

Kiruṣṇaṉ mentions that the loyalty of the *Caṅkam* heroes was not towards a country or even one of the three kings, but towards their master or patron.[30] Kailasapathy assumes that 'Tamils', in the sense of the heroes of classical literature, means the aristocracy or at least respectable society (*cāṉṟōr*), but not, for example, servants, peasants, shepherds, or 'unfree' persons, who according to the *Tolkāppyiam* are explicitly excluded as heroes of literature.[31] Yet Kailasapathy then goes on to describe the very wide range of social groups with which the *Caṅkam* literature deals, and from which are drawn those it depicts as heroes and therefore as *cāṉṟōr*. Among these are, most prominently, poets, singers and bards, but also shepherds, farmers and such like.[32] The question then is how far did the respectable society of *cāṉṟōr* extend in breadth and depth, and it seems that it extended further than assumed. Kailasapathy points out one very significant fact: a 'Tamil', a hero of the literature, could only be a 'free' person, free to choose their own way of life and of death.[33] But this criterion did not include only the aristocracy or a leisured class. Unlike the term 'Sinhala',[34] the concept of a Tamil does seem to have comprised a wider range of societym, and not only the ruling dynasty or dynasties. Later the term contracted: some Tamils became more Tamil than others.

In spite of there being no term for the group, in *Caṅkam* literature a strong impression comes through of people belonging together, of people bound not only by a common language, space, and culture, but by a common fate. There is, as both Kailasapathy and Zvelebil argue, a

[29] Kiruṣṇaṉ, *Tamiḻ nūlkaḷil*, p.87-89; Kailasapathy, *Heroic Poetry*, p.51.

[30] Kiruṣṇaṉ, *Tamiḻ nūlkaḷil*, p.113; similarly Ramanujan, *Poems of Love and War*, p.288. Graul, *Reise*, mentions the intense loyalty of the Tamils towards their (extended) family and to nobody else: ibid., p.202. He also says that this family loyalty is a substitute for national or patriotic loyalty!

[31] Kailasapathy, *Heroic Poetry*, pp.50, 228 ff.

[32] Ibid., pp.24 and 60 ff.

[33] Ibid., p.258.

[34] R.A.L.H. Gunawardene, '"The People of the Lion": Sinhala consciousness in history and historiography', in *Ethnicity and Social Change in Sri Lanka* (Colombo, 1985), pp.55-107.

strong feeling of incipient 'nationalism'.[35] Kiruṣṇaṉ infers a feeling of unity and belonging together, from the fact that one language was spoken, and from the efforts of the singers and bards, who travelled the length and breadth of the Tamil-speaking country and were therefore able to see not only the common features behind more superficial differences and feuds, but also to point them out to their audience.[36] Motifs, such as the three kings, the five landscapes, and kingly or chiefly largesse and patronage, were common to every group or tribe who shared the space of Tamiḻakam. Anybody who listened to their bards' songs implicitly was drawn into a community of time, space and language. 'Nationalism' might be too strong a term for this perception, but it would have fostered a perception of shared identity.

The feeling of belonging based on place and language acquires even more significance during the next centuries, that of devotional and epic literature. However, the significance of language changes at the same time. From the language spoken in Tamiḻakam with probably magico-religious properties, Tamiḻ becomes the sacred language of the Tamils. *Being* Tamil and revering the language becomes more important than speaking it.[37] The authors of *bhakti* literature exhort the people to defend the language against the depredations of other religions who now no longer use Tamil.[38] Kiruṣṇaṉ explains the enhanced primacy of language during this time in the fact of foreign dynasties (Pallavas and Kalabhras) were trying to foist a foreign language (Prakrit) onto the people as the language of Buddhism and Jainism. Both religions had a rich Tamil literature which was now pushed into the background. This led to a vernacular backlash which emphasised Saivism, in which Tamil and eventually Sanskrit became holy and sacred languages.[39] What seems to be implied here is that it was the foreign language that made the religion repugnant and not the other way round.[40] This argu-

[35] Kailasapathy, *Heroic Poetry*, p.76; 'a country of different language', a stock phrase in the poems, ibid., p.161; Zvelebil, *Companion Studies*, pp.137-8.

[36] Kiruṣṇaṉ, *Tamiḻ nūlkaḷil*, pp.34-40; 86f; but also Kailasapathy, *Heroic Poetry*, pp.60-1.

[37] Kiruṣṇaṉ, *Tamiḻ nūlkaḷil*, p.104.

[38] Ibid., p.106.

[39] Ibid., p.132 ff.

[40] This raises interesting questions about 'truth languages', conversion,

ment does seem a bit strained, and might look like a back projection of modern conditions. Yet Tamil *was* an important vehicle carrying religious messages, as is made clear by these quotations from the medieval religious literature:

God has created me the way I am [as myself], so that I render him in sweet Tamil [so that by me he is made sweet Tamil)], and similarly God [is one who] has created me well, so that Tamil [language] makes [shows] him well.[41]

These statements are surely not merely a product of the overheated imagination of some European scholars, but express some genuine assumptions by the Tamils of that time about themselves and their language. They show that the Tamils of the *bhakti* and the Puranas did define themselves strongly through language. The medieval grammatical treatise *Akapporuḷ* for the first time defines Tamil as both sweet and a woman.[42]

There is another aspect to the question of the significance of language and of being a Tamil, which has been brought out recently by Zvelebil. He argues that identity could be derived from sound or language; which would be a very basic feature of distinction.[43] This is nothing unusual and has happened in other civilisations. It could be that language distinctions were the first and foremost to be perceived. The term *mleccha* in Sanskrit conveys 'unintelligible babble', and so does the Greek 'Barbara'. Likewise, the Tamils used language to differentiate themselves from the people from the north: those from the north spoke *vaṭamoḻi* (northern language), and those from the south Tamil or *teṉmoḻi* (southern language). But Zvelebil goes further: language is a feature that pervades Tamil society and Tamil culture, indeed all aspects of Tamil life in a way which has no equivalent in most other cultures. This is the concept of *muttamiḻ*,[44] (literally 'the threefold

Luther's translation of the Bible and religious instruction in sacred as distinct from vernacular languages, which unfortunately we cannot go into here.

[41] *Nālāyirat Tivviya Pirapantam*, 3425, *Tirumūlar.*

[42] Kiruṣṇaṉ, *Tamiḻ nūlkaḷil,* p.126.

[43] Zvelebil, *Companion Studies*, p.xi.

[44] Ibid., p.95, a detailed discussion, pp.140-3, and passim; see also p.251: 'The growth of Tamil self-consciousness was nourished by the "primordial identities" of language, ethnic origin, and religion...or by the "primordial sentiments" of blood, speech and custom...'.

Tamil'—the three kings were called *muttamiḻ vēntar* until the time of the *Cilapatikkāram*).[45] This threefold Tamil comprises more than language—that is to say, music, drama, and *civilisation* in the sense of a life regulated by certain 'grammatical' rules. Language equalled the grammar of life.[46] In medieval literature, language has turned from an inward-looking feature into an outward-looking one. To call this essentialism would be to misunderstand what language meant for the Tamils of both the classical and medieval age, though we can perhaps tentatively term it *Wesen*.

One other point follows: in *Caṅkam* times, Tamil as a language was bounded by time and space. This changed in later centuries. The sacred Tamil was uncreated or created by Siva before time, and, as such, it was in principle not geographically bounded either. As will be discussed below, this consideration is extremely important for modern interpretations and definitions of 'Tamilness' which transcend borders. We also have to decide whether language was the *only* feature to define a Tamil. This point of view has been strongly argued by a variety of scholars, but it is not at all uncontested. Difficulties arise immediately with regard to the Brahmans, who are often singled out for comment in the literature, though without doubt they spoke Tamil. We shall deal with that question too a little later, but may state here that language was a necessary, but not a sufficient, condition for being a Tamil.

We have now a somewhat fluid definition of a Tamil as someone speaking Tamil and living in Tamiḻakam. Did this mean that anybody could be or become a Tamil? Against this Kailasapathy argues for the importance of lineage and descent.[47] Of equal importance would have been the *type* of Tamil spoken. It needed to be a refined, literary language. Though it is uncertain what this refined Tamil was like, it was probably standardised in the region around Madurai;[48] and it has been argued that it was 'pure' in the sense of not containing foreign, Sanskrit, loanwords. In any case to be able to speak 'proper Tamil' was

[45] Kiruṣṇaṉ, *Tamiḻ nūlkaḻil*, p 121.
[46] Compare Zvelebil, *Companion Studies*, p.142.
[47] Kailasapathy, *Heroic Poetry*, p.248.
[48] Kiruṣṇaṉ, *Tamiḻ nūlkaḻil*, p.83; Kailasapathy, *Heroic Poetry*, p.183.

important, and some groups did this better than others.

Vellalars

Most authors on the *Caṅkam* age describe Tamil society as clearly stratified in a rudimentary form of caste system with limited endogamy, but few interdictions on commensality.[49] In the Middle Ages Brahmans had attained the top position and were endowed with land and gifts by the kings. How was this possible? A look at *Caṅkam* times might again be helpful. We have seen that it was the prerogative of kings and patrons to exert largesse in donating gifts to the bards, singers and musicians who praised them in poems or played for them. Kailasapathy mentions, however, that gifts of land were unusual.[50] We should now look a little more closely at the persons who gave these gifts.

Beside the kings there were seven, probably mythical, famous patrons and chiefs who were known for their largesse. Every patron was called upon to imitate these. Patrons had to possess land and a certain amount of wealth. The people who enabled poems to be sung, who enabled singers to survive, who upheld culture and society were chiefs (*vēḷir*) and landowner or farmers. At first glance this seems an ambitious statement; it is, however, borne out by several songs in the *Puṟanāṉūṟu* (*Puṟam*)[51] that denote the importance of agriculture and farmers for the good of the whole country. *Vēḷir* later became the Vellalars, the farmer caste of the time of the imperial Colas. In the *Manudharma*, these are termed Sudras, and they were later considered as such by the British rulers. But they never called themselves Sudras, and to apply that term to them was totally to misunderstand the status of *farmers* in Tamil society. In North India people who *actually worked the land* were indeed the lowest of the low Sudras, due to the prevailing nomadic ideology. But this did not apply in Tamil society. The society of the five landscapes was predominantly an agricultural and livestock-

[49] Ibid., p.60; similarly Hart, *Poems*, p.125.

[50] Kailasapathy, *Heroic Poetry*, pp.222-3.

[51] *Puṟam* 35 and 182, which says that the world exists because some men live who do not strive for themselves but for the good of the world (cf. translation in Ramanujan, *Interior Landscape*, p.157. Kailasapathy mentions explicitly that agriculture and agriculturalists were 'respectable' and 'free'; *Heroic Poetry*, p.264.

producing society where owners of agricultural wealth were highly respected. Kailasapathy sees the heroes of the *Caṅkam* as aristocrats given to the life of surplus and leisure. However, the very standardised tropes and motifs of the poems hint at quite a different reality: cattle-raiding was practically a declaration of war, fields and land had to be defended against predators both human and animal (elephants, tigers), heroes had to leave their lovers and wives to acquire wealth in foreign parts. Farmers, warriors and chiefs must have been in many cases identical. These motifs hint at a pastoral-agricultural society fighting for space. Farmers create order out of the sacred and dangerous disorder of the forest and drive away pollution. They cause irrigation works to be built, and make the land fertile. And they can, as Karkatta (cloud-bringing) Vellalars attract rains by instituting ritual and sacrifice.[52] Their activities and good-will therefore guarantee the life and well-being of all. Ultimately the world. Vellalars or *Vēḷaṉ* can plausibly be derived from *Vēḷaṉmai* (productivity), as well as from *vēḷvi* (sacrifice) or *vēḷir*. Like weavers they provide basic material and ritual necessities. *Puṟam* 35 tells the king, that unless he honours the cultivators, the most important people in his realm, he will not prosper. It is not warriors or singers or priests who are important, but *farmers!*[53]

Access to land meant high status and power, and land was therefore rarely given as gift. The consensus is that *Caṅkam* literature turns around a conflict of two models of society: an earlier tribal society of chieftaincies, and the emerging Brahmanically-influenced one of kings. We see then in the *Caṅkam* an attempt to come to terms with conflicting views of society, and a society at the point of synthesis. The Brahmanical society won out in the end because the Brahmans took the place of bards and singers, and aligned themselves with the emerging kings.[54] But the former chiefs held their own in more ways than one:

[52] E. Thurston, *Castes and Tribes of Southern India* (Madras, 1907), pp.368 and 379.

[53] The king is admonished to protect *the protectors who cultivate and herd cattle.* His kingdom came to him because the farmers made the soil fertile. Note that till this day, in Sri Lanka and Thailand the king (symbolically) ploughs the first furrow at the beginning of the agricultural year.

[54] Kailasapathy, *Heroic Poetry,* p.251.

they turned into the Vellalars, who, by their work, their donations to Brahmans, and their *enabling of* the ritual, maintained the social and religious order. They patronised temples, arts and literature, settled disputes, endowed Brahmans, and so on.

Thurston records a particularly interesting myth of origin in this regard: that the Vellalars gave up their right to rule and occupied themselves with farming, in exchange for the right to crown (that is, to choose) the king.[55] This seems clearly to refer to the struggle between *vḷir* chiefs and the supreme king ,when the former became, like the poligars in later centuries, Vellalar landowners instead of chieftains. Despite the respect they commanded, the Brahmans in turn desperately needed the Vellalars to survive, just as the bards and minstrels of a former time would have been lost without the kings and chiefs who patronised them. While in Aryan society the separation of functions led to high priests and warriors and lowly agriculturalists, in the South the reverse happened: warriors became degraded as mercenaries and 'criminal tribes', and instead the landowners and farmers were elevated to the highest status after the Brahmans. Access to, control over and working of the soil became the preconditions for high status, and were combined with language to define a Tamil. Vellalars became culture carriers and preservers.

From an occupational and ruling group the Vellalar thus emerged, between the ninth and twelfth centuries, as a clearly named and powerful caste group, distinguished both from the Brahmans and kings and from those below them, and, one assumes, not without say in questions of royal succession. The caste of kings is seldom explicitly stated beyond thir not being Vellalar. They may have been lowly warrior castes or marauding tribes engaged by the Vellalars to protect them against other tribes and for protection money. Such a scenario seems probable when we consider what Dirks has to say about the myths of origin of the Putukkottai kings, who were Maravars.[56]

[55] Thurston, *Castes and Tribes*, p.361ff.

[56] Compare Nicholas B. Dirks, *The Hollow Crown. Ethno-history of an Indian kingdom* (Cambridge, 1987). Graul, *Reise*, claims that the Sudra-Vellalars are the 'moral core of the people', p.207. They fill in the south all functions of farmers and Vaisyas, from trade to agriculture; ibid., p.168. Also p.171 ff.: they

The status and role of the Vellalars predestined them to claim the status of Tamils *par excellence* in the nineteenth century,[57] something which neither Brahmans nor low castes were able to call themselves. Was this then an instance of 'caste as 'race' or 'race' as caste' as Inden calls it? If we look at the foremost propagator of Vellalars as 'essential' Tamils, Maṟai Malai Aṭikaḷ, we might be tempted to affirm this, especially as he does talk about the Vellalar *Iṉam*. In 1923 he published a book on the Vellalars, called *Vēḷāḷar Nākarikam*, first given as a talk in Jaffna, in which he terms them 'the civilised agricultural class of the Tamils'.[58] Vellalars were the ultimate Tamils, and Brahmans were explicitly excluded from being Tamil. A look at Thurston, however, gives a different picture: '...what a mixture of blood arises...and how puzzling the variations in the cranial measurements of Vellalars taken at random are likely to become.'[59]

Let us also follow Maṟai Malai Aṭikaḷ's argument a bit further. He proceeds from the basic equality of all humans or at least all Tamils in early times, who, he says were all in a state of similar savagery. Some groups among these became 'civilised' because they discovered agriculture and conducted the sacrifice; others remained barbaric.[60] This again shows the prime importance attached among the Tamils to agriculture, probably from very early times, a trait that we can also discover for the Goyigamas among the Sinhalese: the ideal Sinhalese is a rice-growing peasant.[61] Maṟai Malai Aṭikaḷ goes on to say that because of this differentiation, division into several *iṉam* came about.[62] He does not use *cāti* to describe what in effect was a caste division, but *iṉam* which were characterised primarily by cultural and occupational,

---

are the most honourable, make the land fertile and build tanks!

[57] P. Arunachalam, 'Population: the Island's races, religions, languages, castes, and customs', in Arnold Wright (ed.), *Twentieth-century Impressions of Ceylon* (London, 1907), p.352.

[58] Maṟai Malaị Aṭikaḷ, *Vēḷāḷar Nākarikam* (Madras, 1923), p.12. He equates Tamiḻ and Vēḷāḷar: ibid., p.6.

[59] Thurston, *Castes and Tribes*, p.376.

[60] Maṟai Malai Aṭikaḷ, *Vēḷāḷar Nākarikam*, p.113 (Tamil numeration).

[61] Mick Moore, *The State and Peasant Politics in Sri Lanka* (Cambridge, 1985), p.28 and passim.

[62] Maṟai Malai Aṭikaḷ, *Vēḷāḷar Nākarikam*, p.113.

not physical differences. The Vellalar *iṉam* was Tamil as much as any other *iṉam* only more so. It distributed the right to the soil: Vellalars did not depend on others; others depended on them.[63] Moreover, this *iṉam* was not immutable or fixed: anybody could become a Vellalar and thus an exemplary Tamil, if they followed the Vellalar Saiva creed. This statement was directed explicitly against some among the Vellalar who wanted to keep caste purity.[64] Maṟai Malai Aṭikaḷ considered this attitude extremely harmful, stating that Vellalars had always been replenished by people from other groups. This was not totally wishful thinking, as shown by the well-known Tamil proverb *mella mella ellām Veḷḷāḷarkaḷ ākiṉṟaṉa.*[65] Thurston's inability to assign the Vellalars to a 'race' anthropometrically reflect their real diversity. Vellalars were the most numerous caste in Tamil Nadu, as in Jaffna, but, unlike in Jaffna, they were split up into a large number of distinct and non-commensal subgroups. In Jaffna, they were the absolute majority, which (as we will see) may explain some differences in development between the two regions. Maṟai Malai Aṭikaḷ makes it quite clear that Vellalar-hood does not depend on birth, but on life-style, comportment, occupation and ideology. In his view, anyone who gave up low professions, turned to agriculture, and became vegetarian could be a Vellalar. He does not, incidentally, exclude other castes or professions from being 'Tamil', but states that the Vellalars, because of their 'sacrifice' and life-style, are the Tamils whom other castes should try to imitate. This was not a closed society, like that of the Brahmans, but open and flexible: in theory, anyone with access to land could become a Vellalar, but no amount of Sanskritisation would make anyone a Brahman.

Though language was a defining feature in classical and devotional literature, it may seem to have been pushed back in Tamil ideology from the late nineteenth and early twentieth centuries. To think that would, however, be a mistake. Maṟai Malai Aṭikaḷ wanted not only to give the Tamils pride in their identity against that of Brahmans and/or Aryans, but he wanted to do this with the help of the Tamil language, a

[63] Ibid., p.8.
[64] Ibid., p.114.
[65] Slowly, slowly, they all become Vellalar.

language which was 'pure' and free from Sanskrit pollution. To speak Tamil was not enough. It had to be, as in earlier centuries, the right kind of Tamil. Language was an explicit means to snatch back from the Aryan Brahmans the respect, rituals and privileges which formerly had accrued to the Vellalars.[66] The resultant identity was not primarily based on ancestry and birth; but—and it is a large 'but'—Brahmans were excluded because they were not of the right *iṉam*. All Tamil *iṉam* could become Vellalars, except the Brahmans, because they were Aryan.[67] Maṟai Malai Aṭikaḷ warns the Vellalars against the Brahmans and their schemes to foster a feeling of inferiority among Vellalars and to make them try to imitate the Brahmans. Such efforts, he says, are not only corrupting and degrading; they are also fruitless: non-Brahmans can never become Brahmans. It is degrading because according to Brahman (Aryan) ideology all Vellalars are Sudras and thus children of prostitutes and concubines.[68] Maṟai Malai Aṭikaḷ denounces Aryan law-givers who termed agriculturalists low and despised.[69] Who and what, however, are these Aryan Brahmans, and why can they not be Tamil? We now have to look at the Tamil perception of others, of outsiders.

Tamils and others

If we define Tamils of the *Caṅkam* and mediaeval times broadly as people who spoke Tamil and had access to and control over land, we can then begin to look at the question, who was *not* a Tamil, who was outside this charmed circle, and why? Obviously whoever did not speak Tamil, did not live in the country and did not exercised control there was not a Tamil. But what were these people called and what were their

[66] Maṟai Malai Aṭikaḷ, *Vēḷāḷar Nākarikam*, pp.34, 49-50, 118 and 121-2.

[67] Ibid., pp.14-15 (Arabic numeration).

[68] Ibid., pp.89-90. This refers to *Manudharma* where Sudras are termed the offspring of liaisons between Brahmans and Kshatrıyas, to the custom referred to in the literature that kings took Vellalar women as concubines, and to several famous maintenance cases in Madras where maintenance was denied to Vellalar women because they were Sudras and thus concubines of Brahmans. Some memory of this seems to have informed the denigration of the last Jaffna king Caṅkili in the *YVM*, where all sorts of evil deeds are attributed to him and it is said that he had no right to the throne since he was the son of a *Vellalar* concubine! See.also *Kerala Mitran*, 11 March 1882, on Nambudiri Brahmans and their 'Sudra' mistresses!

[69] Maṟai Malai Aṭikaḷ, *Vēḷāḷar Nākarikam*, p.90.

other characteristics? Were they perceived as friendly, neutral or hostile? Non-Tamils were indeed quite clearly described: we find basically three major groups mentioned: the Vatavar or Northerners, the Møriyar (Mauryas), the Yavaṉar or Greeks. These were three groups the authors of this literature were familiar with and considered as clearly differentiated. As Kiruṣṇaṉ demonstrates, there was hardly a term for 'foreigners' as such: they were nearly always mentioned by their proper—ethnic—names, though we do find the term *milīccar* (mleccha) occasionally applied to them.[70] The terms for outsiders, even *milīccar*, do not seem necessarily to have conveyed a concept of 'impurity'.[71] This is interesting, because Aloka Parasher demonstrates persuasively that it is possible to derive the Sanskrit *mleccha* itself from a Dravidian root denoting people living in the West or in Mesopotamia. Only in Sanskrit usage did the word take on a pejorative connotation.[72] The Greeks—and Romans—were known as traders and sometimes as (despised) mercenaries for the king.[73] During the time of *Tolkāppiyam*, contact with foreigners seems to have been rather restricted, and they were not perceived as hostile. In *Caṅkam* times the contact and differentiation increased, but still wars were fought more often within the Tamil community than with outsiders, while in the epic *Cilapatikkāram,* Tamil kings fought with northern rulers for supremacy in northern areas.[74] The term *āriyar,* though known, was seldom used for 'northerner' in *Caṅkam* literature. We have here a conception of three broadly different groups interacting in a given geographical space and differentiated by language and culture, and clearly outside any understanding of 'Tamil'.

While this might look like a clear distinction, two problems arise. We mentioned the tension in the *Puṟam* songs between two views of society. The songs probably show these two world-views at the point of

[70] Kiruṣṇaṉ, *Tamiḻ nūlkaḷil,* p.26.
[71] Kailasapathy, *Heroic Poetry*, p.39.
[72] Aloka Parasher, *Mlecchas in Early India. A study in attitudes towards outsiders upto AD 600* (New Delhi 1991), pp.63-5. On the impurity of mlecchas cf. p.15. Note, however, that Parasher in her further discussion questions the automatic impurity of a mleccha!
[73] Kailasapathy, *Heroic Poetry*, p.39.
[74] Kiruṣṇaṉ, *Tamiḻ nūlkaḷil,* pp.5-33, 73 and 106.

struggle and assimilation. But there is also another kind of song in the *Puṟam* (namely 183 and 192) which Ramanujan calls 'lessons' and which have less to do with war than with the presumed universality of mankind.[75] These are thought to be Buddhist or Jain influenced. Their 'universality' has been controversial (especially because of its use and abuse for modern-day political purposes). Zvelebil wants to interpret Puṟam 192 in a new way as hinting at the 'incipient' nationalism and a feeling of communality of all Tamils.[76] Kailasapathy argues similarly that mankind in these songs of course did not mean *all mankind*, but only the *cāṉṟōr*, and that this is not a democratic ideal. The point, however, is facetious: neither the Greek democracies, nor for that matter the American constitution, meant all mankind when speaking about the rights of man: the Greeks implicitly excluded the unfree and slaves, and the fathers of the American constitution would have been very indignant indeed if they had been told that their rights of man also applied to women and blacks. Nevertheless both ideals could be and were taken as the basis for the extension of rights to formerly-excluded groups.

There is another way these songs can be interpreted, one which has been popular in the last decades: they might have been directed against the new, Brahmanic ideology of exclusiveness on the basis of purity, pollution, and caste. The stanzas then seem to be opposed to the new idea of Brahman superiority, which squeezed out the bards, singers, sages and soothsayers who had formerly occupied the most respected places, acting also as priests, scholars, and magicians. Puṟam 183 seems to argue against this Brahman supremacy when it states that it is education which makes the person, so that even the lowliest persons will be respected if they are learned. Kiruṣṇaṉ derives from this emphasis on learning the idea that only educated people could speak properly and were therefore Tamils.[77]

[75] For example, 192, the famous stanza that starts *yātum ūrē yāvarum kēḷir* (every place my place, everybody my kin); and 183 which praises the value of wisdom and education over age and caste (a stanza written by the 'Pāṇṭiya king who overcame the āriya army).

[76] Zvelebil, *Companion Studies*, pp.138-9, Kailasapathy, *Heroic Poetry*, pp.134, 260 ff.

[77] Kiruṣṇaṉ, *Tamiḻ nūlkaḷil*, pp.46-7; compare *Puṟam* 183.

Returning to the problem of the Brahmans, we find that Kiruṣṇaṉ states that only at the time of the Saiva saint Appar (ninth to tenth centuries) were the Brahmans explicitly called Aryans, a term until then reserved for northerners and rarely used.[78] In *Caṅkam* literature they are called *pārppāṉ*, from *pār*, to see. As priests they had the title *Antaṉār* (*Tolkāppiyam*). As *pārppāṉ* they are sometimes singled out for comment or even ridicule despite their presumed high rank. These comments and comparisons turned on their different look, their way of dressing, and hairstyle. Does this argue for an origin outside the Tamil country? Our problem of determining their ethnic identity and status is compounded by the fact that quite a few of the *Caṅkam* poets were obviously Brahmans (including Kapilar, who ironically wrote one of the most scathing and unkind descriptions of a Brahman[79] and got the title *pulavar*, the wise or learned one). Hart attributes the conflicting evidence about Brahmans to their having arrived in successive waves. The first ones assimilated thoroughly to Tamil society, and later ones stuck to vedic beliefs. Both groups associated closely with kings and rulers, and usurped the place of singers and bards.[80] This is an accepted view, but the interesting fact is that Hart never questions that the Brahmans were from the North—that is were Aryans—since they are termed 'of the four Vedas'.[81] Whether these northerners who came to live among the Tamils were really Brahmans is, however, quite another question. If we take analogous evidence from Sri Lanka and South East Asia, it is much more likely that they were fairly low adventurers pretending to higher status in the new society. Why else should they imitate the lifestyle of what were, in Hart's view, lowly bards in order to get favours from the king.[82]

To sum up, there were clear and quite early distinctions between 'Tamils' and 'non-Tamils' which did not necessarily involve hostility The Brahmans obviously did occupy an ambiguous place in this scheme: they spoke Tamil, they were singers of songs, but they were

[78] Kiruṣṇaṉ, *Tamiḻ nūlkaḷil*, p.145.
[79] Ramanujan, *Interior Landscape*, p.208, *Kalittokai* 65.
[80] Hart, *Poems*, p.56.
[81] Ibid., p.55.
[82] Ibid., p.148ff.

seen as somehow different. Kiruṣṇan̲ claims that Tamil consciousness awoke first with the coming south of the Aryans.[83] This might well be. But the classical view of Brahmans as distinct itself differs from the anti-Brahmanism of *bhakti* (around the sixth to ninth centuries) which was founded on the rejection of caste in religious devotion and on the sanctity of Tamil. Moreover, the perceived differences were obviously not based on colour, preoccupation with which we find nowadays all over India in the shape of contempt for people who do not have very fair skin-colouring. On the contrary, we find 'red' gods who are beautiful, and even maidens with 'black loveliness' and a beauty 'dark as a mango leaf' [84]

The 'discovery' of the Dravidians

How do we get, in the nineteenth century, from Tamils, Vellalars and Northerners to Aryans and Dravidians? The term Dravidam (*Tirāviṭam*) had been around at least since the Middle Ages as a *Sanskrit* term denoting the South and, in Vaisnava literature, as the language spoken there.[85] At the beginning of the nineteenth century, Colin McKenzie collected several palm leaf manuscripts which dealt with the history of the '*Tirāviṭatēcam*'. The term is, thus, not a European invention. What European scholars did in applying the term was to conflate the place and language with an assumed 'race', and in the same breath to treat the language as a debased dialect derived from Sanskrit. Moreover, the juxtaposition of 'Aryan' and 'Dravidian' as antonyms was entirely attributable to European scholarship. Therefore, when Caldwell 'discovered' the Dravidian family of language, this was progress. The German missionary, Karl Graul, who travelled in South India in the 1840s, did not use the term 'Dravidian', but nevertheless expressed high admiration for the literary and cultural achievements of the Tamils *sui generis;* to my knowledge, he was the first to compare their heroic literature to that of the Greeks.[86] As Tamil identity had been closely

[83] Kiruṣṇan̲, *Tamiḻ nūlkaḷil*, p.74

[84] Hart, *Poems* p.164, transl. *Aiṅkuṟunūṟu* 454; *Kuṟuntokai* 27, transl. Ramanujan, *Interior Landscapes*, p.69.

[85] Kiruṣṇan̲, *Tamiḻ nūlkaḷil*, p.193. I shall not enter into the controversy over the etymology of the term here.

[86] Graul, *Reise*, p.193. '*...nur...ein...Halbbruder des griechischen Genius...*',

connected with language for centuries, the battle-cry was eagerly taken up by Tamil scholars who now set out to establish who and what a 'Dravidian' was. 'Race' was aligned with 'language' in a totally new way. The Tamil scholar, Sundaram Pillai, who lived in the second half of the nineteenth century, called Tamil the mother of Dravidian languages, and wrote the Tamil anthem. In this very anthem he changed *Tirāviṭam* from a language into a geographical unit, a country:[87]

Therein [in the continent of Bharat] the Dekkhan and in it the wonderful land of *Tirāviṭa* form her dainty crescent brow, adorned with the *tilak* [Tamil], the *tilak* that spreads sweet knowledge all over the earth; the fame of Lady Tamil pervades the earth; entranced by your eternal purity, Lady Tamil, we praise you.[88]

As in *Caṅkam* literature, language and country are here congruent. On the basis of this, 'Aryan' pretensions could now be repulsed. And these seemed to be embodied in the Brahmans, who had long denied the worth of any Tamil literature that was not narrowly based on Saivism and heavily Sanskritised. Now the equal sanctity of Tamil and Sanskrit, postulated in *bhakti* and Saiva Siddhanta texts, but lost during the intervening centuries, was proclaimed once again. Maṟai Malai Aṭikaḷ and his followers went a step further. They put the Dravidians up as models of civilisation and virtue, and the Vellalars at the apex of this system, as superior to the allegedly barbaric, savage, and 'primitive' Aryans. All that is good in Aryan civilisation, says Maṟai Malai Aṭikaḷ, was stolen from the Dravidians by the Aryans and then claimed as their own achievement.[89] This is quite a step away from attempts to deny that the Tamils are 'Dravidians' and to assign them 'Aryan' ancestry, efforts which went on in Jaffna until the 1930s and beyond. The perception of Aryan superiority also explains the fury with which other 'Dravidian' states in India have rejected being lumped with the Tamils and have even rejected the 'Dravidian' label: they do not want to be associated

p.198; on heroic poetry of Tamils and their former martial virtues see ibid., p.197. Pope drew the comparison only in 1885, Kailasapathy, *Heroic Poetry*, p.VIII. Graul postulated a non-Aryan '*Urelement*' in South Indian languages, which he derived from the 'Turanian' family, pp.148-9.

[87] Kiruṣṇaṉ, *Tamiḻ nūlkaḷil*, pp.209-10.

[88] Suntaram Pillai, *Tamiḻt tāy vāḻttu* fom *Maṉōṉmaṇiyam*.

[89] Maṟai Malai Aṭikaḷ, *Vēḷāḷar Nākarikam*, pp.49 ff., 80 ff.

with those 'lowly' people, and instead stress their 'Aryan' heritage. The efforts of Maṟai Malai Aṭikaḷ and others changed the self-perception of 'Dravidian' Tamils from inferiority to pride, but did not have the same effect on other Dravidians.[90] There were, however, powerful incentives to help restore 'Dravidian' pride. The discovery of the treasures of classical Tamil literature, hardly 'sullied' by Sanskrit, were discovered, as were the powerful Tamil empires of the Colas and Pandyas. Maṟai Malai Aṭikaḷ drew on these to substantiate pride in Dravidian identity.

The the question of the Brahmans was brought to the fore with a new urgency by the Aryan-Dravidian divide. Indeed, while the controversy seemed to be being fought in such terms, in reality it was a conflict between Brahmans and Dravidians (Tamils). In the nineteenth century it was increasingly about access to resources, education and civil service jobs.[91] Brahmans were considered and considered themselves the Aryans par excellence, a perception strengthened by the Tamil name for a Brahman priest: Ayyar. A substratum of respect, fear and resentment seems to accompany the perception of Brahmans throughout Tamil literature, and it came to a head in the nineteenth century. Brahmans were now seen as the outriders of Aryan oppression in the South and as not belonging to the soil. Efforts thus to exclude the Brahmans were a general feature of the late nineteenth century.[92] Brahmans (it was said) could never become Tamils, even if they spoke Tamil and identified with Tamil culture, and this put them even further away than the lower and untouchable castes who were eventually termed Adi-Dravidas and could be accepted into the fold. Except for this exclusion of Brahmans, the concept of the *Tirāviṭar iṉam* was one that unified rather than divided. It was based on the essential similarity

[90] Even before this, South Indian kings have tried to claim Aryan ancestry to enhance their status: note the Aryachakkravatis of Jaffna, though in this case the term Aryan was probably used in its original meaning of noble, human. Ayyar for Brahman is probably derived from the same root, denoting that they were noble, but also from another group. The racial discourse is at present being repeated in the arguments of the B.J.P. and V.H.P.

[91] David Washbrook, *The Emergence of Country Politics. The Madras Presidency 1880-1920* (London, 1976); see also Zvelebil, *Companion Studies*, p.207.

[92] R. Suntharalingam, *Politics and Nationalist Awakening in South India 1852-1891* (Tucson, 1974).

and equality of the Dravidians who had supposedly been divided by Aryan perfidy. This perception was facilitated by the undoubted exclusivity of the Brahmans, and by the fact that they were divided on the issue of 'race'. While many and often the best Brahman scholars identified themselves as Tamils and thought the racial divide at least irrelevant or even non-existent, another group prided itself on the Brahmans' supposedly 'Aryan' ancestry,[93] an attitude which later helped the Dravidian movement to exclude them.

Of course the 'Aryan myth' of the Brahmans was also fostered by the colonial power for its own purposes, but it has to be said that the perception of superior Aryans and inferior Dravidians was taken up with zest by both 'Tamils' and 'Brahmans'.[94] Western interpretations of ancient categories were both accepted and contested. Between Brahmans and non-Brahmans, caste differences became ethnic differences. Even when the model of the inferior Dravidian was rejected, this rejection was still argued in terms provided by Western scholars: the 'virtues' of the Aryans were claimed for the Dravidians and the Aryans termed 'barbaric'. Only the Dravidian movement began to move beyond this. The categorisation of the Dravidian languages led to a strange conclusion. 'Dravidian' had always been more of a linguistic and geographical term until Europeans made it into a 'racial' distinction. But when the Dravidian language family was discovered, this gave the racial differentiation a boost (which was logical according to most current European thinking), instead of reducing it to its true significance, which would have been more in accord with Tamil perceptions and also with Max Müller's dire warnings against the equation of language and race.[95]

[93] Compare Zvelebil, *Companion Studies*, p.46: while describing the damage done to classical Tamil literature by Brahmanic orthodoxy in intervening centuries, this quotes Charles E. Gover with critical acclaim, 'The Brahmans corrupted what they could not destroy.'

[94] A look at the papers of the time bears witness to this: for example, when *Tattuvavivecini* condemns the Ilbert Bill because it will enable Brahman judges to sit in judgment over non-Brahmans and apply vedic and Manu's laws and superstitions to them, 24 March 1883. Or when another paper (*Vivekavardhini*, May 1881) demanded Brahman cooks in hospitals, because otherwise Brahman patients would not enter them.

[95] Compare Inden, *Imagining India*, pp.60-1.

The Dravidian race or *iṉam* as a concept of unity had to fight hard in the nineteenth century against other 'races', *iṉam* and jātī or *cātī*, that tried to discover racial differences along caste lines. Papers were founded that cater to these different 'races' and their interests; the list is endless.[96] The Paraiyars had a paper of their own, the *Paraiyan* (1893), which voiced their concern and grievances (and which seems to have died a sad death around 1898), whereas the *Dravida Nesan* published the interests and opinions of the high castes and especially Vellalars. As mentioned above, in many cases *cāti* is explicitly translated as 'race', but it seems that with growing consciousness about the Dravidians and the gathering Dravidian movement, the Tamils decided instead to choose another translation, more akin to their perception what 'race' was and should be, namely *iṉam*. To continue the former usage, this should have been a definition based not on birth, but on culture and language; but we shall presently see that, in a different way, *iṉam* came to be based on 'birth' just as did the Dravidian movement. Nonetheless it is important to remember that, in the end, *iṉam was* accepted as a *collective term* for all Tamils of all castes, if not for all Dravidians.

The Dravidian movement

Scholars in the nineteenth century had understood 'Dravidian' as determining country, language, and implicitly people. In the 1920s this connection was consciously severed by E.V. Ramasami Naicker (called Periyar, the great one), the founder of the Dravidian movement. He did not say this explicitly until the 1940s, but it is clear much earlier from his other statements. He rejected identification on the basis of language: Tamil was a language, Dravidians a race, he said, and not everybody speaking Tamil was a Dravidian.[97] It was he, too, who in the 1940s took

[96] Namely *Vettiyakodaiyan* (1874), *Dravidavartani* (1884), *Arya Jana Paripaliny* (1889), *Kshatriya Janapalini* (1893), *Hindu Nesan* (1902), *Dravida Pandyan* (1896), *Dravida Bhanu* (1895), *Tamil Selvan* (1892), *Dravida Nesan* (1891), *Dravida Mandir* (1893), *Āriyat Tarmam* (1922), *Veḷḷāḷa Mittiraṉ* (1929), *Ceṉtamiḻ* (1922), *Tamiḻmoḻi* (1925), *Tamiḻar Nīcaṉ* (1930), *Tamiḻt Tāy* (1935), *Tamiḻar* (1925), *Tirāviṭar Mittiraṉ* (1934), *Catholic Nesan* (1891), *Pāṇṭiya Nīcaṉ* (1891), and so on.

[97] Vē. Aṉaimuttu, *Periyār Ī. Ve. Rā. Cintaṉaikaḷ* (Tiruchirappalli, 1974), p.548.

the name Dravidian as the name of a movement: *Tirāviṭak Kaḻakam*, the combination of the Justice Party and his own Self-Respect Movement (*Cuyamariyātai iyakkam*). And it was probably Periyar who made the term *iṉam* popular in public usage.[98] He posited a dichotomy between *cātī and Iṉam*:, the proud Dravidian *iṉam* has in Aryan perception become the Sudra *cātī*-.[99] The purpose in all this was two-fold. First, it substituted a positive term for the negative 'non-Brahman' which did not help self-respect. Second, at the same time it marked Periyar's refusal to use the term 'Tamil', which defined Tamils as only those born in Tamil Nadu and Tamil-speaking.[100] That was not enough! What was needed was a definition based on something more basic and 'natural': biological race. Only this would prevent the Dravidians from splitting up into castes and self-serving groups, and destroying their racial pride. Dravidian consciousness should unify, not separate the whole *iṉam* against the Aryans—Aryans in this case were both North Indians and Brahmans.[101] Periyar was nearer here to Maṟai Malai Aṭi-kaḷ than many might care to admit, given the decisive differences between the two in other, especially religious, respects. It is important to keep this definition in mind, as it diverges from that employed in the later Dravidian movement. To the present day, of course, we find the term Dravida in the names of the regional parties and associations in Tamil Nadu and Pondicherry.

Maṟai Malai Aṭikaḷ had rejected the equation of Vellala with Sudra, and likewise Periyar rejected the equation of Dravidian with Sudra. He denied that any Tamils had ever been Sudras, and termed this idea a nefarious Aryan scheme to humiliate the southerners.[102] Never before had Aryans and Dravidians been juxtaposed so clearly by the Tamils themselves. The Dravidians, in Periyar's account, had been subjected to racial, not *cultural* suppression by the Aryans and their foremost fifth column, the Brahmans, who had tried to foist their language and social

98 Ibid., pp.42-3.
99 Ibid., p.710.
100 Ibid., p.26.
101 Brahmans are, however, never even an *iṉam*, they are always a caste.
102 Ibid., pp.240-1.

system on to them and to erase their race consciousness.[103] Again and again he calls for *iṉa uṇarcci* (race consciousness) in the Dravidians.[104] His support for atheism can also be explained by his rejection of Aryan race-suppression by means of a superstitious and irrational religion. Brahmans, he holds, will never belong to the Dravidians, even if they are Tamil-speaking. They will forever remain Aryan and thus alien.[105] The racist-sounding stridency of these remarks is tempered by the consideration that Periyar did not advocate the superiority of one race over another, but on the contrary demanded equality for all. He was also one of the few reformers who not only talked about the integration of the harijan castes, but actively took steps to achieve it. Thus the unification of Tamils on the basis of the Dravidian *iṉam* went a step beyond Maṟai Malai Aṭikaḷ's unification on the basis of caste or occupational group: Vellalars turned into Dravidians, and now low castes could be included even more readily. While the Justice Party had looked on untouchables with faint distaste, Periyar explicitly called them to his side.

The anti-Brahman part of his ideology has often been misunderstood, but it is a very important part. What Periyar objected to was not the fact that Brahmans were Brahmans but that they were Aryans. The point was that Brahmans defined themselves as Aryan and therefore as superior. Periyar hit back in a quite ingenious way by not denying or doubting the Aryan origins of the Brahmans, but by admitting them and then denigrating the Brahmans, putting their alleged racial allegiance and superiority to ridicule and shame, and openly excluding them from the privilege of being Dravidian.[106] Dravidians could attain their rights only in an independent Dravida Nadu, and, implicitly, Brahmans could never belong and be part of this: it was Dravida Nadu for the Dravi-

[103] For the contradictions in Periyar's argument and on his programme in general, see D. Hellmann-Rajanayagam, *Tamil—Sprache als Politisches* (Wiesbaden 1984).

[104] Aṉaimuttu, *Periyār Ī. Ve. Rā*, p.544.

[105] Ibid., p.244.

[106] It is interesting that today, even otherwise level-headed and perceptive Brahman scholars in Tamil Nadu still tie themselves in knots trying to ridicule Periyar as a phony and hypocrite (not at all difficult), and dismiss his achievements as ephemeral and short-lived. Obviously Periyar hit where it hurt!

dians.[107] Periyar, moreover, did not believe in an Indian *iṉam* [108] ironically echoing British assumptions of half a century earlier.

After independence and with the entrance of the Dravidian movement into politics, perceptions changed again. The rejection of the allegedly degrading Dravidian label by non-Tamil Dravidian groups meant that the all-Dravidian concept fell flat; it was a heavy blow for Periyar. A faction of the movement had broken away in 1949 under Aṉṉāturai who found the focus on race and social reform stifling. The new D.M.K. (Dravida Munnetra Kazhagam; *Tirāviṭa Muṉṉēṟṟk Kaḻakam*) emphasised the unity of *Tamils* on the basis of language and culture more than of race.[109] Other South Indian states' rejection of their 'Dravidian' overtures did not throw them off balance. But the D.M.K. had to come to terms with the rejection, and did so in two connected ways. One was to retreat into Tamil identity and redefine the Tirāviṭa *iṉam* as the Tamiḻ *iṉam*; the second was at the same time to call the Tamils the original and oldest and therefore the only 'real' Dravidians. For the earlier D.K. (Dravida Kazhagam, Federation) this had always been self-evident, since the Tamil language is the oldest Dravidian language, from which all other Dravidian languages developed. Moreover, it was the 'purest' Dravidian language since it had the fewest Sanskrit additions. We should, however, again be cautious about accepting the equation of language and people. As postulated by the D.M.K., Dravida Nadu for the Dravidians became Tamil Nadu for the Tamils. A further development was that, with the combination of Tamiḻ and *iṉam* the latter was less frequently translated as 'race' than as 'ethnicity', a meaning which now nearly completely predominates. Tirāviṭa *iṉam* , meaning Dravidian race, turned into Tamiḻ *iṉam* , meaningTamil ethnicity. The movement thus again came round to a belief in the primacy of language over race or ethnicity—that is, that anybody can be a Tamil who speaks Tamil or accepts Tamil culture. Brahmans could

[107] Aṉaimuttu, *Periyār Ī. Ve. Rā*,p.718.
[108] Ibid., p.545.
[109] Hellmann-Rajanayagam, *Tamil*, passim. I have been told that there exists a difference between Tamiḻ *iṉam* which excludes Brahmans and Tamiḻ Makkaḷ which includes all Tamil-speaking people; personal communication from Dr. P. Kothandaraman.

again be included within this purview if they give up their adherence to Sanskrit and Aryan culture. This went against the grain of everything that Periyar had ever said, and he denounced the D.M.K. in no uncertain terms. Though he also retreated to Tamiḻ *iṉam* and equated Tamil with Dravidian,[110] he tried to keep the definition biological and geographical, at the same time denouncing Tamil language and literature, in terms that scandalised his audience, as barbaric and useless. Yet, the 'imposition' of Hindi was resisted by D.K. and D.M.K. alike as another instance of attempted racial and religious suppression.[111] Many have been puzzled by this turnabout, which contradicted some of Periyar's earlier statements on language. However, we should see it in the context of the development of the Dravidian movement. Periyar saw earlier than most what would happen to language under the D.M.K.: language as cult, language purity, language as essence.[112]

Tamils in Sri Lanka

Before we discuss this latest development, we should briefly compare the situation in Tamil Nadu with that in Jaffna. Tamils in Sri Lanka followed a different path in defining themselves and broadening their base; one could almost term it a case of arrested development. There were no Brahmans there, and also the Tamils never felt inferior to or oppressed by the 'Aryan' Sinhalese, until rather late—quite the contrary. In Sri Lanka, however, Tamils were equated with Vellalars, farmers with control over land, long before Maṟai Malai Aṭikaḷ said they were. And though the Sinhalese Goyigamas spoke a different language and were thought to be Aryans, at least they were the same caste with similar values. There was no room to develop a 'Dravidian' identity, since the Tamils were the only Dravidians anyway. Lower castes entered into consideration only with the constitutional reforms of the 1920s which gave parliamentary seats on a 'communal' basis. It became necessary to widen the concept of Tamil in order to broaden the electoral base: Ñāṉappirakācar, a Catholic priest, published a small

[110] Aṉaimuttu, *Periyār Ī. Ve. Rā*,.1969.

[111] Hellmann-Rajanayagam, *Tamil*, pp.59-68. The most damaging insult against Hindi was that it was not old enough and undeveloped.

[112] Aṉaimuttu, *Periyār Ī. Ve. Rā*, pp.983ff. (1967).

book on the civilisation of the Tamils in which he explained that all castes were originally termed Vellalar, with different prefixes to mark subsequent separations, and that later the 'Vellalar' was dropped.[113] At one stroke Ñāṉappirakācar could thus make everybody who *spoke* Tamil into a *real* Tamil by making them into a Vellalar. Maṟai Malai Aṭikaḷ's ideology of *Vēḷāḷar nākarikam* was taken on board, as a whole, a sort of conscious, voluntary variation of the '*meḷḷa, meḷḷa*' process.

From 1933-4 the Jaffna paper *Īḻakēcari* ran a series of widely-read articles on the origin and status of Vellalars in India and Jaffna. The two most important points were that they were *never* Sudras, and that they had come to Jaffna as settlers under the Cola emperors.[114] The solidarity of the Tamils was based not on assumed race, ethnicity, or language, but on assumed caste. Tamils could by definition be only of one caste, the agricultural one, and the way to equality was not the removal of these caste barriers, but their widening to include everybody in the same caste. In this debate, it was the Sinhalese who wanted to set themselves off from the Dravidian Tamils as Aryans and implicitly as superiors. The strategy used by the Tamils to counter this threat differed from that used in India against the Brahmans. A division on the basis of caste was difficult, because Goyigamas, unlike Brahmans, were so patently the same caste as Vellalars. But if that was the case, there could be a next step. The Tamils attempted a strategy of inclusion. They tried to prove that the Sinhalese were not Aryans at all, but primarily Dravidians—that is, had Dravidian blood due to their connections with the Pandyas and so on.[115] The language factor was dismissed in favour of an ethnic one. Caste became ethnicity, ethnicity equalled caste. For the Jaffna Tamils this was the only way to deal with the political and social problems that had arisen at that time. It was, however, a singularly unsuccessful strategy, because the Sinhalese, like the Telugus and Malayalis, fiercely resisted any suggestion that they might be anything but 'pure' Aryans with no 'savage blood' in their

[113] C. Ñāṉappirakācar, OMI, *Tamiḻiṉ Pūrvacarittiramum Camayamum* (new edition; Jaffna, 1932), pp.19-22.

[114] *Īḻakēcari,*9 August 1934; 22 January 1933; 28 May 1933.

[115] The clearest formulation of this theory we find in S. Rasanayagam, *Ancient Jaffna* (Colombo, 1926), pp.178-80, 315 ff. and passim.

veins.[116] The reason for this is simple: in spite of all arguments, Dravidian was still seen as an inferior category, and this impression was reinforced by some Western discourse that of course did not openly peddle Aryan superiority, but implicitly seemed to mock the Sinhalese, saying: 'you have nothing to be proud about; you are Dravidian yourselves and thus as 'lowly' as the Tamils', and denying them not only a perception of excellence, but also association with an 'Aryan' West still deemed superior.[117] The 'reduction' of the Sinhalese to Dravidian status will achieve nothing as long as this hidden agenda remains. The inclusive strategy has also been unsuccessful within the Tamil community itself: the Karaiyars, who have not only led the militant struggle, but usurped the role as culture preservers, did not do so as honorary Vellalars, but as people for whom Vellalar is an irrelevant category, as a caste equal to the Vellalars, and as Tamils, as members of the Tamiḻ *iṉam,* located in a clear geographical space: Jaffna and the East.[118]

The Tamil 'race' and the Tamil Wesen

If we want to sum up the meaning of *iṉam* we have to state that differences in its conception are less important than similarities. Existing perceptions of differences changed over time, and different features were at different times deemed more or less significant. The basic feature, however, remained the same: a Tamil spoke Tamil, lived in Tamiḻakam and had control over land. This gave rise to 'sons-of-the-soil' theories in Tamil Nadu after independence, though these were never seriously pursued. In the Indian Union it is less living in Tamil Nad or having land there that is important; language has now acquired supreme importance. The notion of female chastity and of purity of blood, always vital for Tamil *caste* and *lineage* identity, has been displaced onto language: chaste Tamil has to be spoken and Tamiḻt tāy defended against her Sanskritic molesters, who outrage her modesty.

[116] Ananda Guruge, *Anagarika Dharmapala: return to righteousness* (Colombo, 1965), pp. 394 and 479.

[117] This impression is very strong in a recent publication, William McGowan, *Only Man is Vile. The tragedy of Sri Lanka* (Calcutta, 1993).

[118] D. Hellmann-Rajanayagam, 'The Jaffna social system: continuity and change under conditions of war', *Internationales Asienforum* (in press).

Attempts to reduce Tamils or Dravidians to a biological 'race' were in the last resort unsuccessful, not least since they invited hostility from other groups so defined. In Tamil Nadu nowadays, identity is strongly based on language: anybody who speaks—pureTamil—and acknowledges the supremacy of Tamil can theoretically, at least in the end, become a Tamil. This is the explicit strategy of the D.M.K.,[119] but it is also a recent development. Tirāviṭa *iṉam* has become Tamiḻ *iṉam* defined by language. And here we come back to Inden's critique of essentialism. It seems to me that the Tamils do define *themselves* very clearly in this 'essentialist' way, (or should I say, by this *Wesen*?). Inden's critique becomes valid with regard not to European, but to Tamil perceptions of themselves.

But that is only one aspect. On the other, the definition of language as the salient feature has been liberating in so far as it did put aside differences of caste, religion, domicile, and even ethnicity.[120] It has, however, also become confining, since language (and a certain type of language: 'pure' Tamil) is the *only* feature that defines a Tamil and the only one worth preserving: Tamil as form, not as content; Tamil as cult, immutable, unchangeable, 'pure' essence. Whatever you say—this attitude implies—as long as you write it in Tamil, it is all right. Tamiḻ *iṉam* is Tamiḻ *moḻi*, not *muttamiḻ*. This was what Periyar foresaw when he thundered against Tamil as early as 1967.

The equation of Tamil-speaking with Tamil sounds simple, easy and persuasive; anybody who wants to be a Tamil only has to acquire the language. But what about the other way round: people who speak Tamil but do not define themselves as Tamil? This applies to the Muslims in Sri Lanka, but also, with a question mark, to the Brahmans from whom we never seem able to escape. The D.K. denied them membership of the Tamiḻ *iṉam*. The D.M.K. granted it, but do they want it? It is argued by some Tamils, that Brahmans will never acknowledge Tamil culture on an equal footing with Sanskrit, and that they therefore can never be 'real' Tamils. Brahmans, it is said, consider themselves nowadays not

[119] That of the A-I.A.D.M.K. is different: anybody who is a member of the Puratci Talaivi fan-club can be a Tamil!

[120] The last two chief ministers have been non-Tamils, and one (Jayalalitha) is a Brahman.

as Aryans, but as Indians par excellence, with a tradition rooted in the North and a purity of blood that continues from old. They define themselves as something apart and above the Tamils, their proud label 'South Indian Brahmans' notwithstanding. Indeed that label denotes a certain severe orthodoxy or a purer purity than the North, similar to that of the Jaffna Tamils who consider themselves the purest of the pure. Given this self-perception, it is asked, how can the Brahmans be Tamils, and being rootless, how can they be Indians? Their alleged all-Indianness is only Hindi imposition in a different guise. This argument implies an attempt to define the Indian identity by language, which is deemed unacceptable, though the Tamils do just that for themselves. However, they do not *force* anybody to speak Tamil or become a Tamil. The Brahmans, on the other hand, now seem to deny the Indianness not only of anybody outside the 'Aryan Brahman' fold, but also of anybody who adheres to regional roots and cultures. At least that is as many Tamils see and violently resent it.[121]

In spite of the primacy of language, the definition of a Tamil as belonging to the soil and having control over it has not vanished. It has, so to speak, gone underground: Dirks and Daniel report that certain (Vellalar) castes consider themselves as belonging to and compatible with a certain place, a certain sort of soil, and believe that if they are uprooted from it or are unable to occupy it, misfortune and maladaptation will occur.[122] The discussion of who is a Tamil and what is meant by *iṉam* rages on. In a way this is a redeeming feature, because it affords flexibility and the possibility of change and adaptation. Let me end with a quotation which to me seems to sum up who are the Tamiḻ *makkaḷ*:

> Nowadays, political victory and religious victory depend on each other. However, there is no doubt that among the people who adhere to Tamiḻnāṭu there arises a unanimous culture [mind-set]. For that reason, while all sorts of foreigners—Kaḷappirar, Pallavar, Mukammatiyar, Nāyakkar, Airōppiyar—ruled

[121] This perception is to some extent confirmed in Sudipta Kaviraj, 'Writing, speaking, being: language and the historical formation of identities in India', in Hellmann-Rajanayagam and D. Rothermund (eds.), *Nationalstaat und Sprachkonflikte in Süd- und Südostasien* (Stuttgart, 1992), pp.25-68.

[122] Dirks, *Hollow Crown*; E. Valentine Daniel, *Fluid Signs. Being a person*

this country, the Tamiḻ *iṉam* flourishes and stands its ground till this day without its uniqueness being destroyed.[123]

The Tamiḻ *makkaḷ* always know who they are.

---

the Tamil way (Berkeley, 1987).

[123] Kiruṣṇaṉ, *Tamiḻ nūlkaḷil*, p.214.

Chapter 5

RACIAL IDENTITIES AND POLITICS IN EARLY MODERN SRI LANKA

John D. Rogers

Many scholars have acknowledged the importance of Victorian ideas of race for identity formation in colonial South Asia. Racial ideology is said to have influenced various late nineteenth-century social and religious movements, and contributed to the rise of communalism. These movements are commonly portrayed as indigenous reactions to colonial rule, although writers disagree on the relative importance of cultural, economic, and political factors. More recently, 'post-Orientalist' interpretations of South Asia's past have begun to appear.[1] These works generally shift the origins of cultural and ethnic nationalist ideologies to the late eighteenth and early nineteenth centuries, the first years of British rule. Post-Orientalists place great importance on the role of British discourse, which is said to have located South Asians in social categories that served to maintain British power. According to these scholars, late nineteenth-century social movements were based upon these colonial categories, and the identities they propagated were strengthened and hardened by the infusion of European racial ideology. In their more daring moments, post-Orientalist scholars dismiss the past two hundred years of South Asian intellectual and political history as derivative of colonial knowledge.

Scholarship on Sri Lanka has not yet produced any sophisticated and detailed account that covers the role of Victorian racial ideology in the

[1] See, for example, Nicholas B. Dirks, *The Hollow Crown: an ethnohistory of an Indian kingdom* (Cambridge, 1987); Bernard S. Cohn, 'The command of language and the language of command', in Ranajit Guha (ed.), *Subaltern Studies IV: writings on South Asian history and society* (Delhi, 1985), pp. 276-329; Partha Chatterjee, *Nationalist Thought and the Colonial World: a derivative discourse?* (London, 1986); Gyanendra Pandey, *The Construction of Communalism in Colonial North India.*(Delhi, 1990); and Ronald B. Inden, *Imagining India* (Oxford, 1990).

formation of Sinhalese or Tamil cultural nationalism.[2] None the less, many scholars have referred to the importance of this process.[3] It is generally accepted that the mid-nineteenth-century Orientalist classification of Tamil as a Dravidian language, and Sinhala as Indo-Aryan, inclined many late nineteenth- and twentieth-century intellectuals, both Sri Lankan and European, to classify Tamils as members of the Dravidian race and Sinhalese as Aryans. In other words, language was equated with race. During the twentieth century this racial distinction became a component of common-sense knowledge for most Sri Lankans.

Since around 1980, when Sri Lanka became increasingly polarised along ethnic lines, some writers have adopted self-consciously 'modernist' interpretations of Sinhalese nationalism, which aim to undermine historical assumptions behind contemporary Sinhalese nationalist beliefs. Since the racial component of Sinhalese nationalism is perhaps the most vulnerable to such attacks, it has received a good deal of critical attention. Scholars have marshalled considerable evidence that undermines the notion of some two thousand years of Sinhalese racial purity.[4] For some of these writers, giving weight to the racial aspect of Sinhalese nationalism has other advantages. It associates Sinhalese nationalism with a discredited strand of modern social thought, and it portrays Sinhalese nationalism as foreign and colonial, without authentic roots in pre-colonial Sri Lanka. Not all scholars, however, accept the

[2] The more informative general accounts of Sinhalese and Tamil social and cultural movements under British colonialism include Kitsiri Malalgoda, *Buddhism in Sinhalese Society, 1750-1900: a study of religious revival and change* (Berkeley and Los Angeles, 1976); Michael Roberts (ed.), *Collective Identities, Nationalisms, and Protest in Modern Sri Lanka* (Colombo, 1979); K.N.O. Dharmadasa, *Language, Religion, and Ethnic Assertiveness: the growth of Sinhalese nationalism in Sri Lanka* (Ann Arbor, 1992); and Dagmar Hellmann-Rajanayagam, 'Arumuka Navalar: religious reformer or national leader of Eelam', *Indian Economic and Social History Review* 26 (1989), pp.235-57.

[3] See, for instance, John D. Rogers, 'Historical images in the British period', in Jonathan Spencer (ed.), *Sri Lanka: history and the roots of conflict* (London, 1990), p.95.

[4] The most influential such work is R.A.L.H. Gunawardana, 'The people of the lion: the Sinhala identity and ideology in history and historiography', in Spencer (ed.), *Sri Lanka*, pp.45-86. A more radical modernist interpretation is Elizabeth Nissan and R.L. Stirrat, 'The generation of communal identities', in ibid., pp.19-44.

modernist interpretations, and there are important arguments that picture Sinhalese nationalism as at least in part the expression of an old identity in new contexts. Some of these scholars acknowledge that Victorian ideas of race played a significant role in the modern reconstruction of Sinhalese identity, but most tend not to assign this process such a central place.[5]

At the present level of scholarship, it remains difficult to define with any precision the significance of Victorian racial ideology. Did it form the basis of a new mode of social categorisation, or did it merely provide a useful justification for categorisations that were developing independently? If the latter, to what extent were these identities the product of ideas current in the eighteenth century, and to what extent the result of changes that took place under British rule during the nineteenth century? Were Victorian notions of race accepted so eagerly because they resonated with earlier ideas of social difference, or did they instead represent a qualitatively new way of distinguishing groups of people?

This essay addresses some of these issues through an examination of the role of racial identities in politics in the seventeenth and eighteenth centuries. Following the working definition discussed by Peter Robb in the introduction to this volume, 'race' is taken to include 'any essentialising of groups of people which held them to display inherent, heritable, persistent or predictive characteristics, and which thus had a biological or quasi-biological basis'. I argue that there were indeed, in the two centuries before British colonialism, politically-significant identities that fit this broad definition of race. On the other hand, these racial identities were by no means the only important political identities, and the adoption of Victorian ideas of race entailed changes beyond the mere strengthening of earlier ideas of social difference. Nineteenth-century racial identities differed significantly

[5] Two important such approaches take different positions regarding the importance of modern racial ideology. Steven Kemper, *The Presence of the Past: chronicles, politics, and culture in Sinhala life* (Ithaca, 1991), assigns it an important role; but K.N.O. Dharmadasa, '"The People of the Lion": ethnic identity, ideology, and historical revisionism in contemporary Sri Lanka', *Sri Lanka Journal of the Humanities* 15 (1989), pp.1-35, does not believe that its influence was significant.

from those present in the two previous centuries.

Politics in early modern Sri Lanka (c.1597-1815) was marked by the presence of two principal centres of political influence. The coastal areas were controlled by European powers, first the Portuguese (1597-1658), then the Dutch (1658-1796), and finally the British (1796-1815). The interior was dominated by the Kandyan kingdom, which viewed itself as the successor to earlier Sinhalese polities. There were also local rulers, in generally lightly-populated areas on the east coast, in the north-central dry zone, and along the west coast between Negombo and Mannar. Some of these rulers offered allegiance to the European colonial powers, and some to Kandy. Local notables in the area between the south-west coast and Kandy also sometimes shifted their loyalty between one or another of the two principal powers. This political structure ended in 1815 when a British-supported rebellion of Kandyan nobles culminated in Kandy's accession to the colony of Ceylon. Island-wide administrative unity was imposed in 1833, with all central institutions located in the capital, Colombo.

Racial identities in seventeenth- and eighteenth-century Kandy

Central to the ideology of kingship prevalent in Kandy was the notion that only a Kshatriya was fit to rule. In Sri Lanka the label of Kshatriya had long implied royalty, and had never encompassed a substantial number of inhabitants. Even the Radala, the highest-status group among the Goyigama (cultivators), who wielded most political and economic power in Kandy, did not claim Kshatriya status. Kshatriya identity was conceived as largely given at birth, and it could not be adopted explicitly on the grounds of a change in belief or life style. The king's ritual status was inherent, and it both justified his kingship and demanded kingship of him.[6] In practice Kshatriya identity was in part behavioural—there were appropriate and inappropriate ways for a Kshatriya, or king, to act—but claims to Kshatriya status had to be backed up by genealogies, real or invented.

The importance of Kshatriya status for claims to the throne is clear

[6] H.L. Seneviratne, *Rituals of the Kandyan State* (Cambridge, 1978), p.2.

from an examination of Kandyan politics.[7] In 1592 a Goyigama seized power in Kandy and assumed the name Vimala Dharma Surya. He subsequently married a prominent Kshatriya widow, Kusumasana Devi (also known as Dona Catherina), who was the daughter of the king who had been deposed in 1582 when Kandy was annexed temporarily by the neighbouring kingdom of Sitavaka. Vimala Dharma Surya used the marriage to justify his claim to the throne.[8] His mother's sister's son and successor, Senarat (1604-35), also married Kusumasana Devi, and after her death married two of her daughters from her first marriage. Vimala Dharma Surya and Senarat sought to enhance, and perhaps even create, their Kshatriya status through marriage to royal women. Later Kandyan kings had to look beyond Sri Lanka for Kshatriya brides, because by this time there were no other royal families on the island. Beginning with Rajasimha II (1635-87), queens were brought from Madurai in southern India. When Narendra Simha (1707-39) died without any royal issue, he was succeeded by his wife's brother, Vijaya Rajasimha (1739-47), who became the founder of the Nayakkar dynasty, which takes its label from the family of the women brought to Kandy as Kshatriya brides. The Nayakkar were originally from the Telugu-language area of peninsular India, but by this time their primary language was Tamil. Vijaya Rajasimha was preferred for the throne even though Narendra Simha had a son, Unambuwe Bandara, from a relationship with a Radala woman. Although some Radala supported Unambuwe, Kshatriya status proved central, and his mother's status debarred him from ruling. The Nayakkar dynasty ruled until 1815, and its claim to Kshatriya status remained central to its legitimacy. When a group of Radala aristocrats sought to overthrow Kirti Sri Rajasimha (1747-82) in 1760, they planned to place a member of the Siamese royal family, rather than one of their own number, on the throne.[9] In 1782, when Kirti Sri Rajasimha died, he was succeeded by his elder brother, even though he had children by a Radala woman whose rela-

[7] The standard account of Kandyan politics is Lorna S. Dewaraja, *The Kandyan Kingdom of Sri Lanka, 1707-1782* (Colombo, 1988).

[8] H.L. Seneviratne, 'The alien king: Nayakkars on the throne of Kandy', *Ceylon Journal of Historical and Social Studies* 6 (1977), p.57.

[9] Dewaraja, *Kandyan Kingdom*, pp.119-26.

tives had much influence at court.[10]

Kshatriya status alone was insufficient to establish royal legitimacy in Kandy. The king was a bodhisattva, who would one day become a Buddha, and the dominant ideology dictated that he carry out the role of a Buddhist ruler.[11] This requirement was primarily behavioural, not racial. The Nayakkar kings, for instance, all adopted Buddhism and supported the monkhood, but they made no attempt to hide their Saivite family background, and many of their relatives who lived in the capital exhibited little interest in Buddhism. Some Nayakkar rulers also participated in Saivite worship, a practice that offended much of the Buddhist intelligentsia. Such eclecticism, however, was prevalent among the general Sinhalese population; many worshipped Saivite gods, who were integrated into the fabric of popular Buddhism. It was also common in earlier Sinhalese kingdoms, where Buddhist kings such as Parakramabahu VI of Kotte (1411-66) offered patronage to other religions.

Although the Kandyan king's Buddhist role was central in maintaining his legitimacy, Buddhism was not the 'national' religion in the sense that all subjects were expected to adhere to the Buddhist faith. Kandy welcomed Muslim immigrants, integrating them into its social structure, without attempting to alter their religion. Muslims were tenants in many temple villages. In one of these, Rambukandana, land was set aside for the maintenance of a Muslim priest.[12] Roman Catholic missionaries were also welcomed in Kandy in the late seventeenth and early eighteenth centuries, though in 1745 their attempts to gain converts by attacking Buddhism led to the expulsion of all priests.[13]

The exercise of power at levels below that of the king was influenced strongly by racially-based ideas similar to those which dictated that the ruler be Kshatriya. Most senior officials, notables, and monks, both at the court and in the countryside, were drawn from the Radala, and most other influential positions were filled by other Goyigama. In

[10] Ibid.

[11] Seneviratne, *Rituals*, pp.96-97.

[12] Lorna S. Dewaraja, 'The Muslims in the Kandyan kingdom (c.1600-1815): a study of ethnic integration', in M.A.M. Shukri (ed.), *Muslims of Sri Lanka: avenues to antiquity* (Beruwala, 1986), pp.218-21.

[13] Dewaraja, *Kandyan Kingdom*, pp.102-03.

addition to the state's territorial organisation, there was another level of administration that organised people into occupational departments (*badda*).[14] Most of the *badda* were constituted by hereditary occupational groups that came to be defined as castes in the nineteenth century, but the Muslims, who were later labelled the Moor race, were integrated into the Kandyan administration in a similar manner. The *madige badda*, which was concerned with trade and transportation, included in its ranks both Muslims and the Karava, a predominantly Low-Country and Sinhalese group of which the traditional occupation was fishing, but which was also involved in many other activities, including commerce. Most Muslims and Karava were relative newcomers to Kandy; the Muslims, who were the more numerous, had greatly increased their presence in the interior in the sixteenth and seventeenth centuries, when they were subject to various degrees of Portuguese and Dutch persecution in the Low Country. The Kandyan king sometimes appointed Muslims to positions of authority within the *madige badda*; the authority of these officials was not limited to Muslims, but also covered Karava.[15]. Muslims appear to have been regarded as racially distinct from, say, the Goyigama, in much the same manner as the Goyigama were from the Karava. However, the grouping of Muslims and Karava together in the *madige badda* did not imply that Muslims and Karava were the same type of people, though it did indicate that they had a similar status.

The Radala in particular and the Goyigama in general did not claim a history of closed racial purity, but the immigrants and outsiders that played a prominent role in some family myths of origin, such as Brahmans brought from India to Sri Lanka by medieval kings, were of high status. The racial ideology that underpinned status-group differences in Kandy had an important universalist element. Although the details of varna ideology were little known in early modern Sri Lanka, varna labels were sometimes employed to make claims to higher status.[16]

[14] Ibid, pp.228-34

[15] Dewaraja, 'Muslims', p.217.

[16] A.P. Kannangara, 'The rhetoric of caste status in modern Sri Lanka', in Peter Robb (ed.), *Society and Ideology: essays in South Asian history* (Delhi, 1993), pp.115-23.

Their use implies a general belief that there were groups outside the island, about which little or nothing was known, whose status was broadly equivalent to various Kandyan groups. Maintaining status involved not the preservation of closed racially-pure groups, but rather marriage connections with persons of the same, equivalent, or higher status. Such ties could extend between Kandy and the Low Country, and between Sinhala-speaking and Tamil-speaking families.

The Kandyan kingdom was a Sinhalese kingdom, which claimed to be the lineal descendant of earlier Sinhalese kingdoms, most notably those of Anuradhapura, Polonnaruva, and Kotte. In the nineteenth century, Sinhala speakers came to be characterised as part of a Sinhalese race or nation, which was thought to provide the social base for the classical and medieval kingdoms.[17] In recent years this assumption has come under question, and the meaning of the label 'Sinhalese' over the centuries is now an issue of great historical controversy.[18] The available evidence seems to indicate that the term functioned as both a cultural and political label in the later pre-modern period, but that it did not imply any belief in shared ancestry. Certainly the Kandyan Goyigama believed that their origins were distinct from those of other Kandyan Sinhalese groups, who had their own myths of origin.

What meaning then did Sinhalese identity carry in Kandy? Among the intelligentsia there was a belief in a continuous tradition of Sinhalese polity and culture, but this tradition may well have been conceived as something that was more the product of the efforts of kings, monks, and other remarkable individuals than that of a community of Sinhalese people. Although the Sinhala language was undoubtedly associated strongly with the idea of Sinhalese culture, some Radala saw nothing amiss in using the Tamil script when signing important documents.[19] They saw no need to assert individual Sinhalese identities through the use of the Sinhala script, even though they regarded them-

[17] Rogers, 'Historical images'; John D. Rogers, 'Colonial perceptions of ethnicity and culture in early nineteenth-century Sri Lanka', in Robb, *Society and Ideology*, pp.97-109.

[18] Gunawardana, 'People of the lion'; Dharmadasa, '"The People of the Lion"'.

[19] Gunawardana, 'People of the lion', p.67.

selves as Sinhalese. Sinhalese cultural identity was not defined with any precision, and the ways in which it was applied were variable and contextual. Similarly, the political side of Sinhalese identity was flexible, and did not necessarily coincide with cultural identity. It was often defined narrowly. An eighteenth-century Pali chronicle, for instance, refers to Kirti Sri Rajasimha as 'our Sinhalese ruler', despite the fact that he was a Nayakkar who was not racially or culturally Sinhalese.[20] The term Sinhalese was used here in a narrow political sense, synonymous with the polity, in the manner in which the term was probably used in classical times.[21] The cultural and political aspects of Sinhalese identity were not necessarily conflated, and they did not serve to group all Sinhala speakers into an exclusive community that sought political and cultural unity.

Racial identities in seventeenth- and eighteenth-century Low-Country polities

The Portuguese, Dutch, and British polities in early modern Sri Lanka differed significantly from Kandy. None of the European powers adopted indigenous models of kingship, though they sometimes accommodated them for pragmatic reasons. The Dutch, for instance, for some time accepted that they held their territories in trust for the Kandyan king, but neither they nor the Portuguese took on the ceremonial role of the Sinhalese king, and neither ever claimed Kshatriya status. On the other hand, all three colonial powers were conscious of their status as Europeans, and made political distinctions based on the degree to which an individual was perceived as European.

It was always assumed that the captain-general or governor of colonial Ceylon would be a national of the European mother country, born in Europe. This requirement was also necessary or desirable for many other senior posts. More broadly, the Portuguese often assumed that the progeny of Portuguese men and Asian women would create a group of loyal residents. The Dutch too were conscious of racial differences between Europeans and Asians, and made various efforts to maintain a

[20] Kemper, *Presence*, p.97; Gunawardana, 'People of the lion', p.68.
[21] Ibid., pp.46-65.

racial hierarchy.[22] Evidence from the eighteenth century points to four levels among those with a claim to a European heritage: (1) the Europeesch, those born in Europe, (2) the Casties, who were born on the island but whose parents were born in Europe, (3) the Mixties, who were of mixed European and Asian origin, and (4) the Pusties, who were descendants of Casties. The distinction between Casties and Pusties points to the notion that a prolonged stay in Asia on the part of Europeans inevitably led to degeneration.

In practice Dutch racial categories proved difficult to apply with any consistency, and were shaped not only by parentage but by religion, class, and culture. All four groups with a claim to European heritage were often included under the general label 'Hollandsche', who were in turn divided between Vrijburghers (free citizens) and the employees of the Dutch East India Company. In the late seventeenth century the government was often anxious to make distinctions between the Hollandsche and Asian converts to Christianity, who were denoted by the term 'Tupass' (or 'Topaz'). But by the mid-eighteenth century the terms 'Tupass' and 'Mixtie' were often used interchangeably, to denote persons of mixed European and Asian ancestry. The task of classification was further complicated by attempts to make distinctions between persons of northern European and Portuguese descent. Despite the efforts of the government to maintain a racial hierarchy, families moved from one category to another, and categories sometimes collapsed into each other. Many marriages created offspring with an ambiguous status, and the adoption of cultural symbols or practices sometimes moved a family from one category to another. Towards the end of Dutch rule, for instance, the Council of Colombo defined Vriburghers as persons who wore European clothing and were not on the government payroll.[23] Religion, occupation, or dress often pushed a family into a particular racial category.

The Portuguese and Dutch also recognised quasi-racial distinctions

[22] Michael Roberts, Ismeth Raheem, and Percy Colin-Thomé, *People In between: the Burghers and the middle class in the transformations within Sri Lanka, 1790s-1960s*, vol.1 (Colombo, 1989), pp.35-44.

[23] Ibid., p.43.

among their Asian subjects. Most of the south-western Low Country had been part of the kingdom of Kotte before the establishment of Portuguese rule. Kotte society included hereditary status and occupational groups similar to those found in Kandy, and the European powers continued to use these groups, most of which became known as castes, for administration and taxation. However —perhaps because the European powers, unlike the Kandyan Nayakkar, Radala, and Goyigama, were outside the ideological framework that justified these social distinctions—the colonial administrations adopted somewhat more dynamic and pragmatic policies towards them. Both the Portuguese and the Dutch called upon castes to perform labour in occupations not previously associated with the caste in question.[24] Such innovations also occurred under Sinhalese kings, but the colonial powers seem to have been less cautious in these matters, and to have been more willing consciously to change a group's status for economic or political purposes. They also occasionally intervened in customs that shaped group boundaries. For instance, children from a liaison between a higher-caste man and a lower-caste woman normally took their mother's caste, but the Dutch, who sought to increase the number of Salagama (cinnamon peelers) for economic reasons, decreed that all children fathered by a Salagama should take on their father's status, irrespective of their mother's social position.[25]

The Portuguese and Dutch occasionally departed from the Kandyan practice of placing Goyigama in posts with territorial authority that extended beyond a single homogeneous settlement.[26] Perhaps more significantly, they also bypassed Goyigama officials and established direct relations with other castes.[27] Although most smaller castes were ruled through Goyigama intermediaries, by the eighteenth century the larger or more influential castes contracted directly with the Dutch to provide

[24] Michael Roberts, *Caste Conflict and Elite Formation: the rise of a Karava elite in Sri Lanka* (Cambridge, 1982), pp.50-54

[25] Ibid., p.38, n.11.

[26] S. Arasaratnam, 'Elements of social and economic change in Dutch maritime Ceylon (Sri Lanka)', *Indian Economic and Social History Review* 22 (1985), p.40.

[27] D.A. Kotelawele, 'Some aspects of social change in the south west of Sri Lanka', *Social Science Review* 4 (1988), pp.63-76.

the state with specific services, and in return received a good deal of control over their internal affairs, independent of Goyigama officials. Among the castes that took this route were the Salagama, Karava, Durava (toddy tappers), and Hunu (lime burners). These castes had much more independent control over their own affairs than provided for by the *badda* system in Kandy. The leaders of these castes received important headmanships, opportunities for accumulating wealth, and the right to a life-style similar to that of Goyigama officials. From the Dutch point of view, these arrangements were advantageous because they reduced the power of the Goyigama aristocracy and built up loyalty among the castes concerned. Some of these castes, especially the Salagama and the Karava, were able to make claims to higher status as a result of these changes.

It is probable that neither the Portuguese nor the Dutch took the racial aspect of caste very seriously. They maintained caste distinctions because they were at the core of the existing system of administration and taxation, and because they provided the Europeans with opportunities to play one group off against the other. Moreover, while there were many concrete reasons to make specific changes in caste relations, there was no particular reason, either economic or ideological, to launch a frontal attack on caste. Accounts of caste conflicts in the eighteenth and early nineteenth centuries indicate that a belief in the quasi-biological basis of caste remained prevalent among the general population.

All three colonial administrations maintained self-consciously Christian administrations.[28] The European captain-general or governor, unlike the Kandyan king, had no direct religious role, but religious faith was used to a greater extent than in Kandy to determine a subject's political loyalty. Unlike caste status, religious identity was conceived as a matter of behaviour, not something fixed by birth. The early modern colonial states divided their subjects into three broad categories: Christian, heathen, and Muslim. For the Portuguese, adoption of Christianity was a test of political loyalty, and, under both the Portuguese and

[28] Tikiri Abeyasinghe, *Portuguese Rule in Ceylon, 1594-1612* (Colombo, 1966), pp.192-223; K.W. Goonewardena, 'Dutch policy towards Buddhism in Sri Lanka and some aspects of its impact, c.1640 to c.1740', unpublished paper.

Dutch, profession of the Christian faith had many advantages. It made employment in the administration more likely, enabled local men of influence to have their positions confirmed by the colonial power, and offered preferential treatment in many dealings with the state. A Christian religious establishment also received financial support.

While earlier Sri Lankan polities had taken note of religious differences, these had been of importance primarily for high politics, including the performance of state rituals and the relative levels of patronage to be given to different shrines or other institutions. Important as these disputes were, they did not extend to a sustained concern with shaping and classifying the religious faith of the mass of the population. The Portuguese undertook an aggressive campaign to make converts, and, while the Dutch were less vigorous in seeking conversions, they spent considerable energy attempting to control the religious practices of nominal Christians. This preoccupation with the worship of laymen, however ineffective it often was in practice, had no precedent in Sri Lanka. It came about because Christianity was a religion that actively sought converts, and because many European officials took their religious faith seriously. The colonial powers had a direct stake in propagating Christianity that at times was not far removed from the Kandyan elite's stake in the maintenance of status distinctions.

The position of Muslims was different in the Low Country from that in Kandy.[29] For purposes of administration and taxation they were often treated as a caste. In formulating broader policies, however, the Europeans tended to treat Muslims as a special case, distinct from other occupational and status groups. In part this was due to the European perception that the Muslims were really foreigners—many of them were traders who went back and forth between the ports of Sri Lanka and southern India, and between the Low Country and Kandy. The commercial interests of these traders sometimes conflicted with those of the colonial state, and governments were suspicious that many

[29] K. W. Goonewardena, 'Muslims under Dutch rule up to the mid-eighteenth century', in Shukri, *Muslims*, pp.189-209; D.A. Kotelawele, 'Muslims under Dutch rule in Sri Lanka, 1638-1796', in ibid., pp.167-209; Tikiri Abeyasinghe, 'Muslims in Sri Lanka in the sixteenth and seventeenth centuries', in ibid., pp.129-45.

traders were politically close to foreign powers. Portuguese and Dutch attitudes towards Muslims were also shaped by their broader concern with the religious composition of their subjects, and by Islam's clear identity as a rival to Christianity. The Portuguese in particular had an established prejudice against Islam that stemmed from Christian-Muslim conflict in Iberia and North Africa, and it was commonly believed that Muslims were more difficult to convert to Christianity than the other residents of the island. As a result, under Portuguese and early Dutch rule, Muslims were sometimes singled out for harsh treatment. When, around the middle of the eighteenth century, Dutch hostility faded, the government continued to treat the Muslims as a group apart. Around 1770, for instance, it introduced a legal code for Muslims. Overall, while the Dutch often treated the Moors as a caste-like entity in day-to-day administration, they made important distinctions between Moors and the Sinhalese castes. It is likely, for instance, that the Dutch saw racial distinctions between Moors and Goyigama as greater than those between Goyigama and Karava.

There remains the question of the role of Sinhalese identity in the Low Country. The only Sinhalese polity, at Kandy, claimed sovereignty over the entire island, and a majority of the inhabitants of the Low Country were culturally Sinhalese. There is little evidence, however, that Sinhalese cultural identity generated political support for Kandy among the low-country population. Kandy's political appeal was based more on its claim to represent Sinhalese kingship, and on its patronage of Buddhism. These claims had little impact in the coastal areas north of Colombo, which were predominantly Christian. In the mostly Buddhist areas to the south of Colombo and in the interior, links with Kandy were much stronger, but in the late eighteenth and early nineteenth centuries the kingdom's position as the protector of Buddhism along the coastal strip was undermined when the Salagama, Karava, and Durava successfully defied the Kandy-based monastic establishment, which limited higher ordination to Goyigama, by sending missions to Burma that resulted in new fraternities of monks.[30] These orders carried the approval not of Kandy but of the Dutch and British

[30] Malalgoda, *Buddhism*, pp.82-100.

colonial governments.

The Portuguese and Dutch were not preoccupied with distinguishing the Sinhalese from other like groups; this question had little practical significance for them. Caste distinctions were important because they were central to administration and taxation, and religious distinctions were important because they were central to European ideas of identity. The Portuguese, in particular, favoured religious and status distinctions over what later came to be defined as racial ones. In 1626, the Count of Vidigueira, who had served a term as president of the India Council at Lisbon and then was viceroy at Goa for seven years, still believed that Jaffna was populated by Sinhalese.[31] Eight years later the Lisbon authorities made a similar assumption.[32] The scholar, V. Perniola, in the introduction to his comprehensive collection of Catholic documents relating to the Dutch period, notes that the papers do not portray 'any racial distinction between Sinhala and Tamils', but 'rather the division into various castes.'[33] There had been substantial movements of people from southern India to the Low Country between the thirteenth and seventeenth centuries, and in the eighteenth century the Tamil language and script was still widespread in the coastal area north of Colombo, even though by this time most residents regarded themselves as Sinhalese.[34] There is no evidence that any political tension was generated by this situation; the boundaries of Sinhalese identity were of little political importance.

Although neither Sinhalese nor Tamil identity played a important role in politics, eighteenth-century Dutch writings often assume that Sinhala speakers constituted a Sinhalese group, which was a significant social entity.[35] Moreover, the late eighteenth-century efforts to codify

[31] Tikiri Abeyasinghe, *Jaffna under the Portuguese* (Colombo, 1986), p.27, n.31.

[32] Ibid., p.27.

[33] V. Perniola (ed.), *The Catholic Church in Sri Lanka: the Dutch period*, vol.1 (Dehiwala, 1983), p.xxiv.

[34] R. L. Stirrat, 'Caste conundrums: views of caste in a Sinhalese Catholic fishing village', in Dennis B. McGilvray (ed.), *Caste Ideology and Interaction* (Cambridge, 1982), p.10; Roberts, *Caste Conflict*, p.26.

[35] See, for example, S. Arasaratnam (ed.), *François Valentijn's Description of Ceylon* (London, 1978); the original was published in 1726.

laws for Jaffna Tamils and Muslims may have contributed to a sense among officials that their Asian subjects could be broadly divided into three main groups: Sinhalese, Tamils, and Muslims. Although this idea had little practical impact on politics or administration at that time, variants of it were passed on to the British when they took control of the Low Country in 1796. None the less, it would be another 35 years before the British, who were far more interested than the Dutch in systematically gathering information about the island's inhabitants, would construct an authoritative colonial sociology for Sri Lanka.[36]

Concepts of race in early modern and modern polities

I have argued that there were heritable, inherent identities that can be construed as racial in early modern Sri Lanka, and that these identities had important political implications. In Kandy the general idea that persons carried an inherent status was reflected both in the ideology of kingship, which dictated that the ruler be Kshatriya, and in the system of administration and taxation, which was organised around inherited membership in status and occupational groups. In the Low Country there was no king, but the European powers propagated a racial hierarchy based on degrees of European heritage, and among the population in general they maintained status distinctions similar to those found in Kandy. On the other hand, there were also important identities that cannot be construed as racial. The most striking of these were the profession of Christianity in the Low Country and the Buddhist role of the king in Kandy.

In the nineteenth century, Western racial ideas were applied not to the bulk of the social categories that had quasi-biological connotations in the previous two centuries, but to a limited set of identities: Sinhalese, Malabar (Tamil), Moor, Burgher, Malay, and European. By the early twentieth century a distinction was also made between the Indian Tamils, who were from families that emigrated to Sri Lanka from southern India after the commencement of British rule, and the Ceylon Tamils, who had deeper roots on the island. It is for the smaller groups—the Moors, Burghers, Malays, and Europeans—that the

[36] Rogers, 'Colonial Perceptions'.

stronger cases can be made for continuity in racial ideology.[37] Sinhalese identity, in contrast, had little racial connotation in the early modern period. The British classification of the Sinhalese as a race was a consequence of their own assumptions about history and political organisation; they failed to understand the narrower cultural and political connotations that Sinhalese identity carried in earlier periods. It was in the early nineteenth century that the most significant change in Sinhalese identity took place: the conflation of existing cultural and political identities into a single identity that was assumed to be central for cultural, social, and political purposes. At this time British concepts of race were as much cultural as biological, and terms other than race—community, class, and nation—were used interchangeably with race. As the nineteenth century progressed and racial ideas became more prominent in Western social thought, racial identities took on more and more of a biological character.

What happened to the quasi-biological status groups that were found in early modern Sri Lanka? Most of them were labelled castes, and were removed from official discourse after 1833, when the government decided to largely ignore caste distinctions. This policy was based in part on the assumption that among the Sinhalese caste was unnatural because the dominant religion was Buddhism, not Hinduism. Although the government often took caste into account when making administrative appointments, this practice was not alluded to directly, at least in public. Caste was not tabulated in the decennial censuses that began in 1871, and, by the late nineteenth century, many prominent Sinhalese contrasted the backwardness of caste with the modernity of race and nation. This attitude became dominant in twentieth-century public discourse. None the less, caste remained an important factor in elite and local politics in the nineteenth and early twentieth centuries. After around 1920 its political importance declined gradually, but, even in the closing decade of the twentieth century, it is significant in specific contexts. A similar public marginalisation of caste took place among

[37] For the construction of the Malay race, see B.A. Hussainmiya, 'Princes and soldiers: the antecedents of the Sri Lankan Malays', in Shukri (ed.), *Muslims*, pp.279-309.

Tamils, though this process began later and proceeded more slowly than among Sinhalese.

In sharp contrast to caste identities, Buddhist identity maintained a high profile in modern public discourse. At one level, the universalist aspect of Buddhism was acknowledged and maintained: nobody claimed that only Sinhalese could be 'real' Buddhists. On the other hand, the fact that virtually all Sri Lankan Buddhists were Sinhalese led to the integration of Buddhist symbols into the rhetoric of Sinhalese nationalism, and the idea that 'real' Sinhalese are Buddhists has been a consistent strand in Sinhalese nationalist thought. The position of non-Buddhist (mainly Christian) Sinhalese has been rendered ambiguous: they are members of the Sinhalese race, but do not bear the authentic cultural traits of their race. Late twentieth-century political rhetoric often uses the terms 'Buddhist' and 'Sinhalese' interchangeably; this device both incorporates Christian Sinhalese into the ruling race, and asserts Sinhalese-Buddhist hegemony over them.

The power of racial ideology lay not only in its association with modern ideas of progress and nation, but in its ability to provide a seemingly clear-cut sociology that incorporated the myriad of identities available to Sri Lankans. Until the late twentieth century, racial identities in Sri Lanka were usually seen as unifying rather than divisive. Sinhalese nationalists, for instance, focused on bringing diverse religious and caste groups fully into the Sinhalese race; the fact that Tamils and Moors were left outside was seen as natural and inevitable, and its political consequences were not considered with any care. It was not until the 1980s, when Tamil resistance to Sinhalese hegemony turned violent, that Sinhalese nationalists were forced to re-evaluate this issue.

Nineteenth-century racial ideology introduced striking changes, but it was not built on a blank slate. Ideas of difference with a quasi-biological character were already prevalent before the beginning of British rule, and many of the symbols and labels propagated in the name of racial ideology were drawn from earlier periods. On the other hand, modern racial ideology was selective in its appropriation of existing symbols and labels, and often used them in ways that fundamentally altered their meaning. Modern ideas of race were also more powerful than early modern ones, in part because they were dynamic, and sought to unite diverse peoples rather than maintain existing social divisions.

Chapter 6

CASTE AND 'RACE' IN THE COLONIAL ETHNOGRAPHY OF INDIA[1]

Susan Bayly

In recent years Indian historians and anthropologists have amassed a set of widely-shared assumptions about 'orientalist' knowledge and colonial perceptions of caste. Like African and Pacific specialists, Indianists now find much common ground in the debunking of colonial ethnographic stereotypes, and the portrayal of anthropological data-collection as a cornerstone of imperial dominion.

Two points in particular emerge from recent accounts of caste and its place in the official or outsiders' understanding of India. First, there is the notion that caste as we understand it is not a primordial ethnographic fact of Indian life, but a mere invention, an exercise in the Western 'essentialising' of India. By the end of the nineteenth century, European theorists and officials are supposed to have constructed a ludicrously flawed understanding of caste as the all-pervading 'essence' of the Indian social order. In Ronald Inden's bracingly acid account of the crimes of past and current scholars, a motley collection of European romantics, empiricists and miscellaneous 'essentialisers' are held to have created an 'imagined' India in which caste was a mere fabrication, designed to demean and subjugate the supposedly dreaming, politically impotent Indian 'Other' (Inden, 1990).

This fits well with the view that the great Victorian enterprise of data-collection was a one-sided exercise of 'hegemonic' power (Dirks, 1989). Many Indianists are also following Ashis Nandy's lead in debunking 'orientalist' scholarship as a farrago of destructive, white male fantasies (Nandy, 1983). To 'know' India in this systematic

[1] For valuable insights and criticisms I am grateful to Ajay Skaria, Richard Drayton, and Christopher Pinney, and especially to Miles Taylor who generously shared with me his unpublished data on membership of the nineteenth-century ethnology societies.

'scientific' sense was to subjugate it; to name, class and number its castes was to fragment a complex and dynamic society, and to draw strategic gains from its atomised constituent elements—recruiting the 'martial races', pacifying and subduing the 'criminal tribes', dividing 'Brahman' from 'non-Brahman' in the new arena of representative constitutional politics, and so on.[2]

But a second and quite different point also emerges from recent and extremely sophisticated work on caste and colonial rule. Here the emphasis is on complex interactions between the institutions of a manipulative colonial state, and the responses of Indians to the process of data-collection and classification by tribe, caste and community. In the 1970s Washbrook and Baker attacked the prevailing anthropological view of 'traditional' and 'modernising' caste identities, offering what now seems a crude picture of symbiosis between the British census-taker and the opportunist Indian magnate and caste association boss (Washbrook and Baker, 1975). Much has now been done to improve and refine this picture of caste, not as an invention in Inden's terms, but as a meeting ground between Indian reality and colonial knowledge and strategy. Recent studies have added new dimensions to this anti-'culturologist's' view of caste and tribe, in which representatives of the colonial state reshape or 'create' caste in various domains. Alavi (1991) and Singha (1900) have shown how military recruitment and the actions of colonial law-makers Brahmanised or in other ways artificially regulated 'caste' categories or relationships; Skaria (1992) has similarly transformed our understanding of the 'wild' forest tribes.

No one wishing to write credibly about caste today would accept the colonial ethnographic literature as a source of neutral, 'scientific' observation and fact. Nevertheless, there is much to be gained by taking a fresh and far from dismissive look at the so-called colonial discourse of caste. The analytical literature from the nineteenth and early twentieth

[2] Compare Fox, 1985. Among the many studies dealing with Western data-gathering and the colonial encounter, see Thomas, 1989, 1990; Comaroff and Comaroff, 1992; Sahlins, 1985; Prins, 1980. There is of course a large literature on the construction of Indian 'colonial knowledge', but it would be beyond the scope of this essay to give a full account of these diverse and sophisticated works and the debates they have engendered.

centuries is richer and more diverse than one might expect. It engages in fascinating ways with a wider world of British and continental scholarship and experimental science, leading the India specialists into complex theoretical controversies in fields such as medicine, natural history, geology, linguistics—and, above all, in the infamous Victorian 'pseudo-science' of evolutionist racial ethnology.

This is the first of two main points to be made in this paper. Setting aside for the moment what actually happened within Indian society, it is time to correct a major error in our understanding of the so-called colonial perception of caste. Current scholarship has missed out on a central theme in nineteenth- and early twentieth-century analysis: in effect, we have misperceived the colonial misperceptions which have been taken for granted in assessing the nature and impact of British rule. This major element in the portrayal of colonial thought about Indian society is the theme of race. The ethnographers who are still cited as observers of regional castes and 'caste systems,' such as Ibbetson, Hunter and Risley, are much better seen as men who sought to make their mark in a wider learned world which had come to be dominated by ethnological debate. These debates about the definition and significance of race were applied to an extraordinarily wide range of issues in contemporary science and social theory.

The works of scholar-officials with Indian careers are full of allusions to ethnology and its techniques. In speculating about what they understood as the 'castes', 'races' or 'nations' of the subcontinent, the scholar-officials were trying to place themselves in the vanguard of contemporary scientific thought. India for them was not a self-contained and ethnographically separate 'other', and certainly did not constitute a domain of purely localised imperial or strategic significance. Although they are often caricatured as 'orientalists', all monotonously portraying India in the same terms as a childlike, passive, and hierarchical 'caste' society, the colonial theorists and fact-gatherers did not think alike. A close reading of their works reveals something more complex and colourful, often more intellectually sophisticated, than a uniform colonial 'discourse' that worked to invent or fabricate the ideology and the social reality of caste.

Far from representing a monolithic consensus on 'caste', the most significant approach to India as an ethnographic problem in the colonial period was the theme of race, with its accompanying and to us abhorrent notions of evolutionary racial hierarchies and historic race conquests, its belief that civilisation was the unique achievement of ethnologically 'advanced' races, and its insistence on eternal deep-seated antipathies between so-called higher peoples and those of inferior or debased and degenerate 'blood'.[3] It may come as a shock to find that writers who are thought of now as compilers of *caste* data often treated the values and ideologies of 'caste' as a subsidiary issue, of significance to only some of the Indians they were describing and classifying. These analysts were much more concerned with a wider body of speculative scholarship in which the biological and moral qualities of 'race' were perceived as universal human endowments.

The concept of race changed dramatically from the late eighteenth century, when theorists speculated about the distinguishing political and moral character of the so-called 'Aryan' and and non-'Aryan' races whom they defined linguistically and environmentally, rather than in evolutionary terms. From the mid-nineteenth century, new 'scientific' evolutionary concepts were invoked to answer a much wider range of questions about the threat of so-called racial 'degeneration' in European societies, about the supposed dangers to national identity posed by large-scale overseas migration, and about the likely outcome of the so-called global 'struggle for mastery' at a time of explosive international crisis. Collectors of Indian ethnographic data looked to those avowedly scientific ideas about race for the means to interpret their material. In doing this they arrived at complex and unexpected decisions about how to mark and define what they understood as the 'races' of India. Furthermore, they reached equally complex conclusions about the relationships between these distinct racial groups, and also about their relationships in 'racial' or evolutionary terms with the white so-called 'Aryan' Britons who ruled them.

This leads on to the paper's second main point. Colonial theorising

[3] On the history of Western race theory see, for example, Banton and Harwood, 1975; Stocking, 1968; Boas, 1934.

was not just an empty intellectual exercise, or a spurious 'imagining' of India. However distortedly, these colonial perceptions, and, crucially, Indian reactions to them, reveal a great deal about the fluidity and complexity of India's regional societies. In the work of Hunter (1897) and Ibbetson (1916), for example, it is important to distinguish between the spurious premises of nineteenth-century race theory, and the acuteness of at least some of these theorists' observations about the regional societies in which they worked. The ethnologically-informed 'experts' drew on empirical investigations of south India, the Punjab, Bengal and other key regions of the subcontinent which they recognised as being ethnographically distinctive, and quite unlike all the alleged 'colonial' stereotypes of fixed pan-Indian caste hierarchies and all-pervading Brahmanical value systems.

Once it is recognised that Western data-collectors subdivided Indians by so-called 'race' into those who were and those who were not 'fettered' or dominated by supposedly rigid and hierarchical caste values, it becomes clear that debates about so-called 'caste' were often themselves subdivided into two or more components. First, there were debates about who generated 'caste' as a system. Around whom was 'caste' ordered? Was it 'the Brahman' or the 'kingly' Rajput? Such thinking often separated the moral or political critique of 'the Brahman', from a second area of 'colonial' analysis which concentrated on the relationships between the so-called 'castes'. For some, notably Hunter and Risley, these were ethnologically-defined relationships: castes were really 'races', and the distinction between high and low caste was really a distinction between peoples of supposedly superior and inferior racial endowment. There were powerful alternatives to this view, as demonstrated by Ibbetson's work (to be discussed below.)

The importance of ethnological or race scholarship to 'colonial' analysts can be observed by looking at the standard ethnographic literature such as the gazetteers, census reports and journals like the *Indian Antiquary*, as well as the empirical studies of scholar-administrators like Ibbetson and Hunter. Even more can be learned from works which are not much used by Indianists—especially metropolitan publications such as the *Journal of the Ethnological Society* and the *Memoirs of the*

Anthropological Society of London, and their continental counterparts like the *Mémoires de la Société d'Anthropologie.*

For many pre-independence ethnographers of India, what were thought of as the new, progressive and scientifically-verifiable insights of race theory outweighed or at least sharply modified notions of 'caste' as a fundamental fact of Indian history or Indian social organisation. Theorists like Hunter, George Campbell (n.d.) and Walter Elliot (1868-9), who were widely read in official circles, were supporters of an emerging ethnological orthodoxy which portrayed India as a composite social landscape in which only certain peoples, those of superior 'Aryan' blood, had evolved historically in ways which left them 'shackled' by a hierarchical, Brahmanically-defined ideology of 'caste'. At the same time large numbers of other Indians—those identified in varying racial terms as Dravidians, as members of 'servile' classes, aborigines, wild tribes, and those of so-called 'mixed' racial origins—were portrayed as being ethnologically distinct from this so-called Aryan population, and were *not* all thought to belong to a ranked Brahmanical caste order. Furthermore, by the end of the nineteenth century, the ethnological understanding of caste had evoked powerful opposition from other Indianists, notably Ibbetson, who were equally active in the great venture of colonial data collection and taxonomic theorising, but whose mapping of Indian 'caste' categories sought to reverse or to move beyond the principles laid down by the ethnological theorists.

Today the discipline of racial ethnology is best known in its applied anthropometric form, with its logging of cranial measurements, nasal indices and skin colours, and its arcane vocabulary of 'antero-posterior diameters' and 'zygomatico-mandibular' measurements (Hunt, 1863-4, p.17; Karve, 1948, p.9).[4] Indeed—with its inconsistencies, its mechanistic determinism and its conception of race as an endowment of physiological and moral proclivities—ethnology is widely thought of as the great intellectual dead-end of the Victorian age. But Kuper (1988) and Stocking (1968) have identified a complex array of ethnological themes

[4] The medically-trained theorist Robert Knox, quoted by his disciple James Hunt (Hunt, 1863-4, p.17), and Karve, 1948, p.9.

and related historical suppositions underpinning the scholarship of some of Britain's most influential nineteenth-century historians, social theorists and scientists—including those whom we now take for granted as seminal analysts of the Indian social order, notably Maine and Baden-Powell.

Kuper has shown how nineteenth-century ethnological scholarship drew on models of human history which emphasised a kind of political taxonomy of humankind (Kuper, 1988). In this new science only certain 'well-defined' races—those with more 'voluminous brains' and more highly-evolved features and mental faculties—were thought to be capable of achieving the state of moral and political order which constituted 'civilisation' (Hunt, 1864-4, pp.3, 10). By the mid-nineteenth century the contributors to British ethnological journals were engaged in vigorous debates about the means to interpret masses of data which were supposed to throw light on the physiological, moral and intellectual markers of human race and type. This literature abounds in the so-called 'essentialising' which characterises the period's studies of Indian 'castes' and 'tribes'. It should be recognised though that these moralistic dissections of character, physiology and intellect, which are so often portrayed as a ludicrous and demeaning use of 'colonial' knowledge, were a commonplace of writings which were not ostensibly 'colonial' at all.

The problems being 'solved' in ethnological enquiries were not simply 'imperial' problems, though of course they readily lent themselves to colonial purposes. Britain and other 'advanced' societies also had ethnological stories to tell. One aspiring pioneer, the Bristol physician John Beddoe, borrowed the anthropometric classification system devised by France's leading ethnological propagandist, Paul Broca, to compile a survey of his hospital patients' eye colours. The aim was to construct an 'ethnographical history' of the west of England; the name he chose for his statistical device, 'the Bristolian index of nigrescence', will certainly make him a candidate for the anti-culturologists' rogues' gallery (Beddoe, 1865-6).[5]

[5] This would supposedly show the merging of 'civilised', fair Teutonic invaders with dark Celtic indigenes. Medics, like military men and members of

But it is clear that Indian ethnological projects, such as attempts to identify so-called martial races, belonged to a much wider genre of data-collection and theory, in which medics and other aspiring 'men of science' debated such questions as why—in ethnological terms—Britons made better prize-fighters than 'Teutonic' (German) peoples (Pike, 1865-6, pp.153-88), or how the 'Negro race' was to be 'assigned' its proper 'station' in the ladder of ethnological precedence and advancement (Hunt, 1863-4). The aim of Victorian ethnology, then, was to use rigorous 'scientific' methodology to define and rank all humankind, white *and* non-white, to trace its racial interactions according to criteria which equated civilisation with a physiologically-determined bent towards the creation of 'advanced', libertarian, morally-progressive political institutions.[6]

Orientalists and 'ethnology'

The Victorian race theorists owed much to the orientalist scholarship of Sir William Jones and his contemporaries. The term race was widely used in the late eighteenth and early nineteenth centuries, but its meaning was linguistic and cultural, rather than 'ethnological' in the later Victorian sense, when notions of progressive evolution had emerged as a generalised theory of human racial 'type'. Jones's discourses in the journal *Asiatick Researches* spell out the historical significance which he attached to his famous revelations about the shared familial roots of the Indo-European or Indo-Aryan languages (Jones, 1807).

The speakers of the primordial Aryan mother tongue, the 'mother of the Sanskrit...as well as the Greek, Latin and Gothic', were for him a 'race' of conquerors, 'the Hindu race' (sometimes also a 'nation')

---

other Victorian occupations emphasising formal professional training and statistically-based 'scientific' methodologies, were prominent contributors to the Victorian ethnological journals. For the techniques of Broca, founder of the Paris Society of Anthropology and a leading anti-'miscegenist', see his 'Instructions générales' of 1865.

[6] On the classification schemes of nineteenth-century ethnologists see Deniker, 1900, ch.8; and Topinard, 1878. Hunt saw ethnology itself as a test of national or racial initiative and worried that Britain was lagging behind France, Germany and the USA in the field (Hunt, 1893-4). On Social Darwinism and themes of racial struggle and conflict in European ethnology and 'folk science', see Stocking 1968, pp.60-5.

(Jones, 1807, p.64). In this work he reaffirms the all-important Aryan conquest myth which became a cornerstone of ethnological thought about India, and provided later theorists with a parallel between the 'Hindu' Aryans and later Roman, Mughal and British conquerors and dominion-builders.

Jones's Aryans were heroes of a great adventure of migration and conquest 'at the earliest dawn of history', 'expanding' from their west Asian homeland to implant their shared religious and moral heritage across far-flung new new zones of dominion, including the Indian subcontinent (Jones, 1807, p.65). The 'pure', 'primeval religion' of these ancient Aryan-speakers sanctified the teachings of a divine law-giver, Mahabad or Menu, who was identical to India's primordial 'legislator' Manu, and 'who divided the people into four orders...to which he assigned names unquestionably the same in their origin as those applied to the four primary classes of the Hindus...' (Jones, 1807, p.59).

Linguistic kinship thus proved the historic 'racial' kinship of those who came to be identified with this legacy of shared Aryan or Indo-European migration, religion and political culture both in Europe and in Asia.[7] James Forbes, author of *Oriental Memoirs* (1813), built on Jones's claim that a linguistically-defined 'race' or 'nation' of Aryans from west Asia had implanted in India the divinely-sanctioned principles of the varna scheme. Forbes proposed further subdivisions into 84 'classes or castes', each separated by rigid laws of endogamy, and each therefore differing from one another 'in features, dress and appearance, as much as if they were of different nations' (Forbes, 1813, i, pp.60-1).[8]

Furthermore, like the later nineteenth-century ethnologists, and like many indigenous theorists of caste difference, Forbes points to distinc-

[7] On Jones's distinctions between Aryans and other 'races' of Asian origin (Huns, Tartars, Arabians, 'Hyperboreans', etc.), see Jones, 1807a, p.65, and note his 'confident' assumption that 'the Goths and Hindus had originally the same language...and adored the same false deities, performed the same bloody sacrifices and professed the same notion of rewards and punishments after death' (Jones, 1807b, p.12).

[8] Forbes also insists on the complex social reality of 'caste' which cannot be encompassed within the ideal textual scheme of varna (Forbes, 1813, i, p.284). See Marshall and Williams, 1982; Emmer and Ross, 1991.

tions of skin colour as markers of rank within this Brahmanical varna scheme of classification: 'the inferior castes are of a darker complexion than the superior Hindoos...' (i, p.72). But *Oriental Memoirs* gives priority to a totally different means of classifying Indian peoples. This is a notion of climate, terrain and physical environment as a determinant of human character. Its roots were not in Indological speculation, but in the works of the eighteenth-century social theorists of the Scottish Enlightenment who constructed environmental schemes of analysis as a means of accounting for differential human attainments. The environmental theme was then taken up by Victorian ethnologists as part of the language of racial classification in which so-called 'civilised' and 'savage' races were distinguished from one another on the basis of habitat.

Civilisation, for Forbes, was an attainment of inherently virile populations interacting over time with bracing, temperate climates. Tropical terrain was a corrupting and enervating milieu, and the enemy of progress towards fully 'civilised' human development. Foreshadowing the environmental categories of many later theorists, Forbes says that Indians from tropical southern India suffered from 'a want of curiosity, enterprize [sic] and vigour'. This is attributed to the 'heat of the torrid zone' which 'debilitates the body and enervates the mind'. In South India, 'civilisation...has long attained its height'; Tamils and Malayalis have been 'for some thousand years in the same state of mediocrity: producing no new designs in building, no alteration in manners or dress, no improvements in art of science' (i, p.381). 'Their inclinations are chiefly passive: indolence constitutes their happiness, and you can not impose a severer task than mental employment' (i, p.382).

Pronouncements like this became a commonplace in the literature on India's so-called martial races which distinguished between 'wily', 'soft', 'seditious' Bengalis, for example, and warlike, manly 'loyal' uplanders such as Gurkhas and Sikhs—thus providing the basis for fierce counter-claims by Bengali and Maharashtrian martial revivalists and early nationalist campaigners, from the 1890s onwards (McLane, 1977). In its later manifestations, and also in Forbes's work, the environmental idea of human types distinguishes between habitats, and also between active and inactive races or peoples—that is, between historically progressive as opposed to immobile, static cultures.

'With the exception of the warlike Nairs, they [the South Indians] pass days, months and year, in swinging on their verandas...chewing betel, and singing dismal ditties, without a reflection on the past, or a plan for the future' (Forbes, 1813, i, p.382).[9] In *Oriental Memoirs*, as in ethnological works of the later nineteenth century, the terms caste, tribe, nation and race are used interchangeably and imprecisely: 'the Nairs, or nobles [of Travancore]...a well-made handsome race, of fairer complexion than the lesser castes' (i, p.384). These terms are also often applied to populations that would now be treated as *sanyasi* (ascetic) orders or sectarian groups. Forbes was writing at a time when Indian 'castes', especially those thought to be 'gipsy'-like, 'degenerate' or 'thieves', indeed Indian corporate units in general, were seen in much the same terms—that is, as an exotic and possibly threatening manifestation of the society's distinctive atomising tendencies (Richardson, 1801). This explains why Forbes saw the *sanyasi* orders as representing caste-like ethnographic divisions, as in a reference to 'fakeers, or yogees, of the Senassee [*sanyasi*] tribe' (Forbes, 1813, i, p.68).

What is constant in Forbes's writing are his determinist notions of habitat, with their accompanying oppositions of civilised and uncivilised peoples, for example the shrieking, predatory 'Bheels and wild mountaineers' who sweep down from their upland milieu as fiendish despoilers of the plainsdweller's ordered agrarian domesticity (i, p.203). But cutting across these environmental typologies, Forbes also portrays some peoples or regional societies as possessing a pernicious 'attachment' to Brahmanically-defined values of purity, endogamy and hierarchy. Bengalis, for example, display 'deeply rooted prejudices and attachment to *caste*' (his italics: ii, pp.24).

[9] *Oriental Memoirs* was based on the author's travels as a Bombay Company servant in 1765-82. Forbes assigns one group from the hot south, the Maravas of the dry hinterland poligar country, to the ranks of virile 'noble' peoples, even venturing an incongruous classical parallel by comparing Marava women, renowned, he says, for their 'heroic propensity for self-immolation' with stoic Roman matrons (Forbes, 1813, i, p.383).

This distinction between casteless mountaineers and caste-'fettered' tropical lowlanders became a major theme in the racial classification schemes devised by ethnologists of the later nineteenth century (see below). Predictably, however, it is in what Forbes calls 'delightful' temperate Rajasthan that he finds the most important of his valorous, freedom-loving people, for whom caste 'prejudices' supposedly do not prevail. The Rajputs are to Forbes the ultimate specimens of environmentally-shaped nobility, 'a noble race of Hindoos, divided into distinct tribes...' (ii, p.258). The vocabulary of race, tribe and caste is again imprecise and inconsistent. But the later theorists' vision of progressive, freedom-loving, casteless martial people is already present in Forbes's environmental and moral categories. Rajputs 'make the best soldiers in the country'; they are 'imbued with a noble spirit, great energy, and athletic form' (ii, p.258). In contrast to Bengal and other torrid locales, rugged Rajasthan evokes a comparison with Switzerland, one of the favoured noble milieux of the European romantics. Forbes's Swiss parallel expresses this romantic equation of upland, picturesque locale and romantically noble human spirit: 'like that once free and happy country' (Switzerland), Rajasthan 'may be considered, more than any other oriental region, the nurse of liberty and independence' (ii, p.46).

The early orientalists who ascribed 'purity' and 'sublimity' to ancient Hinduism were denounced by evangelical Christian commentators like the Rev. William Ward of the Serampore mission. Ward's influential polemic, *The History, Literature and Religion of the Hindus* (1817-20), sought to explode the sympathetic myth-making of Jones and his supporters with a lurid account of the 'human depravity', 'oppression', 'degradation' and 'immorality' of contemporary Hindu society.[10] As in other evangelical writing on India, the primacy of Brahmans and a Brahmanically-focused ideology of varna was axiomatic for Ward. Hindu society was a Brahmanical tyranny; Hindu belief and ritual a 'fabric of superstitions' concocted by Brahmans, 'the

[10] Ward was a celebrated linguist and Bible translator and addressed his admiring audience with the dual authority of an impassioned Christian proselytiser and an acclaimed expert on contemporary Indian morals and manners.

most complete system of absolute oppression that perhaps ever existed' (Ward, 1817-20, iii, p.69) in which tyrannised victims cowered in their deluded 'state of degradation' (i, p.lxv). Much was made of practices such as the 'monstrous polygamy' of the Bengal Kulins; Brahmans in general were portrayed as exploitative voluptuaries, prone to 'licentious intrigues' (iii, p 80ff.; i, p.lxv).[11]

Ward's vision of an immoral Brahman despotism clearly drew on the period's popular Protestant mythology of a priest-ridden, tyrannised papist Europe, awaiting liberation by the triumph of the Reformation spirit. He therefore highlighted the supposed depravity of those in the indigenous society whom he identified in conventional evangelical terms with failed or fraudulent pastoral care. Far from being refined philosophers or authentic spiritual guides, Brahmans as gurus 'are notorious for their covetousness and impurity' (i, p.lxv); Brahmans as seekers, as practitioners of yogic disciplines, were mere sensualists, 'rehearsing' in their minds merely 'the form of the god, his colour, the number of his heads, eyes, hands...nothing more', thus blind to any sense of true divinity or morality (i, p.lix).

Nineteenth-century Christian polemics like Ward's were clearly a major if unacknowledged source for later theorists, including many modern anthropologists, who came to regard the Brahman as arbiter and moral centre of the 'Hindu' social order. But what has been overlooked in debates about the so-called 'core' values of Indian society, is that they have synthesised what were once at least two separate debates. Those like Ward who attacked the role of Brahmans as a corrupt priesthood were raising questions about public morality under Company rule, and often had no conception of India as a society which was integrated or governed by 'caste' ideology. By the same token, later colonial debates about the significance and origins of 'caste', often focused on notions of polity and race which were only distantly related to nineteenth-century theorising about Brahmans and so-called Brahmanism.

The arguments of Ward the evangelical, focus on Brahmans as

[11] Forbes too sees Brahmans as shameless voluptuaries (Ward, 1817-20, i, p.389).

tyrants and corrupters of free will: 'Like all other attempts to cramp the human intellect, and forcibly to restrain men within bounds which nature scorns to keep, this system [varna]...has operated like the Chinese national shoe, it has rendered the whole nation cripples' (iii, pp.64-5). It is striking that Ward anticipates Dumont's position on the radical subordination or encompassment of kingly power by Brahmanical religious authority. Anyone acquainted with 'the Hindoo system', says Ward, will accept that it is 'wholly the work of bramhuns [sic]; who have here placed themselves above kings in honour, and laid the whole nation prostrate at their feet' (iii, p.65).[12]

Ward thus foreshadows later commentators (vilified by Inden), who portray Indians as people who 'know nothing of patriotism' (Ward, iii, p.287) and lack political will. Despite their differences, both Forbes and Ward, with their assertions about 'prostrate', 'fettered' Hindus, share the same preoccupation with abstract concepts of liberty and freedom which particular peoples either do or do not possess. This universalising political motif became a paramount theme in later ethnographic writing on India. And in these early examples of the genre, the nature of caste as a distinctive Indian institution is a subsidiary matter. The overriding concern is to identify the proportions of 'freedom', 'restraint' and 'oppression' which prevail in Indian political culture.

While the portrayal of a Brahman-centred, caste-driven India served a particular purpose for evangelical Christians, its champions also shared many concerns with Forbes and the other orientalists. Evangelicals like Ward used the Brahman-tyrant model to call for anglicising social 'reform' in the name of Christian morality, 'liberty', and beneficent 'good government'. The same theme also had a lasting effect on ostensibly secular debates about state power and policy. The

[12] Ward too uses 'race' very loosely: as in the 'race' of Brahmans (ibid.,p. lxiv) as well as the 'present race of Hindoos' (i, p.lxvi). He denounces the oppressiveness and falseness of 'caste' for degrading the 'Sudras', although a few individuals have thrown off 'bramhinical fetters' (sic) under 'beneficent' British rule (iii, p.65). He also makes 'orientalist' biological and environmental distinctions. The 'Hindoo' is 'mild and timid' and given to 'effeminate pleasures' (cf. Nandy, 1983); but the fair, 'handsome', 'higher orders' in the 'upper provinces' are more 'robust and independent' than the lowlanders of Bengal (Ward, 1817-20, iii, pp.185-6).

evangelical's licentious Brahman tyrant returned repeatedly to colonial polemical writing, in changing costume to suit the concerns and crises of the moment. His secular equivalent in the early nineteenth century was the wily government 'service Brahman' who supposedly entrapped and corrupted European officials. In 1857 he reappeared as the Brahman conspirator fomenting rebellion amongst his fellow sepoys. And perhaps his final colonial manifestation was as the seditious nationalist Brahman who was to be neutralised through the patronage of client 'non-Brahman' political collaborators.

Evolutionary race theories

But while this polemical Christian account of 'Brahmanism' had a long afterlife, it still represented only one strand in the pre-independence ethnographic understanding of India. By the mid-nineteenth century, the universalising, comparative study of race provided quite a different ethnographic language, and a distinct set of concerns, for those writing about India. The background to this was a series of wide-ranging debates amongst the major Victorian social theorists. In 1866, for example, the *Anthropological Review* carried a fierce attack on John Stuart Mill by the ethnologist Robert Knox, denouncing Mill for promoting a false 'daydream of racial equality' (xiii, 1866, pp.113-35). Mill's error was his indifference to the supposedly immutable evolutionary facts of physiology and intellect which separated race from race. According to Knox, who was another of the medically-trained practitioners of the new racial science, 'The higher races are inherently more qualified for both political and individual liberty than the lower' (p.126).

Knox was primarily concerned with the construction of global, comparative schemes of racial ranking. Ethnologists used notions of anatomical development and physiological 'type', as displayed by so-called head-forms and cranial capacity, to rank Asians in general, and Indians in particular, in the ethnologist's politically-defined 'scale of being' and civilisation. Knox's article cites widely-accepted nineteenth-century classifications ranking the so-called negro racial 'type' in relation to Asians or 'mongol' races. Asians, he says, possess comparatively 'advanced' physiological characteristics. Using avowedly 'modern' scientific methods of physiological measurement and comparison, the 'type' of the 'negro' was to be assigned to the lowest evolutionary category, which was termed 'foetal'; the physiological 'type' of the so-called mongol was classed on a comparatively higher level as 'infantile' (p.120). Intellect and social institutions were supposed to correspond to these stages of physiological evolution. Thus,

> as the type of the Negro is foetal, that of the Mongol is infantile. And in strict accordance with this we find that their government, literature and art are infantile also. They are beardless children, whose life is a task, and whose chief virtue consists in unquestioning obedience (p.120).

Such theorising obviously generated what Inden and Nandy regard as the white ruler's stereotype of the childlike, impotent colonial subject. But for the ethnologist, the immediate concern here was not imperial dominion, but the classification in supposedly neutral and scientific terms of human evolutionary 'specimens'.

The influence of early orientalists like Jones is clear in the race theorists' concerns with polity as a marker of human race and type. Asia, says Knox, has been 'immemorially the seat of despotism'. Its 'codes' were merely 'the successive edicts of absolute sovereigns'. In their 'outlines' and 'fundamental principles',

> ...they were the products of a single legislator, some divinely inspired Menu [sic], Moses or Mohammed, who derives his authority not from without but within, not from the people but from God, and whose short but effective preamble was 'thus saith the lord' (p.122).[13]

Mid-Victorian ethnologists like Knox assigned Indians, or sometimes 'Hindus', to a *single* racial classification within their broad global schemes of rank and precedence. Their categories were vast and crude, and were rooted in a notion of the historical immutability of 'savage' or 'backward' races. The distinction between higher and lower or civilised and uncivilised peoples was a matter of initiative, of historic dyna-

[13] 'Were Mr. Mill an anthropologist, we might point out to him the very important physiological fact, that an immemorial civilisation has utterly failed to Caucasianise either the Chinese or the Japanese, they being still as essentially Mongolian as the rudest nomad of the northern steppes' (Knox, 1866, p.120).

mism, as Knox's colleague Hunt proclaims. 'We know it to be a patent fact that there are races existing which have no history...' (Hunt, 1863-4, p.29). Such people have, 'since remote antiquity', been 'without a progressive history', eternally lacking in the capacity to mature, to develop the 'advanced' morals and political institutions which define the civilised races of mankind, and render them 'fit for places of power' (pp.28-30).

Like other ethnologists, Hunt defines the 'European' as 'the conqueror and the dominant race' (p.31). Dynamism—particularly imperial expansion—is the indelible mark of this superiority. This leads to the inevitable conclusion that as an empire-builder, the European, 'forever restless' (p.31), could be seen as fulfilling his ethnological destiny. By conquering alien peoples, the European was conforming to a racial pattern which linked him historically to his Aryan forbears in India, and to his Roman and Norman imperial predecessors. One of the unexpected features of the period's ethnological writing is this unresolved tension produced by the 'orientalist' Aryan invasion myth. Many ethnologists saw the descendants of India's invading 'Aryan' peoples in ambivalent terms as true though distant and 'debased' kin of the 'advanced' white Europeans (Kuper, 1988).

For Hunt, comparisons with the racial history of the 'Hindoo' provide a powerful means of pointing up strong but still ambiguous ethnological distinctions between Indian and European. He makes this comparison by quoting a bizarre piece of quasi-poetic, evolutionist speculation by the ethnologist Franz Pruner, a continental physician whose sojourns in Ottoman territories led him to style himself Pruner Bey. Writing in 1847, this eccentric theorist drew on the supposed correlation between skull shapes, environment and levels of human evolution, musing:

> What has the noble Hindoo become under an Indian sun, drowned in a sea of spiritualism the most obscure, with his cranium, which by its admirable harmony, its graceful mould, seems exactly to resemble the organic egg which received the divine breath of Brahma? He has, it is true, fulfilled an eminent task; but for many centuries he has been a being severed from terrestrial

regions, and of little use to his fellow beings (Hunt, 1863-4, p.50. note).[14]

In contrast to the flamboyant Pruner Bey, with his attempt to marry proto-Darwinian precepts of natural selection and species adaptation, to a mélange of utilitarianism and orientalist romanticism, the aspiring British ethnologists from the Indian army and revenue administration seem rather a prosaic lot.[15] But when they sought to make *their* mark amongst the metropolitan ethnologists they often broke with the orthodoxies of generalisers like Knox and Hunt. For example, a Major Owen of the Bengal Army argued in the *Memoirs of the Anthropological Society of London* that the 'Hindu mind' was not an immutable, static slave of 'superstition' as other ethnologists claimed (Owen, 1865-6, p.202). His evidence was not supposedly eternal marks of race such as cranial shape or 'primordial' legal institutions. Instead, he focused on a slice of contemporary local history demonstrating what he saw as change and 'advancement' among the Hindu *literati* of upper India.

Owen's ethnological excitement was aroused by the activities of the 'native gentlemen' whom he had seen participating in the lively new learned societies of Benares. He claims that these 'children of Brahma' (p.203) were an evolutionary Indian vanguard, bravely challenging Hindu 'superstition' and thus following in the path of earlier Western pioneers who had 'thrown off the chains' of 'mental slavery' at the time of the European scientific revolution.[16]

[14] For his racial classification methods see Pruner, 1868. Ethnologists who ranked human 'races' on a physiological ladder of precedence equated the 'negro' brain (and intellect) with that of a *male* European infant. For Hunt, *all* female brains were smaller and therefore inferior to *all* male brains within each racial category, so the appropriate female counterpart to the 'negro' brain in ethnological terms was the brain of an *adult* European female (Hunt, 1863-4, pp.15-17).

[15] Apart from members of the increasingly professionalised secular services and occupations, missionaries also influenced and were influenced by ethnological ideas (see, for example, Sherring, 1872). Like law and medicine, missionary work acquired an increasingly institutionalised, bureaucratic character and a dedication to statistics, data-collection and structured, hierarchical forms of organisation during the nineteenth century.

[16] The hero of Owen's paper, a Maharashtrian mathematician and Sanskrit scholar, demonstrated the 'errors' of traditional sastric astronomy by using Western scientific techniques to recalculate the tables of planetary movements by which Hindu temples timed their sacred rituals (Owen, 1865-6).

These things are worthy of our notice. If we remain unacquainted with this dawn of a new day in the east, we shall not know that the Hindu race—a race in which we, as Englishmen, especially take a great interest—is advancing; at least, the first steps have been taken, in...the right direction (p.205).

Here then is a European in India for whom racial 'progress' and evolution were real ethnological facts, not just for the 'advanced' white race, but for the so-called 'Hindu' race as well, despite the profound differences between them. This did not shake Owen's commitment to racial analysis. He managed to combine a belief in the capacity of (some) races to 'progress' in moral and intellectual terms, with a conventional ethnologist's faith in the principle of separate racial endowments: '...the two races [white and 'Hindu'] do not think in the same channel...' (p.205). As a result the pandit's 'scientific' challenge to received wisdom is all the more impressive because of what Owen calls the tremendous '*vis inertia* [that] must have been exerted to set in motion such a ponderous mind as that of the Hindu—a mind comparatively stationary for ages, and to which has clung an abundance of stagnant vegetation' (p.205).

Racial ethnology could thus produce a surprisingly diverse and unpredictable 'discourse' of Indian 'differentness', and one which certainly did not think of Indians solely in static, universal caste categories. Furthermore, it is sometimes forgotten that Indians entered into these debates and contributed to this historical and evolutionary analysis of caste and race. For example, in 1872 the Assistant Collector of Fatehpur in the North Western Provinces appealed in the *Indian Antiquary* for data on 'the origin of the caste of Khattris', proposing that there was a 'close analogy' between the histories of the 'two races' of Khattris and Rajputs, indeed a possibility that Khattris, Rajputs and Jats all shared a common descent or ethnological 'origin' (White, 1872, p.289).

This was an important question for nineteenth-century Indianists, raising questions about differential endowments of 'nationhood' and libertarianism which were still being debated well into the twentieth century by scholars like Ibbetson. In this case, the item on the Khattris prompted an angry rejoinder from a correspondent who identified himself as one Kasi Nath, a 'member of that caste (Dehliwal Khattri)', from Sirsa in Allahabad. It seems likely that the letter really did come from an Indian reader, and that the ethnographic journals were read by people who belonged to the sort of Indian intelligentsia praised by Owen. It is therefore striking that this correspondent took up and used the current racial idiom, not uncritically, but with his own distinctive perspective on the ethnological understanding of caste. 'The Khatris are descendants of a warlike race', he declares (Kasi Nath, 1873, p.27). 'Judging from their physiognomy, they are of pure Aryan blood' (p.26).

Here the claims about the superiority of Khattri antecedents are in tune with European ethnological principles: 'next to Kashmiris' the Khattris 'are the fairest race in Hindustan' (p.26). But Kasi Nath combines arguments based on Western ethnology, with its emphasis on physiological 'race' markers, with indigenous Hindu moral categories. He argues that Khattris possess an inherited superiority because they have a long-standing affinity for 'advanced', scriptural forms of religion. 'Next to Brahmans', Khattris 'are the most religious class, reading much of the Hindu scriptures' (p.26).

His definition of Khattri superiority is not simplistically Brahmanical, however. Guru Nanak was a Khattri, says Kasi Nath; as the 'patron saint' of all Khattris, whether Hindu or Sikh, Guru Nanak and the other Sikh gurus shaped Khattri 'morals, manners and customs', 'weaning' them away from the 'superstitions' followed by other Hindu 'tribes'. Khattris were 'genuine Hindus' (p.26), but did not belong in the same ethnological category as Jats. Kasi Nath cites marks of distinctive identity which point up the Khattris' superiority to the supposedly low, common Jat, who is 'denominated' as 'Sudra' or 'Mlechha' by Brahmans. Khattris are 'scrupulous' about preserving the 'purity' of their blood; they are proverbially lavish in their feeding of fakirs, and their benefactions to the *mahants* of the *akhara* (monastic foundation) at Nirmal give them prestigious connections with the great melas (festivals) of Hardwar and Allahabad. Furthermore, 'pious Brahmans' will take cooked food from their hands, but not from Jats (p.26).

Kasi Nath's arguments suggest the appeal to at least some Indians of an indigenous reworking of Western ethnological categories which involves something quite different from a one-sided 'colonial' fabrication of 'caste'.[17] Since the nineteenth century there has been a persistent and very complex interaction between Western race theories, and a wide range of indigenous intellectual and cultural movements. Indeed the influence of Victorian theories of race and blood purity, and the orientalist myth of Aryan race conquest, is still apparent today. Their most obvious modern manifestation is to be found in the propaganda of the present-day Hindu supremacists who wish to redefine Indian nationhood as the exclusive province of a so-called Hindu 'race', with the pure blood of Ram in their veins (Bayly, 1993).

It is striking that journals like the *Indian Antiquary* welcomed dialogue with educated 'native gentlemen' on ethnological topics. But while the aspiring ethnologist Owen attached such significance to the formation of European-style learned societies amongst educated 'progressive' Indians, to many of his contemporaries the vigour of contemporary European ethnographic scholarship proved just the opposite. Owen saw signs of a new racial dynamism amongst 'Hindus' under the improving rule of the raj. To other racial theorists, the very ability to think ethnologically, and to take part in an associated scholarly world of learned societies and ethnographic publications, was *itself* the mark of European—or British—racial supremacy.

These notions obviously harmonised with imperial aims and strategies, but this alone does not situate ethnological analysis in its full historical context. In fact the same claims about superiority of intellect were also a commonplace amongst ethnologists whose aim was to distinguish, on 'scientific' racial grounds, between Britons and the racially distinct 'nations' of continental Europe. Thus a typically smug article on the 'Psychical characteristics of the English people', in the *Memoirs of the Anthropological Society of London* (Pike, 1865-6), rhapsodises about the all-pervading 'sense of decency' which characterises the English in contrast to their continental neighbours (p.167). The author,

[17] The Urdu-Hindu language debate was one arena in which Indian polemicists appropriated European ethnological ideas. The Nagri propagandist Babu Shiva Prasad denounced Urdu as a debased and alien 'semitic' implant with 'degenerative' consequences for 'Aryan' Hindu India. See King, 1992.

L.O. Pike, finds comfort in the anatomical differences which allow him to distinguish between the moral and intellectual qualities of Englishmen and those of their uncomfortably energetic 'Teutonic' rivals (p.185).

From its earliest manifestations, ethnology had reflected changing trends in European intellectual fashion, and its aims had also been shaped by political change, not just in colonial societies like India, but in Britain and other European states. Thus undoubtedly the background to Pike's ethnological musing about Englishmen and 'Teutons' was the drive to German national unification, the achievements of Germans in science and the arts, and rivalries within Europe and in the new domains of overseas 'informal empire' for political and economic advantage. It is not surprising that Pike's ethnology proclaims the accomplishments of Britons as prosaic but morally upright empire-builders who must ultimately win out against thrusting, competitive Germans:

> The Germans emigrate, but do not colonise—precisely as they carry a new discovery to further results more frequently than they make the discovery itself England is the great coloniser; but wherever England sends colonists, Germany sends migrants (p.185).

For Pike this difference reflects crucial distinctions of intellect and character. For the English ethnologist, Germans and other continentals were unstable and immoderate by nature. The comparisons here are reminiscent of later nineteenth-century colonial stereotypes. French colonial propagandists summed up the British approach to empire as dull, plodding 'Lugardism'. British observers caricatured the French in the age of Lyautey as unstable, militaristic visionaries, lusting for glory and impracticable 'civilising mission'. Thus for Pike:

> ...the steady scientific method of the English is characteristic of the people, and is essentially opposed to the method of the Germans.... The English know the true value of facts; they know how to arrange them, to classify them, to utilise them. They know also the value of theories; they know how to verify them, to apply them, to utilise them. The Germans...value facts for their quantity rather than their quality; they value theories for their mysticism, for the satisfaction they can afford the theoriser rather than for their agreement with established

facts (pp.183-4).[18]

This would appear to be a celebration of the Englishman as colonial master and clear-headed, scientific fact-gatherer which precisely fits the formulations of Said and Inden. The English coloniser deserves his ascendancy because he belongs to a vigorous race with an 'athletic spirit' (p.158), and has a racial predisposition to use his intellect in a distinctive, assertive fashion—arranging, classifying, taxonomising. These, of course, are the special skills which the new racial ethnologists claimed for themselves. It is no wonder that so-called 'colonial' knowledge-gathering is so often portrayed as a 'hegemonic' assertion of power and dominion.

Mid-nineteenth-century ethnographers in India often expressed themselves in precisely these terms. John Beames of the Bengal Civil Service provides an example of these 'orientalist' convictions. People in N.W.P. are not 'safe guides...to their own past history', he asserts. For Beames, India's history is the history of race, and it is this that Britons are uniquely qualified to unravel from the subcontinent's inadequate and chaotic historical sources—including what he calls 'grotesque and...disgusting fables' (Beames, in Elliot, 1869, pp.viii). This obviously fits Inden's characterisation of so-called orientalists as believers in Western man's virile rationality and rigorous sense of true 'factual' history, with India as Europe's mirror image, a land of legend instead of history, a domain of dark, feminine, mystical, a-historical mentalities (Inden, 1990).[19]

For Beames, contributors to the great ethnographic enterprise in India were participating in a noble venture with an elevating, even a

[18] For a more flattering picture of 'race-proud Teutons' as preservers of the 'Aryan genius for political civilisation', see Stocking, 1968, p.50, quoting the nineteenth-century American ethnologist Brinton. And compare the French ethnologist Topinard on the unique 'genius' of the French: this was supposedly derived from fruitful racial mixing which had endowed the nation with a combined legacy of Celtic martial brilliance, Teutonic 'sober devoutness' and Roman talent for organisation (Topinard, 1878, p.410).

[19] From Beames's preface to the 1869 edition of Elliot's 1844 classic, *Memoirs...of the Races of the North Western Provinces....* Victorian ethnologists often bemoaned the a-historical Indian's lack of 'acquaintance' with 'his' history. See, for example, Hunter, 1897, p.3.

regenerative purpose. History, he says, 'in the true sense of the word, does not begin for India until the advent of the Musulman on the scene...' (Beames, in Elliot, 1869, p.ix). But for the scholar's purposes, this is 'too late'; by the time of the medieval Muslim chroniclers, '...Indian society was fixed, wars and migrations had taken place, legends had sprung up, the work of disintegration [into '*that* exaggerated state of social disunion known as caste' (p.viii)] had wrought its full results of evil'. Therefore, all who 'have the good of India at heart' must hope that 'it may yet be given to European skill and perserverance to lift the veil, to build up the perfect statue from the scattered fragments lying hidden under the rubble of time' (p.ix).

This is quite a different 'orientalism' from the nineteenth-century 'imaginings' denounced by Inden. Beames was a scholar-official with an active career in Indian administration, not a German intellectual or a distant English follower of abstract continental speculation. And it is from this official mind, and the minds of missionaries, medics and other professional men, that we can derive a much fuller picture of the so-called 'colonial' understanding of India. Beames argued that there was an honourable and concrete purpose to 'orientalism' in this form — that is, the pursuit of hard ethnological fact, systematically arranged by Englishmen (pp.viii-ix). Indians themselves were not equipped to recover their past. But if enlightened Britons did this for them, 'orientalism' would not so much subjugate, as empower and liberate a grateful client-people who would thus be returned to a realisation of their glorious historic heritage. Once again, this was a vision which depended on belief in the common Aryan heritage of India and Europe, despite the Aryan 'race's' historic divergence into its separate Western and 'Asiatic' branches. For Beames, Britons were to live up to the moral responsibility of empire by uplifting their fellow members of 'the Aryan nation' and restoring these distant racial cousins to their proper greatness.[20]

[20] See Kuper, 1988. Dirks, 1989, notes that no Indian was thought to be mentally equipped to carry on Mackenzie's ethnographic survey work; and see Pick, 1989. Beames's view of caste as a purely 'Aryan' institution which was devised at a time of racial 'degeneration', was taken up by Hunter (see below). Unlike Hunter, Beames celebrates the 'English' fact-gatherer as an unromantic

The new regional taxonomies of 'race'

So what was the response to these appeals for Britons in India to 'serve science' through precise data-gathering and systematic local observation of Indian habits, customs and race markers? In 1869, the Ethnological Society of London invited specialists to map the ethnological composition of individual Indian regions according to the established 'scientific' criteria of ethnology—'physical character', 'language', 'civilisation' and 'religion' (Huxley, 1868-9, p.89). Significantly, the meeting was held in what was then called the Museum of *Practical* Geology. It was accompanied by displays of ethnographic photographs, geological samples, flint axes and other 'specimens'. All this today would be associated with the intersection of European laboratory science, technology and museum-collecting as expressions of the triumphant Victorian intellect and the subordination of the 'Other' (pp.89-90).[21]

The ethnology presented in these 'hegemonic' surroundings portrayed an India in which race coexisted uneasily and ambiguously with what we now think of as caste. For Darwin's champion, T.H. Huxley, unlike Owen or Pike, India was not the domain of a single 'Hindu' race, but a land of two separate racial groupings whose conflicts, migrations and interbreeding had marked out the subcontinent into zones of separate culture, language and racial 'type'. The 'proper' population of the Deccan, says Huxley, has no 'analogue' in north-eastern or north-western Asia. 'They are long-headed, dark-skinned, and dark-eyed men, with wavy black hair.' They speak Dravidian languages, 'and where they have been left in their primitive condition are thorough savages'. The population of the rest of 'Hindostan', he says, exhibits 'obvious signs of the influence of the pale-faced Aryans, who...stretch from the waters of the Indus to...the North Sea, everywhere speaking languages allied to the Sanscrit [sic], which forms the

---

and pragmatic figure, unlike the learned textual scholars of the early orientalist tradition. This notion of the scholar's imperial task also differed from that of the French colonial champions of '*mission civilisatrice*'. It is hard to see in these debates any signs of a uniform Anglo-French imperial consensus' on the ethnography of India (Inden, 1990).

[21] See Mitchell, 1988.

basis of all the dialects of civilised India' (pp.92-3).

The fate of these primordial 'Dravidians'—'through long ages of battle' with the stronger Aryan invaders—was for some, a process of racial 'mixing' which modified their physical features, as well as their language and religion, 'into endless shades of diversity'. The rest of the so-called Dravidians were 'extirpated' or 'driven to the shelter of their savage fastnesses among the hills of the Dekhan...[remaining] like the Celts of Brittany and Wales, a fragmentary and dispossessed primitive population'—known to modern scholars as the 'hill tribes' of the southern peninsula (p.93). Thus this rehearsal of the Aryan conquest myth emphasises the ethnologist's motif of universal race confrontation. Strong pale Aryan conquerors confront and subdue lesser dark peoples, with an explicit equation of European and Asian racial history in the analogy between 'tribal' Celts, and marginalised Dravidians.

Walter Elliot's paper on South India was the most striking of the sessions' detailed regional ethnographies. He too begins with a complaint about the failure of 'the Hindu mind' to document its own ethnology.[22] But elsewhere he too rejects generalisations about a single Hindu 'race' and portrays South India as an immensely complex ethnological terrain populated primarily by so-called non-'Aryan' peoples of Dravidian 'type', whom he subdivides into no less than six distinct racial categories. There is no sign here of a 'hegemonic discourse of caste' in Inden's terms (Inden, 1990, p.58). Indeed 'caste' has no ethnological reality for Elliot. In his view the bearers of a particular 'caste' title were never marked off from other caste groups by the physiological marks and endowments on which ethnologists relied to classify what they thought of as higher and lower 'types' and 'races'. 'Parias', he says, were sometimes 'fair and tall' with 'good' features; other members of the same 'nation' (Elliot, 1868-9, p.103) were 'black and squat', with 'the lowest and most debased cast of countenance' (p.122).

Thus for Elliot there could be no reason to classify his six groups in

[22] '...[E]minent as the Hindu mind has shown itself to be, in the cultivation of speculative knowledge, it is strangely deficient in habits of accurate observation' (Elliot, 1868-9, p.94). As usual it is for Britons to remedy this defect.

hierarchical 'caste' terms. South Indians are not all said to rank themselves according to universal Brahman-centred principles of purity and pollution. The basis of Elliot's taxonomy is racial; he classifies people according to their physiology, their moral attributes, and their level of 'civilisation', meaning their greater or lesser endowments of freedom-loving libertarianism. On this basis Elliot assigns to the first of his six categories the Kurumba hill people of Malabar and other so-called 'simple' hunting and pastoral groups. Included in this Group 1 classification are people who he says are known as 'Kurubars' in Kannada, and 'Dhanzars' in Hindi and Marathi (p.104). By comparing their chief 'moral attributes', 'social customs' and 'religious observances', establishing for example whether they worship 'tutelary deities' or mere demonic 'spirits' (p.95), Elliot 'proves' ethnologically that these people are close racial kin of the Bengal Santals. For Elliot the chief ethnological trait of all such so-called 'pre-Aryan' people, whom he calls both a single 'caste' and a 'race', is, paradoxically, that they are 'free and unfettered by caste' (p.104), sharing a common descent from a single 'highly-civilised' population with a marked ethnological taste for 'freedom' (p.109). Their modern descendants inherit from these 'free' tribal ancestors the crucial moral attributes of the sturdy, valorous, freedom-loving highlander. They thus occupy the slot assigned variously to 'free', virile, 'tribes' of Germans, Aryans, Celts, Scots, Swiss and other representatives of the 'primitive' free peoples of the past and present, who figured so crucially in the ethnological mapping of race and political evolution around the world.

In contrast to other South Indians, whom he assigns to separate categories of unfree, servile, predatory and 'civilised' people (p.95), Elliot asserts that the Kurumba were formerly 'independent princes' of Malabar; in the Carnatic the same people formed a 'federal community' of 'twenty-four states or castles' (p.108). The sad modern plight of these once-strong warrior-pastoralists is for Elliot a demonstration of yet another ethnological principle for the racial theorists. This is the principle of the decay or degeneration of races, a result of various phenomena including racial 'miscegenation' and the superseding of free, 'democratic' government by 'despotism'.[23]

Elliot's vision of free tribal republicanism is strikingly reminiscent of Maine's discussion of primordial Indian 'village republics'. Elliot therefore applies to 'Dravidian' South India a form of evolutionary political analysis that was already being spelled out in the works of theorists concerned not just with India, but with all societies in which particular legal and constitutional forms were regarded as markers of free 'citizenries' and 'republican' liberties, both in the past and amongst living 'primitives' (Kuper, 1988, pp.3-41).[24]

The ethnological view of Indian polity has not been much explored in the analysis of colonial attitudes to 'caste'. But far from belonging to some self-contained 'discourse' of Indological legal and political theory, the theorists of race and type were major arbiters of the Victorian debate about the nature and sources of the primordial Indian 'village republic'. In the work of Elliot's contemporary George Campbell, for example, the 'old Aryans' whose descendants were to be found at the four extremities of the subcontinent in Kashmir, Bengal, Maharashtra and Ceylon, were members of a 'good-looking', 'intellectual' 'Bramin race' whose institutions were 'less democratic' than 'those of the races that followed them' in colonising these areas (Campbell, 1868-9, pp.134-6). In none of these regions, Campbell claims, 'does the true Indian village flourish' (p.136). In the Punjab, on the other hand, it was another wave of migrants, the 'advancing Jats', 'robust and warlike' members of a 'fresher' race (pp.137-8), whose institutions are to be hailed for their superior ethnological qualities. 'In their institutions they are extremely democratic; every village is a perfect little republic'

[23] On 'degeneration' as an ethnological theme, see Pick, 1989, and Knox, 1863. According to Elliot, the ancestors of the Kurumba displayed their freedom-loving qualities by embracing the egalitarian teachings of Buddhism. They thus attained a 'high state of civilisation' until their free 'republic' was annihilated by the medieval Chola kings of Tamilnad. He claims that 'horrible tortures' depicted in south Indian temple carvings provide a record of these anti-Buddhist 'martyrdoms'. Reproductions of these grisly scenes were thoughtfully provided for Elliot's audience (Elliot, 1869, pp.108-9).

[24] This explains Elliot's insistence that India's recent 'despotisms' were an alien implant, that the 'idea of an Indian republic' was a primordial fact of *south Indian* life, and 'the Indian village' was 'the germ of a perfect municipal system' (ibid., p.108, note).

(p.138).

This picture of 'fresh', vigorous, 'democratic' Jats had a strong impact on Denzil Ibbetson's portrayal of caste, tribe and 'race' in the Punjab. Campbell's language is virtually identical with Maine's, and clearly notions of republican polity as manifested in the mythical Indian 'village republic' were a crucial link between Victorian racial ethnology and what many Indianists still think of as the 'respectable' historical speculations of Maine, Baden Powell and even Marx.[25]

Like Hunter and Owen, Elliot drew ethnological conclusions from contemporary history, in particular from the so-called Santal Rebellion of 1851. For Elliot (as for Hunter), these events provided nothing less than a vision of Santal nationhood. This profoundly romantic notion of nationality was another crucial element in the ethnology of race. A spirit of instinctive, race nationality was for Elliot a natural outgrowth of the distinctive moral endowments which characterised his casteless Kurumba and other 'Group 1' people. To prove the point, he quotes descriptions of suicidally selfless displays of Santal valour in the 1851 rising. According to a Major Jarvis, the Santals 'did not understand yielding...as long as their national drums beat, the whole party would stand and allow themselves to be shot down.... They were the most *truthful* set of men I ever met, brave to infatuation' (p.107; italics in original).

This is a far cry from the stereotype of like-minded 'colonial' theorists assigning all Indians to uniform schemes of caste rank and varna affiliation. To Elliot Brahmanical caste-ranking schemes are an alien and comparatively recent phenomenon in South India. They fit badly and with much unevenness into the region's prevailing ethnological make-up. Elliot argues that to look at the region ethnologically is to recognise that most of its population was shaped by strong qualities of libertarianism and a vigorous racial heritage of nobility, independence,

[25] Many ethnologists shared with Maine an evolutionary view of English history which became their reference point in the analysis of Indian society. 'The Rajpoots seem, like the Normans [in England], to have frequently found their way in small numbers among inferior races', and, by a process of amalgamation and intermarriage, 'to have considerably raised the position of such tribes' (Campbell, n.d., p.8).

'nationhood' and republican polity. (This includes people he calls 'predatory' such as Kallars and Maravas in the poligar country, so he is not offering a simplistic two-fold classification of caste 'Hindus' and casteless so-called 'tribals') (pp.112-3).

The five other groups in Elliot's Dravidian taxonomy are also analysed on the basis of these politically-defined moral qualities. Group 2 includes what he calls the 'barbarous tribe' of Konds (p.96) who live in more remote areas than the people in his Group 1 classification. This, he says, allowed the Konds and other members of this group 'to retain their nationality' (p.95). Group 3 sounds very different: they comprise the 'servile classes who have been reduced to slavery, and attached as cultivators to the soil' (95). But Elliot applies his ethnological religious test to the two groups, and decides that Group 2 (who include the Konds) and Group 3 (Paraiyans, Holeyas, Chamars and other 'slave' groups) are ethnologically identical, while Group 1 represents a completely separate 'type'.

This claim is based primarily on the Konds' supposed predilection for human sacrifice. Lurid reports about the 'barbarous' Konds were widely circulated in this period in missionary journals and contemporary travel literature. For Elliot, Kond sacrifice constituted a 'primitive' version of the rites of buffalo sacrifice which he said were central to the religious life of the 'servile classes' of Group 3 (pp.96-102).[26] Thus according to Elliot, the 'servile' Chamars and Paraiyans and the forest-dwelling Konds were all descendants of a single 'aboriginal race' (p.103) who followed the same bloody sacrificial religion, but who had diverged historically. The majority were 'reduced to slavery' by more powerful and 'civilised' ruling groups and, presumably, lost their conscious sense of 'nationality'. The others, who became the 'free' Konds of the forests, kept their sense of shared 'nationality', and retained until comparatively recent times their original 'barbarous' rites of human sacrifice, now being 'abolished' under

[26] Elliot's account of the buffalo sacrifice—with its portrayals of men 'of good caste' rolling in 'putrid gore' (pp.97-100) is comparable to Bishop Whitehead's better-known diatribe against the supposed horrors of south Indian religion (Whitehead, 1921).

the humane influence of British social reformers (p.96).[27]

For Elliot the apparent differences between the 'free' forest Konds (Group 2), and the 'slaves' of Group 3—including the Tamil-speaking Paraiyans and the Holeyeas of the Kannada country—disguise an underlying racial unity which can be 'proved' by the ethnologist, and which also links these people by race and origin to groups such as the North Indian Chamars. Thus Elliot does not refer to these people in terms of Brahmanical concepts of low rank or ritual pollution. Instead, members of this 'great and numerous race' (p.103) all have 'tolerably similar' physical characteristics. The Kond and the 'Paria' are 'rather below...the middle height... In disposition they are lively, impulsive, somewhat irascible and noisy, but good-humoured; industrious when engaged in work, but ready...to enjoy idleness and amusement' (p.102). And it is clear why they cannot be placed in the same category as the truth-telling, drum-beating Santal 'nation': 'They are greatly addicted to drunkenness, and have little regard for truth' (p.102).

The same underlying distinction between political freedom and unfreedom shapes the rest of Elliot's classifications. His fourth group of South Indian peoples comprises what he calls both 'the predatory tribes' and 'the predatory classes' of South India (pp.95, 112). Because they supposedly worship 'Siva and Durga', rather than the 'primitive' deities of Groups 1 and 2, he thinks that these so-called 'predatory' people are descended from relatively recent, and presumably non-'Dravidian' migrants to South India, possibly 'Indo-Scythian invaders' who occupied North India and parts of the Deccan at the time of the ancient kings 'Kadphises' and 'Kanerki' (p.114). The chief ethnological characteristic of these 'predator' groups is that 'they still maintain a considerable degree of independence' (p.95), and he identifies them as 'a third well-defined race mixed with the general population' (p.112).

Here we have a striking manifestation of the Victorian theorists' fas-

[27] Campbell too portrays Indian history as a series of power struggles between peoples whom he defines ethnologically as free and unfree, 'civilised' and uncivilised: 'in every part of India...a Helot race exists under the free races ...not slaves, but politically and socially subject...'. These include the 'Chumars' of 'Hindostan', as well as others of 'non-Aryan' blood, such as south Indian Paraiyans, and 'Mhars' in Maharashtra (Campbell, 1869, p.139).

cination with people such as the Tamil Kallars and Maravas, the North Indian Gujars, and other so-called 'predator' groups and 'warlike' pastoralists who are described today as 'castes' within a ranked and integrated regional caste 'system'. To a modern observer, Elliot's Group 4 would seem to bundle together an even more unlikely collection of people than his other groups. He seems indifferent to the sort of distinctions that would now be made between 'caste' and 'tribal' names, on the one hand, and terms like 'poligar', on the other. 'Poligars' would now be thought of as holders of a political title denoting 'little kingship' in the warrior-ruled domains of pre-colonial South India. But for Elliot those classed as poligars are members of an important Indian racial group who have an ethnological identity of their own, and cannot be lumped in with agrarian populations possessing what are now thought of as conventional caste values. Furthermore this is another Indian 'race' which has members both in South India, and also amongst important groups of non-'Aryans' in North India, such as the 'turbulent' Kolis and Gujars.[28]

In the South...[the members of the 'predatory classes'] are called Poligars, and consist of the tribes of Marawars, Kallars, Bedars, Ramusis; and in the North are represented by the Kolis of Guzerat [sic], and the Gujars of the North-west Provinces. All of these present the same characters, physical and moral... (p.112).[29]

Again there is no reference to caste rank or Brahmanical theory. Instead, Elliot characterises these people in the same terms as early nineteenth-century writers who described the inherently 'warlike' and violent Kallars and Maravas extorting *kaval* dues from 'industrious' cultivators belonging to 'sturdy' South Indian peasant castes. Similar stereotypes of 'predatory' pastoral people as the natural enemies of the worthy 'settled' castes are a commonplace in accounts of the 1857

[28] Elliot was probably drawing on the work of John Shortt, another medic with ethnological interests, who served as Surgeon-General to the Madras Army and Superintendant of Vaccination for Madras; he described the Maravas as a 'low-caste tribe' and emphasised their traditions of pre-colonial warfare and kingdom-building (Shortt, 1867-9).

[29] Despite the inconsistencies in his use of the terms race, nation, tribe and caste, Elliot insists that none of his 'Dravidian' and 'Indo-Scythian' racial groups possess 'Aryan' blood or values.

Rebellion, which emphasise the depredations of innately 'refractory' and 'criminal' Gujars, against 'gallant' sedentary Jat villagers in the North-western Provinces.[30] For Elliot, these tensions too have a racial basis. The 'predatory classes'—'brave, athletic, warlike, addicted to robbery, and fond of the chase' (p.112)—will, 'unless thoroughly reformed', remain 'an element of danger in times of difficulty' (p.114). Their inherited racial qualities make them naturally inclined to an 'independent' way of life which is incompatible with what the Raj defines as 'good government' (p.113). But they have their own ethnological heritage of sovereignty as rulers of the former poligar chiefdoms, and if left in what Elliot thinks of as their native state, they remain natural foes of all external political authority (pp.112-4).[31]

Like other theorists who reached similar conclusions about the 'alien' nature of 'Aryan' or Brahmanical caste values in regions such as Bengal and the Punjab, Elliot insisted that his findings had great strategic significance. In the wake of the 1857 mutiny-rebellion, he argued that the 'simple', truth-telling, 'free' or 'casteless' peoples of South India should be recruited more widely into the army and administration, in preference to the now widely distrusted 'wily' North Indian Brahmans, and others of high 'Aryan' caste. Such people could be shown on ethnological grounds to be inherently risky as collaborators in imperial rule (Alavi, 1991). Arguing that the 'pre-Aryan' people of South India had already shown themselves to be more 'open' to Christianity, 'the surest road to civilisation', than other Indians (p.128), Elliot predicted

[30] On the 'rebel' Gujar and the 'gallant' Jat, see Stokes, 1986, pp.153-61. Elliot took this line about the 'turbulent' Gujars 'resuming' their customary 'rapacious instincts' during the 1857 Rebellion (Elliot, 1868-9, p.114). And compare Elliot's attempt to classify the ethnological traits of the 'predatory' Bhils, well known in colonial anthropology as the 'wildest' of all so-called forest 'tribes' (p.114) (Skaria, 1992).

[31] Elliot's fifth and sixth groups are the only ones identified with an 'Aryan' vocabulary of varna divisions and Brahmanical purity and hierarchy (Elliott, 1868-9, pp.59, 116, 124). His discussion of agrarian 'castes' such as Kammas and Reddis, 'now under Brahminical control' though still virile and soldierly in ethnological terms (p.116), is interesting for its insistence that south India's Brahmans are not of 'Aryan' blood but are descendants of 'proselytes' who were 'raised' to 'Brahman rank' during an ancient 'Aryan' campaign to 'reduce' and subordinate the rest of the population (p.123).

that these 'Dravidian' southerners would eventually establish themselves are 'the most assured supporters of the present state of things. The truthfulness, honesty, and bravery of some of the [Dravidian] races afford the best materials for useful administrators and faithful soldiers' (p.128).

Colonial power and racial 'regeneration'

Elliot was one of many Victorian theorists to argue that South India consisted primarily of 'races' who had been 'oppressed' for centuries by imposed Brahmanical notions of caste. To recognise this, and to follow its implications, would be to fulfil the duties of restoration or 'regeneration' which were cited in so many ethnological accounts of England's racial destiny, and her obligations to a kindred but 'debased' or 'degenerate' India.[32] This is clearly an early ethnological justification for official sponsorship of what would later be called the 'pre-Aryan' or 'non-Brahman' peoples of South India, as a prelude to the day when India would be 'made over to the rule of her own sons' (p.128).

Strikingly similar views appear in Hunter's more widely-known *Annals of Rural Bengal*. Hunter was an extraordinary stylist, and his ethnological portrait of Bengal is steeped in passion and high drama. Bengal for him was a living ethnological battleground shaped by titanic warfare between 'noble' 'Aryans' and rude 'aboriginal races'. The region's configurations of habitat and terrain mark the different evolutionary stages of this epic. The 'Beerbhoom highlands' were a 'theatre' of one of the great 'primitive struggles of Indian history' (p.3). These 'bracing' uplands comprised an 'ethnical frontier' between the descendants of 'tall', 'noble' invaders (p.90) and the 'inferior tribes', who were overrun in 'the primitive time' (p.90) by the bearers of an alien 'Aryan civilisation' (p.3). This imagined racial 'collision', and the

[32] 'The larger acquaintance we are obtaining of the pre-Aryan population, ought to have an important bearing on the destinies of our Indian empire. It is an imperative duty to elevate these long-oppressed races, to enable them to assume their just position in the regeneration of their country...if treated with justice...now...[these 'neglected people'] may acquire equal celebrity [with their princely ancestors] in the future history of their own country, when India is made over to the rule of her own sons' (ibid., p.128).

picturesque terrain in which it occurred, are described with a naive excitement that combines the romantic's enthusiasm for 'noble scenery' (p.2) and 'heroic' peoples, with a celebration of scientific discovery, especially geology as a pioneering counterpart of Victorian 'scientific' ethnology (p.109).

Reading Hunter's descriptions of this primordial race epic and its stark moral message, it is impossible to preserve the stereotype of the 'colonial' ethnographer as a prosaic compiler of statistics and census tables. Of course Hunter can be seen in the familiar guise of the 'orientalist' treating India as a mute anthropological showcase, to be arranged and interpreted by the trained observer (Pinney, 1990). But far from serving as a static display of conventional 'caste' relationships, Bengal's 'specimens' provide Hunter with a picture of grim, degenerative racial catastrophe. His understanding of Bengal's race history thus confirmed widely-held ethnological convictions about the consequences of forming a racial 'composite' through the merging of people from separate racial 'stock' and 'very unequal degrees of civilisation' (p.89) (Knox, 1863).

According to Hunter, 'Our earliest glimpses of the human family in India disclose two tribes of widely different origin, struggling for the mastery' (Hunter, 1897, pp.89-90). The incoming Aryans 'came of a conquering stock' and were 'imbued' with 'that high sense of nationality which burns in the hearts of a people who believe themselves the depositary of a divine revelation' (p.90). Hunter shares Elliot's vision of superior 'race qualities', pitted in an invisible war against 'savagery' and 'corrupting' ethnological forces (Hunter, p.134). In Bengal, the once-noble Aryan conquerors became degenerate, he says, contaminating their 'enlightened' faith with 'degrading superstitions' derived from what he called, revoltingly, the 'squat black [aboriginal] races' (p.98). These views about the supposed perniciousness of inter-racial contact were shared by ethnological generalisers like Robert Knox, who proclaimed the 'mysterious unextinguishable dislike of race to race' (Knox, 1863, p.248), and uttered wild jeremiads against what they called racial 'hybridisation'.[33]

[33] Thus in the Americas, particularly in Mexico, 'unequal' racial mixing be-

Hunter insisted that Indian caste had been misperceived as a static, ancient system dividing all Indians into the all-encompassing varnas of classic Indological theory (pp.96-7). Caste for him was quite different—a 'cruel' (p.101) but diverse and regionally specific creation of relatively recent *race* history. He argues that caste appears in India in two distinct forms. First, caste in its 'true' sense was a creation of the Aryan 'race' in Gangetic upper India. Hunter's account of these Aryan 'invaders' in their 'fatherland', the Gangetic plain (p.105), is an ethnological recapitulation of the early orientalists. Europe and 'Aryan' India were linked by powerful bonds of racial kinship. The same 'prolific race' founded the great dynasties of ancient Persia and central Asia. Other Aryans had made their mark as early colonisers of Europe, and 'Aryan speech' was 'now conquering for itself the forests of the New World, and carrying Indo-Germanic culture to island empires in the Southern Ocean' (p.91).[34]

So what was the sad fate of Europe's 'Aryan' kin in India? In its early pristine state, when the 'Indo-Aryan race' (p.92) was still a strong, 'fresh' and virile 'confederacy of fighting tribes' (p.104), the Aryans' 'national mind' (p.117) had attained spiritual insights which foreshadowed the 'truth' of Christian revelation (p.113).[35] It was in comparatively recent times, Hunter claims, that this enlightened Aryan faith 'degenerated' into the 'degrading superstitions' of contemporary Hinduism (p.127). Having established their dominion in the Gangetic plain, the original Aryan 'fighting tribes' gradually 'subsided' into soft degeneracy, becoming a society of 'mild-eyed philosophers' strolling aimlessly in their mango groves, creating pointlessly elaborate rituals

---

tween settlers and 'inferior' indigenes had produced 'a 'worthless rabble' of mulatto 'hybrids', 'proving' that when 'advanced' races migrate and mix with 'savages', they 'alter', 'deteriorate' and 'wither away' (Knox, 1863, pp.247-53).

[34] For Hunter, 'The history of the ancient world, as understood by classical scholars, is the history of a few Aryan settlements on the shores of the Mediterranean; and that wide term, modern civilisation, merely means the civilisation of the Western families of the same race' (Hunter, 1897, p.91).

[35] They also possessed a more 'profound' conception of 'man's destiny' than the comparatively 'uninspired' philosophers of Greece and Rome (ibid., pp. 122-3).

and wrangling over empty points of sectarian doctrine (p.97). This, for Hunter, was the counter-evolutionary development that produced 'caste' in its 'true' Aryan form, that is as a 'national code', 'disfiguring' the strengths of unified Aryan 'nationhood' and 'ruining' the 'Sanskrit people' (pp.93-5).

In sharp contrast to this is Hunter's account of caste in Bengal. Here, says, Hunter, what Europeans described as caste had been confused with caste in the 'true' form created by hegemonic 'Aryans' in upper India. Society in Bengal had been 'deformed' by something even more pernicious than caste in its Gangetic form. What was called caste in Bengal represented the opposition of 'high' and 'low' races, the 'conquerors and the conquered'. It did not represent 'social distinctions between various ranks of the same [superior] people', as in 'Aryan' upper India, but 'distinctions between too widely diverse and long hostile races' (p.111).[36] For Bengal, measurements of rank expressing criteria of ritual purity and pollution could be explained in evolutionary racial terms. The rules of a high 'caste' lifestyle such as vegetarianism reflect the 'higher' race's deep-seated abhorrence for the 'black-skinned, human-sacrificing, flesh-eating forest tribes' (pp.131-4). Bengalis, he says, reacted to the collision of radically discordant racial 'unequals' by producing an extreme ideology of stratification.[37]

[36] In Bengal, as in Rajasthan, Kashmir and other regions outside 'Aryan'-dominated Gangetic India, Hunter saw caste in the form of the 'Brahmanised' four-fold varna scheme as a late and alien importation (ibid., pp.100-2). There had been 'fierce religious warfare' when 'Brahmanised Hindus' had tried to 'force' their 'fellow-countrymen' to accept their 'system' (p.103) and so 'the rigid four-fold classification of society laid down by Manu' is still 'practically unknown' in some areas, as in lower Bengal (p.108).

[37] The Aryans 'deeply felt that repugnance which the white man everywhere entertains to the black' (ibid., p.114). These views reflected 'progressive' and 'scientific' thought until well into the twentieth century. Hunter defined Bengal's social divisions as an 'ethnical compromise' rationalising the population's ethnological plight. Modern Bengalis were a 'composite people' who had 'evolved from two stocks' (p.89) representing the 'highest and the lowest types of humankind' (p.88). The 'Aryan invaders' 'assumed the the rank of Brahmans' (p.111) and ranked their 'inferiors' according to measurements of the 'purity' or 'impurity' of their racial identity. The 'tribes' of the 'aboriginal' population were thus inevitably placed below the 'tall olive-coloured Brahman', conscious of 'pure' 'Aryan' descent (p.134).

Surprisingly, perhaps, Hunter decided that Bengal and 'Aryan' India in general were ripe for what he called 'regeneration'. This theme receives two different treatments in Hunter's work. Like Elliot, Hunter celebrated the inherent 'nationhood' of dynamic non-'Aryan' hill people, in particular the Santals. He too drew ethnological conclusions from the so-called 1851 rebellion in which Santal 'rebels' supposedly displayed distinctive racial qualities of valour and 'nationality'. For Hunter the Santals were 'a distinct ethnical entity' among Bengal's 'aboriginal races' (p.147), part of the sizeable 'tribal' population which had 'preserved their primitive descent intact' (p.140). Their hardy physiology and low foreheads indicated that they were a race 'created to labour rather than to think' (p.146), and Hunter's account contains all the familiar stereotypes of the 'feckless', 'simple' tribal with his 'happy disposition', his 'sociability' (p.215), and his freedom from 'cringing' (p.126). The 'ignorant and honest' Santal therefore presents a stark ethnological contrast to the devious, 'keen and unscrupulous' Hindu of the wider society (p.228). Hunter denounces the Bengal authorities for allowing Hindu traders to dispossess the Santals of lands which they had been encouraged to settle from the early nineteenth century, as part of the policy of 'pacifying' other 'warlike' tribes of the northern Rajmahal hills (pp.220-9; see Alavi, 1992). The 'revolt' was therefore an assertion of race: British officials had failed to read the signals emitted by people whom they should have cherished as valuable intermediaries between the 'lawless and savage' lower 'tribals' of the Rajmahal region, and the 'timid' Hindu plains-dwellers who had hitherto failed to 'civilise' and cultivate a domain of wild tribal 'predators' (Hunter, 1897, p.222).

As in Elliot's appeal for patronage and recruitment of South India's vigorous 'nationalities' Hunter proclaims his ethnological vision of partnership between the colonial state, and non-'Aryan' groups possessing strong, dynamic 'nationality'. Throughout east Bengal, he says, Santals and other 'hill-men' may be found, 'living apart from the Hindus, and preserving their national customs...' (p.226). 'Patient of labour, at home with nature', as pioneer cultivators and seasonal indigo-workers, such people 'furnish the sinews by which English enterprise is carried on in Eastern Bengal' (p.227). This, then, for Hunter, is a worthy race that was driven only temporarily into rebellion: on ethnological grounds, he saw ample scope for 'regeneration' and thus healthy strategic and economic bonds between the British and the Santal 'nation'.

These theories of inherent 'tribal' nationality would seem to contradict Hunter's second vision of regeneration, expressed with equal fervour elsewhere in the work. Although this is hard to reconcile with his vision of racial collaboration with non-'Aryan' Santals, he argues the Bengali Hindus and 'Aryans' in general were also ripe for 'regeneration'. Unlike England, which was thought to have evolved as a 'nation' from a much more favourable amalgam of Celts, incoming Teutons and other compatible races, Aryan India had for Hunter been retarded in its move towards 'national advancement' because of this history of unfavourable racial mixing (p.139). 'Two races, the one consisting of masters, the other of slaves, are not easily welded into a single nationality' (p.136). But although stagnant, 'effeminated by long sloth' and therefore vulnerable to conquest by their 'Tartar' and 'Mughal' racial 'inferiors', India's Aryans were still of 'noble stock' like their British colonial rulers (p.139). Therefore under enlightened British government, they could be 'regenerated' and helped to recover their old ennobling vision of nationhood. In due course, India would overcome the debilitating fragmentation which had manifested itself for Hunter in the atomising ideology which other theorists had misleadingly called 'caste'. Nationhood would then be reborn in India (p.140).

This picture of a 'weak' divided India subdued by her inferiors will be familiar to Indianists as a theme uniting an otherwise disparate array of Hindu revivalists, Gandhian nationalists and Muslim separatists by the early twentieth century. Thus although it has been usual to think of Third World nationalism, especially in India, as deriving from the liberal, secular traditions of Western constitutional politics, it is important to recognise how powerfully ethnological concepts of race appealed to spokesmen for nationalist organisations in India, and indeed in many other parts of the colonial world. Consciously or not, and however divided on other matters, South Asian nationalists invoked ethnological themes in their visions of a recovery of Indian greatness through spiritual, physical and moral regeneration. The polemical writings of the Arya Samaj, for example, are steeped in ethnological principles. The Hindu revivalist concept of *Aryavarta*, the homeland of the true or pure Indian, has clear roots in an appropriated version of Western race theory (Jaffrelot, 1992).

Indeed, across a wide spectrum of nationalist thought, ethnology was attractive because it told Indians with the voice of modern science that they could take pride in a heritage of classical 'Aryan' civilisation. Race theory was therefore enlisted to 'prove' that India possessed a deep, authentic unity which could override its all-too-visible diversities of caste, language and region. For those nationalist leaders who were themselves men of high caste, this was an ideal way to claim affinity with all other Indians on the basis of eternal bonds of race, as a people of one blood, belonging to one great caste, not many. Thus what was thought of as a new progressive science could be used to oppose all those who still portrayed India as an atomised, caste-fettered society, unequipped for nationhood.

Ibbetson's counter-ethnology of the Punjab

Hunter's ethnological understanding of caste held the high ground in Indological theory until well into the twentieth century. His insistence on race as the paramount 'ethnographic fact' of Indian society echoed the preoccupations of Western social theorists whose concerns were quite remote from India or the imperial setting. Paradoxically, Hunter's vision of race as a universal force linking the history of India to the evolutionary struggles of 'Aryans' throughout the world, was also rooted in his local expertise. Thus his *Annals* in effect described two Bengals. One was Bengal as a mere backdrop to the epic of unending race conflict which to the ethnologist explained the evolutionary history of all mankind. The other was Bengal as a distinctive Indian milieu in which he as an Indianist sought to account for configurations of 'caste', race and tribe which were unique to Bengal, and which therefore allowed him to challenge the stereotypes of current pan-'Indian' caste theories.

Ibbetson, whose *Panjab Castes* was first published as part of the 1881 Panjab census, reached profoundly different conclusions from Hunter's. The deep gulf between these two theorists should dispel once and for all the notion of a uniform 'colonial' consensus on caste. Furthermore, there is a subtlety and historical dynamism in Ibbetson's account which should go far to undermine the myth of the cardboard colonial fact-grubber.[38]

The Punjab and North-West Frontier regions for Ibbetson were open societies where to be a 'Rajput' was not a matter of 'blood' or fixed ethnological fact, but a fluid representation of status as claimed by men of power. His interpretation of 'caste' was therefore based on distinctions of occupation and political resources, rather than concepts of higher or lower 'types' and 'races'. He insisted that the standing of different groups in a particular locality was governed by political considerations, that is the distinction between those who ruled and those who were politically 'subject' (Ibbetson, 1916, p.5).

Here then was another analyst who perceived Brahmans and Brahmanical standards of rank, purity and hierarchy as a marginal feature of the society, with only limited and intermittent significance to most people. Like Hunter, Ibbetson found that the corporate affinities and ranking schemes in 'his' region could not be made to fit the widespread 'popular' understanding of caste based on a theory of four fixed varnaṣ (pp.1-2). But unlike his contemporaries who denounced caste as a static 'Chinese show', 'fettering' the Indian spirit with its tyrannical rigidities, he foreshadows many modern theorists in his account of caste in the Punjab as 'unstable', prone to great variations from locality to locality, and undergoing continual subtle changes reflecting shifts in religious affiliation and ideology, as well as alterations in political and economic circumstances.

[38] Hunter and Ibbetson were in print at the same time, and Hunter's views had a second lease of life as a major source of Risley's racial theories of caste, as expounded in the influential 1901 census. Ibbetson did share some of Hunter's cherished ethnological principles. He regarded 'civilisation' as a universal given (Ibbetson, 1916, p.3) and accepted the supposed distinction between 'Aryan' and non-'Aryan' racial 'stock' in India (pp.3, 40). But he dismissed most of the premises of racial ethnology (pp.97-100) and made little use of the term 'race' in its evolutionary or biological sense.

Ibbetson was alert to debates amongst contemporary social theorists about the evolutionary advancement of humankind from 'primitive' to 'advanced' institutions (p.2). In proposing occupation (rather than race or Hindu religious ideology) as the basis of caste, he cites the findings of 'modern authorities' who theorised an evolutionary path from 'primitive' societies bound by ties of blood and kinship, to more 'advanced' societies in which the individual's 'calling' comes to take precedence over considerations of 'descent' (p.3). He does hark back to the orientalist cliché of an ancient 'priest-ridden' Aryan society to explain why contemporary India had supposedly failed to follow this 'rule' of human evolution. But for Ibbetson the supposed Brahman alliance with Aryan kings explains why India retained a supposedly archaic understanding of occupation as an inherited form of identity, even though the society had otherwise reached an 'advanced' stage of evolution and should therefore have lost this 'primitive' link between 'community of blood' and 'community of occupation' (p.3; Kuper, 1988).[39]

This is no simplistic evangelical caricature of crafty Brahman law-givers foisting caste on their tyrannised inferiors. Ibbetson has a more subtle notion of Brahmans 'almost unconsciously' evolving teachings that sustained their claims of inherited ritual supremacy. This slowed but did not stop the 'separation' of 'occupation' from 'descent'. India was thus the scene of an exceptional development in human evolution, that is the application of religious sanctions to a principle of hereditary occupation which existed in a secular form in all 'primitive' societies. For Ibbetson this explains the creation of 'that tangled web of caste restrictions and distinctions, of ceremonial obligations, and of artificial purity and impurity' which collectively constitute 'what we know as caste' (Ibbetson, 1916, p.4). What he thinks of as the 'strictness' of 'Brahmanical teaching' which rigidified a more open and flexible

[39] The 'special circumstances' of India's evolutionary stalemate were thus the powers supposedly granted to Brahmans by Aryan kings, allowing the Brahman to 'exalt his office' and 'degrade' all other 'conditions and occupations of life' (ibid., p.3). Eventually Brahmans became too numerous to remain a 'priestly' occupational group. They 'ceased to be wholly priests' and 'a large proportion of them became mere Levites' (p.4).

tradition of occupational movement within this structure of 'caste', was a comparatively modern development. This modification of earlier forms appeared in the 'dark ages' of Hindu history when 'Brahminism' was substituted for 'Hinduism', and the religion became 'a chaos of impure and degraded doctrine and sectarian teaching' (p.4).

Although some of this echoes the standard 'colonial' clichés about lascivious Brahmans and 'degraded' Hindu 'ritualism', Ibbetson's historical speculations produce a dramatically different understanding of caste from those of earlier analysts. For Ibbetson the Punjab was a society in which the aspiring theorist of caste had to explain the distinctively non-'castelike' features of much of the rural population. What he called the 'upper or yeomen classes' of landowners, cultivators and pastoralists, who constituted as much as half the Punjab population (pp.5, 26), were open and flexible in their deployment of 'caste' names such as Rajput, Jat, Meo, Gujar and Thakur. To him these titles signalled distinctions of political power which were fluid and variable, not closed units of hierarchical 'caste' identity. Furthermore, unlike many 'colonial' theorists, Ibbetson insisted on a portrayal of 'caste' that included Sikhs and Muslims, who together nearly outnumbered Hindus in the Punjab. It is one of the strengths of his analysis that he refuses to treat as simplified 'hangovers' from 'Hinduism', the paradox of supposedly 'casteless' egalitarian Muslims identifying themselves as Rajputs (as well as Saiyids, Qureshis and 'Arabs'), or of Sikhs retaining a consciousness of Jat, Khattri or 'untouchable' identities.

Ibbetson's Punjab landed people are anything but passive, tyrannised victims of received 'Brahmanical' orthodoxies. 'Caste' as a Brahman's vision of the world, a vision emphasising rank, purity and what he calls 'artificial' criteria of lifestyle, is a known reference point to which these rural 'yeomen' may or may not defer. This depended in part on whether they lived in the Sikh-influenced central regions and Muslim-dominated western plains and Salt Range, where Brahmans were few and marginal to the political order, or in the plains east of Lahore where the Brahman-centred ideal had assumed greater importance (pp.5-6, 11). (These 'artificial' criteria of lifestyle include practices defining 'high-caste' status such as vegetarianism, the seclusion of women and prohibitions on widow-remarriage.)

In this sense 'caste' was not just a reflection of regional political culture, but also a measurement reflecting the external realities of territorial power and resources. A kin group might choose to disregard the expensive and 'irksome' rules of the high-caste Brahmanical lifestyle, even though it had acquired sufficient control of land and manpower for its members to follow this lifestyle if they wished, and thus claim high 'caste' rank (pp.5-6).[40]

Thus 'tribe' for Ibbetson is the universal fact of rural life in the Punjab, not 'caste' (p.31). His 'upper or yeomen' people define themselves first and foremost as holders of 'more or less compact' agrarian territories: these are the basis of their shared 'tribal' affiliation (p.5). He regards 'tribal' affiliations like 'Chauhan', 'Sial' and 'Punwar', which relate to the factual and visible realities of power and land control, as being 'far more permanent and indestructible' (p.16) than the open and variable measurements of status embodied in the use of 'caste' titles like Jat or Rajput.[41]

Again the analysis seems astoundingly sophisticated if one thinks of Victorian ethnographers as crude empiricists unreflectively labelling and ranking all Indians by 'caste', 'tribe' or 'race'. Ibbetson spoke for a wide range of scholar-administrators with experience of village-level revenue administration and military recruitment. These men thought of caste in historical terms which emphasised not ethnology, but the complex links between indigenous political power and the fluid dynamics of status and office. Thus Ibbetson quotes a report by a district settlement officer, Lyall, who describes chiefs and kings as 'the fountain of honour' in the Punjab hills. It was the raja who 'promoted'

[40] 'There is the widest distinction between the dominant and the subject tribes; and a tribe which has acquired political independence in one part of the country, will there enjoy a position in the ranks of caste which is denied it in tracts where it occupies a subordinate position' (ibid., p.5).

[41] 'Barar' and 'Sidhu' are 'tribal' names used by those we would call 'Jat' by caste. A further refinement is that the localised territorial units Ibbetson calls 'tribes' amongst these rural 'yeomen' groups are not static: he describes a complex process of continuous tribe formation as smaller kin-based groups separate off from the 'parent' tribe and form new territorial units (ibid., pp.17-18).

tribes and individuals to new or enhanced caste rank as 'Rathis', 'Thakurs' or 'Rajput'. He also quotes Campbell, who rejects any notion that Rajputs possess a fixed 'racial' or ethnological identity: 'there is no such things as a distinct Rajput stock.... In former times, before caste distinctions had become crystallised, any tribe or family whose ancestor ...rose to royal rank became in time Rajput' (p.7).

For Ibbetson the title 'Rajput' was not a measurement of superior 'Aryan' blood, but a reference to the indigenous 'occupational' facts of kingliness and power, and the bonds of affiliation and patronage through which a lord acknowledged the services of his retainers (p.7).[42] The 'process' of shifting and realigning 'caste' rank is 'going on daily around us', says Ibbetson (p.8). These complex reconfigurations register changes in religious ideology including the growing 'Islamisation' of many Punjab landholding 'tribes', as well as alterations of power and livelihood. In his account Muslims and Sikhs as well as Hindus were still moving back and forth among an array of fluid 'caste' designations which reflected the same standards of measurement, whether the group in question called itself by 'Hindu' titles such as Rajput and Jat, or more consciously 'Islamic' designations like Shaikh and Qureshi. Thus Ibbetson points to people of Chauhan 'tribe' in the Karnal region whose fathers were 'born Rajputs', but who had taken to weaving and had 'become Shekhs'. There were 'Wattu Rajputs' from the Sutlej region who were asserting Qureshi origin, and 'Rajput' tribes of the Salt Range claiming 'Mughal or Arab identity'.

> On the frontier the dependence upon occupation of what there most nearly corresponds with caste, as distinct from tribe, is notorious. A Machhi is a Machhi so long as he catches fish, and a Jat directly he lays hold of a plough. There are no Rajputs because there are not Rajas; and those who are notoriously of pure Rajput descent are Jats because they till the land (p.8).

For these areas Ibbetson also says that particular 'tribes' from the broad Jat-Rajput-Gujar continuum of 'caste', form up or reconfigure

[42] Cunningham's *History of the Sikhs* was another important source for him: 'In Sirsa...clans who were a few generations ago accounted Jat [are] now... generally classed as Rajputs, having meanwhile practised greater exclusiveness in matrimonial matters, and having abandoned widow remarriage...' (ibid., p.7).

themselves into more firmly defined caste-like groupings around the cults of the Punjab's innumerable Muslim *pirs* or cult saints (p.112). This suggests a striking parallel with South India, where over many centuries Islam manifested itself amongst pastoral and warrior groups such as the Kallar in the form of Muslim *pir* cults which provided a similar focus in the shaping of what we now call 'caste' (Bayly, 1989).

Thus for Ibbetson, the Punjab contains at least four distinct manifestations of 'caste', once again overturning the idea of the dim 'colonial' taxonomiser forcing all Indians into the same stereotyped jati or varna classifications. These four different forms of caste in Ibbetson's analysis may be summarised as follows: (1) caste as a bond of blood association; (2) caste as an homogenising designation for immigrants; (3) caste as a Brahmanical measurement of rank for those opting into the game of competitive status-marking; (4) caste as an occupational or trades-guild classification.

Under the first of these headings, Ibbetson discusses 'caste' amongst Muslims in the arid, pastoral west as the bond of blood and 'tribal association' that united what he called the 'ethnic or national castes'. The most prominent of these 'national castes' were the 'fanatical' Pathans and the 'fairly truthful' Baluchis (p.42). These he called 'the two great frontier races', but not in Hunter's sense of race (p.10).[43]

As in areas of strong Sikh influence, 'Brahmanical' criteria of caste lack authority in these Muslim-dominated areas, and so considerations of 'tribe' are paramount. New claimants to Shaikh or Saiyid rank are more readily assimilated amongst longer-standing holders of these titles, and '...the immediate question is, not is a man a Rajput or a Jat, but is he a Sial or a Chhadhar, a Janjua or a Manhas?' (p.10). In frontier areas dominated by these 'tribal' Muslims, he says, one also sees the form of caste which was summarised above under heading No.2. Here small colonies of 'foreigners' such as Kashmiri or Bengali immigrants to the region set aside the more complex gradations of caste which they may have observed at home. Once in the Punjab, they simply took on collective regional or communal designations which become their accepted 'caste' identities. These homogenising designations some-

[43] He is frankly dismissive of ethnological theorising (ibid., p.10).

times even lumped together all Hindus or all Sikhs amongst large populations of 'tribal' frontier people (p.12).

The next heading, No.3, relates to caste as the set of categories which refer to Brahmanical measurements of relative rank and status. Rajput, Jat and Gujar as well as Brahman and Banya are designations of caste in this form, and some (but not all) dominant 'tribes' opt into the game of competitive status-marking that gives these titles and designations their true significance. Thus 'the same tribe is known as Rajput in a tract where it has, and as Jat in a tract where it has not risen to political importance; but the tribal name, indicating a far stronger and more enduring bond than that of common caste, still remains to both' (p.17).

The fourth of Ibbetson's manifestations of 'caste' returns him to the primary occupational focus of his analysis. Caste in this form, which he calls the 'occupational' and 'trades-guild' types of caste (pp.12-13), is found amongst urban artisans, many of them Muslim, who use occupational titles like '*darzi*' (tailor) as caste-like designations, as well as Hindu 'menial' and 'artisan' groups including Chamars, Nais (barbers) and Chuhras (p.13). The impurity attaching to such people is a function of their 'occupations and habits', he says. All those in his broad rural 'yeomen' category would regard people like the Chamars as ritually polluting. But he makes the important observation that his dominant 'upper' agrarian groups would not apply the same precise calculations of hierarchy and ritual purity to measure distinctions between their fellow-landowners and cultivators, that is between Jats, Gujars, Ahirs and even Rajputs (p.25). This is the aspect of his analysis that would be attacked especially fiercely by a modern Dumontian. However the Punjab in this period clearly was a society of complex, contradictory or parallel values and status systems, with only some 'caste' relationships being measured by the 'religious' standards of pollution and purity. Here Ibbetson certainly was providing an accurate and subtle picture of contemporary social reality.[44]

[44] See also Ibbetson's account of the 'village community', in which he goes far beyond theorists of universal evolutionary laws and idealised free 'citizenries'. The supposedly all-pervading village community is not a feature of the

These subtleties inspire considerable confidence in Ibbetson's approach to the mapping of 'caste' and 'tribe'. He certainly does not deploy terms like 'Jat' as static and eternal 'caste' titles; he does not think that they have fixed universal meanings for the census-taker to record as established facts of ethnographic life for the entire population. He does refer to the 'great Jat race' (and, confusingly, the 'great Jat tribe'), as well as the Rajput, Pathan and Baluch 'races' (pp.26, 34). But the term 'race' is little more than a figure of speech in his analysis. Both Jat and Rajput are for him 'occupational' rather than precise 'ethnic' or 'ethnological' categories (pp.26, 100). Towards the west where Brahmanical criteria are least significant, 'Jat' is merely a designation for anyone who cultivates, and this can reflect quite rapid shifts in identity amongst descendants of what he calls polluting 'menials', that is Chamars or Chuhras (p.30).

Far from being 'separate wholes', or distinguishable descendants of different waves of 'Aryans' or 'Indo-Scythians', Jats and Rajputs for Ibbetson are a 'blend' whose ethnological antecedents are uncertain, and whose relationships in contemporary society raise 'social' rather than racial questions (p.100). People of this 'common stock' are therefore in a position to become known as Rajputs once they attain 'political importance'. By definition these are people who choose to assert themselves in caste terms, that is in terms which are those of a ranked, hierarchical model of precedence. To be a Rajput is to adhere to the known lordly lifestyle of the Rajput, that is to marry appropriately and avoid widow-remarriage so as to preserve blood purity, and to shun 'degrading occupations (p.100).

This is the logic of the key Rajput-Jat occupational distinction for Ibbetson. The Rajput male never labours and never touches the plough; his women are secluded. These are the characteristics which distinguish

Western Punjab, he says, where fields and pasture lands are shared out according to 'tribal' criteria of landholding, as one would expect amongst semi-nomadic peoples with a strong pastoral tradition (ibid., p.22). Where so-called 'true' village communities are found in their full 'vigorous perfection' to the south-east, he insists that they are not atomised 'republics' but components within well-defined 'tribal' units of territory which were recognised in Mughal revenue administration as *thapas* or linked groups of villages sharing traditions of common 'tribal' origin (p.23).

him from the 'sturdy', 'free', 'individualistic' Jat (p.102). But this is not Indological 'essentialism'. Ibbetson does not cite these markers of Jat and Rajput identity as fixed moral or ethnological endowments of some eternal 'Jat' and 'Rajput' race or caste. Instead, he insists on the widely varying uses and meanings attached to Jat, Rajput and other 'caste' titles across different regions of the Punjab. In the south-east amongst a largely Hindu population, Jat and Rajput can be seen as terms to be used in tandem, that is as counterparts in a social order where notions or rank and 'caste' hierarchy are clearly defined. Further west, on the lower Indus, Jat is a 'nondescript' term (p.105) applied much more broadly and imprecisely 'to a congeries of tribes, Jats proper, Rajputs, lower castes, and mongrels, who have no points in common save their Mahomedan religion, their agricultural occupation, and their subordinate position' (p.103).

Thus Jat can mean any 'agriculturalist', 'irrespective of his race', indeed all Punjabi-speakers amongst populations of powerful Pushtu-speaking Pathans (pp.105, 109). Ibbetson suggests that 'Jat' was applied historically by groups like the powerful Baluchis near the western frontier to designate anyone they conquered and subordinated who was not a Baluch, Saiyid or Pathan (p.105). This could include subordinate pastoral people such as 'graziers and herdsmen' (p.103). Indeed in much of the western plains the bulk of the agrarian population were pastoralists: to them, the semi-nomadic herding livelihood was the mark of respectable, manly, superior people. These were the people who called themselves Jats, while sedentary cultivating groups were designated by 'inferior' titles such as Arain and Mahtam (p.108). At the same time in the Sikh-dominated central Punjab, the 'Jat' was the familiar 'stalwart and independent husbandman' (p.103), but in this area the rise of the Sikh kingdom meant that 'the Rajput was overshadowed by the Jat', suggesting that the term was used on its own and without the eastern region's implied hierarchical opposition between common, rustic Jat and lordly superior Rajput (p.100; Westphal-Hellbusch, 1975).

Conclusion

The first aim of this paper has been to show that there are striking things to be learnt by looking comparatively at the so-called 'colonial' ethnography that is so often taken for granted by anthropologists and historians. There is astonishing diversity in the literature on Indian 'castes', 'tribes', 'races' and 'nations', and very little of it conforms to the familiar stereotypes about narrow, self-contained, so-called 'hegemonic' knowledge and data-collection. Much of this scholarship was not 'colonial' at all in the usual sense, being conceived as a *contribution* to broad debates in social theory and 'scientific' ethnology, rather than being focused solely on questions of how to 'know' and subjugate Indians as the ethnographic 'other'.

This literature was shaped by complex and rapidly changing debates about human 'race' and 'type'. So the second point to be made here is that so much is now being said about the flawed, demeaning or manipulative 'orientalist' construction of 'caste', that we have overlooked race, in its different intellectual manifestations, as a much more pervasive concept in the analysis of Indian society, until surprisingly recent times.

Racial analysis in its early linguistic and environmental form, with its emphasis on the heritage of primordial 'Aryan' law and polity, had been at the core of the confrontations between 'orientalists' and evangelicals. Early racial analysis also endowed subsequent generations of Western *and* Indian commentators with an understanding of 'freedom', 'tyranny' and 'degeneration' which turned on the supposed role of the Brahman in supposedly 'fettering' the free will of his oppressed 'inferiors'. By the mid- to late-nineteenth century, the new teachings of evolutionary racial ethnology made India an important source of data on the supposed transition from 'primitive' to 'advanced' political institutions in 'Aryan' Europe and its extra-European counterparts. This led scholar-officials with Indian expertise to call on a shifting melange of linguistic, physiological and institutional or moral markers, in their attempts to rank and class Indians in a much more detailed and 'scientific' fashion by 'race', 'type' and inherited political predisposition.

In this enterprise, evolutionary theories of 'civilisation', rather than a narrowly Indological concept of 'caste', defined notions of the Indian social order. Indeed all societies, including those of Europe as well as the non-Western world, were scrutinised for the ethnological story they could tell to the properly-informed scientific interpreter. This led some theorists, such as Hunter, to emphasise an 'Aryan' racial bond between Europeans or Britons and (some) Indians, and a mission of redemptive racial 'regeneration' on their behalf, rather than a static relationship of 'hegemonic' imperial mastery. For specialists who wished to map the ethnological distinctiveness of particular regions such as Bengal or the Punjab, continuing debates about the role of the Brahman were often quite separate from the analysis of 'caste'. These investigators addressed questions which distinguished between Brahmans as a supposedly corrupt priesthood or as subverters of public morality, and 'caste' as a 'cruel' and ethnologically destructive institution which was to be understood as a product of 'Aryan' law-givers or historic racial migrations and 'struggles for mastery'.

In the works of such disparate taxonomists as Elliot and Hunter, 'caste' was seen as a feature of life for some but not all Indians. In ethnological terms, caste was subsidiary to race, and Indians who displayed 'caste' values as opposed to the vigorous, 'virile', 'libertarian' qualities of 'free' nations and citizenries, were those who were racially predisposed to do so. For Ibbetson these ethnological principles were merely a point of departure in what became a far more 'modern' and sophisticated attempt to interpret indigenous classifications of kinship, power and precedence in the different regional settings of the Punjab.

The language and assumptions of the racial theorists is abhorrent to us today. But this must not blind us to the way in which concepts of race shaped the understanding of India and its regional societies. The theorists of race spoke for what was understood for over a century as the progressive, 'scientific', liberating vanguard of social theory and empirical ethnographic research. As such it had a powerful appeal not just for the scholar-officials who have shaped our modern understanding of Indian society and its interaction with colonial power, but also for the many Indians who contributed to learned journals and scholarly debate, and whose concepts of caste, race and national identity interacted in complex and dynamic ways with the changing orthodoxies of evolutionary race theory. Thus there were strong reasons for seeing how powerful this racial perspective has been in marking out the ways in which both Europeans and Indians understood and debated the nature of what we now call caste, and the identities of particular groups and individuals within widely varying schemes of 'caste', 'race', 'tribe' and 'nation'.

Bibliography

Alavi, S. (1991). 'North Indian Military Culture in Transition: c.1770-1830', unpublished PhD thesis, University of Cambridge.

Baker, C.J. and D.A. Washbrook (1975). *South India. Political institutions and Political Change 1880-1940* (Delhi).

Banton, M. and J. Harwood (1975). *The Race Concept* (Newton Abbot, London, and Vancouver).

Bayly, Susan (1989). *Saints, Goddesses and Kings. Muslims and Christians in South Indian Society* (Cambridge).

___ (1993). 'History and the fundamentalists: India after the Ayodhya crisis', *Bulletin of the American Academy of Arts and Sciences* 46, 7, pp.7.26.

Beddoe, John M.D. (1865-6). 'On the testimony of local phenomena in the west of England to the permanence of racial types', in *Memoirs of the Anthropological Society of London* ii (1865-7). pp.37-45.

Boas, F. (1934). 'Race', *Encyclopaedia of the Social Sciences* 13, pp.24-36 (London).

Broca, P. (1865). 'Instructions générales pour les recherches et observations anthropologiques', in *Mémoires de la société d'anthropologie de Paris* ii, pp.69-204.

Campbell, G. (1868-9). 'On the races of India as traced in existing tribes and castes', *Journal of the Ethnological Society of London*, (ns) i, pp.128-40.

__, (n.d.). *The Ethnology of India.*

Comaroff, J. and J. Comaroff (1992). *Ethnography and the Historical Imagination* (Boulder, San Francisco, Oxford).

Cunningham, J.D. (1849). *A History of the Sikhs* (London).

Deniker, J. (1900). *The Races of Man. An outline of anthropology and ethnography* (London) [The Contemporary Science Series, ed. Havelock Ellis].

Dirks, Nicholas (1989). 'The invention of caste: civil society in colonial India', *Social Analysis* 25 (September).

Elliot, H.M. (1869). *Memoirs of the History, Folklore and Distribution of the Races of the North Western Provinces of India* (first published 1844: revised and edited by John Beames, 2 vols, London).

Elliot, Walter (1868-9). 'On the characteristics of the population of central and southern India', *Journal of the Ethnological Society of London* (n.s.) i, pp.94-128.

Emmer, P. and R. Ross (1991). *Race and Racism in European Expansion* (Leiden).

Forbes, James (1813). *Oriental Memoirs* (4 vols., London).

Hunt, James (1863-4). 'On the negro's place in nature', *Memoirs of the Anthropological Society of London* i, pp.1-63.

Hunter, W.W. (1897). *Annals of Rural Bengal* (7th ed., London).

Huxley, T.H. (1868-9). 'Opening address', *Journal of the Ethnological Society of London* (ns) i, pp.89-93.

Ibbetson, Denzil (1916). *Panjab Castes* (Lahore).

Inden, Ronald (1990). *Imagining India* (Oxford).

Jaffrelot, C. (1992). 'The idea of the Hindu race in the writings of the 1920s-1930s' Hindu nationalist ideologues', paper presented to the SOAS Race workshop, 3-4 December 1992; see also in this volume.

Jones, William (1807a). Sixth Discourse, delivered 1789, *Asiatick Researches* ii (5th edn.), pp.43-66.

___ , (1807b). Eighth Discourse, delivered 1791, *Asiatick Researches* iii (5th edn.), pp.1-16.

Karve, Irawati (1948). *Anthropometric Measurements of the Marathas* (Poona).

Kasi Nath (1873). 'Khatris', *Indian Antiquary* (January), pp.26-8.

King, Christopher (1992). 'Images of virtue and vice', in K.W. Jones (ed.). *Religious Controversy in India* (Albany), pp.123-48.

Knox, Robert M.D. (1863). 'Ethnological inquiries and observations', *Anthropological Review* i, pp.246-63.

___, (1866). 'Race in legislation and political economy', *Anthropological Review* xiii, pp.113-35.

Kuper, Adam (1988). *The Invention of Primitive Society* (London and New York).

Marshall, P.J. and G. Williams (1982). *The Great Map of Mankind. British perceptions of the world in the age of enlightenment* (London).

McLane, J.R. (1977). *Indian Nationalism and the Early Congress* (Princeton).

Mitchell, Timothy (1988). *Colonizing Egypt* (Cambridge).

Nandy, Ashis (1983). *The Intimate Enemy* (Delhi).

Owen, Major Samuel R.I. (1865-6). 'On Hindu neology', *Memoirs of the Anthropological Society of London* ii, pp.202-15.

Pick, Daniel (1989). *Faces of Degeneration: a European disorder, c.1848-c.1918* (Cambridge).

Pike, L. Owen (1865-6). 'On the psychical characteristics of the English people', *Memoirs of the Anthropological Society of London* ii, pp.153-88.

Pinney, C. (1990). 'Colonial anthropology in the "laboratory of mankind"', in C. Bayly (ed.). *The Raj* (London), pp.252-63.

Prins, Gwyn (1980). *The Hidden Hippopotamus* (Cambridge).

Pruner F. (1847). *Aegypten's Naturgeschichte und Anthropologie* (Erlangen).

___ , (1868). 'D'observations microscopiques sur la chevelure', *Mémoires de la Société d'Anthropologie* (Paris) iii, pp.77-92.

Richardson, Captain David (1801). 'An account of the Bazeegurs, a sect commonly denominated Nuts', *Asiatick Researches* 7, pp.457-85.

Sahlins, M. (1985). *Islands of History* (Chicago and London).

Sherring, Rev. M.A. (1872). *Hindu Tribes and Castes as Represented in Benares* (London).

Shortt, John (1867-9). 'Habits and manners of the Maravar tribes of India'. *Memoirs of the Anthropological Society of London* iii, pp.201-15.

Singha, R. (1990). 'A Despotism of Law: British criminal justice and public authority in North India, 1771-1837', unpublished PhD thesis, University of Cambridge.

Skaria, A. (1992). 'A Forest Polity in Western India.The Dangs: 1800s-1920s', unpublished PhD thesis, University of Cambridge.

Stocking, G.W. (1968). *Race, Culture and Evolution* (New York).

Stokes, E.T. (1986). *The Peasant Armed* (Cambridge).

Thomas, Nicholas (1989). *Out of Time* (Cambridge).

___, (1990). *Marquesan Societies* (Cambridge).

Topinard, Paul (1878). *Anthropology* (trans.T.H. Bartley) (London).

Ward, William (1817-20). *A View of the History, Literature and Religion of the Hindus* (3rd. ed., 4 vols., London).

Westphal-Hellbusch, S. (1975). 'Changes in the meaning of ethnic names as exemplified by the Jat, Rabari, Bharvad and Charan', in L. Leshnik and G. Sontheimer (eds.). *Pastoralists and Nomads in South Asia* (Wiesbaden).

White, J. (1872). 'Khattris', *Indian Antiquary* (6 September), p.289.

Whitehead, H. (1921). *The Village Gods of South India* (2nd edn., Calcutta).

Chapter 7

RACE, CASTE, AND TRIBE IN CENTRAL INDIA: THE EARLY ORIGINS OF INDIAN ANTHROPOMETRY[1]

Crispin Bates

The year 1989 was the hundredth anniversary of the commencement of the very first ethnographic survey of India, and to celebrate this the government commissioned a new multi-volume survey of all of India's so-called tribes and castes. Despite a renewed emphasis on social and cultural indicators, often absent from the very first surveys, the work of physical anthropologists and the techniques of 'anthropometry', which indeed formed their basis, would not, it was said, necessarily be ignored. The only difference in methodology between the two surveys was that where the British drew a line and refused to include communities of less than 2,000 in number, the new survey would go down to the last 200; and, where cranial measurements were once the key indicator of differing racial type, this time blood groups may more often be preferred as the crucial indicator of physical difference.[2] Such contemporary concerns show that the concept of race has had a powerful effect on Indian scholars and academics.

But that is not to say that the idea of race is unique to contemporary India; indeed, there are ideas of difference, generalised to describe whole communities, that are to be found in a variety of ancient Indian

[1] Thanks are due to Clare Anderson, Nicholas Dirks, Ian Duffield, Jill Duffield, Jean-Claude Galey, Paul Nugent, Christopher Pinney and Peter Robb for their suggestions and comments on earlier drafts of this paper. The records of the Government of the Central Provinces of India referred to in this paper were consulted in the Madhya Pradesh Central Record Office in Nagpur and in the Central Secretariat in Bhopal, India. These archives are referred to as 'MPCRO' and 'BP' respectively. Use was also made of the British Library in London, the Bibliothèque Nationale in Paris, the Cambridge University Library, and the Scottish National Library in Edinburgh. 'IOR' refers to the India Office Records in the British Library, Oriental and India Office Collections; and 'NAI' to the National Archives of India in New Delhi.

[2] Personal interview with A.K. Danda, Deputy Director of the Anthropological Survey of India, Calcutta, February 1989.

texts. Moreover, in India today, amongst academics outside the government-run anthropological survey of India, there may be found a great variety of ways of thinking about cultural, social and political differences amongst Indian communities in the recent as well as the distant past. However, though at one level. the differing abstract ideas of intellectuals on the issue of race do not form a coherent unity, yet a unity of thinking on this issue is to be found in certain organs of the administration as well as amongst the wider population. The mode of thinking has been described as a 'colonial discourse'; and this discourse of race, arising from the period of European colonialism, has been called 'hegemonic'. It was so in the colonial period, despite the great variety of views amongst its practitioners, and the existence of many contemporary critics of nineteenth-century theories of race, because it nonetheless embodied a unity of form and substance: even those who disagreed with it were forced to accept its basic terms of reference. The discourse of race was also hegemonic in that it was universal in its application: colonisers as well as the colonised were classified in the nineteenth-century taxonomies of race, and even those unflatteringly described in such taxonomies were widely convinced of their validity and relevance. Not surprisingly Indian elites were seen to share features in common with their European masters: assets that could doubtlessly be enhanced with the aid of Western education and under the beneficence of British rule. Despite this, it was at the same time undoubtedly an 'orientalist' discourse in that, however universally the 'scientific' theories of race were applied, and no matter how much subtlety or variety might be described amongst the different species to be 'mapped' (or pinned, like butterflies) within the Indian subcontinent, there was always one uneluctable conclusion to be drawn: that the modern European (particularly the Briton) was superior to any other race, and that the degree of difference between the European and other races was simultaneously a measure of the backwardness of the 'subject' (or objectified) population. There was no vast conspiracy, no single conception of the relationship between race and caste, and much disinterested speculation amongst nineteenth-century scholars only indirectly related to the complex business of managing the British empire. Nevertheless, the nineteenth-century conception of 'race' has outlived its critics, and to this day remains fundamental to popular and even some academic conceptions of political, social and cultural difference, both in Britain and India. In this, like the 'science' of anthropology and so many others of the social sciences, it betrays its practical relevance to the political, if not technical, management of modern industrial society.

That the idea of race should be useful, however, does not also make it 'true', and we may in the present be moving towards a time in which the utility and relevance of nineteenth- and early twentieth-century conceptions of race and caste may be on the wane. Controversy in this regard has focused on the issues of positive discrimination and of 'reservation' both in India and in the United States. Amongst historians there has been a shift towards the study of polities and cultures and away from the study of caste and class—with as yet indeterminate effects. The concept of race, however, undoubtedly captured a moment in the history of Western thought, and its influence cannot be overestimated. Indeed the importance of racial theory in the social history of the past two centuries, and in particular in the history of European colonialism, is still underestimated, and India is still often seen to be immune to many of the prejudices and fashions that held sway in other colonial territories in the same period. But India is not unique, in that the conceptions of race, caste and tribe in South Asia have numerous analogues elsewhere in the colonial empires of the nineteenth century.

At the same time I would argue, perhaps more controversially, that there was nothing inevitable about the rise or hegemony of the conception of race with which we are all so familiar: intellectual fashions might at any time have taken a very different course, and it is in the unique relationships and in the transmission of ideas between a relatively small intellectual elite in America and Europe, and in the colonial administrations of Africa, the Middle East and Asia at this time, that we may find the origins of the modern conception of race. In this enterprise the 'laboratory' was not simply India, but the whole of humankind, and although the paradigm of the new science was elitist, both in India and the West, its epistemology had much in common with the 'sciences' in general, whilst its applications were not uniquely imperial but characteristic, much more generally, of the *modus operandi* of the modern, centralised, bureaucratic state.

The genesis of anthropometry

Xenophobia, or the fear of strangers and of the unknown, is a common feature in human society. When strangers are associated together as a group, it is also perhaps natural to assume that any individual will have all the characteristics imputed to that group. People often associate for reasons of culture, appearance, religion or belief. Some may believe that they are a 'chosen people' and superior to other groups of people. These views are all 'racism' of a sort, and are to be found in places at all times in history. Such ideas however must be clearly distinguished from what Philip Curtin has described as 'the full-blown pseudo-scientific racism' which dominated European thought from the 1840s until the middle of this century. The difference lay, as Curtin describes it, in that

> 'science', the body of knowledge rationally derived from empirical observation, then supported the proposition that race was one of the principal determinants of attitudes, endowments, capabilities and inherent tendencies among human beings. Race thus seemed to determine the course of human history.[3]

Whilst the Spanish and Portuguese had very early to form a view of the status of the New World populations, as a result of their experience of direct territorial control (the conclusion of the Catholic church being that the peoples did indeed have souls and were therefore worth at least the effort of conversion), for the British no systematic approach to the question was necessary until the nineteenth century. As a result, much of the early work on racial classification was undertaken by biologists beginning, most importantly, with the work of a Swede, Carolus Linnaeus. Linnaeus's *Systema Naturae*, published in 1735, elaborated the classical idea of a 'Great Chain of Being', according to which God (or Nature) had organised the world so that all living things could be

[3] Philip D. Curtin, *The Image of Africa: British ideas and action,1780-1850* (Madison, 1964), p.29.

classified and fitted into a hierarchy extending from man down to smallest insect. A common Biblical classification of the time was to describe the races of man as descendants of Ham, Shem and Japhet. Linnaeus broke from this by distinguishing four races deduced from growing European knowledge of the extra-European world. These were the Homo Americanus (described as obstinate, contented and free), Homo Europaeus (fickle, keen, inventive), Homo Asiaticus (grave, dignified, avaricious), and Homo Afer (cunning, lazy and careless). Other writers followed this line, with more varied distinctions, but probably the first to postulate measurable (and therefore verifiable) differences was the Dutchman, Pieter Camper (1722-1789). 'Camper's facial Angle', as it became known, was essentially a measure of prognathism, deduced from observation of the human head in profile, and measured by drawing a line from the meeting of the lips to the middle of the forehead, and another from the opening of the ear to the base. The angle between these two lines was then supposedly useful as a means of distinguishing and ranking the races of man, a bigger angle indicating a greater skull capacity and a greater intelligence, assumed to be normal among Europeans.[4]

Although Camper soon fell out of favour, largely because of the difficulty in taking such measurements, new measurements and assessments of racial difference were constantly sought, if only in an effort to make sense of the alarming differences in the habit and lifestyle of populations increasingly being encountered by Europeans in different parts of the world. Such differences were particularly important to adherents of 'polygenesis', a minority position at the time, which contradicted the conventional Biblical view of 'monogenesis', that there was a single creation of the human species and that subsequent variation was largely a product of culture and environment. A significant contribution to this debate in Britain in the late eighteenth century was Edward Long's *History of Jamaica*, published in 1774, an attempt to back up the polygenist perspective using technical (although wholly spurious) biological arguments. Long concluded that there were basic-

[4] Ibid., p.39.

ally three races: Europeans (and others like them), negroes and orang-utan, a view that was quickly harnessed in support of slavery, particularly in the United States. Charles White, an anti-slavery campaigner, disputed Long's views after examining various animal and human skulls and pointing out inconsistencies in his evidence. It was the German, S.T. von Sömmering, however, who first published comparative measurements of Africans and European anatomies, in 1785. Although von Soemmering pointed to numerous similarities, his work suggested the possibility of differences between the intelligence of the two races, which instantly confirmed the prejudices of polygenist theorists.[5]

Baron Cuvier (1769-1832) in Switzerland began to lay the foundations of the modern sciences of comparative anatomy and palæontology, but the evidence available to Cuvier on anatomical variations within the human species was still extremely limited, and his conclusions concerning cranial capacities, based on Sömmering, merely confirmed earlier racial chauvinisms. Others, such as the English physical anthropologist, James Cowles Prichard, with neither the tools nor data to work on, fell back on unmeasurable, aesthetic criteria to construct their theories. It was the science of phrenology, however, which first attempted to link culture and physical features, the science being pioneered by the Viennese, Franz Joseph Gall (1757-1828), who later moved to Paris, and by Gaspar Spunzheim (1774-1832) in Trier in Germany. Gall's six-volume study, *Sur l'origine des qualités modes et des facultées de l'homme et sur les conditions de leur manifestation* (Paris, 1822), was for many years a standard reference work; and there were soon several British practitioners, one of the earliest being George Combe, who was personally converted to the new science by Spunzheim. Combe's *Essays on Phrenology* were published in 1819, the first of many editions.[6]

In Britain, the work of Cuvier helped to undermine polygenesis and

[5] Ibid., pp.45-8.

[6] G. Combe, *Essays on Phrenology* (Edinburgh, 1819). The enlarged, American edition of this book appeared under the title, *A System of Phrenology*, in 1845.

was therefore of some assistance in the campaign against slavery. The campaign itself, however, never went so far as to suggest the *inequality* of the races of man; and, although in defence of slavery the pro-lobby used crude xenophobia and dwelt on the political and economic expediency of continuing the slave trade, it avoided as far as possible making use of the pseudo-science of racial theory. When the slave trade was finally abolished in 1807, of course, slavery was not, and there was nothing then to prevent the development of this field: no sympathetic lobby to dissuade biologists and physical anthropologists from using pseudo-scientific theory to argue the case for maintaining the subordination of already enslaved peoples in America, or elsewhere.

The so-called 'science' of anthropometry, as it became understood, was first devised by American polygenist anthropologists in the 1830s, possibly as part of a more general reaction against political developments across the Atlantic. Foremost amongst these writers was the Philadelphian physician, Samuel George Morton, who was influenced by Combe, and probably enjoyed a higher reputation than any other American scientist of his time. Together with the theoretician, Louis Agassiz, Morton provided a systematic justification for American slavery by arguing, in a series of articles, that the human races were entirely separate, created species. This endeavour was gratefully acknowledged, at Morton's death in 1851, by the *Charleston Medical Journal* which wrote: 'We of the South should consider him as our benefactor for aiding most materially in giving to the negro his true position as an inferior race.'[7] The evidential basis for Morton's arguments was his collection of skulls, reputed to be the largest in the world. These skulls he measured and assessed to arrive at a systematic ranking of human races according to mental capacity. Needless to say, the results of Morton's work, published in three massive volumes between 1839 and 1849, confirmed the whites as the most intelligent race, the American Indian as less intelligent, the Hindus as even less

[7] Stephen Jay Gould, *The Measure of Man* (New York, 1981), p.69. A detailed biography of Morton by Marc Swetlitz is also to be found in G. W. Stocking (ed.), *Bones, Bodies, Behaviour: essays on biological anthropology* (Wisconsin, 1988).

intelligent, and the negro as the stupidest of the lot. Apart from the incorrect association of bodily stature, cranial cavity and intelligence, implicit in this work, subsequent reassessment has shown that Morton consistently (though probably unintentionally), falsified his results. At the time, however, he was highly regarded, his only opponents being the biblically-motivated monogenists, who believed all races to be descended from Adam. Even the monogenists, however, were forced to agree that, even if of the same species, the African was an inferior variety—his degradation being a consequence of the tropical environment.

The publication of Darwin's *Origin of Species* in 1859 undermined the position of both monogenists and polygenists. But at the same time as affirming the essential unity of the human species, evolutionism allowed for the conception of far greater variety than had previously been thought feasible, by establishing extraordinarily long time-scales as the basis for human development. No longer was it thought that the negro's hair might straighten and his skin turn white after prolonged exposure to the more equable climate of the U.S.A.[8] The new orthodoxy established the negro as a related, but previous and probably inferior form of *homo sapiens,* placed halfway between the caucasian and the ape.

In support of this theory the developing science of anthropometry seemed to offer novel and certain proof. A pioneer of this technique was Paul Broca, a professor of clinical surgery, who founded the Anthropological Society of Paris in 1859. It was Broca's conviction that human races could be ranked on a linear scale of mental worth: 'it did not occur to him that human variation might be ramified and random rather than linear and hierarchical'.[9] And since he knew the order already, anthropometry in his hands became a search for characters that would display the correct ranking, rather than an exercise in raw empiricism.[10] Much of Broca's work was carried out

[8] Gould, *Measure of Man*, p.39.

[9] Ibid.

[10] See P. Broca, 'Sur le volume et la forme du cerveau suivant les individus et suivant les races'. *Bulletin Société d'Anthropologie Paris* 2 (1891) (Paris).

using patients in Parisian hospitals as his subjects, and his conclusions, unsurprisingly, were deeply misogynist as well as racist. One of his erstwhile students wrote:

> in the most intelligent races, as among the Parisians, there are a large number of women, whose brains are closer in size to those of gorillas than to the most developed male brains. This inferiority is so obvious that no one can contest it for a moment; only its degree is worth discussion.[11]

Professor Paul Topinard, Broca's chief disciple, explained this phenomenon as follows:

> the man who fights for two or more in the struggle for existence, who has all the responsibility and the cares of tomorrow, who is constantly active in combating the environment and human rivals, needs more brain than woman whom he must protect and nourish, than the sedentary woman, lacking any interior occupations, whose role is to raise children, love and be passive.[12]

Topinard himself acquired a reputation as one of the leading anthropologists of the second half of the nineteenth century, and it was naturally to his authority, and to his English contemporary, Sir William Flower, the Hunterian Professor of Comparative Anatomy and President of the Anthropological Institute (1883-85), that Indian ethnographers deferred in their efforts to quantify and codify the castes and tribes of India.

Colonial anthropology in India

The discourse surrounding the cognitive status of caste in India has a long history; it has been touched upon in a recent article by Rashmi Pant, as well as in the critiques of orientalist indology recently published by Bernard Cohn and Ronald Inden.[13] The earliest use of

[11] G. LeBon, 'Rechèrches anatomiques et mathematiques sur les lois des variations du volume du cerveau et sur leurs relations avec l'intelligence', *Revue d'Anthropologie*, 2nd series, 2 (1879) (Paris), pp.60-2; cited in Gould, *Measure of Man*, p.105.

[12] P. Topinard, 'Les poids de l'encéphale d'après les registres de Paul Broca', *Mémoires Société d'Anthropologie Paris*, 2nd series, 3, pp. 1-41; cited in Gould, *Measure of Man*, p.104. See also P. Topinard, *Anthropology* (London, 1878).

[13] B. Cohn, 'The command of language and the language of command', in R. Guha (ed.), *Subaltern Studies* IV (Oxford, 1985), pp.276-329; R. Inden, *Imagining India* (Oxford, 1990); R. Pant, 'The cognitive status of caste in colonial ethnography: a review of some literature on the North West Provinces and

caste as a basis for interpreting social and demographic data arose from British officials' concern to stamp out female infanticide, which they believed to be customary in western and northern India in the mid-nineteenth century.[14] Later the use of caste at an all-India scale to categorise the population according to occupation and social structure formed a more sophisticated basis for British attempts at social engineering. The criminalisation of certain tribes, for example, provided a means of controlling turbulent populations in the more inaccessible or 'lawless' parts of the subcontinent. According to these laws (most infamously the Criminal Tribes Act of 1871), tribes, such as the Maghyar Doms in Bihar, the Kunjurs or Khangars in Bundelkund and the Ramosi, Mang, Kaikari or Bowrie tribes in the Narmada valley, were described as habitually criminal, and adult male members of such groups forced to report weekly to the local police.[15] Other categories of caste such as moneylending, agricultural or 'martial' were used as a basis for legislation controlling land transfers, the grant of proprietary rights, and the regulation of rents, as well as a basis for distinguishing between the loyal and the disloyal, and for recruiting to the armed forces. Overall, the purpose of this process of categorisation and research was summed up by Denzil Ibbetson as follows:

Oudh', *Indian Economic and Social History Review* (hereafter *IESHR*) 24, 2 (1987), pp.145-62. See also N.B. Dirks, 'The invention of caste: civil society in colonial India', *Social Analysis* 25 (1989).

[14] The Rajputs, the caste believed to be most commonly practising female infanticide, were also those thought to be responsible for the reported incidents of sati (the self-immolation of Hindu widows). The nature of official enquiries into these two phenomena thus shared many features: see Lata Mani, 'Contentious traditions: the debate on sati in colonial India', in Kumkum Sangari and Sudesh Vaid (eds.), *Recasting Women: essays in colonial history* (Delhi, 1989). The campaign against infanticide is notable for marking the first introduction of birth-registration to the subcontinent.

[15] See E.J. Gunthorpe, *Notes on Criminal Tribes Residing in or Frequenting the Bombay Presidency, Berar and the Central Provinces* (Bombay, 1882); also G.W. Gayer, C.P. Police, *Lectures on some Criminal tribes* (V/27/161/16, IOR); A.E.M. Le Marchand, *A Guide to the Criminal Tribes of the Central Provinces* (V/27/161/15, IOR); and M. Kennedy, *The Criminal Classes in India* (Delhi, 1908; reprinted New Delhi, 1985). For a description of the notorious 1871 Criminal Tribes Act and its effects, see S. Nigam, 'Disciplining and policing the "criminals by birth"', parts 1 & 2, *IESHR*, 27, 2 and 3 (1990), pp.131-65 and 257-88.

Our ignorance of the customs and beliefs of the people among whom we dwell is surely in some respects a reproach to us; for not only does that ignorance deprive European science of material which it greatly needs, but it also involves a distinct loss of administrative power to ourselves.[16]

As early as 1841 a new ethnological questionnaire produced by the British Association for the Advancement of Science, based on one published by the Société Ethnologique in Paris, requested detailed descriptions of individual and family life, including the life cycle, details of language and measurements of the head. (The questionnaire was reprinted and enlarged in 1852.) However, such procedures, and particularly the measurement of heads, do not seem at first to have been widely used in India. The earliest forms of classification in the censuses of 1865, 1872 and 1881 were based instead on a Brahmanic theory of caste classification, with the population being divided into Brahmans, Kshatriyas, Vaishyas and Sudras. However, although this categorisation met with the approval of Sanskrit scholars and others well versed in the vedic myths, the simple four-fold varna categorisation neither corresponded to the relationships that existed in practice between the castes, nor served any particularly useful administrative purpose. The 1891 census was therefore based, instead, primarily on occupational criteria, the materialist evolutionary basis for this classification having been first laid down by J.C. Nesfield in a study of the castes of north India, and by Denzil Ibbetson in his introduction to the 1881 census of the Punjab.[17]

Ibbetson summarised the popular and currently received theory of caste as follows: (1) that caste is an institution of the Hindu religion, and wholly peculiar to that religion alone; (2) that it consists primarily of a fourfold classification of people in general under the heads of Brahman, Kshatriya, Vaishya, and Sudra; and (3) that caste is perpetual and immutable, and has been transmitted from generation to generation throughout the ages of Hindu history and myth without the possibility

[16] D.C.J. Ibbetson, *Report on the Census of Punjab, 1881*, vol.1 (Calcutta, 1883).

[17] Ibid.; and J.C. Nesfield, *Brief View of the Caste System of the N.W.P. and Oudh* (Allahabad, 1885).

of change. To each of these points Ibbetson believed there to be a convincing reply. Firstly, he argued, caste was more of a social than a religious institution, and conversion from Hinduism to Islam did not necessarily have the slightest effect upon caste. Secondly, he pointed out, there were Brahmans looked upon as outcasts by those who, under the fourfold classification, would be classed as Sudras; there was no such thing as a Vaishya; it was very doubtful that there was such as thing as a Kshatriya; and Sudra had no present significance save as a convenient term of abuse to apply to someone considered lower than oneself. Finally, Ibbetson concluded that nothing could be more variable and difficult to define than caste, and that

> the fact that a generation is descended from the ancestors of any given caste creates a presumption, and nothing more, that that generation also is of the same caste, a presumption liable to be defeated by an infinite variety of circumstances.

He went on to assert that castes were essentially guilds, and that a guild in its earliest form was nothing less than a tribe, based on common descent. A great many caste divisions or sub-caste units, such as *gotras*, he then argued, were essentially tribal in origin.

Ibbetson was an administrator of immense experience, who later went on to become one of the more successful Chief Commissioners of the Central Provinces, a member of the Viceroy's Council under Curzon and finally the Lieutenant Governor of the Punjab, but his classification of castes, however logical and useful it might have proven, lacked a 'scientific' basis, as well as completely neglecting the problem of status. Equally important was the unpopularity of J.C. Nesfield's uncompromising rejection of 'the modern doctrine which divides the population of India into Aryan and aboriginal', particularly his assertion that a stranger walking into the class rooms of the Sanskrit College at Benares 'would never dream of supposing' that the high-caste students of that exclusive institution (as Risley put it) 'were distinct in race and blood from the scavengers who swept the road'.

Ibbetson's theories are today still widely admired. His ideas were enlarged upon in particular by the Cambridge anthropologists, James Hutton (in the 1940s and 1950s) and Edmund Leach (in the 1960s and

1970s); and they have been cherished by successive generations of non-Marxist, non-Dumontian historians and anthropologists working in the classical British tradition of structural-functionalism, first established by Radcliffe Brown.[18] But, however popular his ideas may have been in certain academic circles in more recent times, they sat awkwardly in the period in which they were first formulated. Arguments such as those of Nesfield, although they were a logical extension of the Ibbetson view, offended Victorian common sense, as well as the social prejudice of the educated English and Indian. The answer to this lay in the revival of 'pseudo-scientific' racism and the importation of new European techniques of anthropometry and racial classification.

The early ethnography of Central Indian tribes

One of the first to exercise an interest in measuring skulls as a means of ethnic categorisation within India had been William Sleeman. Sleeman served as district commissioner of Narsinghpur in the Saugor and Narmada Valley territories in the 1820s, and in 1835, after a period as the magistrate in Jabalpur, capital of the territories, was appointed as General Superintendent of the operations for the 'Suppression of Thuggee'—the dacoit conspiracy which he claimed to have unearthed during his period of service in Jabalpur. Sleeman was convinced, as were many of his contemporaries, that criminality was an inherited tendency, and that the Thugs could be regarded as virtually a separate caste or tribe, being a closely-knit criminal conspiracy, with their own language, customs (including inter-marriage) and religious beliefs

[18] See, for example, J.H. Hutton, *Caste in India: its nature, function and origins* (Oxford, 1963, 4th edn.; first edn. published Cambridge, 1946), and S. Bayly in this volume. Edmund Leach's views on caste are succinctly expressed in E. Leach, 'Introduction: what should we mean by caste?' in *Aspects of Caste in South India, Ceylon and North-West Pakistan* (Cambridge, 1960). Leach suggests that caste might be regarded essentially as a benign division of labour designed to guarantee security of employment to the artisans and labouring class of the population—a naively harmonious view, little different from the description of English social structure to be found in the (now little- used) third verse of the hymn 'All things bright and beautiful' by Mrs. Alexander, in which class ('the rich man in his castle, the poor man at his gate') is seen as ordained by God as a field of influence for patronage and Christian charity, like *jajmani*, the binding forces of Anglican society.

(including worship of the goddess, Kali).[19]

Sleeman's interest in skulls was not unusual, as the study of phrenology was becoming increasingly popular at this time, with phrenological societies and museums being founded in a number of cities, including Edinburgh. One of the most famous was founded by George Combe, who published his influential *Essays on Phrenology* in 1819 and founded the Phrenological Society in Edinburgh in the following year. In 1822 Rammohan Roy sent a selection of twelve 'Hindoo crania' to be examined by Dr. George Paterson, a member of the society, whose findings, published in the society's journal, edited by Combe, pointed to the conspicuous development of 'acquisitiveness and secretiveness' in the Hindu.[20] Sleeman may well have been moved to inquire into the subject by such observations. In 1832, he received a request from a keen Scottish phrenologist, George Swinton (then a Chief Secretary to the Government in India), to assist Henry Spry, a young officer in the Bengal Medical Service stationed at Saugor. Spry forwarded seven of the skulls of convicted and executed Thugs, via Swinton, to Edinburgh for the purposes of study.[21] The skulls were

[19] W. Sleeman, *Ramaseeana, or A Vocabulary of the Peculiar Language used by the Thugs*... (Calcutta, 1836).

[20] Dr. George Murray Paterson, 'On the phrenology of Hindostan', *Transactions of the Phrenological Society* (Edinburgh, 1824), pp.430-48. 'How, then, is this greater cerebral development manifested by the mind of the Hindoo? I might answer this question in a very few words, by replying, that Hindoo is only another term for falsehood, and that love of money is his darling propensity' (ibid., p.443). Observations on the 'secretiveness' of the Hindu were incorporated into later editions of Combe's *Essays on Phrenology*: see G. Combe, *Elements of Phrenology* (9th edn., Edinburgh 1862), pp.75-7. Interestingly, the skull of Rammohan Roy himself was later studied by the Edinburgh phrenologists, following his death in Bristol in 1833. His skull was found to be larger than the average, thus accounting for his 'force and dignity of character'. This was very fortunate since, as Combe confessed, 'had the brain of Rammohun Roy been of diminutive size, the circumstances would have done more to extinguish Phrenology than the whole amount of misrepresentation and abuse which it has been doomed to endure': 'On the life, character, opinions and cerebral development of Raja Rammohun Roy', *Transactions of the Phrenological Society* VIII, XL (Edinburgh, 1834), pp.577-603.

[21] Skulls of blacks and aboriginals in Australia were commonly being collected for phrenological purposes by the late 1820s. See for example I. Duffield, 'The life and death of "Black" John Goff...', *Australian Journal of Politics and History* 22, 1 (1987), p.36. See also P. Fryer, *Staying Power: the*

accompanied by a paper from Spry, describing the occupation and characters of the Thugs. It was subsequently published in the *Transactions of the Phrenological Society*, together with remarks on the skulls themselves by Robert Cox. Not surprisingly, Cox's analysis of the skulls, all smaller than 'the European average', confirmed the interpretations suggested by Spry: it noted, amongst these specimens, an exaggeration of the 'organs of the animal propensities' (including secretiveness) by comparison with the 'organs of moral sentiments' (such as benevolence), and a reinforcement of the obvious propensity to 'Destructiveness and Acquisitiveness' through that 'Veneration and Love of Approbation' which apparently was a weakness of all 'Hindoos'. Taking his cue from Paterson, Cox also found the Thugs to exhibit the characteristics of 'Philoprogenitiveness and Adhesiveness' ('manifested in the Hindoos in the happiness they seem to feel when surrounded by their children...and in their frequent and ardent embraces'), as well as the 'usual' tendency of Hindus to jealousy, polygamy and 'unnatural desires'. Beyond such observations, however, there was little attempt at theorisation or detail.[22]

More sophisticated racial theories about Indian castes and tribes nonetheless developed rapidly in this period. In the late eighteenth century, Sir William Jones had first mooted the idea of a racial difference existing between northern and southern Indians, and between high and low castes, but his theories, particularly that of the so-called 'Aryan invasion', were only weakly supported by linguistic and archaeological evidence: they had not yet received any other 'scientific' proof, or achieved widespread popular acceptance.[23] By the 1830s,

---

history of black peoples in Britain (London, 1984), pp.167-71, for a description of early attempts at racial theorisation using phrenology in the U.K.

[22] Henry Harpur Spry, 'Some account of the gang-murderers of Central India, commonly called Thugs; accompanying the skulls of seven of them and remarks on the skulls and characters of the Thugs by Robert Cox', *Transactions of the Phrenological Society* VII, XL (Edinburgh, 1834), pp.577-603.

[23] Interestingly the scientific proof of the 'Aryan invasion' has still not been found, whilst the archæological and linguistic evidence for it has been seriously contested: see Colin Renfrew, *Archæology and Language: the puzzle of Indo-European origins* (London, 1987); also Léon Poliakov, *The Aryan Myth: a history of racist and nationalist ideas in Europe* (London, 1975).

although the fully-fledged discourse of Indian castes and tribes was not yet apparent, already observed differences of appearance were being recorded, largely in terms of the Brahmanical ideas then being applied. This period saw the contest between the scholarly and the reductive models of Indian society, publicly displayed in great debates between those whom contemporaries referred to as 'Orientalists' and Utilitarians. The latter increasingly monopolised decision-making positions in the East India Company. But, even amongst those not yet immediately party to these debates, an elemental form of racism had already developed, particularly concerning the tribals, the section of the population about which the British were least informed, and from which they felt they had most to fear. As Brahmanical theories of Indian society gradually became more widely accepted amongst British officials, so was the imagined 'tribal' increasingly reified as the natural antithesis of the Brahman. Not only did the 'tribal' or the 'Dravidian' provide the most obvious test-bed for theories of racial difference, but once the idea of separate races, had been accepted, then the degree of miscegenation between indigenous tribals and 'Aryan' Brahmans afforded an immediate, if intuitive, explanation for the proliferation of intermediate castes. Speculative observations of this sort were often first made in the jungle fastnesses of Central India.

The sanguinary nature of early contacts with the tribals, or adivasis, of Central India did not bode well for their future reputation. The first expedition into Bastar by Captain Blunt, in 1795, was attacked and expelled from the country. From this experience may be traced some of the more fearful accounts of the savagery of tribal Gonds.[24] The already-established reputations of the predatory Bhils of Gujarat and the rebellious Santhals and Kols of Bihar also served to colour the expectations of early travellers in Central India. Hindu informants often reported the adivasis there to be practitioners of human sacrifice, and this was widely believed, although no evidence of it was ever uncovered.[25] The density of the jungle and the prevalence of malaria also made

[24] J.T. Blunt, 'Narrative of a route from Chinargur to Yentragoodum, 1795', in *Early European Travellers in the Nagpur Territories* (Nagpur, 1930).

[25] Dr. Henry Spry firmly believed that in the 'wild and unreclaimed hill

any venture into the interior something to be greatly feared. Another early expedition, that of Alexander Elliot and four other officers, who attempted to march from Cuttack to Nagpur and thence to Hoshangabad, between 11 August and 9 December 1778, ended in the death of Elliot and three of his four companions. Only one member of the party, Thomas, actually made it to Hoshangabad, and on the return journey he was considerably harassed by tigers, robbers and 'a treacherous Naig' (sic).[26] In later expeditions, however, expectations were not always confirmed. The large number of Hindus, including Rajputs and 'agricultural Brahmans', resident in Chhattisgarh and the surrounding tracts, was noted with surprise; and the customs and practices of the Gonds were discovered to be not always as bizarre as had previously been described. One expedition of the early 1830s reported:

> It has been suspected by many that the Gonds do not scruple to perform human sacrifices and devour the flesh, but the Hindoo inhabitants whom we questioned exonerated them from the charge of cannibalism. The Gonds whom we met with, far from showing any symptoms of cannibalism, even abstain from beef. The lower classes have no objections to other kinds of animal food, although the chiefs and better sort of folk have adopted the prejudices of the Hindu in this respect.[27]

---

jungles' of central India '...they sacrifice and eat their fellow-creatures. The fact of their doing so is so well attested that there can be no doubt of its correctness'; H. Spry, *Modern India*, vol. II (London, 1837), p.138.

[26] NAI, Survey of India memoirs and field books: M320, Elliot Mission; M272, Route from Cuttack to Nagpur and thence to Hoosingabad, by Wm. Campbell, 1778; M163, Route from Nagpur to Cuttack, 1782, by Thomas (diary of events). See also C.U. Wills, *British Relations with the Nagpur State in the 18th centur* (Nagpur, 1926), which contains extensive quotations from survey records and embassies of this period.

[27] IOR (Map Room), Routes in the Central Provinces, MSS 36: Report on the route from Chunargarh to Amarkant by Lts. Waugh and Renny (1833). The belief that the Gonds practised human sacrifice was one of the most potent myths of this period. Although no evidence was ever found, the allegation was frequently repeated up and until the administration of Bastar came directly under the control of the British in 1911. The issues involved are discussed in C. Bates, '"The invention of perdition": human sacrifice and British relations with the Indian kingdom of Bastar in the 19th century', and 'Dasehra and revolt: problems of legitimacy in 20th-century Bastar', unpublished papers presented at the Centre d'Études de l'Inde et de l'Asie du Sud in the Maison des Sciences de l'Homme in Paris, April 1992.

Richard Jenkins, in his report on the Nagpur territories, formed the impression that while the wildest of the Gonds, the Murias of Bastar, engaged in human sacrifice, the majority of Gonds 'class themselves under the second cast [sic] of Hindoos'. This, he wrote, 'is a stretch of complaisance in the Marhatta [sic] officers, owing, probably, to the country having been so long under the Rajahs of the Gond tribe. They, however, term themselves Coetoor (a corruption of Khutriya)'.[28] This account, attributing Kshatriya status to the Gonds, almost certainly arose from Jenkins' encounter with the Gond Raja of Deogurh in Nagpur. He was a Hinduised 'Raj Gond', then still nominally sovereign over a large part of the Raja of Nagpur's territory, receiving a share of the state's revenues.[29] Jenkins' confusion well illustrates the uncertainty of many writers in this period, but his distinction, between more 'civilised' tribals and those 'others' of whom little was known but who were suspected of the most heinous savagery, is also to be found in the account written by Vans Agnew at this time, concerning the Subah or Province of Chhattisgarh:

> The only tribes I heard of that are peculiar to this part of India are the Kaonds. or inhabitants of Koandwana [Gondwana], Kakair [Kanker], and Bustar, and Binderwa and Pardeea casts found in the hills North-East of Ruttunpore.... The Koands are Hindoos and not particularly distinguished from the wild inhabitants of other jungles, except by the high character they are reputed to possess for veracity and fidelity.... The Binderwas reside in Hilly and Woody Country near Ruttunpore, particularly in the Koorba and Sirgooja Hills, and much resemble the wild savages who have been described as met with in other parts of India. They appear to be so seldom seen by the other inhabitants of the Country that there is much reason to doubt the truth of all that is reported respecting them. They are, however, said to have scarcely any religion; but if they regard any idol, Daby [Debi] has the preference. They go entirely naked; are armed with Bows and Arrows; never build any huts or seek other shelter than that afforded by the Jungles; but sometimes cultivate small quantities of

28 R. Jenkins, *Report on the Territories of the Rajah of Nagpore* (Calcutta, 1827), p.29. Jenkins also noted that 'the different tribes divide themselves, like their Hindu neighbours, into twelve and a half castes; and these, again, branch out into subdivisions, denominated according to the number of the Penates, or household gods' (p.30).

29 See ibid., p.140 et seq. Apparently the Gond rajah still gave the tika, or mark of royalty, to the Bhonsla princes on their accession to the *gadi* (or

the coarse grains; are said to destroy their relatives when too old to move about and to eat their flesh, when a great entertainment takes place to which all the family is invited. Their enemies, and the travellers they may slay, they are also said to eat. It is doubtful that they have the ceremony of marriage.[30]

Descriptions broadly in sympathy with those of Agnew are to be found in William Temple's *Report on the Zamindaris and other Petty Chieftaincies in the Central Provinces in 1863*, although in this and in other reports of the very first Chief Commissioner of the Central Provinces a tendency was shown to dwell on the economic potentialities rather than the savageries of the newly acquired territories.[31] Other accounts of the period continued the anecdotal-cum-scholarly ethnographic mode of enquiry, a good example being the *Papers Relating to the Aboriginal Tribes of the Central Provinces* by the Reverend Stephen Hislop, a missionary of the Free Church of Scotland, based in Nagpur. It was published posthumously in 1866. Hislop referred to the Gonds as a race, but his detailed description of them contains no anthropometric evidence and few descriptions of their physical characteristics. He expounds the theory that there are distinct races of 'Kolarian' and 'Dravidian' tribes, notes the similarities between Gondi and the Telugu and Tamil languages, and speculates that the 'Kolarian' tribes of the Satpura hills may be related to the Karens and other tribal peoples of Burma and Malaysia. Beyond that however he confines himself largely to his professional interests and to descriptions of Gond customs and religious beliefs, the information having been gleaned during his missionary activities with the assistance of a number of 'native Christian' informants.[32]

---

throne) and was entitled to put his seal on certain revenue papers.

[30] P. Vans Agnew, *Report on the Subah or Province of Chhattisgarh* (written in 1820, published Nagpur, 1920), p.5.

[31] For example Temple's extremely up-beat *Report on the River Godavery and its Feeders* (Nagpur, 1863). Reprints of both of these reports, made in the 1920s, are available in the MPCRO, Nagpur.

[32] R. Temple (ed.), *Papers relating to the Aboriginal Tribes of the Central Provinces Left in MSS by the Late Revd. Stephen Hislop* (Nagpur, 1866). In his introduction Hislop gives his characteristically paternalist view of the Gonds and other adivasis: 'There is much in the character of these tribes to attract British sympathies. They are honest and truth-telling; they are simple-minded; though superstitious, they are yet free from fanaticism; they have great physical

Thus, although notions of racial difference and of the distinctive characteristics of so-called 'castes' and 'tribes' were becoming established, no-one had yet attempted actually to measure, codify and standardise these differences in anything other than anecdotal or religious terms. The need for some such codification, however, was becoming pressingly obvious. A number of live specimens of Indian subjects were displayed at the Great Exhibition in London in 1851, and soon after this the Governor-General in India, Lord Canning, commissioned a large-scale photographic survey of *The People of India*, eventually to see the light of day in eight volumes published between 1868 and 1875.[33] At about the same time the Schlagintweit brothers were also commissioned to make a series of life-casts of Indian subjects, their survey of the interior of India and of the Himalayan region being completed between 1854 and 1858. A proposal by Dr. Joseph Frayer in 1867, that the Royal Asiatic Society of Bengal should set up a living ethnological exhibition, was apparently never acted upon.[34] But officials and part-time ethnologists in the Central Provinces were less inhibited. In 1866-67 an exhibition was held at Jabalpur, modelled on the Great Exhibition at Crystal Palace in 1851, at which live 'specimens' were displayed.

The Central Provinces had been seized from the Bhonsle Rajas of Nagpur in 1854 (according to the notorious policy of lapse), but, as the insurrection of 1857 had intervened shortly afterwards, an administrative system independent of that of the North-West Provinces was not properly established until 1861. The Jabalpur exhibition was thus the first real opportunity to take stock of this, the largest new territory to be acquired since the conquest of the Punjab in 1841. Samples of produce,

---

endurance. Their courage is remarkable; the instance is freshly remembered in the Chhindwara District, where an English officer was saved from instant death in the grip of a panther by the bravery of a Gond hunter: and still more recently, a wounded officer on the Godavery was rescued from the wild beasts by his native hunter' (p.vii). Less favourably though, Hislop himself recounts descriptions of human sacrifice elsewhere in the text (p.16).

[33] C. Pinney, 'Colonial anthropology in the "laboratory of mankind"', in C.A. Bayly (ed.), *The Raj* (London, 1991), p.252-63. See also John Falconer, 'Photography in the nineteenth century', ibid., pp.264-77.

[34] Pinney, 'Colonial anthropology', p.254.

archaeological finds and handicrafts were brought to Jabalpur from all over the Central Provinces, together with live examples of the various 'aboriginal tribes' that were judged to be characteristic of the different parts of the territory. The idea of having examples of aborigines at the exhibition was inspired by a circular of the Asiatic Society of Bengal in 1866, detailing information that was being sought by ethnologists concerning the aboriginal tribes of India. Using this memorandum as their model, an Ethnological Committee was then established under the chairmanship of A.C. Lyall, to examine the 'aboriginals'. Their findings were subsequently published. Excluded from the study were all 'races' or 'castes' which were judged to be immigrants to the territory. Also excluded were religious 'sects' such as the Satnamis and Kabirpanthis, and all 'manufacturing and trading classes', even if originating from tribal areas. Instead the focus was on the 'Inferior and Helot' tribes, the 'Wandering Tribes' such as as the 'Mangs', and (principally) the 'waifs and relics of aboriginal tribes' to be found in the thickly wooded hills in the heart of the Provinces. Following George Campbell's recently published ethnological paper,[35] the 'aboriginals' were divided into Kolarians (such as Kols, Bheels, Korkoos, and Bygahs) and Dravidians (such as Gonds, 'Hulba Gonds', Khonds, and Kois). The report provided the briefest of descriptions from respective divisional commissioners, the recording of manners and customs by interview, and a listing of the specimens' habitat, name, age, parentage, and sex. But, significantly, by far the bulk of the report was devoted to measurements: of height, length of upper arm, lower arm, thigh, and leg, breadth of chest and body, colour of skin, eyes, pupils, beard and moustache, length or other peculiarity of heel, any other physical peculiarities, and diet.[36]

[35] G. Campbell, *The Ethnology of India* (1865). Campbell was a civil commissioner in Awadh in the early 1860s, where he first acquired his reputation as a champion of tenants' rights. He went on to serve as Chief Commissioner of the Central Provinces from 1867 to 1868, and as Lieutenant-Governor of Bengal from 1871 to 1874. He was a regular contributor of ethnographic articles to the Calcutta-based *Journal of the Bengal Asiatic Society* and the *Quarterly Ethnological Journal.*

[36] *Report of the Ethnological Committee on Papers laid before them and upon examination of specimens of Aboriginal tribes brought to the Jubbulpore*

At the end of the exhibition, a museum was established at Nagpur to house the more important of the exhibits, including, reportedly, clay models of some of the 'aboriginals'.[37] But, despite the thoroughness of the work conducted by the Ethnological Committee, little said is about the results of their enquiry in the *Gazetteer of the Central Provinces*, written and edited by Charles Grant and published in 1870. Beyond noting that the Committee had concluded that there were 23 'certain' (13 Kolarian and 10 Dravidian) and six 'doubtful' aboriginal races, there is little reproduction of the anthropometric findings of the Committee. The bulk of the Gazetteer's introductory entry on aboriginals in fact relies on Hislop's and Campbell's racial speculations, with only a minimal leavening of descriptive observation. Grant observes that Kurkus are 'mostly black, with flat faces and high cheekbones', and that among the Baigas 'the purest of the race in the Eastern Forests of Mandla approach in feature to the aquiline Aryan type and as a rule...are above the Gonds in stature'. He writes of the 'savage straightforwardness of speech' of the 'Dhur-Gonds' at the very bottom of the Gond community, who nonetheless were still possessed of 'the stalwart limbs and contempt of fear, which are characteristic of the race... and render Gonds useful tools in employment'. Generally Grant is more interested in unquantified speculation about the date of the Aryan invasion and the persistence of 'serpent-worship' amongst the Gonds of Chhattisgarh. This is probably, as confessed in the preface to the volume, due to the Gazetteer's being largely completed before receipt of W.W. Hunter's famous circular commissioning the production of gazetteers for each and every province and district of the empire, a circular which laid particular stress on the need for careful empirical and statistical observation.[38]

Exhibition of 1866-67 (Nagpur, 1868).

[37] Clay models of central Indian 'aboriginal races' were also sent to the International Exhibition held in London in 1874. See MPCRO, Letters to the Govt. of India, 1874, No. 2265/97: J.W. Chisholm, Offg. Sec. to CCCP to GOI, Dept. Agri., Rev. and Commerce.

[38] C. Grant (ed.), *Gazetteer of the Central Provinces* (Nagpur, 1870), pp.cv-cxxvii. Grant's response to Hunter's circular was hurriedly to append a dozen pages of somewhat unreliable area, population and revenue statistics to the very end of his gazetteer.

The lack of precision seen in the first Gazetteer for the Central Prtovinces was, however, repeated again in the census of 1872. It was by far the least structured census ever conducted in the subcontinent and a printer's nightmare, since, rather than fit the population into predetermined categories, census takers asked relatively open-ended questions about religious beliefs and occupations. The result was a proliferation of columns concerning occupations in particular. Individuals appeared as 'con-man', 'pimp', 'prostitute', 'idiot' and 'thief, or however else they might appear or describe themselves. Worse still, castes and tribes were listed as to whether they were 'animist', Christian, Hindu or Mohammedan, with little structure or system beyond the self-representation of the respondents. It was the need for some such order which led to Denzil Ibbetson's functional, occupational categorisation of castes and tribes in the 1881 census.

However, not only did that allow for the possibility of unhealthily egalitarian conclusions about the ethnic mixing of the Indian population, and the possibilities for change in economic and social status, but it also directly conflicted with the racist ideas about Indian social structure that by then had been largely confirmed in the minds of administrators by more than a generation of anecdotal writing. The response was to seek for a new method that would confirm 'scientifically' what were now ingrained prejudices. The immanent discourse of pseudo-scientific racism had already shown itself in early experiments in phrenology, and in the techniques of physical measurement attempted at the Jabalpur exhibition. A major break-through was not possible, however, until the introduction to India of new European techniques of anthropometry, first tried out, at the instigation of Sir Herbert Hope Risley, in the Ethnographic Survey of Bengal.

Herbert Hope Risley and the apotheosis of 'pseudo-scientific' racism

Risley's first experience of survey work was as an Assistant Director of Statistics in Sir W.W. Hunter's Survey of India, the results of which were embodied in the first edition of the Imperial Gazetteer, published in 1881. However, his interest in anthropology largely developed after his marriage in 1879 to an erudite German woman, who introduced him to a wide range of European writings on anthropology and statistics. In 1885 he was then placed in charge of the Ethnographic Survey of Bengal, a project which occupied him for the next six years.

Preliminary anthropometric data on the people of eastern Bengal, consisting of measurements of skin colour, skull size, orbito-nasal indices and overall stature had already been compiled by a Dr. James Wise. This was combined with E.T. Dalton's work on the tribes of Chota Nagpur[39] to produce a four-volume dictionary of the tribes and castes of Bengal, which was finally published in 1891. Two of the four volumes consisted of anthropometric data, a considerable proportion of which Risley had collected himself.[40] The maximum sample size used in Risley's enquiry was 100, and in many cases his conclusions about the racial origins of particular castes or tribal groups were based on the cranial measurements of as few as 30 individuals. Like Professor Topinard, Paul Broca, Le Bron and Morton before him, Risley had a clear notion of where his results would lead, and he had no difficulty in fitting the fewest observations into a complex typology of racial types.

According to Risley the people of India were composed of seven basic racial types: the Mongoloid, the Dravidian, the Indo-Aryan, the Turko-Iranian, the Mongolo-Dravidian, the Aryo-Dravidian, and the Scytho-Dravidian. Each group was the result of incursions by different racial types into the subcontinent, the Scythians arriving from central Asia some time in the second millenium, and sweeping down the west coast, and the Aryans arriving shortly after. The Mongoloid and the Dravidian races were the original inhabitants of north-eastern India and the Dravidians the original inhabitants of the south, and with these races the invading peoples sometimes mixed, and sometimes, apparently, not. Most of those thought to be tribals were described as being of Dravidian or Mongolian stock, whilst the agricultural or peasant classes of north India were either of mixed stock, or were Aryan in origin. All this Risley believed could be proven by the simple act of measurement,

[39] E.T. Dalton, *Descriptive Ethnology of Bengal* (Calcutta, 1872) (later re-published as *Tribal History of Eastern India*).

[40] H.H. Risley, 'Introduction' and 'Ethnographic Appendices', *Census of India, 1901*, vol. I (Calcutta, 1903).

though he admitted that his own evidence, at best, suggested only a three-fold racial division between Aryan, Mongoloid and Dravidian. (Similar arguments about the racial origins of castes were espoused by non-Brahman propagandists for quite different reasons in the late nineteenth century but, as with Risley, these theories were more to do with the appropriation of knowledge for political ends than the product of disinterested scholarship).[41]

Risley also believed that the basic linguistic divisions of the Indian subcontinent could be traced back to racial origins, and wrote: 'the gobbling speech of the people of Chittagong and Eastern Bengal, and their inability to negotiate certain consonants seem to suggest that their original tongue belonged to the Tibeto-Burman family, and that their vocal apparatus must differ materially from that of their western neighbours'.[42] It was views such as these that led Max Müller to denounce what he described as the 'unholy alliance' between comparative philology and ethnology that lay behind the ethnographic survey. Risley however dismissed Müller's criticisms as merely a matter of detail, and went on to pursue his belief that the custom of endogamy amongst certain caste groups meant that even the minutest social distinction could, in time, be traced to some difference in physiognomy, skin colour or bone structure. He thus asserted:

> if we take a series of castes in Bengal, Bihar and the United Provinces of Agra and Oudh, or Madras, and arrange them in the order of the average nasal index, so that the caste with finest nose shall be at the top, and that with the coarsest at the bottom of the list, it will be found that this order substantially corresponds with the accepted order of social precedence.[43]

Risley was highly dismissive of cultural and linguistic indicators since 'the wholesale borrowing of customs and ceremonies...makes it practically impossible to arrive at any certain conclusions by examining

[41] For the importance of these debates (particularly the theory of Aryan invasion) in the emergent ideology of late nineteenth-century Hindu reform movements, see R. O'Hanlon, *Caste, Conflict and Identity* (Cambridge, 1985), ch. 8.

[42] H.H. Risley, *The People of India* (2nd edn., London, 1915), p.9.

[43] Ibid., p.29.

these practices'.[44] However the simultaneous publication of Dr. George Grierson's Linguistic Survey of India seemed nonetheless, and very fortunately, to bear out his results. This was no coincidence, since Grierson himself was armed with the much earlier but as yet unproven hypotheses of Sir William Jones concerning matters of language and race, and was intimately acquainted with Risley's theories of racial origins. Grierson also followed a similar *ex ante* deductive methodology in his research.

Like Risley's caste categories, Grierson's linguistic categories were pre-selected, and the grammar and vocabulary of the languages then ascertained by circulating for translation the parable of the prodigal son, the fatted calf being discreetly changed to a fatted goat to avoid offending religious prejudices. 'Authoritative' translations of this parable, together with a list of common words and phrases, were then used to define the boundaries of the main linguistics groups. However, Grierson's sources were merely the opinion of 'local intelligent persons' who were asked to name the languages of their neighbourhood. Thus, Grierson wrote, 'we are told that Bengali is spoken in such and such a place, but we are not told what is meant by the word "Bengali"'.[45]

A common victim of this methodology was the great variety of local tribal dialects and languages in central India, which were simply lumped together under the title 'Gondi'—meaning, whatever was unintelligible to the educated informant. The Survey was thus not so very different from earlier dictionaries, such as Sleeman's *Ramaseeana*, or Meninski's dictionary of Persian, or dictionaries of the 'secret languages' of the criminal tribes, all of which were highly arbitrary collections of linguistic information, which were needed to achieve administrative ends, but which did not necessarily reflect the authentic language of any particular community.

Following the success of the Ethnographic Survey of Bengal, a scheme for the systematic survey of the whole of India was sanctioned

[44] Ibid., p.20.

[45] G. Grierson, *Linguistic Survey of India*, vol. 1 (Calcutta, 1898), introduction.

in 1901. A Superintendent of Ethnography was appointed for each Presidency or Province, and an allotment of £5,000 provided to every Presidency each year for a period of eight years in order to carry out the work.[46] The data for these surveys were collected firstly by the circulation of questionnaires to local government officers, and secondly by the physical measurement of the population in the manner prescribed by Risley. Few of the later surveys, however, were quite so thorough, even by Risley's standards. One of the most ludicrous was Thurston's study of southern India. Thurston was the curator of the government museum in Madras, and clearly saw the study of racial types among the Indians as an extension of his daily routine of labelling and pinning butterflies, and of collecting and categorising the varieties of plants. Like Risley, Thurston was convinced of the distinctness of racial types, and that several of the tribes of southern India, who were of the race 'Homo Dravida' (as he called it), had more in common with Australian aboriginals than their Aryan or high-caste neighbours. The use of the boomerang by Kallan and Maravan warriors in South India he believed to be convincing evidence of this, whilst the prevalence of tree-climbing amongst the Kadirs of the Anamalai hills, as amongst the Dayaks of Borneo, he clearly believed to indicate that both shared some previous evolutionary origin.

Armed with a similar '*boite anthropometrique*' to that used by Risley—as recommended by Professor Topinard of Paris, and lent for the occasion by the Asiatic Society of Bengal—Thurston would set off in search of suitable subjects in order to carry out his measurements. He

[46] In the Central Provinces the commission was given to R.V. Russell, the Superintendent of Ethnography for the C.P., and Rai Bahadur Hira Lal, an amateur archaeologist and extra assistant commissioner. Extracts from the resolution of the Government of India are given in an appendix to this paper. It is noticeable that Lord George Hamilton, the Secretary of State for India, suggested at the time that in addition to photographs being taken of 'representatives of the different Indian races', 'archaic industries' should be similarly recorded (see MPCRO, Berar, Miscellaneous Dept. 10/190, enclosure 2). This second proposal was eventually dropped, only to be revived and brought to fulfilment by Indira Gandhi in the Indian Crafts Museum in New Delhi (see P. Greenhough, 'Tradition, economy and nation at the Indian Crafts Museum, New Delhi', unpublished seminar paper, Centre of South Asian Studies, University of Edinburgh, November 1992).

relied heavily on his authority as a government officer, there sometimes being no other way, for example, that he could persuade a bewildered villager to strip in order to be measured with the mysterious-sounding 'Lovibond Tintometer'. At other times, however, his methods backfired: he would attract villagers to his camp by playing a phonograph and giving an exhibition of 'American pseudoptics' (or illusions), but those gathered would flee in all directions as soon as he produced his measuring instruments. On other occasions the numbers attending the camp would be so great that he would be able to carry out only the most cursory of measurements. Whole villages sometimes fled in advance of his arrival, and the Boer war having just finished, many took him to be a recruiting sergeant for the army, the bodily measurements being required, it was thought, in order to provide them with uniforms. Others thought that the marks that Thurston made on their foreheads 'to indicate the position of the fronto-nasal suture and bi-orbital breadth' would blister into a number, which would then serve as future identification for the purpose of kidnapping. Others still took the height-measuring platform for a gallows, or believed Thurston to be selecting the finest of them to be stuffed as exhibits for the Madras Museum—a thought which one suspects was not impossibly far from his mind. Despite all these obstacles, Thurston managed to complete his survey, but his conclusions were based on the measurement of only 30 or 60 members of each caste or tribe, and in some cases measurements had been taken from only six or seven individuals.[47]

By the time of the last ethnographic survey, that of the Central Provinces and Berar, which was published in 1916, anthropometry had begun to fall out of favour. The authors—Russell and Hira Lal—relied much more heavily on folk tales and other anecdotal evidence. as had Risley's principal rival and critic, William Crooke, the author of *The*

[47] E. Thurston (assisted by K. Rangachari), *The Tribes and Castes of South India* (7 vols., Madras, 1909), vol.1, introduction. Edgar Thurston was also a 'Correspondent Etranger' of the Société d'Anthropologie de Paris. To get a real sense of his often lurid, orientalist imaginings the best source is his *Ethnographic Notes in Southern India* (Madras, 1906), which is complete with hook-swinging, fire-walking, earth-eating and human sacrifice, in a style that is most revealing.

Tribes and Castes of the North-West Provinces of India.[48] The basic caste categories of the survey, however, still replicated those in the companion volumes by Thurston, Risley and Enthoven.[49] In the case of Russell and Hira Lal, the definition of castes remained essentially racial, but the distinctions were not based on measurement (although such 'facts' were known to be available). Instead, explanations were sought, once more, in vedic texts, the investigators' principal authority being M. Emile Senart's *Les castes dans l'Inde*. From this source Russell and Hira Lal reasoned that the tribals could probably be identified as the Rakshasas (or devils) described in *Mahabharata*, and that they were therefore an entirely distinct community. The Brahmans, Kshatriyas and Vaishyas were Aryan invaders, and the Sudras were the original inhabitants of South Asia, reduced to a subordinate role.

Thus although occupational descriptions were used, particularly in distinguishing the different ranks of Aryans, the hierarchy remained extreme (and definitively racial) in a form that was still probably unrecognisable to most participants in the social system itself at this time.[50] In this way, although Risley's anthropometry had become

[48] R.V. Russell, and Hira Lal, *The Castes and Tribes of the Central Provinces* (London, 1916); W. Crooke, *The Tribes and Castes of the North-West Provinces and Oudh* (4 vols., Calcutta, 1896). See also W. Crooke, *An Ethnograhpic Handbook for the N.W.P. & Oudh* (Allahabad, 1890); *The North-Western Provinces of India: their history, ethnology and administration* (London, 1897); and *Natives of Northern India* (Delhi, 1907). It is notable that Crooke was also responsible for editing the reprinted version of Col. Tod's romantic historical and anecdotal account of Rajasthan, originally published in the late 1820s; J. Tod, *Annals and Antiquities of Rajasthan, or the Central and Western Rajput States of India* (Oxford, 1920).

[49] R.E. Enthoven, *The Tribes and Castes of Bombay* (Bombay, 1920). Enthoven's work in turn depended heavily on the compendious but unsystematic ethnographic researches of Sir James Campbell, conducted over a period twenty years in preparation for the publication of the thirty-four volumes of *Bombay Gazetteers* in 1901, to which Enthoven himself appended an index volume.

[50] The highly anecdotal basis of Russell and Hira Lal, *Castes and Tribes*, is well illustrated by the entry on 'Thugs' in vol. 4, pp.558-87, which is replete with references even to the ill omen incurred if the turban of a Thug should happen to catch fire, substantiated with cross-references to James Fraser's *Golden Bough*. The entry on 'Gonds' also faithfully reproduces, without qualification, nineteenth-century descriptions of the practice of human sacrifice in Bastar and other territories.

unfashionable, his views persisted.[51] Even as far as racial anthropometry was concerned, it had to compete merely with social and cultural perspectives in the field of anthropology, pioneered by Franz Boas, and these, though influential in the United States, made but slow headway in Europe and the colonial territories. In the field of criminology there was little to comtest with Cesare Lombroso's theories on inherited criminality until the 1930s. Anthropometry continued to be used by the Indian police as a means of identifying criminals until the introduction of the Berthillon system of finger-printing, firstly in Bengal and then in Berar, in 1897, and even then finger-printing was adopted only because of the saving it afforded in labour, time and expense. Anthropometric records continued to be compiled for some time ,in tandem with finger-printing.[52] With modifications, the Criminal Tribes legislation also remained in force, and was still being used actively in the Central Provinces and elsewhere in the late 1930s.[53]

Risley himself continued to enjoy a distinguished career. Besides working as Census Commissioner in 1899, he also served on a Commission appointed to enquire into the working of the Indian police, and, in 1909, he became a temporary member of the Governor-General's Council.[54] He was also three times President of the Asiatic Society of Bengal, and, upon returning to England, was appointed to succeed C.J. Lyall as Judicial and Public Secretary in the India Office, as well as being elected President of the Royal Anthropological

[51] For years after Risley's retirement, books such as Bishop Eyre Chatterton's *The Story of Gondwana* (London, 1916), repeated his ideas on the racial origins of Indian castes and tribes, together with all the other paraphernalia of nineteenth-century orientalist discourse on India, including the great myths of thagi and human sacrifice. To this day reports of the Anthropological Survey of India continue to appear with some form of introductory exegesis on 'the seven races' of India: for example, V. Bhall, 'Prospects of Seriological Studies in India', in Hirendra K. Rakshit (ed.), *Anthropology in India,* vol.2, *Physical Anthropology* (Calcutta, 1976), pp.144-64.

[52] MPCRO, Berar Police Department, 1898/36: 'Substitution of the system of identification by finger prints for that of anthropometry'.

[53] See ibid., Berar Police Department, 1936/18-1: 'Rules framed under the Criminal Tribes Act, 1924', a file which details the notification of a number of newly-criminalised tribes in the Berar region.

[54] As Home Minister under Lord Curzon, Risley is remembered particularly (though not very fondly) for his part in the partition of Bengal.

Institute, before his death in 1911.

Contemporary concepts of 'tribe': Africa and India compared

Modern anthropological thought, influenced by the latest developments in biology such as the concept of the cline and the mathematical theory of population genetics, has largely overthrown the notions of race developed by Risley and others in the late nineteenth century. Indeed the view of present-day geneticists is that *homo sapiens* probably originated in Africa, and that, as a consequence, the genetic diversity between Africans (for example between a Zulu and a Masai) is many times greater than that between Africans and Europeans, or even between Europeans and Chinese.[55] African anthropologists have long since rejected the theory of race, and also the concept of the tribe. Both phenomena, when examined closely, reveal the workings of a variety of genetic and social processes, few of which follow one another with sufficient consistency to merit a unitary form of ranking. Any classifications of race, or social grouping, in this way, including the traditional notions of 'tribe', are, in effect, wholly arbitrary.

In the African context, Aidan Southall has cleverly debunked a number of such traditional usages. There are, of course, numerous instances of self-identification by certain groups. However an extraordinary number of ethnic or communal associations have either evolved in response to external pressures, or been directly imposed. In such cases the history of 'tribes' tells us more about the powerful and the elite than about the subject peoples themselves. A well-documented case is that of the Luyia in Kenya. Before the 1930s the region described by Europeans as 'kavirondo' contained as many as seventeen different tribes, but the creation of the North Kavirondo district, later renamed the North Nyanza district, rapidly encouraged the formation of political associations such as the North Kavirondo Central Association and the Bantu Kavirondo Taxpayers' Association. In order to associate

[55] It has also been said that most black Americans are now genetically closer to Europeans than to their African ancestors, due to extensive miscegenation, and that many white Europeans are probably genetically more similar to modern-day African populations.

themselves with these organisations, and to conform to the new administrative boundaries, the seventeen tribes quickly adopted the one name—of Luyia. The choice of this name was easy enough, as roughly translated it refers to the meeting place of the elders in nearly all the languages of the region. Other, so-called tribal names, such as Sukuma and Nyamwezi in Tanzania, refer simply to geographical locations: the Sukuma being 'northerners' and the Nyamwezi 'westerners'. There were in fact at one time more than a dozen different ruling families among the Sukuma and Nyamwezi, each with its own 'chiefdom' or 'kingdom'.[56] Other tribal names simply refer to people who live in a common habitat, such as the bush, the valley, or the jungle, and these people need not necessarily share any common social or cultural characteristics.

The association of people by language is, finally, an even less helpful criterion of tribe, since language is an element that groups within acephalous societies often deliberately manipulate as a means of distinction and identification. Larger tribal polities, such as the kingdom of the Ahom in Assam, have also often incorporated a number of other groups by conquest or assimilation, and in consequence include a variety of languages. In India it is not unusual in some localities for half-a-dozen different dialects or languages to be spoken within an area the size of an English county. In the case of Bastar, the language of every-day communication is that of a small Hinduised tribe, known as the Halba, who once served as armed retainers of the Bastar Raja. But, despite the recently high levels of assimilation and integration within this culture, the local dialects of the Murias, Marias, Dorla, Dhurwa and Bhattra tribes still remain.

Faced with the multiple problems of definition, of illusion, and of transition and transformation, Aidan Southall has argued that the contingent nature of stateless societies (characterised as they are by multi-polities, ritual superintegration, complementary opposition, intersecting kinship and distributive legitimacy) *is of their essence,* and is not something we ought be trying to sweep away by penetrating

[56] J. Abrahams, *The Nyamwezi Today: a Tanzanian people in the 1970s* (Cambridge, 1981).

analysis. Although this sort of argument has its attractions, it nonetheless has little explanatory force, and in reaction some anthropologists have dropped the study of tribes altogether in favour of sub-groups of people who really are lineally related by blood. In this way the Dinka of Kenya were divided by Leinhardt into 25 'groups', three of which contained 27, 10 and 6 lineally related 'tribes', whilst John Middleton has defined as many as 60 sub-tribes amongst the Lugbara.[57]

In India, anthropologists now more often speak of 'sub-castes' or *jatis* as the building blocks of society. However, unless there is a strong element of political control or territoriality associated with such groups these too tend to disintegrate upon closer inspection, as soon as essentially exogamous practices such as hypergamy are taken into account. Needless to say, all such endogamous groupings are increasingly irrelevant when talking about modern India, where large-scale migrations are commonplace, where economic and social change is radically re-shaping society, and where marriage taboos are being overthrown at an accelerating rate.

Custom, property and the theory of 'ancient law'

Quite apart from bone structures or ethnic or racial rankings, Victorian ethnographers also saw in Indian tribal societies an earlier form of their own societies, and the definition of tribal institutions and social organisation became a part of Europeans' attempts to describe their own history and evolutionary origin.[58] Perhaps the most influential of

[57] A. Southall, *Alur Society* (Cambridge, 1956), p.44. See also Southall, 'A critique of the typology of states and political systems', in M. Banton (ed.), *Political Systems and the Distribution of Power* (New York 1965), pp.113-40; Southall, 'Stateless society' in *International Encyclopaedia of the Social Sciences* 15 (New York, 1968), pp.157-68; and 'The illusion of tribe', *Journal of Asian and African Studies* v, 1 & 2 (January-April 1970), pp.28-50. More recent contributions to the literature debunking of the notion of the tribe include L. Vail (ed.), *The Creation of Tribalism in Southern Africa* (London, 1989); W. Samarin, *The Black Man's Burden* (Boulder and London, 1989); and J. Willis, *Mombasa, the Swahili and the Making of the Mijikenda* (Oxford, 1993).

[58] This is, of course, a principal function of 'orientalist' writing of this period, orientalism being a mode of reasoning and a means of situating contemporary understanding of British and more broadly 'Western' society in a global historical and evolutionary context. See G.W. Stocking, *Victorian*

such accounts was Sir Henry Maine's *Ancient Law*, published in 1861. In common with many other thinkers of his time, Maine saw the origins of liberty, freedom and social progress as lying in the growth, out of feudalism, of the private property right. This interpretation of private property was itself in turn founded on the notion of 'possessive individualism' espoused by political theorists such as Hobbes and Locke in the seventeenth century. By the mid-nineteenth century this interpretation had become virtually axiomatic, and the objective of writers such as Maine was merely to locate its evolution and historical origins in the past.

Henry Maine's mode of reasoning was probably not very different from that of many other nineteenth-century writers, such as Bagehot, Herbert Spencer, Engels, Acton or Mill, but his arguments were by far the most brilliant and succinct, and in his own generation were probably also the most influential. Maine's basic thesis, which is familiar to most academics, was that, in the very earliest forms of society, religion and the rule of law were intimately connected, and that the fundamental unit of both law and society was not the individual, but the group, and in particular, the patriarchal family. Within this family kinship was traced through the male line only, and the solidarity of the family group was underpinned by a variety of religious and symbolic rituals. As the family unit gradually broke down, joint holdings and group possessions of land and other forms of property developed, but it was only in later, more progressive societies, that separate, individual holdings and wills became the norm. This gradual break-up of family ties and the emergence of the individual as the usual legal personality was described by Maine, in a now famous phrase, as the transition from status to contract.

India was crucial in Maine's account as a living example of the social and political institutions which he was describing, but which in the West had long since passed into history. Maine was thus fascinated by the debates amongst British officials in India as to the nature of landholding and village structure, and in these debates he saw close

Anthropology (London, 1987) and E. Said, *Orientalism* (London, 1978) and *Culture and Imperialism* (London, 1993).

parallels with European controversies about the origins of the Mark, the manor, and of feudalism, and concerning the history of the Scottish and Irish clans. Maine's concerns with social organisation paralleled those of many others in the eighteenth and nineteenth centuries in attempting to develop typologies of civilisation measured by the yardsticks, variously defined, of material mastery and technological advancement.[59] However fascinating, these were nonetheless largely theoretical questions to Maine; but to other British administrators in India they were questions of immense practical importance. For this reason the comparative theories of Maine and his contemporaries had a great influence, and in many cases were seized upon and applied with vigour. The exponents of both *malguzari* and *raiyatwari* systems of settlement, for example, appealed to the theory of the ancient village community in defence of their pet administrative projects, and in the process a great deal of imaginative rewriting of history took place.[60]

From almost every perspective, however, tribal notions of property were invariably described as simply an inversion of modern bourgeois property rights. Even conservative critics of Maine, such as Bade Powell and Sir George Campbell, who were keen to exorcise the village community of all traces of communism, did so either by appealing to the evidence of diversity, or by arguing that private property *was* to be found, only vested in some other commodity, such as cattle, rather than land. The application of highly teleological theories about ownership in the settlements of the mid-nineteenth century inevitably spawned contradiction and confusion. But this was particularly the case in some of the tribal areas of central India where revenue officers found that the idea of property as understood in the Western sense was completely absent. Thus one divisional commissioner enthusiastically commented

[59] Michael Adas, *Machines as the Measure of Men: science, technology and the ideologies of Western dominance* (Ithaca, 1989).

[60] The authoritative analysis of this question is C.J. Dewey, 'Images of the village community: a study in Anglo-Indian ideology', *Modern Asian Studies* 6, 3 (1972), pp.291-328. The main limitation of Dewey's analysis is his somewhat schematic categorisation of the political views of the nineteenth-century authors whom he describes as being either 'conservative' or 'radical'. See also A. Kuper, *The Invention of Primitive Society: transformations of an illusion* (London, 1988) for arguments parallel to those of this paper.

of tenant rights in Chhattisgarh in eastern Madhya Pradesh: 'surely a more striking example of village communism and of village rights going beyond the ryotwari system of Madras or Bombay could not be imagined'. Yet although officials anguished over the appropriateness of malguzari or ryotwari systems of settlement, none could quite come to grips with the actual function of property rights within tribal societies. Being officials, as were all of Maine's informants for his later work on village communities, they were instinctively drawn to the study of institutions, to the general neglect of the social and economic processes which underpinned them.[61] Nonetheless many of Maine's theories and observations, canonised in the writings of distinguished anthropologists such as L.H. Morgan, have become accepted truths of anthropological theory.[62]

In an effort to fill this lacuna, and taking also their cue from Ibbetson's observations about the connections between caste and tribal society (quoted earlier in this paper), renewed attention has recently been devoted to the history of tribal kingdoms and tribal societies. An early, imaginative attempt to link kin-based patterns of landholding with institutions such as chiefship, and the growth of the tribal state, was made by R.G. Fox with his theory of the 'developmental cycle' of the Rajput lineage. Fox's principal source was the somewhat dubious

[61] See R.G. Fox's insightful comments on this in *Kin, Clan, Raja and Rule: state-hinterland relations in pre-industrial India* (Berkeley, 1971), ch.4. Fox forms the view that the differences between 'feudalism' and 'tribalism' which obsessed nineteenth-century ethnographers arose from an inadequate understanding of superstratification in lineage societies. Thus many societies, he argues, which were apparently 'feudal' were in fact lineage-based. He further claims that the distinction is in any case an artificial one and the product of oriental scholarship, though I suspect his own approach is merely a more subtle interpretation of the 'tribalist' perspective which he found in his sources.

[62] See H. Kuklick, 'Tribal exemplars' in G.W. Stocking (ed.), *Functionalism Historicized : essays on British social anthropology* (Madison, 1984). A much wider debate on the relationship between anthropology and imperialism has of course since developed: see Talal Asad (ed.), *Anthropology and the Colonial Encounter* (London, Ithaca, 1973); G. Huizer and B. Mannheim (eds.), *The Politics of Anthropology: from colonialism and sexism toward a view from below* (The Hague, 1979); Renato Rosaldo, 'From the door of his tent: the fieldworker and the inquisitor' in J. Clifford and G. Marcus (eds.), *Writing Culture: the poetics and politics of ethnography* (Berkeley, 1986), and C. Geertz, *Works and Lives: the anthropologist as author* (Oxford, 1989).

authority of Sir Alfred Lyall, another former officer of the Central Provinces administration, who was one of the more programmatic of nineteenth-century writers on Indian history.[63] Quite apart from the reliability of his evidence, Fox's account is flawed because it tells us nothing about how Rajput kingdoms functioned and reproduced themselves economically. This is no great surprise, as it exactly reflects the obsession of Lyall and his contemporaries with the idiosyncracies of Hindu kinship and religion. But, with the the addition of an economic dimension, the point of division in Fox's account between the ideological framework of the 'clan' and the practical workings of 'lineage' would become far more apparent, and the debates which obsessed nineteenth-century writers, such as whether the joint village was a more or less developed form of the joint property right, would become largely irrelevant.

The study of tribal social structures ought really to begin, therefore, with the study of the practical exigencies of their particular modes of production. Interestingly, however, this approach did not even occur to Indian ethnologists until towards the very end of the colonial period. Perhaps it is no coincidence that this was the period in which colonial development agencies emerged, along with the idea of tribal reservations and the now classical, dichotomous debates as to whether the adivasis should be 'assimilated' or 'preserved', a debate in which participants were pretty much divided along the lines of nationalists versus colonialists. The anthropologists of this period (the exceptions among which may include Verrier Elwin) therefore often continued to

[63] A potted biography of Alfred Lyall is available in R. Owen, 'Anthropology and imperial administration: Sir Alfred Lyall and the official use of theories of social change developed in India after 1857' in T. Asad (ed.), *Anthropology and the Colonial Encounter* (London, Ithaca, 1973), pp.223-43. See also A. Lyall, *Asiatic Researches, Religious and Social* (London, 1894) and Daniel Thorner's discussion of Indian feudalism in *The Shaping of Modern India*, ch.13. Lyall's theories on tribes and feudal society in India were largely developed between 1865 and 1878 when he served in the Central Provinces, Berar and in Rajputana. The other key source used by Fox is C.U. Wills, 'The territorial system of the Rajput kingdoms of medieval Chhattisgarh', *Journal and Proceedings of the Asiatic Society of Bengal*, n.s. XV (1919), pp.197-262. A collection of the papers of Wills, including notes used in the preparation of this article, is kept in the MPCRO in Nagpur.

shed much more heat than light.

Conclusion

Although the colonial discourse of caste and tribe in India may have been hegemonic, it was not always uncontested, and it would be a mistake to regard it solely as the effect of a larger project aimed at 'normalising' the sociology of India in order to render it more susceptible to administrative control. It is doubtful in fact that any anthropologist or historian of South Asia has gone so far as to make this explicit suggestion. On the contrary, there is if anything a tendency, recently described in the African case by Christopher Fyfe, for historians to neglect perceptions of race and racial ideology as explanatory variables.[64] Whatever the nature and purpose of the colonial discourse on castes and tribes, it should not therefore be forgotten that the discourse was situated in a political order in which concepts of race were used quite instrumentally. Contemporaries did not need reminding that in general, in the words of Victor Kiernan, 'the lighter the skin, the sharper the sword'.[65] As Lord Dufferin put it: 'The diversity of races in India and the presence of a powerful Mohamedan community, are undoubtedly favourable to the maintenance of our rule...'.[66] Dufferin went on to disown any intention of exacerbating racial conflicts for political ends, but he said nothing whatever about the relationship between the rulers and the ruled. On this, his predecessor (but one) as Viceroy, Lord Lytton, had much firmer views:

> [G]reat mischief has been done by the deplorable tendency of second-rate Indian officials and superficial English philanthropists to ignore the essential and insurmountable distinctions of race qualities, which are fundamental to our position in India; and thus, unintentionally, to pamper the conceit and vanity of half-educated natives, to the serious detriment of commonsense, and of the

[64] C. Fyfe, 'Race, empire and the historians', *Race and Class* 33,4, pp.15-30 (London, 1992).

[65] V.G. Kiernan, *The Lords of Human Kind: European attitudes towards the outside world in the imperial age* (London, 1969).

[66] Lord Dufferin in a letter to the editor of the *Pioneer*, 1 January 1887, cited in A. Seal, *The Emergence of Indian Nationalism: competition and collaboration in the later nineteenth century* (Cambridge, 1972), p.157.

wholesome recognition of realities.[67]

To divorce colonial ethnology from such views and the context in which they arose, and to treat the discourse of castes and tribes as mere faltering steps on the road towards the formulation of a purer science of Indian sociology, would be gravely mistaken. It is not sufficient for historians to recall the racialism of colonial rule without exemplifying and discussing it, and it is important to recollect the distorted impressions the colonial era has left us of India's pre-colonial past. In the case of the so-called 'adivasis', a description of who they were and where they came from ought not to begin by plucking them as specimens from the colonial era, but by examining their resistance to colonialism, and the previous history of the rise and fall of tribal kingdoms in a period when they were much more largely masters of their own fate. To do so is important, since what is called the sociology of nineteenth-century India is, as Irfan Habib has argued in a related context, above all the sociology of the colonised written by the colonisers. Before asking 'what is caste' therefore we must first ask 'who wants to define it?', and recollect that the discourse of race, caste and tribe was in many ways the Peacock Throne of British India, carried off by the new Constitution of 1950, but still greatly missed by many.[68]

[67] IOR, Lytton Collection, MSS.Eur.E.218/4-3: Lytton to Caird (3 December 1879) and Lytton to Clarke (26 April 1878); cited in S.R. Ashton, *Colonialism in India* (London, 1988).

[68] I. Habib, 'Studying a colonial economy—without perceiving colonialism', *Modern Asian Studies* 19, 3 (Cambridge, 1985). See also Crispin Bates, '"Lost innocents and the loss of innocence": interpreting *adivasi* movements in South Asia', in R.H. Barnes, A. Gray and B. Kingsbury (eds.), *Indigenous Peoples of Asia* (Madison, 1995).

APPENDIX

Extract from the Proceedings of the Government of India in the Home Department (Public), Simla, 25 May 1901

RESOLUTION

In August 1882, when the statistics of the census of 1881 were still in process of compilation the Census Commissioner suggested that steps should be taken to collect full information regarding castes and occupations throughout British India. The proposal was commended to Local Governments and Administrations, and the Bengal government undertook an Ethnographic Survey of the customs of all important tribes and castes in Bengal and an anthropometric inquiry, according to the methods prescribed by the French anthropologists Broca and Topinard, into the distinctive physical characteristics of selected tribes and castes in Bengal, the North-Western Provinces, Oudh, and the Punjab. The results of these inquiries were recorded in the four volumes of *The Tribes and Castes of Bengal.*

In December 1899, when the preliminary arrangements for the census of 1901 were under consideration, the British Association for the Advancement of Science recommended to the Secretary of State, in the letter appended to this Resolution, that certain ethnographic investigations should be undertaken in connection with the census operations. Their proposals may be summarised as comprising:

(1) Ethnography, or the systematic description of the history, structure, traditions and religious and social usages of the various races, tribes and castes in India;

(2) Anthropometry, or measurements directed to determining the physical types characteristic of particular groups; and

(3) Photographs of typical individuals and, if possible, of archaic industries.

The Scientific importance of the investigations recommended by the British Association is admitted in Sir Arthur Godley's letter, dated 16th January 1900, to the address of the Association, and the Government of India are in entire agreement with this view. It has come to be recognised of late years that India is a vast storehouse of social and physical data which only need to be recorded in order to contribute to the solution of the problems which are being approached in Europe with the aid of material, much of which is inferior in quality to the facts readily accessible in India, and rests upon less trustworthy evidence. Mention may be made of Sir Alfred Lyall's Asiatic Studies, of Professor Haddon's Study of Man, of Emile Senart's Les Castes dans l'Inde, and of Dr. W.Z. Ripley's recent work on the Races of Europe, as showing the extensive use that has been made by the ethnologists of data collected in India.

It is unnecessary to dwell at length upon the obvious advantage to many branches of the administration in this country of an accurate and well arranged record of the customs and domestic and social relations of the various castes and tribes. The entire framework of native conduct of individuals are largely determined by the rules of the group to which they belong. For the purposes of legislation, of judicial procedure, of famine relief, of sanitation and dealings with epidemic disease, and of almost every form of executive action an ethnographic survey of India, and a record of the customs of the people is as necessary an incident of good administration as a cadastral survey of the land and a record of the rights of its tenants...

It has often been observed that anthropometry yields peculiarly good results in India by reason of the caste system which prevails among Hindoos, and of the divisions, most closely resembling castes, which are recognised by Mohammadans. Marriage takes place only within a limited circle; the disturbing element of crossing is to a great extent excluded; and the differences of physical type, which measurement is intended to establish, are more marked and more persistent than anywhere else in the World. Stress was laid upon these points by Professor Topinard in reviewing at length the results of the measurements taken in Bengal, the N.W.P. and the Punjab, and by the late Sir William Flower in his Presidential address to the British Association in 1894. The Government of India propose to collect the physical measurements of selected castes and tribes. In Madras the work can be done by Mr. E. Thurston, the Superintendent of the Central Museum, whose ethnographic researches in the South of India are well known, and who it is understood is likely to be selected by the Provincial Government as Superintendent of the Ethnography for the Madras Presidency. For the rest of India it will probably be convenient to employ a Civil Hospital Assistant who worked under Mr. Risley. in Bengal and is stated to have a competent knowledge of the subject. This part of the scheme will cost in all about Rs. 6,000, which will be placed at the disposal of Mr. Risley.

The proposal of the Association to place photographers at the disposal of the Census officers is one which could not be carried out in practice.... It would be very expensive.... Moreover a large collection of photographs already exists at the India Office Library. The government of India are further advised that in comparison with measurements, photographs posses but a little scientific value....

Source: MPCRO, Berar, Miscellaneous, Census Department, 10/1901, Subject: 'Ethnographic Survey of Caste and Tribes in British India'.

Chapter 8

MARTIAL GURKHAS: THE PERSISTENCE OF A BRITISH MILITARY DISCOURSE ON 'RACE'

Lionel Caplan

Introduction[1]

There can be few ideas which convey British imperial attitudes to questions of 'race' as succinctly as the view that martial qualities inhere only in particular populations. While the notion of martial groups may have pre-dated European arrival in South Asia, it was during the latter part of the colonial period that the 'theory' was elaborated to become the principal basis for military recruitment into the (British) Indian army. Moreover, it persisted well into the twentieth century, and in certain instances—I am thinking particularly of the British Brigade of Gurkhas—it endures to this day. In this paper I explore how the martial race idea informed enlistment strategies in respect of the Gurkhas, and more generally British military discourse about these legendary warriors from Nepal. The texts I examine are those written—and still being written—by British officers who have commanded Gurkhas in war and peace: regimental histories, personal war memoirs, autobiographies, and (principally) popular accounts of these soldiers and their exploits which feed the public appetite for military adventure and exotica.

The theory of martiality is too well-known to need elaboration here, and so we might only remind ourselves that it was predicated on the idea that while the 'military instinct' is inherent in Europeans (especially the British), the same could not be said for all the diverse peoples of the Indian subcontinent. The theory had two main strands. One was

[1] Field work in Nepal in 1988 was funded by the Nuffield Foundation, while expenses incurred in Britain in connection with this research were met from a grant provided by SOAS. I am grateful to both bodies for their assistance. I am also indebted to Pat Caplan and David Arnold for comments on an earlier version of this paper.

based on the idea of natural qualities, emphasising that martiality was an inherited trait and therefore an aspect of 'race'.[2] In this conception, a martial race, to quote Cynthia Enloe, flags an ethnic community as inherently inclined towards military occupations; it possesses some special characteristic embedded in its physical make-up, in its 'blood' (1980, p.39). In the nineteenth century, blood was widely regarded as the substance responsible for the transmission of hereditary features, so that all members of a particular race would be endowed with the same qualities (Robb, this volume; Street, 1975, pp.7 and 77). Martiality (along with other characteristics) was thus deemed to be inherited in the blood. In this sense, martial theory did not emerge *sui generis* to meet specific military needs in the nineteenth-century Indian context. Rather, it has to be understood as but one manifestation of the wider European doctrine of biological determinism or scientific racism, which gained at least some of its currency from contemporary anthropological ideas about race, culture and evolution (see Fox, 1985, pp.150-3; Bolt, 1984, pp.129-30; Street, 1975, p.5).

A second strand in martial thinking introduced a climatic-environmental element. The most favoured argument was that we find warlike peoples in hilly, cooler places while in hot, flat regions races are timid, servile and unwarlike (see Creagh, n.d., p.233).[3] Both these strands of martial thought could be and were employed in the designation of Gurkhas as a martial people. So after 1857, the British felt the need to reconsider the suitability of certain previously-favoured groups (such as the men from Awadh) for military enlistment; there was a dramatic fall in the number of battalions recruited from traditional areas in the east and south, and a corresponding rise in the numbers recruited from the north (Omissi, 1991, p.12). The intellectual justification for the revision of enlistment policy was provided by senior military figures such as

[2] In the view of Bingley and Nicholls, authors of a military handbook on Brahmans, 'fighting capacity is entirely dependent on race...', *Caste Handbooks for the Indian Army: Brahmans* (Calcutta, 1918), p.47.

[3] Heathcote points out that this hypothesis, viz. that 'hard countries breed hard men', goes back at least as far as Herodotus and was popular in the post-Mutiny Indian context because of its simplicity, T.A. Heathcote, *The Indian Army: the garrison of British imperial India, 1822-1922* (Vancouver, 1974), p.93.

Field-Marshal Lord Roberts and Lt.-General G.F. MacMunn, whose ideas on martiality were shared, according to Mason, by 'nine out of ten' British officers and 'perhaps more' (Mason, 1974, p.348; Roberts, 1897/2; MacMunn and Lovett, 1911, MacMunn, 1932). Alongside the new bias towards north India, attention was increasingly focused on Nepal.[4]

Martial Nepalis

In Nepal, the notion that some groups are more suited to military occupations than others pre-dates the flowering of martial race theory in nineteenth-century British India. Prithvi Narayan Shah, the ruler of Gorkha at the time of the invasion of Kathmandu Valley in the third quarter of the eighteenth century, and regarded as the 'father' of modern Nepal, is reported to have favoured the idea that only four *jat* ('castes' or 'tribes') should be enlisted in his army—namely, the (caste) Thakuris and Khas (Chetris), and the (tribal) Gurungs and Magars—and that the priestly (Brahman) and lowest ('untouchable') groups should be excluded (Stiller, 1989 [1968], p.44).[5] The ethnic or *jat* composition of the Nepalese army at the time of his conquest of the Valley of Kathmandu is a matter of some uncertainty and much speculation. While there is widespread agreement that Chetris and Thakuris provided the bulk of the officer class, opinions as to the identities of the other ranks are mixed. Bennett, for example, in her study of a rural area in central Nepal points out that the high castes ('Chetri-Bahuns') regard themselves as having formed the bulk of the conquering army of Prithvi Narayan Shah (1983, p.10). This reinforces Kirkpatrick's observation that in the latter part of the eighteenth century, Brahmans and Chetris 'compose[d] the army of the state' (1811, p.183). Others, like Shaha, insist that the Gorkha army included Magars and Gurungs as well as Chetris and Thakuris (1986, p.5), which

[4] Since the focus of this essay is on the specific discourses generated by British Gurkha officers, I cannot consider the varieties of martial race theorising in India, or their development over time.

[5] According to *Dibya Upadesh*, Prithvi Narayan at first planned to include the Brahmans among his army to attack the Valley, but it reports that his uncle advised him that if he did so, there would be 'sin everywhere' (Stiller, 1989 [1968], p.40). Thereafter, the Brahmans were not included in his fighting *jat*.

view accords with that attributed to the Gorkha King himself in *Dibya Upadesh* (see above).

A series of Nepalese government orders issued during the 1814-16 war with the East India Company also suggests that not all groups were expected or allowed to fight. While 'weapons-bearing castes' were instructed to report with their swords, shields, bows, arrows and muskets, members of the ('untouchable') Blacksmith caste (Kami) were required to make themselves available for metal work at munitions factories and forts; Damais (musicians)—also 'untouchables'—were instructed to bring their musical instruments to accompany the troops; and Brahmans were ordered to recite scriptures and pray for victory.[6] Subsequently, most Western (and especially military) authors have come to insist on, though they do not provide much evidence for, a preponderance of Magars and Gurungs in the Nepalese forces at the outbreak of the Anglo-Nepal war (see Vansittart, 1894, p.213; Pemble, 1971, p.26). This may simply be a case of reasoning *ipso post facto*, since following the war, as we shall see, Magars and Gurungs were singled out as pre-eminently suited for military occupations, and became the principal groups enlisted as recruits. One British Gurkha officer, writing about the war, argues:

> we may surmise that the Nepalese troops opposed to [the East India Company's Generals] Gillespie and Ochterlony were the pick of their service and composed to a great extent of the classes (for example Magars) we value so much nowadays (Shakespear, 1913, p.379).

Probably the first European to refer to Nepal's 'martial tribes' was Hamilton (1819, p.19), and from the Anglo-Nepal war, during which the British 'discovered' the fighting qualities of their Nepalese opponents, certain ethnic groups were regularly labelled in this way. Like those in north India, they were believed to have something in their

[6] Regmi Research Series, 16, 1984, pp.11-12. Chakravarti argues that Brahmans served as soldiers and commanders of armies in ancient India and were frequently represented as such in the epic literature (1941, pp.78-9). And of course the Bengal army in the eighteenth and nineteenth centuries included many Brahmans, a fact of which the Nepalis would certainly have been aware. It is therefore possible that while Brahmans were not compelled to bear arms in Nepal, many in fact did so.

make-up, in their blood, which made them inherently inclined towards military occupations. So Nepalese deserters and prisoners were recruited into special Gurkha battalions even during the Anglo-Nepal war, and several decades later, following the Mutiny, the numbers of Gurkha units and recruits increased. Hodgson, who was at the British Residency in Kathmandu during the third and fourth decades of the nineteenth century, labelled particular groups as 'martial classes' (1833, p.220) and urged their recruitment. Hodgson's classification had a very pragmatic political motive (that is, fear of a resurgence of Nepalese militarism), but in time the underlying reason for his plea disappeared in the general rhetoric surrounding the development of martial-race ideas in the Indian army. Significantly, the Nepalese warriors on whom British admiration was lavished were the ordinary soldiers and not their officers. The view was becoming widespread that, as Lord Roberts was later to pronounce, 'eastern races...do not possess the qualities that go to make leaders of men' (1897, p.444). So the Nepalis could only realise their enormous martial potential under the tutelage, supervision, and leadership of British officers (see Northey, 1937, p.196). Shortly after the Anglo-Nepal war, the Nepalese government actually offered to place units of its army—with their own officers—at the disposal of the Company, but the British refused, and insisted on recruiting only ordinary riflemen who would be commanded by British officers.

The notion of Gurkhas as a martial race developed fully towards the end of the nineteenth century. British officers enthusiastically proclaimed the virtues of their soldiers. 'Their fighting qualities', wrote the author of the first handbook on Gurkhas, 'are *nulli secundus* amongst the troops we enrol in our ranks from the varied classes of our Indian Empire' (Vansittart, 1894, p.249). They are, he later added in his revised handbook on the Gurkhas, 'natural fighters', and, moreover, the cool and bracing climate of the Nepalese hills produced a robust character, physically as well as morally superior to that of any Hindu of the plains or valleys (1915, p.10).

By the end of the nineteenth century, regiments were permitted to enlist men only from the martial tribes or classes, described by headquarters. As India had been, Nepal was divided up into ethnic units and a particular set of characteristics was attributed to each on the basis of personal observations. This was especially extemporaneous in the case of Nepalese groups, since British recruiting officers were unable to visit the country (which was closed to all foreigners until after 1951), and so had no first-hand knowledge of it. Nonetheless, a few officers became avid ethnographers, producing handbooks in which ethnic differences were stressed and highlighted (see, for example, Vansittart, 1915; Morris, 1933; Gibbs, 1947). Military authors disregarded the ethnic and linguistic heterogeneity of the various groups inhabiting the middle hills of Nepal (on which all recruitment was concentrated). Differences were rendered insignificant by the premise of a common 'biology' and environment, which transmitted the collective martial inheritance. Indian army handbooks, as Omissi points out, were part of 'the urge to measure, codify and classify the Indian population' so that 'India could be comprehended (and therefore controlled)...' (1991, p.19). The tendency was to attribute to whole groups particular characteristics (like martiality) which, as we have already noted, were thought to be passed on from generation to generation. Stereotyped ethnic identities were thus carefully cultivated over many years, and continually reiterated and reinforced both in the literature produced by military writers, and orally within the informal contexts of British officer interaction (such as the mess).

These strategies of division and classification have been seen as part of 'the instinctive defence mechanism of imperialism, an understandable tendency to seek out those groups who might be relied upon by the colonial power and exclude those who could not' (Omissi, 1991, p.8; see also Enloe, 1980, p.25). But, whatever the practical politico-military implications of these policies, it is important not to overlook or dismiss the content of the martial ideology itself, which came, in time, to be regarded as a 'truth emergent from the nature of society itself' (Des Chene, 1991, p.75).

The martial groups of Nepal

For some years, Hodgson's identification of martial groups in Nepal formed a recruiting blueprint, and mainly ('tribal') Magars and

Gurungs were taken. Indeed, at one point, the Nepalese prime minister is reported to have begged the Indian army not to insist so exclusively on enlisting only members of these two communities, since the areas of western Nepal in which they lived were becoming denuded of their young men (Husain, 1970, p.246). Hodgson's other specified martial class, the (higher caste) Khas (or Chetris)—which implied the (royal caste of) Thakuris as well—whom he deemed to be somewhat less desirable because of their 'brahmanical prejudices' and devotion to the House of Gorkha (Hodgson, 1833, p.220), were lightly recruited before the Mutiny, but hardly at all for several decades after it (Cardew, 1891, p.136). Although a special regiment was formed for high-caste groups in 1893, the Gurkhas still drew their numbers predominantly from among the Magars and Gurungs whom Vansittart asserted were 'by common consent recognised as the *beau ideal* of what a Gurkha soldier should be' (1894, p.223).

Even some 'tribal' groups who shared a common middle-hill environment, as well as many aspects of history, language and culture with the Magars and Gurungs, were not initially labelled 'martial'. Peoples of the eastern hills, like the Rais and Limbus, while acknowledged as good fighters, and taken into para-military units such as the Burma Military Police and the Assam Rifles, were deemed too headstrong and quarrelsome, and so too undisciplined, to be labelled real martial classes. These latter groups, however, were gradually reclassified as martial. Another Tibeto-Burman community, the Tamangs, who were even closer to the Gurungs and Magars, in terms of both geographical propinquity and culture-history, did not acquire a martial label until the middle of this century (see Gibbs, 1947), although the latest Gurkha handbook declares that the Tamang 'makes an excellent soldier' (Leonard, 1965, p.113). While early handbooks tended to blame Tamang dietary habits (they were reputed to eat beef) for the virtual ban on their enlistment, more recent handbooks admitted that the principal region of Tamang settlement in Central Nepal was closed to recruitment on the insistence of the Nepalese government (Gibbs, 1947, p.21). Pahari suggests that these areas were closed because they immediately surrounded the capital, and the country's political rulers exercised a virtual monopoly of Tamang labour which was in 'bondage to the state and Kathmandu elites' Thus while they were relatively numerous in the Nepalese police and army, their number in foreign armies was 'disproportionately low' (Pahari, 1991, p.9). The implication is that British recruiting policy and the theory of martiality on which it was based took account of such circumstances. In similar fashion, they acquiesced in the tea-planters' request not to interfere with their labour pool for the tea-gardens, and for a time recruitment was prohibited in Darjeeling, where members of a number of Nepalese martial communities had migrated (Vansittart, 1915, p.157). By the commencement of World War I, Magars, Gurungs, Rais and Limbus were acknowledged as the principal 'Gurkha tribes', Thakurs and Khas were still being listed as such, and another Tibeto-Burman group, the Sunwars, had been added to the list (ibid., p.47).

Thus, despite the notion that martiality was 'bred in the bone' and/or environmentally determined by the climate of the middle hills, the identity of Nepalese fighting groups—like those in India (Dewey, 1992; Omissi, 1991, p.10)—did not remain static over time, and was subject to various 'external' influences. Nonetheless, martiality was perceived to be the key ingredient in enlistment. Ragsdale estimates that approximately 60 per cent of men entering Gurkha service between 1894 and 1913 were recruited as Magars and Gurungs, 27.5 per cent as Rais and Limbus, while all other ethnic communities (including Khas and Thakuris) contributed about 12.5 per cent of recruits (1990, p.13).

The place of martiality

British officers with the Gurkhas also stressed the importance of 'place' in certifying groups and individuals as 'martial'. Thus, a group which was normally deemed martial, could only be so in its own native territory. There was a belief that when, for example, Gurungs or Magars migrated to the east of the country from their original homes in western Nepal, as many of them did, they somehow ceased to retain the qualities which characterised them as martial in the first place. Military writers make statements such as 'Gurungs of Eastern Nepal are practically not Gurungs at all', or 'the Magars of Eastern Nepal are...very much inferior to those of Central Nepal...in all respects' (Vansittart, 1915, pp.78, 86); or again, Magars and Gurungs outside their native habitat are 'usually of inferior quality and are not normally enlisted' (Northey, 1937, p.94). Such assertions were usually not accompanied by any explanation, but where a reason was given it was that intermarriage had occurred—so the blood which carried the military qualities had been contaminated. Officers with the Gurkhas shared the general British abhorrence of 'miscegenation' and insisted on recruiting 'unsullied' members of the martial classes. Vansittart refers to the Magars' 'proper habitat' west of the Kathmandu Valley, where 'undoubtedly the best and purest Magars are found' (1915, p.82). But one section (the Gharti) was pronounced 'more mixed' than other (pure) Magar sections, and so those responsible for enlistment were warned to be beware when confronted with members of the former group (Vansittart, 1894, p.230). Similarly, recruiters were informed that, whereas Thakurs were 'good material', the Hamal Thakur or progeny of a Thakur and Brahman 'should not be enlisted by any regiment' (Vansittart, 1915, p.62).

British officers in the Gurkhas believed in the idea that character could be fundamentally influenced by place. For years they debated the respective merits and traits of 'western' and 'eastern' Gurkhas (see Smith, 1973, p.40). Men belonging to regiments recruited in western Nepal were thought to be more phlegmatic, but of better humour, while those enlisted from the eastern side of the country were comparatively dour and quicker to anger. While explanations for these attributes were seldom given, when pressed at interview officers might account for the differences in terms of settlement patterns or the productivity of land.

The significance of 'place' also featured centrally in the long-standing debate about the martial quality of 'line boys', the sons and grandsons of soldiers who had been born in the family 'lines' of the Gurkha battalions, had been to school, and had experienced the 'fleshpots' of India before independence, and later those of Malaya, Brunei or Hong Kong, where the regiments subsequently were quartered. The view was widespread among British officers that contact with towns corrupted a Gurkha's purity and simplicity, and so his fighting ability; and elaborate precautions were taken by recruiters to enlist only young men from the more remote parts of the Nepalese hills. The literature is replete with speculations about the extent of martial deterioration as a result of growing up in the lines. MacMunn reasoned that if such a boy had a Gurkha mother he would have 'sucked in' the regimental tradition with her milk, and kept most of the warlike traits of his father for at least one generation (1932, p.199). Similarly, early Gurkha handbooks reported that, while their physique did not deteriorate much in a single generation, their morality did, so that 'they are often men of loose habits, and are not dependable, the chief characteristics of the Gurkha being almost entirely absent from their characters.... There is no doubt that the real Gurkha despises them...' (Morris, 1933, p.126); see also Vansittart, 1915, p.92). Another military author concluded that by the second generation the line boys could hardly achieve the standard of the 'hill-bred article' as far as things like morals and dependability were concerned (Northey, 1937, p.195).

This prejudice against line boys developed fully in the latter part of the nineteenth century alongside the general British preference for what were assumed to be simple villagers, and the distrust of literate or semi-literate urban dwellers. In the middle of last century, the Gurkha regiments had actually seemed anxious to recruit line boys. In a letter to the Deputy Adjutant-General of the Indian army, the then Commander of the Sirmoor (Gurkha) Battalion, reported that he was 'encouraging men to bring their families with them, so as to have boys on the lines. These lads...I find just as good in the Field as the fresh Goorkah from Nepaul...and far more intelligent...'.[7] But within a few decades—and especially following the Mutiny—any idea of favouring men raised in the lines or in towns had disappeared. It was the 'extra wild Goorkhalees' who were now regarded as the 'most trustworthy'.[8] Uneducated youths from the hills were definitely preferred to educated young men from the plains—that is, towns (Forbes, 1964, p.158). 'If we were

[7] Letter Books, 2nd K.E.O. Goorkhas: Major C. Reid to Major Norman, 25 January 1858.

[8] Letter Books, 2nd K.E.O. Goorkhas: Lt.-Col. D. Macintyre, CO 2GR, to Adjutant-General, 1 February 1878.

to judge by the Gurkha soldier', wrote one senior British officer, 'then we would conclude that mankind is happiest and most honest where...civilising influences are least' (Tuker, 1957, p.3). The most severe deterioration in martial qualities was assumed to occur among what one author called the 'flotsam and jetsam who have drifted into the big cities' (Gibbs, 1947, p.5). In Calcutta, we are informed, 'evil communications corrupt good manners', and the Gurkha declines rapidly (Northey, 1937, pp.195-6; see also Morris, 1933, p.126).[9]

Masculinity

The rhetoric of martiality embraced an idealised notion of masculinity. Indeed, the two terms were occasionally used interchangeably. MacMunn, for example, might refer to martial classes as 'manly' classes (1932, p.358). Martial races possessed obvious masculine qualities which the non-martial races lacked. The British, we are told, found the 'fighting races' more attractive than the 'passive, supine Hindus...' (Parry 1972, p.50). Said (1985, p.23) has pointed out that the Orient was routinely described as feminine, and Inden has recently reiterated that imperial India was widely imagined as a female presence, lacking Western (masculine) rationality. Hinduism was seen to exemplify a mentality favouring the passions over reason and will, 'the two inevitable components of world-ordering rationality' (1990, pp.85-9). In the novels of empire, too, the people of India were seen as 'volatile and passionate', quintessentially female qualities (Mannsaker, 1983). Even male dress was described as graceful but essentially feminine (Tarlo, in press). The widely-held perception was therefore of European (masculine) reason dominant over an Indian (feminine) nature.

The military authors who created the discourse on Gurkhas discovered in non-martial India the very antithesis of manhood. The merchants and town-dwellers lacked 'guts' (MacMunn, 1932, p.345), while the intelligentsia were dismissed as effeminate (ibid., p.354). Masters tells us that South Indians, who inhabited what the British

[9] The same prejudice applied to Muslims in north India, who would not be recruited if they lived in towns. Omissi points to the irony of declaring such men to make poor soldiers when they could not be enlisted in the first place (1991, p.10).

termed the 'sloth belt', were all thought timid (1956, p.145). But the Bengalis, as Robb notes in his introduction to this volume, had the worst of it. They were castigated as 'soft' (Roberts, 1897/2, p.383), 'languid and enervated' (Oldfield, 1974 [1880], p.262), and 'hopeless poltroons' (MacMunn and Lovett, 1911, p.130).[10] MacMunn made it plain that the British had little regard for them, reserving their 'respect and affection for martial classes' (1932, p.345).

Nepal came out rather well in the masculinity stakes. It benefited especially by contrast, since it bordered on the homeland of what one military writer called the 'least masculine' of India's people—in Bihar and Bengal (Tuker, 1950, p.626). Nepalis also compared well against the 'effeminate races of the South' (Roberts, 1897, p.442). The contrast between plains and hills, moreover, served almost as a metaphor for masculine-feminine distinctions. The hills bred robust and sturdy men, who looked down on men of the plains as soft and supine (Forbes, 1964, pp.54-5; see also Bayly, this volume, on Elliott). One British officer wrote to his mother, after his transfer to the plains from the regimental station in the hills of what is now Pakistan, that 'all the locals seem half-dead after the Pathans.... [T]he Pathan has his faults but is a man anyway.'[11]

Nepal itself has, since the Anglo-Nepal war, been consistently portrayed by the British very much in masculine terms. Vansittart conveys the image by noting, for one thing, that the purity of Nepal's soil (as compared to that of India) had not been sullied by the 'foot of the Mohamedan conqueror'—it is interesting that he does not consider India's soil as having been 'sullied' by the British conqueror—and, for another, that the Nepalis had fought the Company 'in fair conflict like men'. Even Nepal's lingua franca (Khas-kura or Gurkhali, as the British writers called it) had a hard, masculine quality: 'terse, sim-

[10] The frontispiece of Woodyatt's (1922) book on the Gurkhas contains a photograph of a British Gurkha general dressed (presumably for a costume party) as a 'Native Clerk', with *dhoti* and *kurta*, waistcoat, turban and umbrella. The resident British community of the period would immediately have recognised the stereotype of the 'baboo', and no doubt found it immensely amusing.

[11] Unpublished letters, Oriental and India Office Collections of the British Library.

ple...very characteristic of the unlettered but energetic race of soldiers and statesmen who made it what it is' (Vansittart, 1915, pp.10, 32 and 67).[12]

Military writers also conveyed the manliness of the country in two main kinds of trope. In one, Nepal was seen as a 'military state' in which a military 'outlook' pervaded every section of society, so that the whole ethos of the Nepalese state was perceived to consist in militarism. Hodgson wrote not only of the 'martial propensities' and 'martial habits' of the highland tribes, but more generally of the 'warlike enthusiasm of the people' (1833, p.205). He referred to the 'exclusive military and aggressive genius of the Gorkha institutions, habits and sentiments' (see Hasrat, 1970, p.234). Campbell, the Assistant Surgeon at the British Residency in Kathmandu during much of Hodgson's tenure, also detected a natural propensity for the masculine activity of warfare, and the 'abhorrence of all the military tribes in Nepal to engaging in other pursuits than that of arms...' (ibid., p.226). And the theme was taken up by British military writers. One wrote of the Government of Nepal as a 'purely militarist government of a purely military people' (Bruce, 1928, p.xxiii).

In a second kind of trope, these authors stressed the contrast between what they perceived as the pervasive obsequiousness of Indians—especially those who inhabited the plains—and the spirit of independence found among the martial people of Nepal. It is not only the Gurkha as an individual or member of a martial group who possess the qualities associated with autonomy and self-reliance, but the whole political ambience in which he has lived for generations. These military writers therefore contrast the colonial subjugation of India, on the one side, with what they term Nepal's spirit of independence, on the other—a spirit which was thought symptomatic and generative of the Kingdom's military strength, dignity and, by implication, masculinity. Nepal, wrote Woodyatt, 'enjoys complete independence' (1922, p.158), while according to Morris it is a 'completely independent country and in no way subject to the orders of the Government of India...' (1935,

[12] In his study of masculinity, Seidler points out that masculine language is seen as 'deeply instrumental' (1989, p.63).

p.425). Northey, for his part, insists that, in light of Nepal's independent status, the British Resident in Kathmandu occupies an 'entirely different position from that of a Resident in a native state in India' (1937, p.59). But of course the Treaty of Sagauli, which concluded the Nepal-East India Company war of 1814-16, had imposed the Resident—the only representative of an outside power permanently stationed in the country—who kept an eye on Nepal's internal affairs, and for over a century severely restricted its right to conduct its own foreign policy. Nepal's independence was clearly limited to the extent allowed by the British (Mojumdar, 1973; see also Rose, 1971, pp.171-2; Des Chene, 1991, pp.153-8).

The persistence of martial thinking

Although the martial-race theory was effectively suspended during both world wars—in order to achieve the massive recruitment targets set by the Indian army—the end of hostilities on both occasions saw its return as the main basis of enlistment. Omissi shows that, after the First World War, the Indian army 'returned to its pre-war ethnic mix', and that martial-race thinking was not abandoned. If the theory was no longer the colonial strategy it had once been, it had nonetheless become a 'habit of mind' (1991, pp.21-2). If anything, it received a fillip with the publication in 1932 of MacMunn's volume on *The Martial Races of India*.

Even World War II, in which over 200,000 Nepalis of every description took part, appears not to have seriously shaken the confidence of British military thinkers and authors in the soundness of the theory of martiality, since it persists in providing the basis of recruitment to the Brigade of Gurkhas in the post-colonial British army. The section of the Nepalese population from which recruits are sought continues to comprise only a tiny proportion (some 6 per cent) of the total population of the country, and the area in which this population is found (the middle hills) constitutes about one-third of the total area of Nepal (Edwards, 1978, p.228). Gibbs's manual on the Gurkhas, prepared in 1943 and published just after World War II, defines the 'true Gurkha' as 'a man of the martial clans of Nepal' (1947, p.6), and lists those ethnic groups which provide true Gurkhas. Similarly, Leonard's handbook of 1965—prepared for a post-war, post-Indian independence generation, and recommended to British officers joining the Gurkhas even today—has a table listing the districts in which ethnic groups who supply Gurkhas are to be found, with comments about their martial qualities. Thus, Gurungs in one administrative area are said to be available only in small numbers and 'are not of the best type', while Magars in another area are numerous and 'of good type'. Even particular clans are labelled: in Palpa there are 'excellent' Thapa Magars, but 'careful selection is necessary and the foothills must be avoided' (Leonard, 1965, pp.138-9). These reproduce the kinds of assessments offered by Vansittart in his 1915 handbook: this Thapa clan 'needs careful enlisting' or that Thapa clan 'should not be enlisted' (see above). Thus, on the basis of evaluating a few individuals at one point in time, entire groups inhabiting large tracts of territory continue to be stereotyped as fit or unfit for martial tasks. The latest handbook also indicates the persistence long after the end of World War II of ideas about the significance of place, with statements insisting that, for example, Thakurs in eastern Nepal must be cautiously selected because it is not their 'natural habitat' (Leonard, 1965, p.139). Finally, the underlying theory of martiality is reiterated and reinforced when the same author traces the origin of the martial spirit in Nepal to the 'infusion of north Indian blood into the brave, but unenterprising hill tribes' (ibid., p.27).

Recent military contributors to the literature on Gurkhas still refer to 'martial tribes' (see Bredin, 1961; Davis, 1970; Niven, 1987) and express a traditional view on line boys. Thus, although the prejudice against the latter is said to have eased somewhat following World War I (see Woodyatt, 1922, p.194), Cross continues to insist that because of being raised away from their villages, line boys simply do not possess the 'inherent chemistry engendered by an upbringing in the hills' which enables them to 'make good if they are enlisted', although he shares the widespread opinion that the education they receive in British Army schools 'is useful when technicians and specialists are being recruited' (Cross, 1986, pp.133-4). Writers also continue to refer to the 'demanding environment' of the middle hills which form the 'hard, stoical, self-disciplined but cheerful characteristics of the Gurkhas who join the British Army' (Edwards, 1979, p.222). The image of autonomous and independent men produced by harsh surroundings also endures. According to one military writer, these qualities are found quintessentially among the Gurungs, described as nomadic pastoralists who, like the Pathans, were:

> a tribe of warriors, preferring the spoils of war to the tedium of weaving blankets, tilling the fields and minding their flocks. Moving about amid the remotest Himalayan steeps and valleys.... Perched on the heights, with their flocks... [even today] the more solitary herdsman seldom comes into conversation with other folk (Tuker, 1957, p.33).

Like many an anthropologist, these military writers see in this imagined pastoralism what Rosaldo refers to as the 'idealized characteristics of a certain masculine imagination—fierce pride, a warrior spirit, rugged individualism...' (1986, p.96).

An alternative to the Gurkha as pastoralist free-spirit is the image of the soldier as 'yeoman'. The Gurkhas, writes one post-colonial military author, 'were freehold yeoman farmers' who had 'bred in them a spirit of independence' (Forbes, 1964, p.55). As Green has pointed out, the English also believed themselves to be a nation of yeoman soldiers (1980, p.34), and the label was frequently attached to the martial classes in the Indian and especially the pre-Mutiny Bengal army (see Peers, 1991, p.551). However misleading this application of a category delineating nineteenth-century British society to contemporary South Asian contexts, it is meant to imply, among other things, that these martial people have come from the middle order of the agricultural classes, and thus share the pride and self-esteem thought to characterise the small landowner. As one senior British officer who had served with the Gurkhas commented in an interview: 'We only recruited people with land, and not landless labourers, so we creamed off the best—the independent yeomen'.

Men seeking enlistment in the Gurkhas are by now well aware of these British predilections for rural recruits possessing the idealised characteristics of a martial people. So, although many young Gurungs, for example, nowadays want to join the Gurkhas precisely to escape the village, and to have money to live well in what *they* regard as modern and civilised conditions (that is, the towns), they feel obliged to present themselves to recruiters as rustics, and to stress their martial qualities—that is, to play up to the British image of the ideal Gurkha (see Des Chene, 1991). In other ways too, the Gurkhas reproduce the rhetoric of martiality created by the British. While in Nepal in 1988, I was told by one former soldier that the governments of other countries regularly request Nepal to send quantities of Gurkha semen/seed (*biu*) so as to acquire their martial attributes. Like others labelled martial, then, Nepalis who were, are, or seek to become Gurkhas are, as Fox observes, compelled 'to adapt to British beliefs about them' (1985, p.4).

Discussion and conclusion

Dawson has drawn attention to the durability of the image, within Western cultural traditions, of the soldier as paragon of masculinity. In the Indian colonial context this ideal 'became intimately bound up with...the imagining of imperial identity, in which the Englishman enjoyed a natural, racial superiority over the...peoples who had been subordinated to British imperial power' (1991, p.119). The representation of Gurkhas by their British chroniclers in strongly martial-masculine terms may be seen therefore as a recognition in the Gurkhas of those very qualities which enabled the British to fashion an empire.

The discourse on martiality, grounded in nineteenth-century biological determinism, has survived with some slight modifications into the period of post-Indian independence and quite different scientific presuppositions.[13] Some scholars have from time to time declared the end of martial theory, but it endures in British writings about Gurkhas, although 'races' have become 'tribes' or 'classes', and the language of disdain for non-martial people has turned softer. Certainly, ethnological

[13] Cohen suggests that 'no one believes in this enlightened age in the theory of martial castes' calls for a Gilbert and Sullivanesque response: well, hardly anyone—except the military. Cohen suggests that the theory of martiality is still 'widespread' in independent India (1971, p.47). Though officially discredited, it appears to survive in the ways its soldiers are organised and portrayed. Not only are they still grouped in ethnic regiments, but military authors continue to list the special qualities of each, using terms made familiar by the British (see, for example, Das, 1984).

knowledge has grown as British officers have come into contact with a wider cross-section of Nepalese hill society, and personally gained access to many parts of the country previously closed to them, and this has been reflected in recent publications. Yet the portrait of Gurkha 'character'—in terms of inherent qualities of martiality—has remained remarkably consistent (see also Des Chene, 1991, p.81). Despite the many changes in the home environments from which the soldiers originate, and in the politico-military contexts within which the Brigade itself is situated, the Gurkhas appear caught in a time warp woven by their military chroniclers. While some officers informally contradict, even disclaim, many of the stereotypes offered in the literature, latter-day texts continue to essentialise the Gurkhas in much the same way as they did in the past.

Why should this be so? Why should ideologies generated within and fostered by an imperial context continue to pervade post-imperial military writings? One answer may simply be that images and perceptions of others tend to persist through time, despite the changing political and ideological environments in which they arose in the first place. This is especially so where those who represent others exercise dominion over virtually all aspects of their subjects' lives. The officers, from whose ranks emerge those who perpetuate the discourse on Gurkhas, control the enlistment, training, assessment, promotion, disciplining—and so ultimately the livelihoods—of their soldiers. Such omnipotence would encourage most authors to rest secure in the authenticity of their depictions.

Furthermore, tenacity of discourse is implied in the nature of the relationship between the writer and audience of such militaria. The Gurkha literary 'genre' presupposes certain expectations on the part of the reader, to which the author responds (Green, 1980). There is, in other words, something of a conspiracy between writer and audience to preserve these Gurkha 'fictions', in the sense of their consistency over time.

But the perseverance of this discourse on martiality might also be understood against the background of political and military upheavals following World War II: fundamental changes in the size and role of the British army consequent on post-war economic and power realignments, and the rapid collapse of the empire. These developments had direct consequences for the Gurkhas, which were manifested in the traumatic division of regiments between the armies of Britain and independent India in 1947-48. Some twenty years later the end of 'confrontation' in South East Asia (in which the Gurkhas had played a vital role) had further repercussions for the Brigade. Sometimes described as the British army's last great colonial battle, this was followed not only by dramatic alterations in the size and dispositions of the Gurkha regiments, but by a felt transformation in the officers' attitudes towards their calling, encouraged in part by changes in the composition of the officer corps itself. This period is perceived as heralding the rise of the career officer for whom service with Gurkhas was only one of several possible stages in the course of professional advancement, and the corresponding demise of the regimental officer, devoted above all to his unit, his colleagues, and his Gurkha soldiers. During interviews with former officers who served during the period up to and including 'Confrontation' in South-East Asia, they would invariably refer to the hostility shown by even the most senior officers to 'careerism', perceived as an insidious threat to the regimental focus of the British Gurkha officer. In the words of one: 'In the 1960s we were extremely reactionary. The company commanders in those days were wartime officers who were totally devoted to Gurkhas, and you were distrusted if you went to staff college.' Another recalled: 'In the days of Confrontation we never thought of leaving. Nobody went outside his regiment, thought of going away even for career reasons. It was only when Confrontation ended that people began getting career-minded.'

The great majority of officers who moulded the discourse and authored the literature on Gurkhas—including the most recent texts—spent their formative years in this kind of colonial or neo-colonial setting, and regarded themselves as zealously attached to 'their' Gurkhas. Against the background of what appears to these officer-authors as retrogressive change, the continuity of Gurkha portraits might therefore be understood as their attempt to preserve an image of something which no longer obtains, but which they feel should be cherished. In this respect, these Gurkha depictions are like the pre-World War I travel books which sought to retain the illusion of bygone places which had long since passed out of existence (Fussell, 1980, p.226). Through textualisation, a disappearing world might be preserved (Clifford, 1986, p.112).

Finally, it has to be noted that in numerous ways Gurkhas have been depicted as honorary Europeans, possessing the most endearing qualities of their public-school-educated British officers—courage, humour, honour, and so on. Their virtues, moreover, were consistently emphasised in contrast to the negatively-evaluated qualities of non-martial Indians (and Nepalis) who represented 'Otherness' for these authors (Caplan, 1991). The image of Gurkhas as inherently martial thus reflects the way in which British officers have for a very long time perceived themselves, and the endurance of such an image may be read as an attempt on the part of the latter to situate their own sense of identity in what would seem to be a timeless and unchanging 'racial' essence.

References

Names preceded by an asterisk (*) are British officers who served with Gurkhas.

Bennett, L. (1983). *Dangerous Wives and Sacred Sisters* (New York).

Bingley, A.H. and A. Nicholls (1918). *Caste Handbooks for the Indian Army: Brahmans* (Calcutta).

Bolt, C., (1984). 'Race and the Victorians' in C. Eldridge (ed.), *British Imperialism in the Nineteenth Century* (London).

*Bredin, A.E.C. (1961). *The Happy Warriors: the Gurkha soldier in the British Army* (Gillingham, Dorset).

*Bruce, C.G. (1928). Foreword to W.B. Northey and C.J. Morris, *The Gurkhas: their manners, customs and country* (London).

Caplan, L. (1991). '"Bravest of the brave": representations of "the Gurkha" in British military writings', *Modern Asian Studies* 25, pp.571-97.

Cardew, F.G. (1891). 'Our recruiting grounds of the future for the Indian army', *Journal of the United Service Institution of India* XX, 86, pp.131-46.

Chakravarti, P.C. (1941). *The Art of War in Ancient India* (Dacca).

Clifford, J. (1986). 'On ethnographic allegory', in J. Clifford and G.E. Marcus (eds.), *Writing Culture: the poetics and politics of ethnography* (Berkeley).

Cohen, S.P. (1971). *The Indian Army: its contribution to ther development of a nation* (Berkeley).

Creagh, Sir O'Moore (n.d.). *Indian Studies* (London).

Cross, J.P. (1986). *In Gurkha Company: the British Army Gurkhas, 1948 to the present* (London).

Das, Chand N. (1984). *Traditions and Customs of the Indian Armed Forces* (Delhi).

*Davis, P. (1970). *A Child at Arms* (London).

Dawson, G. (1991). 'The blond Bedouin: Lawrence of Arabia, imperial adventure and the imagining of English-British masculinity', in M. Roper and J. Tosh (eds.), *Manful Assertions: masculinities in Britain since 1800* (London).

Des Chene, M. (1991). 'Relics of Empire: a cultural history of the Gurkhas, 1815-1987', PhD thesis, Stanford University.

Dewey, Clive (1992). 'Racism and realism: the theory of the martial caste', unpublished paper given to the SOAS workshop on 'the Concept of Race in South Asia' (2 December).

*Edwards, J.H. (1979). 'Nepal and the Brigade of Gurkhas', *Royal Engineers' Journal* V, 93, pp.220-30.

Enloe, C.H. (1980). *Ethnic Soldiers: state security in divided societies* (Harmondsworth).

*Forbes, D. (1964). *Johnny Gurkha* (London).

Fox, R.G. (1985). *Lions of the Punjab: culture in the making* (Berkeley).

Fussell, P. (1980). *Abroad: British literary travelling between the wars* (New York).

*Gibbs, H.R.K. (1947). *The Gurkha Soldier* (Calcutta).

Green, Martin (1980). *Dreams of Adventure, Deeds of Empire* (London).

Hamilton, F.H. (1819). *An Account of the Kingdom of Nepal* (Edinburgh).

Hasrat, B.J. (1970). *History of Nepal: as told by its own and contemporary chroniclers* (Hoshiarpur, Punjab).

Heathcote, T.A. (1974). *The Indian Army: the garrison of British imperial India, 1822-1922* (Vancouver).

Hodgson, B.H. (1833). 'Origin and classification of the military tribes of Nepal', *Journal of the Asiatic Society* 11, pp.17-24.

Husain, A. (1970). *British India's Relations with the Kingdom of Nepal 1857-1947* (London).

Inden, R. (1990). *Imagining India* (Oxford).

Kirkpatrick, W. (1811). *An Account of the Kingdom of Nepaul* (London).

*Leonard, R.G. (1965). *Nepal and the Gurkhas* (for the Ministry of Defence) (London).

MacMunn, Sir G. (1932). *The Martial Races of India* (London).

MacMunn, Sir G. and A.C. Lovett (1911). *The Armies of India* (London).

Mannsaker, F. (1983). 'Early attitudes to empire', in B. Moore-Gilbert (ed.), *Literature and Imperialism* (Roehampton).

Mason, P. (1974). *A Matter of Honour: an account of the Indian army, its officers and men* (London).

*J. Masters. (1956). *Bugles and a Tiger: a personal adventure* (London).

Mojumdar, K. (1973). *Anglo-Nepalese Relations in the Nineteenth Century* (Calcutta).

*Morris, C.J. (compiler) (1933). *Gurkhas: Handbooks for the Indian Army* (Delhi).

____, (1935). 'Some aspects of social life in Nepal', *Journal of the Royal Central Asiatic Society* 22, pp.425-46.

*Niven, Col. B.M. (1987). *The Mountain Kingdom: portraits of Nepal and the Gurkhas* (Singapore).

*Northey, W.B. (1937). *The Land of the Gurkhas or the Himalayan Kingdom of Nepal* (Cambridge).

Oldfield, H.A. (1974 [1880]). *Sketches from Nepal: historical and descriptive with an essay on Nepalese Buddhism and illustrations of religious monuments and architecture* (Delhi).

Omissi, D. (1991). '"Martial Races": ethnicity and security in colonial India 1858-1939', *War and Society* 9, pp.1-27.

Pahari, A. (1991). 'Ties that bind: Gurkhas in history', *Himal* 4, 3, pp.6-12.

Parry, B. (1972). *Delusions and Discoveries: studies on India in the British imagination 1880-1930* (London).

Peers, D.M. (1991). '"The habitual nobility of being": British officers and the social construction of the Bengal Army in the early nineteenth century', *Modern Asian Studies* 25, pp.545-69.

Pemble, J. (1971). *The Invasion of Nepal: John Company at War* (Oxford).

Ragsdale, T.A. (1990). 'Gurungs, Goorkhalis, Gurkhas: speculations on a Nepalese ethno-history', *Contributions to Nepalese Studies* 17, pp.1-24.

Roberts, Field-Marshal Lord, of Kandahar (1897). *Forty-one Years in India: from subaltern to Commander-in-Chief* (London).

Rosaldo, R. (1986). 'From the door of his tent: the fieldworker and the inquisitor', in J Clifford and G. Marcus (eds.), *Writing Culture: the poetics and politics of ethnography* (Berkeley).

Rose, E.L. (1971). *Nepal: strategy for survival* (Berkeley).

Said, E. (1985). 'Orientalism reconsidered', in F. Barker *et al.*, *Europe and its Others*, vol.I (Colchester).

Seidler, V. (1989). *Rediscovering Masculinity: reason, language and sexuality* (London).

Shaha, R. (1986). 'The rise and fall of Bhimsen Thapa: the war of 1814-16 with British India and its aftermath', *Rolamba* 6, pp.2-7.

*Shakespear, L.W. (1913). 'The war with Nepal: operations in Sirmoor, 1814-1815', *Journal of the United Services Institute of India* XLII, pp.369-79.

*Smith, E.D. (1973). *Britain's Brigade of Gurkhas* (London).

Street, B. (1975). *The Savage in Literature: representations of 'primitive' society in English fiction 1858-1920* (London).

Stiller, L.F. (1989 [1968]). *Prithwinarayan Shah in the Light of Dibya Upadesh* (Kathmandu).

Tarlo, E. (in press). *Dress and Undress in India: the problem of 'what to wear' in the late colonial and modern era* (London).

*Tuker, Sir F. (1950). *While Memory Serves* (London).

____, (1957). *Gorkha: the story of the Gurkhas of Nepal* (London).

*Vansittart, E. (1894). 'The tribes, clans and castes of Nepal', *Journal of the Asiatic Society of Bengal* 63, 2, pp.213-49.

____, (1915). *Gurkhas: Handbooks for the Indian Army* (Calcutta).

*Woodyatt, N. (1922). *Under Ten Viceroys: the reminiscences of a Gurkha* (London).

Chapter 9

THE EFFEMINATE AND THE MASCULINE: NATIONALISM AND THE CONCEPT OF RACE IN COLONIAL BENGAL

Indira Chowdhury-Sengupta

The year 1900 saw the publication of a biography of a Bengali colonel: Colonel Suresh Biswas.[1] Born in 1861 in the village of Nathpur, in Nadia in Bengal, Suresh Biswas travelled to England in 1874. Among other things he worked in a circus in Kent and later as an animal-trainer in Hamburg. He finally joined the Brazilian army in 1887, by which time (we learn from a letter to his uncle), he had mastered seven foreign languages: English, French, German, Spanish, Portuguese, Italian, Danish and Dutch.[2] He trained as a surgeon at the army hospital in Rio de Janeiro, and by 1894 had been promoted to the position of lieutenant. He had led a small band of soldiers in 1893 in the defence of Rio de Janeiro from rebels, and died there, with the rank of Colonel, in 1902.[3]

The very term 'Bengali colonel' seemed, in the context of colonial Bengal, a contradiction in terms, not only because Bengalis did not serve in the imperial army until World War I, but also because by the turn of the century the stereotype of the effete Bengali with 'the intellect of a Greek and the grit of a rabbit' had become fairly well established.[4] How then had it become possible for a frail Bengali to

[1] Upendra Krishna Banerji, *Karnel Suresh Bishvas* (1900; second edition, Calcutta 1909-10).

[2] Letter to uncle Kailash Biswas from Santa Cruz dated 8 February 1887, reprinted in Upendra Krishna Banerji, *Karnel Suresh Bishvas*, p.197.

[3] His letter to his uncle from Rio dated 10 January 1894, enclosed a photograph of himself in lieutenant's uniform. The letter reads: 'You will be astounded to know that I had to spend one thousand dollars to have this uniform tailored, because of its beautiful material, the feathers and silk and gold braids', ibid., p.204.

[4] Sir Frank Dunlop Smith, private secretary to the Viceroy, 1905-10, in M. Gilbert, *Servant of India* (London, 1966), quoted in John Rosselli, 'The self-image of effeteness: physical education and nationalism in nineteenth-century Bengal', *Past and Present* 86 (1980), p.121.

attain a high rank in the army? The fascinating story of Colonel Suresh Biswas, who served in the Brazilian army, became immensely popular during the Swadeshi movement of 1905 because it seemed to substantiate an identity which the colonial stereotype of the non-martial Bengali had consistently deemed inconceivable. The story unfolds for us the interplay between the twin notions of race and gender as a part of a larger nationalist self-assertion in colonial Bengal.

The biography of Suresh Biswas, which was published together with seven of the letters he wrote to his uncle from Brazil between 1887 and 1894, contained the essential ingredients which could contest the colonial notion of the weak Bengali. As Rosselli has demonstrated, the Bengali nationalist elite took up this racial stereotype and 'strove to overcome its supposed degeneracy through the pursuit of physical culture'.[5] Mrinalini Sinha has revealed how this popular stereotype was part of the 'British response to the political challenge from the Bengali middle class'.[6] Both these important studies, however, have hardly dealt with the emerging nationalist self-definitions which deployed the Orientalist notion of a common Aryan race in order to contest the colonial racial stereotype of the non-martial Bengali. This paper takes up the specific case of Bengal, though other formulations probably emerged in other parts of India.

Suresh Biswas represented a particular heroic identity with which nationalism sought to counter the colonially-constructed image of the weak Bengali. The lack of conviction about the physical capabilities of the Bengali based itself on several notions which originated in the earlier part of the nineteenth century. They emerged out of a complex network of discourses: Orientalist scholarship, social Darwinism, and the British policy of recruiting 'martial races' into the imperial army. More generally, British official attitudes generally labelled Indians as weak, not only because of their physical stature, but also because of what was perceived to be a moral inadequacy. The British 'often

[5] Ibid.

[6] Mrinalini Sinha, 'Gender and imperialism: colonial policy and the ideology of moral imperialism in late nineteenth-century Bengal', in Michael S. Kimmel (ed.), *Changing Men: New directions in research on men and masculinity* (Newbury Park, 1987), p.217.

suspected that Indians were by nature more lascivious than they were themselves. Child-marriage and polygamy seemed to prove it.'[7] The inability to control sexuality was a charge levelled at both Indian men and women. The complex response to such allegations engendered the self-descriptive oppositional discourse which deployed the category 'race', frequently in a generalised sense.

II

The nineteenth century saw the proliferation of the myth of the Aryan in Europe, which had interesting reverberations in colonies like India. By the middle of the nineteenth century, what was an initially philological category became a value-loaded term denoting a superior civilisation.[8] In concert with the prevalent nineteenth-century theory of social Darwinism, it made way for a theory of a superior master race. The Orientalist identification of the Hindus as successors of the ancient Aryans assumed that the rulers and the ruled shared a common racial origin: this was problematic within the colonial context. The manner in which colonial discourse sought to accommodate the identification reveals the complex interaction between discourses of power within the context of colonialism. The indigenous notion of *jati*, which signified race, tribe and caste identity, increasingly accommodated the Hindus' notional origin as nationalists began to deploy the term 'Aryan' as a self-descriptive category.[9] Within the context of nineteenth-century

[7] Kenneth Ballhatchet, *Race, Sex and Class under the Raj: Imperial attitudes and policies and their critics, 1793-1905* (London, 1980), p.5.

[8] Partha Mitter's presentation at the SOAS workshop on the 'Concept of Race in South Asia' [not included in this volume] reveals the way in which European historians of Indian art deployed this transformed linguistic category as a cultural one. Thus a racial theory of culture became the basis of stylistic morphology in accounts about the evolution of art in India. See Partha Mitter, 'The Aryan myth and British writings on Indian art and culture'.

[9] While colonial policy had targeted depraved customs (especially Hindu ones), the researches of the Orientalist scholars had elevated Hinduism as emanating from the venerable site of a flourishing, ancient civilisation. Within such a construction the present degeneration of the Hindu's character into an idolatrous and superstitious one had been induced by Muslim intervention. The Hindu was thus identified as a victim-figure, and his deliverance from colonial imputations, of being ignorant, prejudiced and superstitious, constituted a part of the Orientalist mission. Friedrich Max Müller, in his defence of the 'native

nationalism in Bengal, the term *jati* in its wider sense denoted the greater community of Indians: the nation that was in the making. In its narrower sense, it denoted caste-hierarchy with reference to the local communities among the Hindus themselves. Thus, within events organised by the Hindu Mela, which began functioning in 1867, Aryan racial identity became an overarching theme. Caste identities remained secondary to such grand nationalist projects even though they continued to monitor social events and played an important role in the politics of Bengal. Athough caste became a significant political category by the 1930s,[10] within the broad framework of early nationalism the term *jati* referred to a 'common Indian race'—a term riddled with contradictions.

The nationalist self-definition appropriated Orientalist as well as ethnographic research. Risley's ethnographic work borrowed from Alfred Lyall the idea of a biracial composition of Hindu society, the higher castes belonging to the Aryan stock, and the lower castes being the non-Aryan autochthons of the land.[11] Social Darwinism aided further in elaborating this idea, as is exemplified in indigenous attempts at writing history during this period. The conquering Aryans were seen as settling in ancient India, and the indigenous historical discourse clearly designated these people as the ancestors of the Hindus. Originally, as a nineteenth-century historian tells us, the ancient inhabitants of India lacked ethics and religion. Although very little is available by way of description, says Priyanath Mukhopadhyay, a 'consideration of the uncivilised races like the Santals and the Kols who have descended from them, indicate that huge trees, stones and objects that generated fear were worshipped as gods by them'.[12] With

Hindu' character, therefore evoked the dreadful nature of Muslim rule—'after reading the accounts of the terrors and horrors of Mohamedan rule, my wonder is that so much of native virtue and truthfulness should have survive', F. Max Müller, 'On the truthful character of the Hindus', *Collected Works of Friedrich Max Müller*, vol.XIII (London, 1910), p.72. By positing the Muslims as the repulsive and barbaric Other, Müller established Hinduism as a set of currently corrupted manners that required an urgent rescue.

[10] See Sekhar Bandyopadhyay, *Caste, Politics and the Raj: Bengal 1872-1937* (Calcutta, 1990).

[11] Ibid., p.35.

[12] Priyanath Mukhopadhyay, *Balya Shiksha Banglar Itihas* ('A Children's History of Bengal') (Habra, 1891), p.2.

the coming of the Aryans a superior culture was introduced: 'A race superior to the ancient inhabitants of India arrived here from a northwestern direction. This was the Aryan race; they are our ancestors.'[13] The notion of the Aryan race, denoting a superior civilisation, came to be deployed as a cultural category. Indeed, the Hindutva of early nationalism took much of its justification from this racial identity which fused biology and culture.

Rajnarayan Basu's '*Briddha Hindu asha*', or 'The hopes of an old Hindu', published towards the end of the century, focused this racial-cum-cultural identity in significant ways. Originally written in English in 1881, the pamphlet was translated into Bengali in 1886 and appeared in the periodical *Nabajiban*.[14] This pamphlet can be seen as a progression from Rajnarayan's earlier 'Prospectus for the society for the promotion of national feeling among the educated natives of Bengal' (1866). Rajnarayan envisaged an organisation for Hindus to give voice to their various grievances, and also to safeguard their economic interests. Rajnarayan's definition of what characterises a Hindu illustrated the interactive matrix from which such cultural definitions of race originated. Insisting that Hindutva does not depend on the food-habits or the dress of a people, he asserted that it was dependent on a common origin. Firstly, Rajnarayan claimed an Aryan descent for the Hindus. However, in order to distinguish his position from the Orientalist one, from which it obviously derived, Rajnarayan pointed out that this criterion effectively included all the subordinate groups that Indian Aryans had united under the term Aryan—therefore it signified the Brahmans of Madras as well as other subordinate groups. Secondly, his definition necessarily precluded all communities that did not accept the *Ramayana*, *Mahabharata* and the eighteen *Puranas* as histories of their past. Thus Rajnarayan synthesised a concept of community, using nineteenth-century Orientalist racial and textual terms: he presented the notion of the common Aryan race from which Hindus descended, and the notion of ancient texts which contain the genealogy of that community.

[13] Ibid., p.2.
[14] See Rajnarayan Basu, *Atma Charit* (Calc .tta, 1908), p.96.

The third of Rajnarayan's criteria linked racial origin with language. Thus the Hindus were a community that shared a common mother-language—Sanskrit. Once more drawing upon Orientalist research, Rajnarayan based this nexus of language and race on the theory of the Indo-Aryan family of languages, a theory which viewed most of the languages spoken by the Hindus in India as deriving from Sanskrit. To this Rajnarayan also added those non-Aryan languages which had admitted many Sanskrit words. His final descriptive feature is the acceptance of one supreme godhead, by which definition the Brahmans, the Sikhs, the Vaishnavas, the Kabir-panthis, the Nanak-panthis and the Brahmos all took on a Hindu identity.[15]

The identification of the land of the Aryans—*Aryavarta*—with *Bharat* or India thus set in motion a process of differentiation which marked out the Aryans from the non-Aryans. Thus Muslims and other communities could have no claim to this great racial heritage. In the contemporary context, Rajnarayan saw a political alliance with the Muslims to be desirable and necessary, but he discarded the possibility of a united front:

> Just as racial impediments should not hinder the political alliance of these two groups, the fact that any deep-rooted affiliation with our Muslim brothers is impossible, should not prevent us from establishing our Great Hindu Organisation for the benefit of Hindus.[16]

Rajnarayan's attempt to differentiate and thus marginalise the Muslim population in Bengal was a fairly common 'nationalist' stance. An article in Manomohan Basu's journal *Madhyastha*, in 1873, had expressed the same attitude. Answering criticisms against the National Association, a body precipitated by the Hindu Mela in 1870,[17] for not including Muslims or Christians, the article asserted:

> Dwelling in the same country does not necessarily mean that you belong to the same nation. And just because there are many nationalities in the country, it

[15] See Rajnarayan Basu, *Briddha Hindur Asha: Maha Hindu Samiti name ek maha samiti sthapaner prastab* ('The Hopes of an Old Hindu: a proposal to establish a grand organisation called the Maha Hindu Samiti') (2nd edn., Calcutta, 1892), pp.6-7.

[16] Ibid., p.5.

[17] Jogesh Chandra Bagal, *Hindu melar Itibritta*, p.61.

does not follow that the Hindus cannot append the epithet 'National' to their own gathering. The Hindus are the ancient inhabitants of this land and they have lived here for thousands and thousands of years; they are also the majority; even if they are defeated as a nation, this is their country; not the rash usurpers, but only the Hindus are the true, legitimate children of the *Bharat Mata*. No matter who confiscates their wealth, their dignity, their freedom, their princely status, their landed property, the Hindus will still retain the right to use the adjective 'national'.[18]

The adjective *jatiya* ('national') thus came to denote a Hindu nationality which could trace its genealogy to the ancient Aryans. By an extension of the same argument, the Hindus were the original and, by implication, the legitimate inhabitants of *Aryavarta*. This was seen as reason enough to exclude Muslims and other communities. On the other hand, the conceptualisation of racial heritage in terms of culture rather than biology made possible the occasional acceptance of exemplary figures from other religious groups within the broad category Aryan. This exceptional integration was effected by instituting a false universalism as the essence of Hinduism. Outstanding contemporary figures from other communities were thus accepted provided they demonstrated virtues that were deemed Hindu or broadly Aryan. The Aryan heritage of Suresh Biswas was emphasised while his conversion to Christianity was glossed over. This was specifically a Bengali response.

This configuration of race is clarified further by the Bengali reaction to the theory of what came to be known as the 'martial races' and dictated recruitment policy following the reorganisation of the Indian army after the Mutiny of 1857. It was advocated and put into practice by Lord Roberts, the Commander-in-Chief of the Indian Army between 1885 and 1893.[19] The codification of the theory went hand-in-hand with a definition whereby the fighting instinct was seen as the appropriate expression of manliness.[20] The theory considerably shaped the Ben-

[18] '*Jatiya bhab O jatiya anusthan*', *Madhyastha*, February 1873, p.703.

[19] One of the earliest analytical studies of this theory was by Nirad C. Chaudhuri, 'The "martial races" of India', *Modern Review* xlviii, 1 (1930), pp.41-51, and xlviii, 3, pp.295-307.

[20] David Omissi, *The Sepoy and the Raj: a social and political history of the Indian army, 1860-1940* (forthcoming), ch.I, passim.

gali's defence of his contested self. However, the added gloss of being designated non-martial, from the 1880s onwards, simply intensified an existing sense of humiliation. The exclusion of Bengalis from the Indian army had had a longer history, and had given rise to the stereotype of the effete, unmilitary and cowardly Bengalis.[21] The slight of army-recruitment policy reinforced a repeated categorisation of the Bengali babu as effeminate and weak.

The babus' supposedly cowardly response to the tough and manly task of war formed the core of many jokes which surfaced in different literary genres. Illustrating the self-image of a weakling, Kaliprasannas Sinha burlesqued the meeting held at the Hindu Metropolitan College in May 1857 to condemn the Mutiny and express loyalty to the British government. Assuming the persona of 'Hutom Pyancha' or 'Barn Owl', Kaliprasanna wrote:

> Sniffing danger, the Bengali Babus organised a meeting...to convince the *Saheb* that 'Although a hundred years have passed, they are still...[the] ill-fated chicken-hearted Bengalis—even after years of hobnobbing with the British and imbibing British education...they have failed to become like the Americans. ...Many of their bigwigs are so scared of storms that they do not take a boat ride on the Ganges, if they have to urinate at night they have to be accompanied by their wives or their servants and maids to the toilet...they are frightened even of their own shadows—that these people will fight is absolutely impossible.[22]

In contrast to this caricature, ten years later the *National Paper* carried an article on 'Can the Bengalees be a military nation?' This argued against colonial allegations that the Bengalis under foreign rule were degenerate in mind and body, that they were of a speculative disposition, that they married early and that hence their offspring were weaklings, that they lacked enterprise and daring, and that they were physically weak and effeminate. The article dismissed the first two assertions as untrue, and, while admitting some ill-effects from child-

[21] See Rosselli, 'The self-image of effeteness', and Mrinalini Sinha, 'Colonial policy and the ideology of moral imperialism'.

[22] Kaliprasanna Sinha, *Hutom Pyanchar Naksha* ('Sketches by the "Barn Owl"', 1862), Arun Nag (ed.), *Satika Hutom Pyanchar Naksha* (Calcutta, 1991), p.133.

marriage, asserted that social reform was rapidly changing the custom of child-marriage. The article argued also that, though the urban, educated babu might well be physically weak, the lower classes of Bengalis were employed under zamindars as *lathiyals*, while some others became terrorising dacoits. In conclusion, it asked: 'If Bengali low-class men can be employed for such purposes, why cannot they be brought up for the better purpose of being soldiers?'[23] While 'low-class' men were thus perceived as already possessing the necessary prerequisites for a military career, another article in the same paper argued that the weak babu required preparation before he could 'shoulder the musket', for 'the possessing of strong, robust, healthy constitutions makes *men* and *heroes*'.[24]

The Aryan theme answered this search for 'men and heroes' in certain specific ways. Historians like Rajanikanta Gupta presented to Bengalis the essence of Aryan qualities in his book *Arya Kirti*, or the 'Glorious Deeds of the Aryans' (4th edition, 1887). Rajanikanta's heroes were Rajputs, and included Rana Kumbha, Rai Mal and Rana Pratap. Mainly he followed Tod's *Annals and Antiquities of Rajasthan*, published in two volumes in 1829 and 1832; indeed stories of Rajput valour that circulated in nineteenth-century Bengal usually originated in Tod's *Annals*. Tod's popularity in contemporary Bengal is attested to not only by the several attempts at translation—between 1873 and 1898 at least two different Bengali translations of Tod's *Annals* were published—[25] but also by numerous plays, novels and poems that had Rajput protagonists.[26] Rajanikanta Gupta contextualised the stories in terms of the lack of patriotism in contemporary Bengal. His history

[23] 'Cannot the Bengalees be a military nation?', *National Paper*, 22 May 1867, p.244.

[24] 'Courage and exercise', *National Paper*, 12 June 1867, p.281. Emphasis in original.

[25] These were the anonymous *Rajasthaner Itibritta*, vol.1 (1872), which announced that it would be published every month; Yagneswar Bandyopadhyay's *Sachitra Rajasthan*, vols.1-2 (1882-3), introduced by Mahendranath Vidyanidhi (4th edition, 1906). Mahendranath hailed Tod's *Rajasthan* as 'our flag of victory!', p.iii.

[26] For details of the literary works, too numerous to name here, see Barun Kumar Chakrabarti, *Toder Rajasthan O Bangla Sahitya* (Calcutta, 1984).

seems to be a text representing the nineteenth-century preoccupation with a political self-definition, where the valiant Rajputs demonstrated in physique and in spirit their Aryan ancestry. The constant deployment of Rajput legend in reconstructing an heroic self-image was, as Kaviraj has shown, an attempt by Bengalis to 'see themselves as part of a larger whole.... At the same time, this implies a faint, uncharacteristic, admission of inadequacy, of being unable to cope with British colonialism singlehandedly.'[27]

One of the items *Arya Kirti* defined at the very outset was the nature of 'true' courage. Courage was defined in terms of *nyaya* and *dharma*. Both terms were codified in terms of Hindu standards, whereby *nyaya* refers to justice and an ethical base, and the related term *dharma* connotes adherence to a sacred principle. Both terms become very important in Rajanikanta's delineation of the noble Aryans. For him, physical prowess was only one attribute. Aryans were defined by other qualities as well: 'The deeds of the Aryans did not end with the wars they fought. Together with immense courage, they combined intelligence, truthfulness and charitable qualities and so are still worshipped by the whole world.'[28] Rajanikanta established that the Rajputs were the true inheritors of Aryan qualities, and saw in them the embodiment of true courage.

For the oppositional identity in the making, the Aryan theme thus came to denote more than a racial distinctiveness. It came to signify a cultural superiority. The imagined geographical space occupied by the Aryans was thus a landscape of heroism. The gendering of this self-descriptive discourse of race attempted to challenge the colonial notion of the effeminate Bengali by constructing alternative heroic figures, male as well as female. The process was a complex one. Rajput examples served as a pre-history of the Bengalis. If the Rajput heroes were manly and martial, so were Karmadevi, Rani Durgavati and a host of other Rajput heroines. Padmini and Krishnakumari, who did not

[27] Sudipta Kaviraj, 'Imaginary history', Occasional Papers on History and Society, Second Series No.VII, Nehru Memorial Museum and Library (New Delhi., 1987), p.107.

[28] Rajanikanta Gupta, *Arya Kirti*, p.117.

hesitate to kill themselves to protect the honour of the land, were important figures in Rajanikanta Gupta's depiction of the glorious deeds of the Aryans.

Aryan womanhood, with its heroic capacity to sacrifice, was, as Uma Chakravarti has demonstrated, a construction that suited the goals of nationalism.[29] The dauntless daughters of Aryavarta did not hesitate to defend the land against the enemies of their fathers or their husbands. At times they took up arms like the heroic Karmadevi, while at others they welcomed death, ascending the funeral pyre like Queen Padmini, rather than surrender to the enemy. In either case, the heroism of war, which could be achieved through a patriotic death, was not seen as a male privilege. Rajanikanta Gupta's glorification of Rajput queens and princesses demonstrated that the martial temperament was not exclusively male. These heroic tales played a complex role in the nationalist self-assertion of the late nineteenth and early twentieth centuries.

Yet such constructions of Aryan womanhood—militant, capable and in control, in contrast to the effete babu—were not simple compensatory self-images. The simultaneous nationalist construction of the *birmata*, or the brave mother who was capable of mothering fearless sons, was also linked to the imaging of heroic womanhood.[30] The besieged motherland awaited liberation by her courageous sons. In the mothering of heroes lay the hope for rejuvenating the fallen race of Bengalis. Thus Dwarakanath Gangopadhyay's song, included in Yogindranath Sarkar's anthology of nationalist songs, urged:

Rise, Oh sisters!
Oh wives and mothers of the brave!
Instruct your offspring,
As you nurse them at your breast
In legends heroic!

[29] Uma Chakravarti, 'Whatever happened to the Vedic dasi? Orientalism, nationalism and a script for the past', in Kumkum Sangari and Sudesh Vaid (eds.), *Recasting Women: Essays in colonial history* (New Delhi, 1989), pp.27-87.

[30] See Jashodhara Bagchi, 'Representing nationalism: Ideology of motherhood in colonial Bengal', *Economic and Political Weekly* (hereafter*EPW*), 20-27 October 1990, pp.WS-66-8; and Tanika Sarkar, 'Nationalist iconography: Image of women in nineteenth-century Bengal', *EPW*, 21 November 1987, pp.2011-15.

So the blood vibrates with pride as it flows in their veins.[31]

In the figure of Suresh Biswas nationalism found one such heroic son of the motherland. At the same time this was a compelling oppositional self-image.

The elaborate intertwining of themes—martial competence and gender—articulated a self-definition which could confront colonial denigration. If the British perceived the martial temperament as an expression of masculinity, the self-descriptive discourse of nationalism took the notion of masculinity further. The manliness that expressed itself on the battlefield could not be quantified in terms of military achievements alone: the Aryan definition of courage that refused to swerve from the path of *dharma* became the yardstick of such achievements. It was thus demonstrated that colonial denigration of the Bengali as 'effeminate' displayed a very narrow view of femininity, for, as the oppositional nationalist discourse argued, Aryan women were militant and capable of governing. Far from being despicable, for Aryan womanhood embodied and typified heroism. Thus the medieval Rajput heroines came to represent the response of an affronted Bengali masculinity.

III

By the turn of the century, however, attempts were being made to reinstate Bengali heroism. The focus was now on Bengal and instances of Bengali courage. Prior to Suresh Biswas, this search for Bengali heroism attempted to recall stray incidents of heroism displayed during the Mutiny of 1857. Rajnarayan Basu's recollection of the 'fighting Moonsiff', in his 'Prospectus for a society for the promotion of national feeling among the educated natives of Bengal', which appeared in the *National Paper* in 1866, fused the theme of loyalty with the demand for physical education. Rajnarayan had stressed a new pedagogy for the Bengalis—a process which involved the emulation of historical examples:

[31] Yogindranath Sarkar, *Bande Mataram* (6th edn., Calcutta, 1908), p.136. Sumit Sarkar points out that this anthology of songs went through three editions in September 1905, and the fourth was published the following March. Sumit Sarkar, *The Swadeshi Movement in Bengal: 1903-1908* (New Delhi, 1973), p.290.

> The Society will also publish tracts in Bengalee, giving, by instances quoted from the ancient history of the country, proofs of the military prowess of the ancient Bengalees, and mentioning isolated instances of the existence of such prowess in modern Bengalees also, such as the celebrated 'fighting Moonsiff' who figures in the late Sepoy Rebellion on behalf of the English.[32]

The 'fighting Moonsiff' was Babu Pearymohun Banerjee of Uttarpara, who at the time was munsiff of Allahabad. In the context of nineteenth-century Bengal it is not surprising that the dichotomy between intellect and physical strength should be located at the heart of reports about this incident. Referring to the *Calcutta Review's* accolade for Pearymohun's display of 'a capacity for rule and a fertility of resource', the *Friend of India* retorted:

> We are not slow to scold Bengalees when required, but if in India there is a race to whom God has given capacity, real clearness of brain, it is the Bengalee. Take the most timid quaking wretch of a Kayust you can find, put him in any district in India with a shadow of authority, and if he does not make Punjabee and Sikh and Marhatta and Hindostanee work themselves to death for his benefit, and think all the while it is for their own, he is no true Bengalee.[33]

The 'fighting Moonsiff', the anonymous tract informs us, was not only promoted to Deputy Magistrate and Deputy Collector in Banda, but was also given some jagir land.[34] The theme of loyalty merged here with defiance against the stereotype of the weak but intelligent Bengali. The theme was to remain important even many decades after the Mutiny. In 1907 the courage of the 'fighting Moonsiff' entered a discussion about identity and diet in the historical journal *Aitihasik Chitra*,[35] and Pearymohun found a prominent place in Gyanendramohan Das's compendium of eminent Bengalis in other provinces.[36] Another Bengali to whom Gyanendramohan paid tribute, was Durgacharan

[32] Rajnarayan Basu, 'Prospectus', *Hindu Melar Itibritta*, p.92.

[33] Quoted in *The Mutinies and the People*, p.141.

[34] Ibid., pp.141, 193.

[35] Ashvini Kumar Sen, '*Sipahi yuddhe bhento Bangali*' ('The rice-eating Bengali in the Sepoy Mutiny'), *Aitihasik Chitra*, August-September 1907, pp.211-4.

[36] Gyanendra Mohan Das, *Banger Bahire Bangali: Uttar Bharat* ('Bengalis outside Bengal: North India') (Calcutta, 1915), pp.69-73.

Bandyopadhyay.[37]

However, while Pearymohun and Durgacharan were both strictly-speaking civilians who had proved their martial skill in 1857, Suresh Biswas visibly proved that Bengalis could serve in the army proper. His life could become an occasion to trace the Aryan descent, as also to refute charges that Bengalis were non-martial. The notion of race was thus tied up not only with a civilisational category which encompassed the whole of India, but also with a more specific Bengali identity that was attempting to contest colonial classification. The very existence of a Bengali colonel challenged the colonial stereotype.

The preface of his biography is particularly interesting in the way it unfolds the story of a colonial slight; the author defers his introduction of the hero in order to discuss several issues central to the indigenous definition of race and racial heritage. First of all, he is careful to construct the geographical boundaries within which this particular racial heritage is contained. Identifying India as the sacred birthplace of an ancient civilisation—Aryavarta—the preface tells the story of the transformation of the militant Aryans. Bengal, the setting of the story, was a flourishing landscape of plenty, which had lured even the heroic Aryans into indolent placidity.[38] When the conquering Aryans came to Bengal, they found

> the land fertile and the climate mild and pleasant. Slowly the local landscape began to exercise its captivating influence over these conquering Aryans. They began to harvest plenty of crops without exerting themselves. The sweetness of nature also made them mild and gentle and the more or less forgot the great virtus of the constant enthusiasm for work.[39]

Genealogically the Bengali had an Aryan heritage—not an entirely new concept. The particular genealogy was then deployed in early

[37] Durgacharan had joined as a clerk in the Adjutant Office and was posted along with the regiment to Hansi in the Punjab. In his autobiography, which was serialised in the Bengali journal *Janmabhumi* in 1890-91, he wrote of the amazement of the soldiers (obviously non-Bengali) at his skill in horse-riding and sword-play. They would ask: 'Babu! You do not look like a Bengali. Are you really a Bengali?'; Durgacharan Bandyopadhyay, '*Amar jibancharit*' ('My autobiography'), *Janmabhumi* I(7), 1890, p.371

[38] Ibid., p.4.

[39] Ibid., p.4.

nationalist writings as a rejoinder to the colonial classification of the Bengalis as a people incapable of physical vigour or any substantial degree of heroism. History was seen as containing the basic elements of an evolving nationhood. As Baidyanath Barat stated in the preface to his *Arya Darpan*, written in 1877: 'Wherever you find the word Hindu in this book please understand it to mean Aryan.'[40] Indeed, the correspondence that was sought between the Aryan and the Hindu very often guided the demand for reform by remodelling distorted custom closer to the ancient ideal.

Geographically the territory occupied by the ancient Aryans was seen as corresponding to the present-day northern India, as typified in antiquarian researches of Rajendralal Mitra:

> The Vedic Hindus called themselves aryas, and the tract in which they settled themselves in India has the distinctive name of Aryadesa.... The Aryadesa or Aryavartta [sic!] of Manu is bounded on the north by the Himalaya; and on the south by the Vindhyan chain.[41]

Thus on account of the specific geographical location, as well as shared original customs, the Aryans were envisaged as the predecessors of the present Hindu inhabitants of India. Most historical texts insisted upon this link as firmly as they validated the superiority of the ancient Aryans. Cultural superiority which was thus affirmed constituted the contemporary Hindu's claim to equality with the European. Rajanikanta Gupta, the author of *Arya Kirti*, claimed in another text that this was the reason why, despite their appreciation of Western education, present-day Hindus were not awestruck with amazement. He illustrated this by approvingly quoting from Seeley's *Expansion of England*:

> Many travellers have said that the learned Hindu, even when he acknowledges our power and makes use of our railways, is so far from regarding us with reverence that he very sincerely despises us. This is only natural. We are not cleverer than the Hindu: our minds are not richer or larger than his.... He can match from his poetry our sublimest thoughts: even our science perhaps has few conceptions that are altogether novel to him.[42]

[40] Baidyanath Barat, *Arya Darpan: Arthat Adhyatmik Aitihasik Upanyas* ('Aryan-mirror: Or, a spiritual historical novel') (Calcutta, 1977), preface, p.iv.

[41] Rajendralala Mitra, *Indo-Aryans*, vol.II, pp.438-9.

[42] Sir J.R. Seeley, *The Expansion of England* (1883, reprinted London,

Of particular significance is that the portion chosen by Rajanikanta Gupta deliberately disregarded Seeley's statement on the Aryans in India just two pages earlier. Seeley comments:

The Aryan race did not make so much progress in India as in Europe. As it showed in India an extreme incapacity for writing history, so that no record of it remains except where it came in contact with Greek or Mussulman invaders.... No great political system grew up; there was little city-civilisation.[43]

Rajanikanta made a political choice in ignoring this part of Seeley's argument. It was Seeley's report of the testimony of English travellers in India that Rajanikanta found more useful. He could then go on to argue that the innate superiority of the Hindus justified such testimonies. This argument was then extended to invalidate the oft-reiterated allegation that the Hindu was a slave of Western education: 'On account of the legacy of knowledge that has been extended by the ancient Hindu Aryans, the Hindus have appreciated the education given by England, but have not been overwhelmed with wonder.'[44]

Apart from his cultural heritage, the Hindu, and by extension the Bengali, also had a forgotten military heritage. The numerous attempts at rewriting history in the Bengali language during this, the late nineteenth century, affirm contemporary attempts to reclaim a glorious past—a past where the Bengali could claim virility and manhood, qualities he allegedly lacked. With constant accusations of effeminacy the need to prove Bengali masculinity to the 'master race' thus engendered the self-descriptive discourse on race.

IV

The biography of Suresh Biswas thus begins with Macaulay's description of the Bengali in 1830 as 'feeble even to effeminacy', and one for whom 'courage, independence, veracity are qualities to which his

---

1931), pp.282-3. This passage is quoted in Bengali translation in Rajani Kanta Gupta, *Bharat Prasanga* (Calcutta, 1887), p.212.

[43] Ibid., p.280.

[44] Ibid., p.213.

constitution and his situation are equally unfavourable.'[45] Upendra Krishna, the author of Suresh Biswas's biography, denies such statements' historical legitimacy. Subsequent colonial views of 'weakness and timidity', he points out, 'have been based on Macaulay's wispy fiction.'[46] Notorious amongst others who had helped in the consolidation of such colonial misrepresentations, according to the author, was G.W. Steevens, a journalist who arrived in India on the track of the newly-appointed viceroy, Lord Curzon, in 1898-9. Steevens's description had reiterated Macaulay's basic depiction, combining the physical with the moral:

> By his legs you shall know the Bengali. The leg of a free man is straight or a little bandy, so that he can stand on it solidly.... The Bengali's leg is either skin and bones; the same size all the way down, with knocking knobs for knees, or else it is very fat and globular, also turning in at the knees, with round thighs like a woman's. The Bengali's leg is the leg of a slave.[47]

Notably, Steevens classified the physical attributes of a slave community in terms of a despicable womanliness. He went on to categorise the mental and moral qualities of the Bengali:

> He has the virtues of the slave and his vices—strong family affections, industry, frugality, a trick of sticking to what he wants until he wears you down, a quick imitative intelligence and amazing verbal cleverness; dishonesty, suspiciousness, lack of initiative, cowardice, ingratitude, utter incapacity for any sort of chivalry.[48]

The discussion of the views of Steevens and Macaulay had a distinctive resonance for the framing of an oppositional identity through the persona of Suresh Biswas. The assumptions that lay behind the writing of this heroic biography affirmed and legitimised a self-image that was capable of defying the contemptuous colonial one. Moreover, through the image of the Bengali colonel what was being attempted was the framing of a heroic identity by recharacterising racial stereo-

[45] Thomas Macaulay, 'Critical, Historical and Miscellaneous Essays', *The Works of Lord Macaulay*, vol.V (Boston, 1860), pp.19-20, quoted in Leonard Gordon, *Bengal: The nationalist movement, 1876-1940* (New York, 1974), p.6.

[46] Upendra Krishna Banerji, *Karnel Suresh Bishwas*, p.10.

[47] G.W. Steevens, *In India* (London, 1899), pp.85-6.

[48] Ibid., p.86.

types.

> The great man whose life we have set out to describe today, in the context of which we have entered into such meaningless things—he exemplifies how capable Bengalis are capable of heroism even today and how gifted genius can express itself even in adversity.[49]

Suresh Biswas's adventures in Burma at the age of fourteen when he rescued a woman from a fire, his escapades in England and Germany, and his achievements in distant Brazil, were seen as an important part of the oppositional self-image. Here at last was a real-life example in contrast to the Rajput and Maratha heroes who peopled the contemporary history text books. The biographer of the colonel took great care to emphasise his rootedness in Bengal's cultural traditions, and at the same time attempted to refute the colonial construction of the 'weak' rice-eating Bengali.[50]

The biography also concerned itself with the related problem of defining what constituted civilisation. The Aryan inheritance placed civilisation on a higher plane than the achievements of Western materialism admitted. In this particular assessment, wealth and economy were rejected as inadequate standards, while technology and industry were identified as techniques that aided the domination of the East by the West. In a significant redefinition science was viewed as manifesting itself differently in Bengal: 'The science of Bengal is the science of ethical family-life—Bengal's science is the science of happiness and peace. The aim of Bengal's science is the enrichment and growth of family and society, of human qualities and of peace.'[51]

Read with Steevens's allegations of the excessive family affection

[49] Upendra Krishna Banerji, *Karnel Suresh Bishvas*, p.12.

[50] Bankim Chandra Chatterji's *Banga Darshan* article, '*Bangalir bahubal*' or 'The physical strength of the Bengalis' (1874), reveals the contemporary anxiety about the relation between diet and physical strength. Among reasons for the lack of physical strength among Bengalis, Bankim discusses the role of the physical environment—fertile soil making the Bengalis less hard-working. Heat and humidity also make him indolent. The third cause is the fact that Bengal is a rice-producing state, and rice forms the main diet of Bengalis. Rice does not have adequate nutrients to build the body, and hence Bengalis are weak. Bankim attributes this to the lack of gluten in the diet of the Bengalis, using Johnston's *Chemistry of Common Life*, vol.I (Edinburgh, 1853), as his source.

[51] Ibid., p.18.

that characterised a slave, Upendra Krishna's assertion placed the contested qualities of Bengalis on a different scale of values altogether. The nurturing of human qualities were projected as more important than material achievements. What Steevens had failed to appreciate was the balance inherent in Bengali society. Moreover, given contemporary anxiety about the collapse of the joint family system, this redefinition of 'science' implied a critique of the disruption brought about by colonialism. The 'old' system of social organisation was increasingly seen as leading to the fragmentation of the social structure. By highlighting Bengal's 'science of ethical family life', the oppositional nationalist discourse sought to pinpoint the technology inherent in the social structure of a 'slave' people which was designed to train the human spirit. The courageous colonel was therefore a true son of Bengal—a terrain where spiritual and physical qualities were equally cultivated.

While grit and determination were seen as the defining qualities in the early life of Suresh Biswas, his conversion to Christianity was glossed over by the author. Accounting for the conversion in terms of a trend that characterised the 1860s and 1870s, the narrator stated that the tide had presently turned in favour of the ancient *Arya-dharma* of India. As pointed out above, not only was the Hindu identity promulgated by this discourse defined in cultural rather than religious terms, but also Hinduism, from its Aryan roots, had claims to universality: it included the essence of all religions. Therefore, Suresh despite his conversion was identified in the text as a Bengali from Nabadvip—the major centre of the medieval scholarly tradition of Bengal.[52] Suresh's racial heritage thus affirmed the links between Bengalis and Aryans.

Moreover, in one way, Suresh Biswas seemed a living embodiment of the colonial stereotype. He was every inch the frail Bengali. His biographer informed the reader: 'If one saw Suresh one could not make him out to be a strong man. His frame was frail and his body far from

[52] Another example of a similar inclusion despite conversion to Christianity was that of Upadhyay Brahmabandhab, the editor of *Sandhya*, who described himself as a *sannyasi* , as evidenced in his *Bilat Jatri Sannyasir Chithi* ('Letters of a Sannyasi from England') (Calcutta, 1906).

being muscular. But perhaps his muscles were made of iron.'[53] The paradoxical existence of strength in a weak body was illustrated with a anecdote from his experiences in England. While working a circus in Kent, Suresh had effortlessly defeated an English wrestler in open combat. Later in 1893, as a lieutenant in the Brazilian army, his successful defence of the city of Rio had been with a meagre squadron of 50 soldiers. We learn from his letters to his uncle, written from Brazil, that his deeds and his photograph in a lieutenant's uniform were publicised among family and friends. What made this story particularly attractive to Swadeshi nationalists, who drew inspiration from him, was his physical capability despite his slight frame.

V

In Bengal the interest in Suresh Biswas endured long after his death in Rio de Janeiro in 1902; it coincided with the contemporary search for Bengali heroes. This was being expressed by Sarala Debi in her various nationalist ceremonies. Celebrating the first Pratapaditya Festival in 1903, she attempted to place the humiliated race of Bengalis on the same plane as the heroic martial races:

> We the children of Bengal are being systematically deprived of our national heritage. The lesson which we learn from histories concocted by foreigners...is that the Marathi, the Punjabi and the Rajput are indeed the brave races of India...[and] the Bengalee cannot boast of having inherited any heroic traditions whatsoever.... How proud are the Marathas of Shivaji.... Just as they came to the front and proved their heroism at the time when Shivaji flourished, so did we during the reign of Pratap. Let the Bengalee boy remember this, and hold his head as high up as his Marathi brother.[54]

Sarala Debi's attempts to reinstate the heroic in contemporary Bengal were concurrent with the historical writings which were shaping a specific martial Hindu identity in the Bengal of her times. Her heroes were specifically chosen from Bengal, and their heroism was identified in terms of their resistance to Mughal power—thus simultaneously giving the Hindu-cum-Aryan heroic identity a regional dimension and a

[53] Upendra Krishna Banerji, *Karnel Suresh Bishvas*, p.144.

[54] Sarala Debi Ghosal, 'The heritage of the Bengalee', translated and reprinted in the *Bengalee*, 5 June 1903, p.3.

more emphatic Hindu distinctiveness.

Suresh Biswas continued to be commemorated as an heroic Bengali representing a putative self-image of manliness. By 1940 his biography was to become an archetypal portrayal of Bengali courage—the veritable defiance of the colonial classification 'effeminate'. His inclusion in Upendra Nath Bhattacharya's *Rapid Reader for Schools—Banger Bira Santana* or 'The Brave Sons of Bengal'[55]—illustrates the process by which the self-descriptive category of race was engendered. This book contained brief biographies of Bengali men who exemplified resistance and prowess: Vijayasinha who conquered Ceylon, Pratapaditya and Sitaram Ray—the last described as the real *Karma yogi*. In the last story, about Colonel Suresh Biswas, the colonel is seen to motivate the Brazilian soldiers during the attack on Rio de Janeiro during the civil war of 1893. In his attempt to provoke his meagre squadron of soldiers into action, the colonel's speech brings into play the notion of masculinity, as expressed in the son's defence of the motherland and the putative Bengali identity: 'Can the sons of Brazil ever fear for their lives? Look how a son of Bengal snatches the enemy's cannon!' The authorial comment at the end affirms the nexus between the heroic, race and regional identities: 'He emerged victorious and his heroism did proud the entire Bengali race!'[56] The book ran into 16 editions in five years.

The achievements of the Bengali colonel in distant Brazil were thus mythologised. This particular construction was a part of a larger attempt at defending a contested self-image. Thus racial distinctiveness often came to be perceived in cultural rather than biological terms; the Aryan genealogy of the Bengali race was the source of their latent physical and moral strength. The discourse on race was not separate from the numerous contemporary discourses which were attempting to describe a nationalist self. Such constructions appropriated the Aryan heritage attributed to the Hindus by Orientalist scholars, and at the same time responded assertively to the allegations of being non-martial.

[55] Upendra Nath Bhattacharya, *Banger Bira Santana* (Calcutta 1940; 16th edn. 1945).

[56] Ibid., p.60.

The construction of a twin inheritance—the Aryan and the militant Rajput—thus fused a superior racial heritage for Bengalis. At the heart of this fusion lay a dominant convention of nationalism which attempted to present empowering self-definitions, by recasting Orientalist and official interpretations without discarding the indigenous notion of *jati*. Thus Suresh Biswas came to represent a multi-faceted heroic identity mingling the Aryan, Rajput and Bengali racial heritage. This synthesised racial identity could then challenge the supposed masculinity of the 'master race' as well as redeem the image of the 'effeminate' Bengali.

Chapter 10

PAN-ISLAM AND 'DERACIALISATION' IN THE THOUGHT OF MUHAMMAD IQBAL

Javed Majeed

It has been stressed by scholars that historically the European notion of race drew upon many disciplines and covered a variety of identities and loyalties which were not differentiated from each other.[1] The vagaries of popular discourse apart, on the more abstract level there were a number of competing and conflicting theories of 'race'. Not only was the concept far from monolithic, it was not an analytic notion susceptible of a definition of any consistency; this is especially true during its heyday in the nineteenth and early twentieth centuries.[2] To attempt such a definition would be to pre-empt studying the differing ways in which the concept was used in a variety of concrete contexts. Indeed, it is possible that it was the very vagueness of the notion 'race' that lent it an elasticity which ensured it its tenacity and survival.[3]

Nowhere was this inchoate nature of the European notion of 'race' more evident than in British India, where the term was used to describe a variety of caste, sectarian, tribal and ethnic identities, which underpinned what David Washbrook has called the raj's 'sociology of multiple ethnicity'.[4] The aim of this paper is to describe and analyse an

[1] Bernard Lewis, *Semites and Anti-Semites. An inquiry into conflict and prejudice* (London, 1986), p.95; David Washbrook, 'Ethnicity and racialism in colonial India', in Robert Ross (ed.), *Racism and Colonialism* (Leiden, 1982) pp.143-81.

[2] Michael Banton's *Racial Theories* (Cambridge, 1987) is a detailed study of these competing theories and their embedment in the political and social life of the societies to which their authors and readers belonged.

[3] Ernest Gellner has argued there are no reasons to believe that vague and broad notions whose logical implications for conduct are ill-determined, do not have a powerful and specific impact on actual behaviour; see 'Concepts and society', in Bryan R. Wilson (ed.), *Rationality* (Oxford, 1985), p.19. It can be argued that 'race' was just such a broad and vague notion, whose lack of clarity as a concept contributed to its powerful impact.

[4] Washbrook, 'Ethnicity and racialism', p.157. See also Farzana Sheikh,

instance of how this sociology, underpinned by European notions of community subsumed under the inchoate concept of 'race', interacted with a set of notions for categorising groups that had a geneaology independent of and preceding European colonial expansion. This interaction was at the core of reconstructions of Islam in the Indian context by prominent thinkers and writers from the early twentieth century onwards. The first signs of these reconstructions occur in the aftermath of the annulment of the partition of Bengal in 1911, and become increasingly evident during the Khilafat movement. However, they truly come into their own after the failure of that movement, when an increasing concern with 'race' manifests itself, as thinkers struggle to fashion notions of pan-Islam in the context of the creation of nation-states in the Middle East following the disintegration of the Ottoman empire. The significance of events outside India in influencing the course of these reconstructions of Islam, and also in fashioning the notions of 'race' which were to serve as a foil to these reconstructions, cannot be ignored.

The course of these reconstructions, and their possible uses as political strategies within British India, is evident in all its complexities in the later work of Muhammad Iqbal (1876-1938). Iqbal drew upon two pools of ideas about 'race'; the first an Islamic sphere in which the notions for categorising people originated from before European colonial expansion; the second ideas of type, which formed the core of European notions of race from the early nineteenth century onwards.[5] It was the interaction of these two set of ideas in Iqbal's thought that sharpened his concern with concepts of community in Islam, categories which had been important in early Islam and continued to have an impact in his own day. In many ways, the agenda for thinking about types of communities and their possible relations to each other had been set in terms preceding European expansion, although they were reactivated and partially transformed as a result of it. In this context, it may prove useful to consider the extent to which a thesis such as

Community and Consensus in Islam. Muslim representation in colonial India 1860-1947 (Cambridge, 1989), pp.49-73.

[5] Banton, *Theories of Race*, p.ix.

Richard Fox's, on the internalisation by the Singhs of a British reconstruction of their community, could be applied in a similar way to the case of Iqbal's concern with race and Islam.[6]

'Arabian imperialism' and 'Persian Magianism'

In his presidential address at the annual session of the All-India Muslim League at Allahabad on 29 December 1930, Iqbal cited as one of the reasons for the formation of a Muslim state the need to rid Islam of what he called 'the stamp that Arabian imperialism was forced to give it.'[7] This concern with what he called 'Arabian imperialism' is paralleled by another concern with what Iqbal described as 'Persian Magianism'. What is to be noted here is not just the categories of Persian and Arab as self-evident types, but how these types represent tensions in early Islam between Arabs and non-Arabs. These tensions tended to cluster around concepts of community in Islam. The key words in this context are those whose connotations were discussed by Iqbal in a later debate with Maulana Hussain Ahmed, namely *ḳawm*, *millat*, and '*ummat*,[8] but Iqbal's reference to 'Arabian imperialism' in his 1930 presidential address indicates how the survival of historical tensions between Arab and non-Arab in early Islam had to be negotiated in his reconstruction of Islam.

Such historical tensions are dealt with by Bernard Lewis in his *Race and Color in Islam*. He shows how, with the Islamic conquests, there was a narrowing, specialising and fixing of terms of colour applied to human beings. This is in contrast to pre-Islamic and early Islamic poetry, where, whilst there is an awareness of difference, this is never expressed in rigid categories, and the range of terms is wider and they express a different sense of colour.[9] Lewis shows how this shift in colour terminology takes place in the context of increasing tensions between Arabs and non-Arab converts to Islam, and draws attention to the various incidents of what we would now see as 'racial' tension,

[6] Richard Fox, *Lions of the Punjab. Culture in the making* (Berkeley, 1985).

[7] A.R. Tariq (ed.), *Speeches and Statements of Iqbal* (Lahore, 1973), p.14. Cited hereafter as *Speeches and Statements*.

[8] Ibid., pp.235-46.

[9] Bernard Lewis, *Race and Color in Islam* (New York, 1971) ,pp.7-9.

ranging from the Zanj rebellions of black slaves in Basra in the ninth century, to the so-called 'battle of the blacks' in August 1169 between Saladin's army and the black troops loyal to the Fatimid caliphate.[10] It is in relation to this tension between Arab and non-Arab Muslims that one has to see the operation of the system whereby non-Arab converts had to become the clients or *mawālī* of conquistador Arabs with proven genealogies, and also the emergence of the so-called *shu'ūbīya* movement in the ninth century on the part of groups seeking to distinguish between Arabism and Islam. This movement reflected in particular claims by Persians to social and cultural equality (*taṣwīa*) with Arabs, if not to their superiority (*tafẓīl*) over them.[11] Thus, the reference to 'Arabian imperialism' in Iqbal's speech echoes the tensions between Arab and non-Arab which had been present in early Islam, but which continued to have relevance in his own day.

It might be worthwhile to remind ourselves that medieval Islamic literature on schemes of classification of the natural world included typologies in which 'race' played a part. An instance of this is the thirteenth-century work of Nāṣir ad-Dīn Ṭūsī, the *Akhlāqe Nāṣirī* (or 'Nasirean Ethics'). This text is a valuable conspectus of the significant moral and intellectual preoccupations of the medieval Islamic world, and in particular of that world's engagement with Greek philosophy. The author treats nothing in isolation, and considers all spheres of existence as interdependent; hence hierarchies and ranks based on relations between genera, species, and properties abound. In the section on ethics, he considers 'degrees' in the vegetable, animal, and human world, in order to show how each are related to the other. In this scheme, he writes of the 'utmost of the animal degrees' (*martabā*) which is 'contiguous with' (*muttaṣil*), the 'first degrees of man' (*va martabeh-e aval āz marātib insān badīn martabeh-e muttaṣil*). In this category, the author places 'peoples dwelling on the fringes of the inhabited world, such as the Negroes of the West' (*va ān mardmānī bāshad ke bar aṭrāf 'imārat-e 'ālim sākanand mānand saudāne*

[10] Ibid., pp.66, 72-3.

[11] Ehsan Yarshtar (ed.), *Encyclopædia Iranica* 1 (London, 1985), pp.700-1.

maghrib).[12] The point to be made here is that in an Islamic world, as in a European world, there are some hints of typologies of race, which were part of theoretical discourses that purported to classify and interpret the diversity of all forms of life. While these discourses were embedded in the social and political life of the societies to which the authors belonged, they did stimulate a growth of knowledge that was independent of those societies.[13] At any rate, Iqbal's reference to 'Arabian imperialism' has to be seen both in the contexts of the variety of theoretical discourses on types in God's creation, and the historical tensions between Arab and non-Arab Muslims, which continued to have some validity in his own day in terms of how Muslim cultures related to each other.

As for Iqbal's abiding interest in what he called 'Persian Magianism', in his *The Reconstruction of Religious Thought in Islam* (1934), in the context of refuting Spengler's views of Islam in *The Decline of the West*, Iqbal wrote that the main purpose of his lectures was to 'secure a vision of the spirit of Islam as emancipated from its Magian overlayings'.[14] In the process of doing so, he clearly hints at Shi'ism as one strand of Magian culture which has survived in Islam. This concern with 'Persian Magianism' is also evident in his earlier work, *The Development of Metaphysics in Persia* (1908), which considers the influence of Magianism and Gnosticism in the formation of a distinctive Islam in Persia.[15] The association between Sufism and Magianism in his early work becomes more pronounced in the writings of his later period.[16] Iqbal explicitly defines the Aḥmadīyyā movement as an expression of pre-Islamic Magianism in the guise of Islamic mysticism.[17] It is clear that he considers the main threat of Persian Magianism to lie in its subversion of the idea of the finality of

[12] Nāṣir ad-Dīn Ṭūṣī, *Akhlāqe Nāṣirī* (1235; abridged text Tehran, n.d.), p.21.

[13] Banton, *Racial Theories*, p.167.

[14] Muhammad Iqbal, *The Reconstruction of Religious Thought in Islam* (1934; Lahore, 1986), pp.114-15; *Speeches and Statements*, p.103.

[15] Muhammad Iqbal, *The Development of Metaphysics in Persia. a contribution to the history of Muslim philosophy* (1908; Lahore, n.d.), pp.21, 82, 147-8.

[16] *Speeches and Statements*, pp.103-04.

[17] Ibid., p.120.

Muhammad's prophethood.[18] This is especially evident in Iqbal's series of articles on the Aḥmadīyyā movement.[19] In one instance he links what he sees as the Magianism in that movement with the early Iranian reaction against Islam in the eighth century. This manifested itself from 748 A.D. onwards in a rash of rebellions, led by a string of self-styled prophets in the name of a refurbished Zoroastrianism which implicitly challenged the finality of Muhammad's prophethood.[20]

Ḳawm, millat, 'umma and the move towards 'deracialisation'

Iqbal's continual stress on Islam's message as what he calls 'deracialisation'[21] must therefore be seen in the context of his perception of two powerful strands in Islam, namely 'Arabian imperialism' and 'Persian Magianism', and the historical tensions and conflicts between the two. However, in this context of such historical tensions, Iqbal also refers to Sir Arthur Keith's *The Problem of Race;*[22] indeed, he takes the term 'deracialisation' from Keith's work.[23] Michael Banton has discussed the importance of the latter as pioneering an approach to race in terms of genetic processes.[24] Iqbal points to the choice which Keith offers between 'race building' and war, and achieving peace through countering 'race building'.[25] Keith's own solution to the 'ever-disturbing factor' of race in human life, is to argue that 'evolution is true in practice—as well as in theory'. On the basis of this acceptance, he asserts the need to bring our 'inborn tribal instincts and racial prejudices under the rule of reason.'[26] For Iqbal, however, Keith's pleas for a 'deracialisation' of the world enabled him to define Islam as a force for

[18] Iqbal, *Reconstruction,* p.115. For an examination of this issue in relation to the development of the Aḥmadīyyā movement, see Yohann Friedmann, *Prophecy Continuous. Aspects of Ahmadi religious thought and its medieval background* (Berkeley, 1989), pp.49-82.

[19] *Speeches and Statements,* pp.92-3, 106, 110, 117-20.

[20] Ibid., p.110.

[21] Ibid., pp.134-5.

[22] Ibid., pp.135-6.

[23] Sir Arthur Keith, *Ethnos or the Problem of Race* (London, 1931), pp.89-91.

[24] Banton, *Racial Theories,* pp.93-6.

[25] *Speeches and Statements,* p.136.

[26] Keith, *Ethnos,* pp.9, 91.

deracialisation, and one which had been struggling against various forms of divisiveness, springing from categories used to typify groups of people since the beginning of the Arab conquests.[27] The ubiquitousness of European theories of race sharpened Iqbal's own perceptions of historical and contemporary tensions within Islam, and helped him to define what he argued was its original spirit, namely the construction of an 'ummat which transcended jinsīyā.[28]

It is also on the basis of this view that Iqbal discusses the meaning of the terms *millat, ḳawm*, and *'ummat* in a debate with Maulana Hussain Ahmed.[29] All three terms occur in the *Ḳur'ān* but the first two terms in particular underwent important changes during the late nineteenth and early twentieth centuries.[30] Whereas in the *Ḳur'ān* the term *millet* refers to the religion of Abraham, in post-Ḳur'ānic usage the term appears in the meaning of religion generally. It is in this primary sense that it occurs in official Ottoman documents, where it appears to indicate especially non-Muslim communities of the empire from the seventeenth century onwards. The term became central to the so-called 'millet system', whereby the central administration of the empire perceived individual religious communities in local contexts as parts of religious and juridical communities that had an empire-wide dimension under their respective ecclesiastical leaderships. However, when Turkey came to regard itself as a 'nation', the term *millat* rather than *ḳawm* was used.[31] The provenance of the latter term varied from the Maghrib to Persia and Ottoman Turkey in the nineteenth and twentieth centuries. In Qur'ānic usage the term signified the prophets who were Muhammad's predecessors. More to our purpose here, however, the term *Ḳawmiyya* came to mean the movement of Arab nationalism within the Ottoman dominions in the Fertile Crescent. *Al-ḳawmiyya al-'arabiyya* was a reaction to prolonged Ottoman domination, under

[27] *Speeches and Statements*, pp.6-7, 48-9, 91-2, 195, 227-8.

[28] Ibid., pp.235-40.

[29] Ibid., pp.235-46.

[30] What follows is drawn from the entries in the *Encyclopedia of Islam*, which trace in detail the genealogy and development of these terms in various parts of the Islamic world from the early Islamic period to the twentieth century.

[31] *Encyclopedia of Islam* 7 (Leiden and New York. 1993), pp.61-4.

which the question of national identity within the *'umma* (or community of believers) had not arisen.[32]

The details of Iqbal's debate in March 1938 with Maulana Hussain Ahmed are of less interest here than the fact that the debate itself reflected the way in which key terms of community were being changed. That Iqbal himself was aware of this is clear from his article. Thus, he contrasts the way the terms *ḳawm*, *millat*, and *'ummat* are used in the *Ḳur''ān* with the meanings they have acquired in the contemporary world.[33] He also quibbles with the Maulana's interpretation of how these terms are used in the *Ḳur'ān* and discusses in detail their significance in Ḳur'ānic usage, again in the context of comparing the changes that have occurred in the scope of their meanings.[34] He argues that his own use of the word *millat* as 'nation' is in accordance with its usage in modern Arabic, Persian, and Turkish languages, where it has come to mean nation, rather than law and religion as in the *Ḳur'ān*.[35] The rest of Iqbal's article attempts to establish a hierarchy of identities based on *ḳawm*, *millat*, and *'ummat* , but it is not clear how successful he is in doing this. However, his unease about nationalism is expressed explicitly:

> I have been repudiating the concept of Nationalism since the time when it was not well-known in India and the Muslim world. At the very start it had become clear to me from the writings of European authors that the imperialistic designs of Europe were in great need of this effective weapon—the propagation of the European conception of Nationalism in Muslim countries—to shatter the religious unity of Islam to pieces.... [This] has now reached its climax in as much as some of the religious leaders in India lend their support to this conception.[36]

Iqbal also argues that if 'nation' is simply a 'geographical term', then he has no objections to it. In that sense, it is safe to say that 'We are all Indians and are so called because we live in that part of the world which is known by the name of India'. However, it is when the

[32] Ibid., 4, p.794.
[33] *Speeches and Statements*, pp.229, 236-7.
[34] Ibid., pp.237-41.
[35] Ibid., p.229.
[36] Ibid., p.230.

word 'nation' ceases to be a geographical term and becomes a 'political concept' signifying a 'principle of human society',[37] or what he describes elsewhere as 'a structuring principle of solidarity',[38] that the problems arise. This is mainly because, in his view, Islam's purpose was to create a community which ignored all 'national and racial' distinctions. Its aim was 'to unite and organize mankind, despite all its natural distinctions'.[39] It is for this reason that Muslims cannot be a nation in the political sense of the word except in terms of their being a *millat*.[40] It is perhaps significant that Iqbal ends his article by associating (in a rather confused way) the European notion of nationalism with the Aḥmadīyyā movement. He describes the conception of nationalism as having the same role as the rejection of the finality of Muhammad's prophethood has in the beliefs of Qādianīs. In other words, those who advocate nationalism of this type are in effect urging Muslims to take up a position outside the prescriptions of the 'divine law'. Whilst nationalism is a political concept, and the Aḥmadīyyā position on the finality of prophethood is a theological issue, nonetheless there is 'a deep inner relationship between the two'. However, Iqbal does not spell out what this relationship is. Instead, he states that this relationship can only be demonstrated 'when a Muslim historian gifted with acute insight compiles a history of Indian Muslims with particular reference to the religious thought of some of their apparently energetic sects'.[41] Nonetheless, the nub of his position in this context appears to lie in associating an attack on the finality of the prophethood in Aḥmadīyyā beliefs, with an attack on the centrality of religious belief as a whole in defining a transnational Muslim community.

The association in Iqbal's work of what he saw as a modern form of a Magian belief with European nationalism, points to his simultaneous exploration of the historical tensions between Arab and non-Arab in Islam, and the notions of race and nationalism. This exploration is undertaken in the context of considering what it is that actually consti-

[37] Ibid., p.231.
[38] Ibid., p.136.
[39] Ibid., p.232.
[40] Ibid., p.235.
[41] Ibid., p.245.

tutes a Muslim community Iqbal's concern with these historical tensions, and with race and nationalism, can also be traced in his artistic work. At one point in his 1932 Persian epic poem, the *Jāvīd Nāma* ('Book of Eternity'), the poet Zinda Rūd ('living stream') laments how Iran has fallen into the 'ring of a trap' (*halqa-e dām*), and how, in its paradoxical attempt to define for itself a modern national identity on the basis of a pre-Islamic past, it belittles the Arabs and fails to recognise their benefaction.[42] This aside on the Arab-Persian tensions in Islam is part of a larger concern in the *Jāvīd Nāma* with the new forces of nationalism, and, in particular, the creation of nation-states in the Middle East following the break-up of the Ottoman empire. One of the characters the poet meets, on his Dantesque journey through the cosmos in the poem, is the pan-Islamicist Sayyid Jamal ad-Din al-Afghani (1838/9-1897), who has been described as 'one of the outstanding figures of nineteenth-century Islamic history'.[43] The predominant themes in al-Afghani's discourse in the *Jāvīd Nāma* is the incompatibility between the rival ideologies of pan-Islam and the European notion of nationalism:

lurd-e maghrib ān sarāpā makr vā fan
ahl-e dīn-rā dād ta'līm-e waṭan
ū befikr-e markiz va tu dar nafāq
beguzār az shām va falastīn va 'irāq.[44]

This concern with nationalism reflects the increasing threat that the latter posed as a rival ideology to pan-Islam in the period between the breakdown of the Khilāfat movement and the outbreak of the Second World War.[45] It was this period which saw the laying of the founda-

[42] Muhammad Iqbal, *Jāvīd Nāma* in *Kulliyyāt-e Fārsī* (Lahore, 1985), p.174/3, p.175/3; hereafter JN. The page reference is to the separate pagination of the poem which begins on p.589 of *Kulliyyāt-e Fārsī* the number after the slash refers to the couplet on that page.

[43] Nikki R. Keddie, *Sayyid Jamal ad-Din al-Afghani. A political biography* (Berkeley, 1972), p.1.

[44] 'The Lord of the West, cunning and artful from head to toe / Gave the knowledge of nationhood to the people of religion / He is thoughtful of the centre and you are in discord / Pass by Syria and Palestine and Iraq' (JN p.62/5-6).

[45] Jacob M. Landau, *The Politics of Pan-Islam. Ideology and organization* (Oxford, 1990), pp.217-8.

tions of a novel state system in the Middle East that reorganised existing forms of associations and solidarities, and transformed the focus of political vocabularies which had their roots in more traditional discourses.[46] Whilst it is now clear that pan-Islam cannot mount any serious challenge to the existing state-structure in the Middle East,[47] at the time Iqbal was writing, this process of transformation was taking place and was not yet fully accomplished. The rivalry between nationalism and pan-Islam was already evident in the use which Sultan Abdulhamid II had made of pan-Islam as a policy within the Ottoman empire, namely to check nascent nationalism within the empire, and in particular, to reinforce the loyalty of Arab groups within it to the Turkish sultanate/caliphate.[48] Now, with the disintegration of that empire and the carving up of the Middle East by Britain and France into states which bore little resemblance to the Ottoman administrative units, there was an increasingly sophisticated approach to nationalism on the part of such pan-Islamists in the 1920s and 1930s as Hasan al-Banna (1906-49).[49]

Thus, Iqbal's reassessment in his March 1938 article of the various terms used to categorise communities in Islam, such as *millat*, *ḳawm*, and *'ummat*, is significant for a number of reasons. First, it shows the extent to which Muslim intellectuals at the time were self-consciously rethinking these concepts, often aware of the genealogy of such terms, and the more recent meanings they had acquired in the twentieth century. Hence Iqbal's discussion of what such terms meant in the *Ḳur'ān* and his contrast between their *Ḳur'ānic* usage and their present day usage. Secondly, an important part of the context for this discussion is the Muslim Middle East, where the European concept of nationalism is seen to be doing its most dangerous work. A pan-Islamic position emerges in part against the European notion of nationalism *per se*, as well as against its influence on the development of nationalism in the

[46] Roger Owen, *State, Power and Politics in the Making of the Modern Middle East* (London, 1992), pp.19-23; M.E. Yapp, *The Near East since the First World War* (London, 1991), pp.2-5.

[47] Yapp, *Near East*, p.45.

[48] Landau, *Politics of Pan-Islam*, pp.23, 37-8, 42-3.

[49] Ibid., pp.223-4.

Middle East. Furthermore, given Iqbal's explicit denunciation of nationalism, it is difficult to see how Muslim separatism in India can be reconciled with this position without the crucial pan-Islamic element in the equation.[50] Thirdly, a pan-Islamicist position also emerges in reaction to a notion of race; hence Iqbal's repeated references to his own conception of an Islamic community which transcends both national and racial divisions. Finally, the association between what Iqbal saw as a modern form of Magianism and the European notion of nationalism points to his concern to negotiate a path between the wider tensions and conflicts inherited from early Islam, and the powerful influence of the political concept of a nation.

As far as Iqbal's engagement with the notion of 'race' is concerned, we might tentatively conclude that it is the interplay between European notions of race and a set of terms in a Muslim context, of an independent genealogy which forms the background to Iqbal's equation of Islam and 'deracialisation'. It would seem that this interplay is a negative one, in so far as Iqbal uses notions of race in a negative way, to define an Islam in contrast to these categories. In this sense, a thesis such as Richard Fox's in the case of a Singh identity runs counter to Iqbal's views on race and Muslimhood. Far from internalising an imperial construct of Muslimhood, Iqbal attempted to define Islam against European categories. Nowhere does Iqbal assume that Indian Muslims, or Muslims anywhere, form a single 'race'; rather, the '*ummat* consists of a wide variety of such groups, who are united in their adherence to certain religious codes. It is difficult to find in Iqbal any reference to the racial underpinnings of a Muslim *ashrāf* culture to which Farzana Sheikh has drawn detailed attention.[51] Indeed, it might be more useful to see Iqbal in terms of his distance from, and not his proximity to, such a culture and some of its assumptions. From the perspective of such classical points of reference in high Islamic culture, Iqbal was after all only a Punjabi Muslim (albeit of Kashmiri origin) of unexceptional social background, who would have easily qualified as being an '*ajam* (the Arabic equivalent of the Greek *barbaros*, applied

[50] This is discussed in more detail below.
[51] Farzana Sheikh, *Community and Consensus in Islam*, pp.93-6.

specifically to Persians in early Islam).[52] His reconstruction of Islam using the notion of race as a foil has to be seen not only in the context of tensions between Arab and *'ajam*, but also in terms of his own situation, which did not afford him much opportunity for an unqualified personal investment in the classical reference points of high Islamic culture and their possible racial underpinnings.

The All-India Muslim League and 'race'

There is also some evidence to suggest that the vocabulary of race began to creep into the observations on the conflict which accompanied the dismemberment of the Ottoman empire by some members of the Muslim League. For example, in the All-India Muslim League papers, there are a few instances where the term 'race' is used in a strident way, which sometimes suggests a view of the clear-cut nature of 'race' to which certain types of conflict give rise. So, in the memorial of 1 January 1919, addressed to the British Foreign Secretary, reference is made to the 'racial conflicts' in Eastern Europe, where Muslim minorities are vulnerable victims, and to the hope that 'no racial or religious prejudices' would determine the attitude of the victorious Entente powers to the settlement regarding the dismemberment of the Ottoman empire.[53] In fact, there is further evidence to suggest that, for some Indian intellectuals, one crucible for their thinking about race was not India at all, but South Africa. It was in the predicament of the Indian settlers in South Africa that the starker realities of racial perceptions had earlier been evident. It is ironic that the Muslim League papers show much concern for this predicament, irrespective of the religious affiliations of the Indian settlers; the development of racial segregation in South Africa in the early twentieth century, with its broader notions of 'race', paid no heed to finer details of caste, communal, or ethnic identities. The predicament of Indian settlers in colonies of European

[52] The word comes from the verb *'ajama*, to speak indistinctly, to mumble, and was applied to non-native speakers of Arabic.

[53] All-India Muslim League papers (Quaid-e Azam Academy, Karachi; hereafter 'AIML papers'), vol. 503: memorial presented to British Secretary of State for Foreign Affairs by Aga Khan *et al*, 1 January 1919.

settlement abroad pointed to the fundamental discrepancy between the two empires of the Indian raj and the colonies of European settlement. Thus, at the All-India Muslim League's annual session of 1912, the League recorded 'its deep appreciation of the gallant fight that the Indian settlers in South Africa, Australasia, and British North America are maintaining under depressing circumstances for their inalienable rights as British citizens', and it entered a plea to the imperial government to ensure that its Indian subjects received 'the full rights and privileges of British citizenship by the removal of racial distinctions within the Empire'.[54] This discrepancy between the rights of citizens of the same empire is stressed again, when the position of Indians abroad as citizens of the British empire is described as 'very delicate; theoretically we enjoy the same rights and are amenable to the same laws as the English themselves and their kith and kin in the colonies, but in practice even the most elementary rights are denied us'.[55] The position of Indians in the Transvaal was especially pointed to as further evidence of this,[56] a position earlier protested against in view of the Asiatic Registration clauses of the Transvaal Immigration Act.[57] It was obvious discrepancies such as these between the positions of citizens from different parts of the Empire which also revealed the weakness of the imperial centre in dealing with local colonial and settler designs to create 'white' states. In fact, in some ways the ideal of the Commonwealth was defined to negotiate these very discrepancies. The Commonwealth position not only attempted to bridge the gap between the Indian raj and the colonies of European settlement; it also developed a form of multi-racialism which had the advantage of blurring differences

[54] AIML papers, vol. 64: Resolution 8 for annual session, 3-4 March 1912.

[55] AIML papers, vol. 65: Reports and Proceedings of the Annual Session of the Muslim League, 1912.

[56] S.S. Pirzada (ed.), *Foundations of Pakistan. All India Muslim League documents: 1906-1947* (3 vols.; Karachi, 1969): Presidential Address, 5th Session, Calcutta, 3-4 March 1912, 1: pp.244-5.

[57] AIML papers, vol. 4: 1908 Central Committee Meetings, letter from Hamidia Islamic Society, Johannesburg, to President of Muslim League, 25 November 1907, and subsequent resolution passed by Central Committee (in English nd Urdu).

between policies on race developed in different parts of the empire.[58] As early as 1915, Lionel Curtis, one of the most significant thinkers of the Round Table group responsible for disseminating the conception of a commonwealth after the Union of South Africa in 1910, wrote of the need for 'equality of rights' between the two parts of the commonwealth. However, he failed to tackle the indentured labour system head on, and continued to oppose the settlement of Indians in the dominions and European colonies. Although all indentured labourers in British colonies were freed on 1 January 1920, it was issues such as these which hampered the smooth evolution of the Commonwealth, and which continued to point to the inequality in rights between different parts of the British empire. [59]

Thus, when considering the interplay of European notions of 'race' with Islamic notions of community, it is well to reiterate that the arena for this interaction was wider than India itself. There was the global imperial arena, in which the position of Indian settlers in colonies of European settlement pointed to the discrepancies between the statuses of citizens of the British empire. There was also the arena of the Middle East in which the foundations of the nation-state system were being laid. Finally, there was the arena of British India itself in which the Muslim League, amongst others, struggled to form an all-India Muslim constituency by playing a pan-Islamic card to bolster the status of Indian Muslims as a minority.[60] For a time, though, this process was usurped by the Khilafat movement, which pushed the League to the periphery of significant politics. As Gail Minault has argued, it was in the Khilafat movement that a pan-Indian Muslim constituency was formed through the use of pan-Islamic symbols.[61] However, there were earlier signs that this strategy was emerging in the aftermath of the annulment of the partition of Bengal in 1911. This was particularly clear in the reactions to Montagu's speech in the House of Commons of

[58] Paul B. Rich, *Race and Empire in British Politics* (1986; Cambridge, 1990), p.55.

[59] Ibid., pp.59-60.

[60] Landau, *Politics of Pan-Islam*, p.306.

[61] Ibid., p.214; Gail Minault, *The Khilafat Movement. Religious symbolism and political mobilization in India* (New York, 1982), pp.208, 211-12.

25 April 1919, in which he asserted that it was a 'mistake to talk of the Mahomedans of India as though they were a homogeneous nationality. The Mahomedans of Eastern Bengal and the Hindus had little or no relation with those outside Bengal.' The Secretary to the Muslim League responded to this statement by describing it as an attack on 'the unity of Muslims all over India, not to say all over the world, on the basis of religion, of political rights and social homogeneity'. Not only were the interests of Muslims in one province the same as in another, the interests of Muslims in India were identical to those Muslim communities who lived beyond the frontiers of India.[62] The construction of an all-Indian Muslim constituency went hand-in-hand with a pan-Islamic notion of a global Islamic community, both of which were pitted against the 'racial' heterogeneity of India.

'Abul Kalam Azad on the Caliphate and the question of race

The three arenas in which European notions of 'race' were manifested on different levels, and in which they played a variety of roles, were also the arenas in which reconstructions of Islam were mounted. All of these had one common thread, namely the defining of Islam as a cultural force inimical to the notions of race.[63] Iqbal was not alone in grappling with the notion of race in his reconstruction of Islam, nor indeed was he alone in considering the tensions between what had come to be seen as the Arab and non-Arab threads in Islam. These

[62] AIML papers, vol. 91: Council Meetings, 1912, circular letter of Secretary, 27 April 1912, which cites the passage above from Montagu's speech. See also the resolution passed by the Punjab Muslim League to the effect that this speech represented 'an unwarranted departure form a recognised principle of Imperial Indian policy which has hitherto accepted all Indian Musalmans, irrespective of locality and origin, as consituting one community', and that the interests of Punjabi Muslims are identical to those of Bengali Muslims (Resolution enclosed in circular letter of Secretary. All India Muslim League, 8 May 1912).

[63] For some examples of these definitions, see Landau, *Politics of Pan-Islam*, pp.84-6, 189-92, 223-4, 335-41; see also Appendix I, which contains the text of a 1910 pamphlet by Ahmed Hilmi. See also AIML papers, vol. 10 (Morley-Minto Reforms): 'The Reform Scheme' from the *Observer* (Lahore), November and December 1907; vol. 65: Reports and Proceedings of Annual Session of 1912, 'Turkey and Persia'; vol. 91: Council Meetings, 1912, Madras Presidency Muslim League to All-India Muslim League (London branch), 19 June 1912.

concerns were writ large in 'Abul Kalam Azad's *Maslāh-e Khilāfat va jazīrāh-e 'Arab* ('The problem of the Khilafat and the Arab peninsula').[64] The breadth and depth of the argument of this work, and its ambiguities, make it a key text for understanding how the issues which are the subject of this paper were negotiated by Muslim intellectuals at the time. Here only two broad and interrelated points can be stressed. The first is Azad's anxiety to show that there is nothing in the *ḥadīth* or the Ḳur'ān for the basis of the view that the Caliphate must be limited to the Qureish or the Arabs generally. The sophistication of Azad's argument (not least in the interpretative strategies he brings to bear in his reasoning), and the sometimes tortuous way he arrives at his conclusion cannot be examined here. Suffice it to say that he shows how the view that the Caliphate must be limited to the Qureish arose, and how it had to be placed in the historical circumstances of the time. He also argues that this view was partly based on a reading of *ḥadīth* which failed to see those portions of it relating to the Qureish and the Caliphate as predictions (*paish goī*) and not reports (*khabar*).[65] He concludes that there is no evidence in Islamic doctrine that the Caliphate was limited to any nation (*ḳawm*) or family (*khāndān*) or lineage and race (*nasl*).[66] Having argued that the Caliphate can be held by an *'ajam* as well as an Arab, and that historically this has been the case,[67] Azad moves on to his second point, namely a consideration of what the correspondents of European papers had called 'pan-Islamism', and, in particular, their claim that Abdulhamid II fostered the notion of pan-Islam in order to buttress the prestige of the Turkish sultanate among Muslim groups living outside the confines of the Ottoman

[64] This was a discourse delivered in Urdu before the Bengal Khilafat conference in 1920; for my purposes, I have relied on an edition published in 1963 by Khalid Book Depot, Lahore.

[65] Abu'l Kalam Azad, *Maslāh-e Khilāfat va Jazīrāh-e 'arab* (Lahore, 1963) pp.111, 116. For the need to establish a priority of credence on the basis of distinguishing different types of dictum in Islamic law and in ḥadīth see especially pp.102-4.

[66] Ibid., p.97; the word '*nasl*' originally meant lineage and pedigree, but came to mean race too.

[67] Ibid., pp.94-5; Azad uses the word '*ajam*. See also p.105.

empire.[68] In rebutting this claim, Azad reiterates a point he has stressed all along, that the brotherhood of Islam pays no heed to distinctions of nationality, race, or country.[69]

The question of anti-semitism

Thus, there were parallels between Iqbal's concern with race and pan-Islam and the reconstructions of other thinkers;[70] significantly, some of these reconstructions took place in the context of negotiating the historical differences between *'ajam* and Arab in the Islamic world. This has to be understood not only in the context of the emerging state system of the Middle East, but also in the light of the evidence of the increasing penetration of a starker concept of race into the Middle East, namely the importation of European anti-semitism into the region. By the early twentieth century, through a variety of means and methods, the basic texts of European anti-semitic literature were available in Arabic, ready for use and wider dissemination.[71] One major step in the dissemination of European-style anti-semitism came in the aftermath of the 1908 revolution of the Young Turks, whose opponents accused them of Jewish links, an accusation encouraged by such European diplomats as the British ambassador in Constantinople, Sir Gerard Lowther. This accusation was further used during the First World War, when the imperial powers at war with Turkey attempted to discredit the Ottoman empire and the Young Turk regime with anti-semitic propaganda directed against Arab groups in particular.[72] Whilst the penetra-

[68] Ibid., p.135.

[69] Ibid., p.135; see also p.97 for a strong statement of Islam as opposed to specificities of lineage and nation (*'ikhtasas ul-nasl va ḳawm'*) and racial distinctions (*'imtīāz ul-nasab'*), and pp.98-100. For an interpretation of the hijrat in accordance with these views on Islam and race, see pp.52-3.

[70] There were, of course, major differences between the thought of Iqbal and Azad; for example, in broad terms between Iqbal's system of *khūdī* and Azad's comments on *infirādīyyat* (individuality) in *Maslāh-e Khilāfat*, p.52. However, these major differences make the similarities between their work all the more significant. For an examination of the metaphysics of *khūdī* see J. Majeed, 'Putting God in His place: Bradley, McTaggart, and Muhammad Iqbal', *Journal of Islamic Studies* 4, 2 (1993) pp.208-36.

[71] Lewis, *Semites and Anti-Semites*, pp.132-7, 139.

[72] Ibid., pp.137-8.

tion of anti-semitism in its European form was slow and limited, and did not become a major factor in the Middle East until the late 1950s and early 1960s,[73] during the interwar period under consideration here the colonial expansion of European powers in the region was beginning to have an impact upon changing attitudes to Jewish groups.[74] These changes were reinforced by Nazi propaganda in the 1930s, and, most importantly of all, by the question of a Jewish state in Palestine.[75] Thus, whereas there was nothing in Islamic history preceding this period to parallel the expulsion of Jews from Spain in 1492 and the Inquisition, or the Russian pogroms and the Nazi holocaust,[76] in this period there was a shift of attitudes consequent upon changing conceptions of loyalties and identities, and the importation of a European notion of Jews as a separate race.[77]

Some of the memorials prepared at the height of the Khilāfat movement indicate an awareness of the changes that were taking place in these attitudes, and reflect not only a nostalgia for the older discourse in which this tone of racial hostility against Jewish groups was absent, but an awareness of the different sta· dings of Jewish groups in Islamic and European history. Thus, in the memorial of 3 March 1919, submitted to A.J. Balfour, the British Foreign Secretary, reference is made to the Balfour declaration of 2 November 1917, and it is pointed out that the creation of a Jewish state in Palestine would result in considerable unrest and resentment. It is also added that 'History proves that the Jews can live in closest amity with their Mussulman fellow-subjects under Muslim rulers and enjoy exceptional privileges not conceded to them even now by many European nations'.[78] In another memorial of 31 July 1919 submitted to David Lloyd George, the expulsion of the Jews from Spain is unfavourably compared to the standing of Jews as a *millat* in the Ottoman empire.[79]

[73] Ibid., p.197.
[74] Ibid., p.125-6.
[75] Ibid., p.28, 146, 164-87, 259.
[76] Ibid., pp.121-2.
[77] Ibid., p.164, 131-2.
[78] AIML papers: vol. 503, Khilafat memorials, memorial submitted to A.J. Balfour by Aga Khan, Amir Ali *et al.*, 3 March 1919.
[79] *AIML papers*: vol. 503, Khilafat memorials, cutting from *Daily Telegraph*,

Conclusion: sight in the Jāvīd Nāma and Iqbal's engagement with race

What is interesting about Iqbal's thinking around these issues is that his work reveals signs of both an attempt to define Islam by using the notion of race as a foil, and of the increasing acceptance of European notions of race as self-evident concepts. Despite his identification of what he calls the 'race idea' as inimical to his definition of Islam,[80] and despite his castigation of Attaturk's 'Pan-Turanianism' for resting on an assumption of the 'absoluteness of races',[81] Iqbal sometimes wrote as though races were self-evident categories. This is partly because he needed some sort of notion of race in order to define a pan-Islamic community which transcended racial groups but did not collapse into them. This is clear in his statements on the nature of pan-Islam, and in his characterisation of Islam as 'stooping to conquer without itself becoming a race-making factor' [82] This also emerges in his attempt to define a hierarchy of allegiances on the basis of *qawm*, *millat*, and '*ummat*.[83] However, Iqbal was also at pains to endorse what David Washbrook has called the British 'vocabulary of a sociology of ethnicity' as it was applied to India.[84] Hence, he repeatedly emphasises the heterogeneity of the subcontinent in terms which almost exactly mirror this sociology, in order to deny the validity of any form of Indian nationalism.[85] Furthermore, he sometimes expresses in biological terms his aversion to the sort of India envisaged by the Indian National Congress, as when he points to the possible 'fusion of the communities in a biological sense'.[86] He also at times refers to 'martial races' as self-evident categories when he considers what the future security arrangements in a federal India might look like, whilst simultaneously

2 August 1919, containing text of memorial submitted to Lloyd George by Aga Khan, Ameer Ali *et al.*, 31 July 1919.

[80] *Speeches and Statements*, pp.195, 207.

[81] Ibid., p.136.

[82] Ibid., pp.207, 135.

[83] Ibid., pp.235-46.

[84] Washbrook, 'Ethnicity and racialism', p.170.

[85] *Speeches and Statements*, pp.9-14, 27, 35, 42, 63, 67-8, 94-5, 110, 169, 182.

[86] Ibid., p.214

arguing that the British have used such notions of race for their own political ends.[87] This parallels his perception of the British creation and manipulation of a rural-urban divide in Punjab,[88] and what he takes to be their creation of Zionism in the Middle East.[89] Iqbal's simultaneous reliance on categories of race, whilst attempting to escape from them in his definition of Islam as a force of 'deracialisation', affords a poignant example of how, like many others, he was sometimes trapped in the very categories he sought to challenge, and how that challenge was often launched on the same premises as the concepts he sought to undermine.[90]

To a certain extent, there are signs of this predicament in the imagery of sight which forms one of the main threads of the *Jāvīd Nāma*. This concern with different types of sight is part of Iqbal's engagement with Sufism. The recurring stress in the *Jāvīd Nāma* on a transforming vision which yields a different world reflects Iqbal's exploration of the concept of *¢auq* (literally: taste, enjoyment), which he had earlier discussed in the context of Sufism as an 'inner perception' that reveals atemporal and non-spatial planes of being.[91] In the *Jāvīd Nāma* there are frequent references to the glances of the powerful which convert motes into suns and rend all veils:

zarah-hā āz yek nigāhī āfdāb
yek nigāh sho tāshavad haq be-hijāb![92]

One of the key distinctions the poem makes is between the immediacy of the gnostic's vision and the mediatory nature of hearsay that forms common religion;[93] and indeed part of the poet's quest is to approach the station of visionary sight which transforms what it gazes upon:

87 Ibid., pp.20, 22. For a lucid exposition of theories of martial race, see David Omissi, '"Martial races": ethnicity and security in colonial India 1858-1939,' *War and Society* 9 (May 1991), pp.1-27.

88 *Speeches and Statements*, p.97.

89 Ibid., pp.218-9.

90 Washbrook, 'Ethnicity and racialism', p.159.

91 See his *Development of Metaphysics in Persia,* p.111.

92 'From one glance motes become the sun / Be one in vision so that the truth becomes unveiled!' (*Jāvid Nāma* , p.96/11).

93 'He said what is the religion of the common people? I said it is hearsay / He said what is the religion of gnostics? I said it is true sight' (ibid., p.37/13).

nau'e dīgar bain jahān dīgar shavad
īn zamīn va āsmān dīgar shavad.[94]

However, this preoccupation with transforming sight is matched by an emphasis on the consequence of becoming the object of someone else's gaze, namely, losing one's autonomy by becoming transfixed by their stare. Thus, there are instances of gazes that are trapped by the very objects they look upon,[95] whilst the central mood of the concern with sight is captured by the following couplet:

Har zamān bar naqsh-e khūd band va naẓar
Tānagīrad loḥ-e ū naqsh-e dīgar.[96]

The concern with sight in the *Jāvīd Nāma* can clearly be placed in the context of Iqbal's engagement with Sufism. However, the fear of being the object of another's gaze and so losing one's autonomy, can also be placed in the context of having one's identity defined and therefore fixed by the gaze of the more powerful. Indeed, Iqbal's engagement with Sufism had political implications as well; the *Jāvīd Nāma* is an instance of how Iqbal tried to combine the ecstatic and rhapsodic mode of Sufi poetry with political polemic aimed at the colonial state and its global ideologies.[97] This play-off between different modes of seeing in the *Jāvīd Nāma* points to the oscillation in Iqbal's work as a whole between a seemingly self-conscious and critical use of the notion of race, in alliance with a set of terms of independent genealogy drawn from an Islamic sphere of influence, and a succumbing to the notion's apparently self-evident nature as a category of differentiation. This oscillation is itself indicative of the processes of internalisation by the Indian intelligentsia which Washbrook has discussed in detail.[98] Iqbal's use of such categories also points to the fluidity and imprecision of the

[94] 'View the world otherwise, and it will become other / This earth and heaven will become other' (ibid., p.109/13).

[95] 'Science casts its gaze on the past and present / Love cries "Glance at what is coming!"' (ibid., p.120/6). 'They fasten their eyes on the past? And would kindle their hearts from an extinguished fire!' (ibid., p.144/3).

[96] 'He always fixes his gaze on his own image / Lest his tablet recieve another's image' (ibid., p.69/13).

[97] For an attempt to examine these strands in the *Jāvīd Nāma*, see Majeed, 'Putting God in His place', pp.232-6.

[98] Ibid., pp.158-9.

notion of race, which permitted it to be used for a variety of purposes and in a number of conflicting contexts, in which biological, political, and cultural significances are fused together, and theoretical discourses stand in complex relationships with 'folk' concepts.[99] But in the context of British and Muslim India, it is in the interplay between notions of European origin and reconstructed Islamic notions of community that the more interesting relationships lie. These relationships show how a set of notions of 'race', European in origin, partially transformed a pool of concepts about communities that preceded European colonial expansion, without completely supplanting them. Above all, by focusing on the processes in which these relationships were embedded, we can avoid the dangers of an exclusive concern with notions of European community in the context of South Asia. Iqbal's work reminds us of the continued relevance of concepts with histories and genealogies in languages and discourses independent of, as well as preceding, European colonial expansion.

[99] Michael Banton, *Racial Theories*, pp.vii, xi-xiv. On race as lineage, type, subspecies, status, and class, see pp.1-167.

Chapter 11

THE IDEA OF THE HINDU RACE IN THE WRITINGS OF HINDU NATIONALIST IDEOLOGUES IN THE 1920s AND 1930s: A CONCEPT BETWEEN TWO CULTURES

Christophe Jaffrelot

Students of early Indian history and the Great Tradition indicate that at that time autochthons' ideas about the Other were based on cultural and linguistic rather than racial distinctions and that these differentiations were blurred. Wilhelm Halbfass emphasises that in ancient India 'the *mlecchas* are nothing but a faint and distant phenomenon at the horizon of the indigenous tradition. They do not possess an "otherness" against which one's own identity could be asserted or in which it could be reflected'.[1] This peculiar 'xenology' stems mainly from the fact that the society is seen, in the Brahmanical tradition, as maintaining a relationship of homology with the *dharma* as a universal norm. This theme is very clear, for instance, in the *sloka* of the *Rig Veda* narrating the sacrifice of the primordial man (*Virat Purusha*): his mouth became the Brahman, his arms the Kshatriya, his thighs the Vaishya, and his feet the Shudra.[2]

This organicist and self-universalising view of society explains partly why the racial criterion has been downplayed in this tradition. According to Romila Thapar, the *mleccha* were discriminated against because they did not observe the rules of the *varna vyavastha* and the vedic rituals, being ignorant of the language (Sanskrit) in which the latter were performed.[3] The discrimination was a function of the degree of ritual purity rather than ethnicity and the 'Aryas' were taken to be a 'noble people' rather than a racial group. Therefore, the frontier

[1] W. Halbfass, *India and Europe—an essay in understanding* (New York, 1988), p.187.

[2] 'Rig Veda X-90' in *Hymnes spéculatifs du Veda*, notes and introduction by Louis Renou (Paris, 1956), p.99.

[3] R. Thapar, 'The image of the barbarian in early India' in Thapar, *Ancient Indian Social History* (New Delhi, 1978), p.155.

between the Aryas and the *mlecchas* was a relatively open one: the progeny of inter-caste unions formed a new caste included in the social system, in the Shudra category,[4] and foreigners could also be integrated if they accepted the ritual rules of which the Brahmans were the custodians. The successive invaders (the Greeks, Shakas and Huns who adopted local religious beliefs and practices) were thus recognised as Kshatriyas. As a result, 'from about the ninth century onwards references to large numbers of indigenous peoples as *mlecchas* beg[a]n to decrease'.[5]

The inner logic of the caste system demonstrates here its capacity for assimilation of the Other at a subordinate level: in so far as its hierarchy reflects a graduation of status based on the concept of ritual purity, any group can be attributed a rank according to its degree of purity, orthopraxy or conformity with the social rules.[6] This assimilation-and-subordination is more than an opportunity: it is a necessity, because the 'traditional Indian xenology', as Halbfass terms it, does not enable the Aryas to conceive anything beyond them; every community is supposed to be integrated to their social system to maintain the cosmic order. This world view, however, is primarily promoted by the Brahmanical order whose attitude, according to Sheldon Pollock, citing Geissen, amounts to a 'pre-form of racism',[7] as evident in the exclusion of the Shudras from knowledge of the Vedas. Yet the author emphasises the absence of eugenic grounds for this exclusion in the *Mimamsa*:

While a biogenetic disqualification is sometimes adduced elsewhere, sudras and other despised communities are here not excluded from vedic literacy on the grounds of physical or intellectual inferiority. On the contrary, 'sudras are as capable of learning as the twice-born are'; in the matters of this world, aryas and mlecchas have equal capabilities [according, respectively, to Kacaspati and

[4] Ibid., p.157.

[5] Ibid., p.173.

[6] On this point, see L. Dumont, *Homo Hierarchicus—le système des castes et ses implications* (Paris, 1966), p.242.

[7] Cited in S. Pollock, 'Deep orientalism? Notes on Sanskrit and power beyond the raj', in C.A. Breckenridge and P. van der Veer (eds.), *Orientalism and the Postcolonial Predicament* (Philadelphia, 1993), p.107.

Kumarila].[8]

As a result, Pollock describes the restrictions on high-culture literacy as part of 'a program of domination'.[9] This assessment, combined with the idea of a 'pre-form of racism', is close to the notion of 'upper-caste racism'—a term coined by Gyanendra Pandey—[10] which I shall try to apply to key Hindu nationalist ideologues. In effect, these men drew some of their inspiration from the 'Great Tradition'.

However, these ideologues had also been exposed to many European ideas about race. Interestingly, philosophers and sociologists working on racialism sustain that the racial theory was born in an article of 1664 by François Bernier, a French doctor who travelled extensively in India. This article, entitled *Nouvelle division de la terre, par les différentes espèces ou races d'hommes qui l'habitent*, was the first attempt to divide the world according to the racial criterion.[11] But, though Bernier's travelogues were translated into English as early as 1671, this article apparently was not; and, therefore, the first proto-racialist theories evolved by Europeans using the English medium must probably be located in the late eighteenth century. In 1792, William Jones had deduced from the discovery of the Indo-European linguistic family the notion of a common, original race whose branches had migrated towards Europe and India.[12] This theory was developed during the nineteenth century by many German philologists such as Albrecht Weber, R. Roth, A. Kuhn and J. Möhl (whose books were published in the 1840s and 1850s). In their writings appear the notions of 'Sanskritic race' or 'vedic people'. These speculations reached India from the late 1850s onwards through Max Müller, who tended to be somewhat more cautious, and William Muir who published, in 1860, a study on 'The trans-Himalayan origin of the Hindus, and their affinity

[8] Ibid., p.110.

[9] Ibid., p.111.

[10] G. Pandey, 'Which of us are Hindus?', in Pandey (ed.), *Hindus and Others: the question of identity in India today* (New Delhi, 1993), p.252.

[11] L. Toth, 'Existe-t-il une doctrine traditionnelle de la race?', *Politica Hermetica* 2 (1988), p.23.

[12] P.J. Marshall 'Introduction' in Marshall (ed.), *The British Discovery of Hinduism in the Eighteenth Century* (Cambridge, 1970), p.15.

with the western branches of the Aryan race'.[13]

The first Hindu revivalist thinkers were clearly influenced by these European reconstructions of the past. Swami Dayananda Saraswati, according to Jordens, 'did his best to keep abreast of what European scholars were publishing'.[14] In 1868 or 1869 he employed a Bengali to read to him Max Müller's translation of the *Veda*, about which his knowledge seems to have been rudimentary till then.[15] The theses of the Western orientalists about the vedic period probably shaped the views he expressed in *Satyarth Prakash*, the Light of Truth, few years later. In this book, the vedic Aryas are described by Dayananda as a primordial and elect people to whom the Veda has been revealed by God and whose language—Sanskrit—is said to be the 'Mother of all languages'.[16] They would have migrated in the beginning of the world from Tibet—the first land to emerge from the Oceans[17]—towards the Aryavarta. This territory, homeland of the vedic civilisation, covered the Punjab, Doab and Ganges basin. From this position, the Aryas would have dominated the whole world till the war of the *Mahabharata*, a watershed opening a phase of decadence. The national renaissance implied precisely, for Dayananda, a coming back to the vedic Golden Age. The Arya Samaj is probably the first movement in India defining nationalism in terms of ethnicity: in Dayananda's

[13] I am most grateful to Bruce Graham for the information contained in this paragraph which he developed in still unpublished chapters; see his book on the Jana Sangh where the argument is summarised in one page: B. Graham, *Hindu Nationalism and Indian Politics—the origins and development of the Bharatiya Jana Sangh* (Cambridge, 1990), p.44.

[14] J.T.F. Jordens, *Dayananda Sarasvati—his life and ideas* (Delhi, 1978), p.170.

[15] Ibid., pp.56-7.

[16] Swami Dayananda, *The Light of Truth* (Allahabad, 1981, translated and introduced by Ganga Prasad Upadhyaya), p.249.

[17] The idea that the Tibet, and more generally the Himalaya, was the birth place of the Aryan race was first developed by European writers. Originally, geographers of the eighteenth century, alleging the effects of the Deluge, explained that the ancestors of the humanity could only come from high mountains. Since the highest mountains surrounded Tibet, philosophers such as Kant and Herder evolved this thesis, obviously borrowed by Dayananda from European authors. See L. Poliakov, *Le mythe aryen. Essai sur les sources du racisme et des nationalismes* (Bruxelles, 1987 [1971]), pp.210-13.

writings, the Hindu are clearly the descendants of the Aryas, even if he called his followers not to register themselves as Hindus—because of the decadent shape of Hinduism—before the census of 1881. This stance was reversed by his successors before the census of 1911.

The idea of world domination by the Hindus was elaborated around that time by another Arya Samajist based in the Rajasthani British enclave of Ajmer, Har Bilas Sarda (1867-1955).[18] In the second chapter of *The Hindu Superiority* (1906), entitled 'Hindu colonization of the world', this author rejects the Central Asia theory of emigration (a point to which I shall return) and asserts that the Aryavarta was the birth place of a race which spread and settled in Egypt, Ethiopia, Persia, Asia Minor, Greece, Rome, Turkistan, Germany, Scandinavia, Hyperborean countries, Great Britain, Eastern Asia and America.[19] This geography is precisely the one suggested from another point of view by W. Jones: beyond the linguistic links between the Greek, the Gothic, the Celtic, the Persian and the Sanskrit, this author indicated that the Scythian, Hyperborean and Scandinavian philosophies and mythologies might have been introduced or shaped by 'a foreign race' from the East.[20] As far as America is concerned he adds:

> It is very remarkable that the Peruvians, whose Incas boasted of the same descent, styled their greatest festival Ramasitoa; whence we may suppose, that South America was peopled by the same race, who imported into the farthest parts of Asia the rites and fabulous history of Rama.[21]

The similarities in the inscriptions on Abyssian, Ethiopic and Indian monuments led Jones to conclude that 'Ethiopia and Hindustan were peopled or colonised by the same extraordinary race'.[22] Har Bilas Sarda, who quotes Jones abundantly along with Colebrooke, Kuhn,

[18] This Arya Samajist leader—who organised the celebration for Dayananda's birth centenary in 1924—became a Hindu Sabhaite in the 1920s; R. Gopal, 'Har Bilas Sarda, a sketch' in H.B. Sarda, *Speeches and Writings* (Ajmer, 1935).

[19] Har Bilas Sarda, *Hindu Superiority—an attempt to determine the position of the Hindu race in the scale of nations* (New Delhi, 1975), pp.109-63.

[20] William Jones, 'On the Hindus' in Marshall, *British Discovery of Hinduism*, pp.254-5.

[21] Ibid., p. 256.

[22] Ibid., p. 257.

Muir, Müller, Roth, A. Weber and the Theosophists, uses such claims to prove that most of the civilisations originated in the Hindus-Aryas, a race which colonised the whole world before the *Mahabharat* war.

The same themes appeared at the same time in the second book by Bal Gangadhar Tilak, *The Arctic Home in the Vedas* (1903). The author, known for his Hindu nationalist leanings, claimed that the Aryans had their original home near the North Pole in palæolithic times and that they migrated from this place southwards into Asia and Europe because of changes in the climatic conditions.[23] Interestingly, Tilak refers often to Muir and Müller to substantiate his theory.[24]

Obviously, the first Hindu nationalist ideologues of the late nineteenth century and early twentieth century borrowed heavily from the European orientalists. Among other themes, the one they used assiduously related to the common racial origin of the European and Indian peoples, and its corollary, the southward migration which they interpreted to prove that the Hindus were the first race and that they once dominated the whole world. This myth helped the first Hindu revivalists to regain a certain self-esteem by claiming that their ancestors were the first inhabitants of the world. But the argument was not developed beyond this point. It seems that these authors hesitated to resort to the themes of racial purity as such, and this is the issue I would like to analyse now, especially because this attitude proved to be perennial.

A similar kind of ambiguity in the use of racial theories can be observed in the case—on which I shall focus—of Hindu nationalist ideologues of the 1920s and 1930s, when such theories were so much in vogue in Europe. The reason for this restraint seems to lie in the contradiction between the Western influences and the 'traditional Indian xenology': the leaders of the inter-war period inherited an hierarchical but integrative view of society into which the racial theories did not fit easily.

[23] S.L. Karandikar, *Lokamanya Bal Gangadhar Tilak—the Hercules and Prometheus of modern India* (Poona, 1957), p.193.

[24] J. Leopold, 'The Aryan theory of race', *Indian Economic and Social History Review* 7, 2 (June 1970), p.275.

The Hindus as a race and the Western influence

V.D. Savarkar was probably the most influential ideologue of Hindu nationalism in the 1920-1940 period. His book *Hindutva—who is a Hindu?* has been recognised as a treatise of Hindu identity by many followers; published in Nagpur in 1923, it was one of the influences which prompted Hedgewar to create the Rashtriya Swayamsevak Sangh in 1925. This book shares the perspective of those written by Swami Dayananda and Tilak. Savarkar had been given a grant to study in England thanks to the recommendation of the latter,[25] and the hostel where he lived between 1905 and 1910 in London, India House, was being looked after by a staunch Arya Samajist from Bombay, S.K. Verma,[26] whose interest in Herbert Spencer's theories was evident in his journal, *The Indian Sociologist*.[27] Savarkar inherited the Hindu revivalist ideas of the late nineteenth and early twentieth centuries, but he extended them and developed their racial aspects.

Near the end of *Hindutva*, Savarkar offers the following definition of the Hindu:

A Hindu, then is he who feels attachment to the land that extends from Sindhu to Sindhu as the land of his forefathers—as his Fatherland; who inherits the blood of the great race whose first and discernible source could be traced from the Himalayan altitudes of the Vedic Saptasindhus and which assimilating all that was incorporated and ennobling all that was assimilated has grown into and come to be known as the Hindu people; and who, as a consequence of the

[25] V.S. Anand, *Savarkar—a study in the evolution of Indian nationalism* (London, 1967), and Chitragupta, *Life of Barrister Savarkar* (Bombay, 1987 [1926]).

[26] Home Department (Political) Proceedings for the year 1914, P/9460, 1 December 1914, Pro. no 169, IOLR. During his stay in London, he introduced a nationalist pledge that the inmates of India House would collectively repeat every night a bedtime prayer in which the word race appeared along with five other concepts: 'One God, one nation, one language, one race, one form, one hope'; H. Srivastava, *Five Stormy Years—Savarkar in London* (New Delhi, 1983), p.64. At that stage, 'race' was not used to designate a special community but, as in many European writings at that time, as a rather loose synonym for 'nation'. In the India House, Arya Samajists such as Har Dayal and Bhai Parmanand, and Muslim leaders like Asaf Ali and Sikandar Hayat Khan, shared the same type of non-religious, revolutionary nationalism.

[27] I. Yajnik, *Shyamaji Krishnavarma—life and times of an Indian revolutionary* (Bombay, 1950), see ch.IX, 'Herbert Spencer Lectureship', pp.103-19.

foregoing attributes, has inherited and claims as his own the Hindu sanskriti [culture], the Hindu civilization, as represented in a common history, common heroes, a common literature, common art, a common law and a common jurisprudence, common fairs and festivals, rites and rituals, ceremonies and sacraments.[28]

Obviously, Savarkar attaches most importance to the concepts of territory and race. The first draws its name, Hindustan, from the fact that it is girdled by the sea and seven rivers (*sapta sindhus*, mainly the Indus and the Brahmaputra). The second, coming from the mountains where these rivers have their source, is said to have settled in this land at the dawn of the world. Savarkar insists on this primacy and ascendancy of the Hindus: 'They are not only a Nation but also a race-jati.... All Hindus claim to have in their veins the blood of the mighty race incorporated with and descended from the vedic fathers...'.[29]

The myth of the vedic Golden Age is reactivated and reinterpreted to the extent that Savarkar puts the emphasis more on its racial dimension than on the cultural or religious aspects which are presented as derivative. This emphasis seems to be easy to explain: Savarkar tries desperately to demonstrate that an original unity underlies and orders the cultural diversity of the Hindus:

And no word can give full expression to this racial unity of our people as the epithet, Hindu does. Some of us were Aryans and some Anaryans; but Ayars and Nayars [according to the South India terminology]—we were all Hindus and own a common blood.[30] Some of us are Brahmans and some Namashudras or Panchamas [untouchable castes]; but Brahmans or Chandalas [one generic term for the untouchables]—we are all Hindus and own a common blood. Some of us are Daxinatyas [from the South] and some Gauds; but Gauds or Saraswatas [*smarta*—orthodox—Brahmans]—we are all Hindus and own a common blood. Some of us were Rakhasas [demonical beings perceived as the original settlers of India] and some Yakshas [supernatural beings having some elements of divinity]; but Rakshasas or Yakshas—we are all Hindus and own a common blood. Some of us were Vanaras [inhabitants of the forest, tribals as well as monkeys] and some Kinnaras [denizens of the *antariksha* or atmospheric region]; but Vanaras or Naras—we are all Hindus and own a

[28] V.D. Savarkar, *Hindutva—who is a Hindu?* (Bombay, 1969), p.100.

[29] Ibid., pp.84-5.

[30] I shall return to this contradiction in terms in the second part of the paper.

common blood. Some of us are Jains and some Jangamas [shaivite sect]; but Jains or Jangamas—we are all Hindus and own a common blood. Some of us are monists, some pantheists; some theists and some atheists. But monotheists or atheists—we are all Hindus and own a common blood. We are not only a nation but a Jati, a born brotherhood. Nothing else counts, it is after all a question of heart. We *feel* that the same ancient blood that coursed through the veins of Ram and Krishna, Buddha and Mahavir, Nanak and Chaitanya, Basava and Madhava, of Rohidas and Tiruvelluvar courses throughout Hindudom from vein to vein, pulsates from heart to heart.[31]

This incantatory piece of rhetoric is indicative of the whole ideological strategy of Savarkar: belonging to a community divided into many castes and sects, he tries to imbue it with a nationalist consciousness by arguing that beyond all the visible differences there exists an invisible bond—blood. (However, he acknowledges that the reality of this common blood is less important than the *feeling* of its national meaning, a point to which we shall return in the second section.)

The way in which Savarkar employed a racial criterion stemmed probably from Western influences which we must now analyse. During his stay in England, Savarkar had obviously been exposed to evolutionary theories. In his autobiography, books by Darwin, Spencer, Tyndall, Haeckel and Huxley are mentioned: they were among his readings in the Andamans prison where he was kept for anti-British activities between 1911 and 1921, and where he conceived *Hindutva.*[32] All these writers share a common interest in evolutionist theories. The work of the German zoologist, Ernst Haeckel, even belongs to the bio-evolutionist school of thought, since he justified the domination of races considered to be incapable of progress.[33] In the late 1930s, soon after his liberation from jail in 1937, Savarkar expressed a certain attraction for European fascism. In 1938, the year after he became president of the Hindu Mahasabha, he congratulated Hitler during a

[31] Savarkar, *Hindutva*, p.89.

[32] V.D. Savarkar, *My Transportation for Life* (Bombay, 1984), pp.269-70. The references are to Charles Darwin (1809-1882), Herbert Spencer (1820-1903), John Tyndall (1820-1893), Ernst Heinrich Haeckel (1834-1919), and Thomas Henry Huxley (1825-1895).

[33] P.-A. Taguieff, *La force du préjugé. Essai sui le racisme et ses doubles* (Paris, 1987), p.335.

public meeting at Delhi for having 'liberated' the Sudetans who shared the 'same blood and same tongue'[34] as the Germans. At the same time, *Hindu Outlook* (the Hindu Mahasabha mouthpiece) and *Mahratta* (one of Tilak's newspapers, edited by N.C. Kelkar, an active Hindu Sabhaite) praised Franco[35] and Mussolini,[36] as well as Hitler.[37]

Some Hindu Sabhaites had had direct contacts with European fascists since the early 1930s. When Moonje (Tilak's lieutenant at Nagpur, who became president of the Hindu Mahasabha in 1927) journeyed to London to attend the first Round Table Conference, he went to Italy in order 'to see the working of the Ballila movement'.[38] It seems that he met Hitler and had an interview with Mussolini, who was pleased to show him his military institutions.[39] After coming back to India, Moonje laboured to establish a military school. It opened in 1938 at Nasik, thanks to the support of many Maharajas.[40]

But the main Hindu movement generally perceived as stemming from European inter-war fascism is the Rashtriya Swayamsevak Sangh. In fact, its foundation took place in 1925 before the first contacts of Hindu nationalist leaders with European fascists, and its model was more the sect than the totalitarian party.[41] However, the ideological influence seems to have been real, as indicated by the use of the concept of race in *We, or our nationhood defined,* the first central text of the R.S.S. written in 1938 by M.S. Golwalkar, who became head of the organisation in 1940. Drawing his inspiration explicitly from

[34] *Hindu Outlook*, 12 October 1938, p.13.

[35] Ibid., 2 November 1938, p.5.

[36] 'A Great Dictator—Signor Mussolini at work', ibid., 30 November 1938, p.7.

[37] *Mahratta*, 6 January 1939, p.10.

[38] M.N. Ghatate (a prominent R.S.S. worker at Nagpur, and Moonje's secretary during his European tour) 'Dr. B.S. Moonje—tour of European countries', in *Dharmaveer Dr. B.S. Moonje Commemoration Volume* (Nagpur, 1972), pp.68-9.

[39] Reminiscences of V.G. Deshpande, in ibid., p.25.

[40] Moonje Papers, NMML (Microfilm section), reel no.10, letter from Moonje to Appasahib Kelkar, 25 February 1936.

[41] I developed this argument in *The Hindu Nationalist Movement and Politics in India c.1925-1993. Identity-building, implantation and mobilisation* (London, 1995), ch.1.

'Western political scientists',[42] this author distinguished five criteria as defining a nation: land, race, religion, culture and language. Among those, by contrast with Savarkar's *Hindutva*,[43] the racial factor is given more prominence than the territorial.

This emphasis on the racial criterion stems clearly from the influence of the Nazi model which attracted attention in the 1930s:

> The ancient Race spirit which prompted the Germanic tribes to over-run the whole of Europe, has re-risen in modern Germany. With the result that the nation perforce follows aspirations, predetermined by the traditions left by its depredatory ancestors. Even so with us: our Race spirit has once again roused itself as is evidenced by the race of spiritual giants we have produced, and who today stalk the world in serene majesty.[44]

The concept of 'race spirit' used by Golwalkar corresponds most probably here to the German notion of '*Geist*'. It refers to a conception of the nation based on ethnic qualities: the nation bears a special genius expressed in its culture and its language. This kind of nationalism had been developed by Herder and Fichte without racial references; and, apparently, Golwalkar, in the wake of the Hindu revivalist writers, took it over and added the word 'race'. However, another passage of his book would appear to indicate that Golwalkar borrowed more than an ethnic model of nationalism from the German national socialism:

> German pride has now become the topic of the day. To keep up the purity of the Race and its culture, Germany shocked the world by her purging the country of the semitic Races—the Jews. Race pride at its highest has been manifested here. Germany has also shown how well nigh impossible it is for Races and cultures, having differences going to the root, to be assimilated into one united whole, a good lesson for us in Hindusthan to learn and profit by.[45]

Here, Golwalkar draws from the eugenic core of the European fascism. He openly suggests that minorities can hardly be assimilated and, therefore, must be eliminated. The trouble with this often quoted pas-

[42] M.S. Golwalkar, *We, or our nationhood defined* (Nagpur, 1947), p.21.

[43] However, it seems that *We, or our nationhood defined* is an abridged version of an essay by the eldest brother of V.D. Savarkar; see W. Andersen and S. Damle, *The Brotherhood in Saffron—the Rashtriya Swayamsevak Sangh and Hindu revivalism* (New Delhi, 1987), p.43.

[44] Golwalkar, *We, or our nationhood defined*, pp.39-40.

[45] Ibid., p.43.

sage is that it is the only place, so far as I know, where Golwalkar refers to racial purity. He does not seem to have evolved a systematic racial theory based on eugenic or biological principles. This is probably largely due to the fact that Golwalkar drew most of its inspiration from European writers who cannot be termed 'racist' in biological terms. Among the 'political scientists' quoted by Golwalkar we find 'Hole-Combe' (in fact Arthur Norman Holcombe), 'Bluntsley' (in fact Johann Kaspar Bluntschli), 'Gumplovic' (in fact Ludwig Gumplovicz) and Burgess (John W. Burgess).[46] None of these writers was a hard-core eugenist. Holcombe, in the very book quoted by Galwalkar,[47] writes that 'modern anthropologists and ethnologists have not succeeded in classifying mankind upon the evidences of relationship by blood, so as to enable the political scientist to identify nations with particular races'.[48] This assertion is somewhat shaded by the polysemy of the word 'race' in Holcombe's writings (like in so many others at that time). About 30 pages later, he writes that:

> in general, Oriental nationalism is blended with the larger problems arising out of the rivalries of races. The doctrine of self-determination may be understood, not as the self-determination of nations, but as racial self-determination. It has been so understood, for instance, by the more radical leaders of the movement for self-government in India.[49]

Despite this lack of conceptual rigour, Holcombe remained an exponent of a non-ethnic form of nationalism. By contrast, Gumplovicz,

[46] He also mentions a certain 'Getel'; in fact Raymond Garfield Gettell who published an *Introduction to Political Science* in 1910.

[47] Golwalkar cites the following definition of nationalism by Holcombe by omitting the words of the original in parentheses: 'Nationality (regarded as a force in modern politics) is a corporate sentiment, a kind of fellow feeling or mutual sympathy relating to a definite home-country (and binding together the members of a human group, irrespective of differences in religion, economic interests, or social position, more intimately than any other similar sentiment). It springs (as Lincoln eloquently suggested) from a common heritage of memories, whether of great achievements and glory or of disaster and suffering'; A. Holcombe, *The Foundation of the Modern Commonwealth* (New York, 1923), p.133. This definition largely borrows from Renan's universalistic definition of nationalism—which Holcombe himself cites; but Golwalkar omitted an interesting part of it.

[48] Ibid., p.129.

[49] Ibid., p.161.

who wrote *Der Rassenkampf* in 1883, was influenced by Gobineau's theories. However he also criticised the idea of classifying races—none of them being pure—and did not consider races as primary elements but as constructs, products of the fight between groups striving for domination.[50] In addition, Golwalkar mentions Gumplovicz en passant. He quotes more extensively 'the famous German writer', 'Blunstley', a passage (its origin not indicated by Golwalkar) which comes from Bluntschli's *The Theory of the State* which was published in English in 1885 and republished in 1892, 1895, 1897, 1898, 1901 and 1921. The excerpt selected by Golwalkar is revealing of the influences to which he was most receptive:

> [A nation] is a union of masses of men of different conceptions and social states, in hereditary society of common spirit, feeling and race bound together especially by a language and customs in a common civilization which gives them a sense of unity and distinction from all foreigners, quite apart from the bond of the state.[51]

This definition is chiefly illustrative of the German kind of 'ethnic nationalism' based on inherited cultural features. 'Race' appears here as one criterion among others. The racial dimension was emphasised by other writers as early as the late nineteenth century, but Golwalkar did not borrow primarily from them.

More generally, no other Hindu nationalist ideologue has been able to assimilate the biological logic underlying the fascist version of racialism. This must be scrutinised, not to congratulate oneself on this incapacity, but in order to identify the Hindu nationalist variety of racism, which is probably less dramatic but more enduring than the eugenic or biological one. This particular racial theory seems to be rooted in the 'traditional Indian xenology' and to have been adapted to the specific needs of ideologues such as Savarkar and Golwalkar in

[50] See *La lutte des races* (Paris, 1893), pp.179-92; Taguieff, *La force du préjugé*, p.577, and I.L. Horowitz, 'The sociology of Ludwig Gumplowicz (1838-1909)', introduction to L. Gumplowicz, *Outlines of Sociology* (New York, 1963), pp.10-17.

[51] J.K. Bluntschli, *The Theory of the State* (English translation from the 6th German edition; Oxford, 1885), p.86; cited in Golwalkar, *We, or our nationhood defined*, p.21.

terms of (Hindu) nation-building.

Social racism rather than bio-racism or the persistence of traditional xenology

The historical account of the formation of the Hindu people by Savarkar excludes the notion of a pure race. True, to emphasise the uniformity of the Hindu blood throughout the society, he invokes the legality of inter-caste marriages through the customs of *anuloma* and *pratiloma* (the first when the male's status is higher than the female's, and the second when the female's is higher than the male's),[52] and, on the same reasoning, he denied that the Shakas and the Huns were integrated in the Hindu matrix: they were opposed straightaway.[53] But as mentioned, his Hindu race includes Aryans as well as non-Aryans. This is an implicit acknowledgement of the way the former conquered the sub-continent. As the Aryans penetrated the sub-continent, 'different peoples of other highly developed types began to be incorporated into their culture'.[54]

Savarkar rejects even the idea of a pure Hindu race:

> After all there is throughout this world so far as man is concerned but a single race—the human race kept alive by one common blood, the human blood.... Even as it is, not even the aborigines of the Andamans are without some sprinkling of the so-called Aryan blood in their veins and vice versa. Truly speaking all that any one of us can claim, all that history entitles one to claim, is that one has the blood of all mankind in one's veins. The fundamental unity of man from pole to pole is true, all else only relatively so.[55]

This repudiation of the very idea of a Hindu race, so strongly stressed elsewhere by Savarkar can be explained from two points of view: first, the Aryan theory was not thought nationalistic enough; and, second, that social integration which dominates the hierarchical view of the world in Brahmanical Hinduism, remained a very strong priority for the Hindu nationalist ideologues.

(1) *The Aryan theory is not nationalistic enough.* The Aryan theory

[52] Savarkar, *Hindutva*, p.85.
[53] Ibid., p.21.
[54] Ibid., p.11.
[55] Ibid., p.90.

had been very much used by Indian writers, in order to regain their lost self-esteem, from the end of the nineteenth century till the beginning of the twentieth century. Alleging racial links with the dominant white power and invoking the colonisation of the world by Indian Aryans were factors nourishing nationalist pride. But in the 1930s and 1940s, the Aryan theory seems to have been counter-productive from this very same Hindu nationalist view point.

First, it seems it was not able to unite the Hindu nation beyond the castes, sects and regionalisms (as Savarkar tried to show in some parts of his book) because it introduced a division between the Aryans and the peoples who used to live in India before the Aryan migration, mainly the Dravidians and tribals whom Savarkar are considered part of the Hindu nation from other points of view such as culture and geography. According to Joan Leopold, this divisive impact of the Aryan theory had been the main cause of its rejection by many nationalist writers even before Savarkar.[56] In Savarkar's nationalism the emphasis is put above all on the land. The territory being the main basis of Hindu nationalism, the pre-Aryan tribes are automatically recognised as Hindus, independently of their race:

> Therefore, the Santals, Kolis, Bhils, Panchamas, Namashudras and all other such tribes and classes are Hindus. This Sindhustan is as emphatically if not more emphatically, the land of their forefathers as of those of the so-called Aryans; they inherit the Hindu blood and the Hindu culture; and even those of them who have not as yet come fully under the influence of any orthodox Hindu sect, do still worship deities and saints and follow a religion however primitive, are still purely attached to this land, which therefore to them is not only a Fatherland but a Holyland.[57]

For authors such as H.B. Sarda or Golwalkar, the Aryan theory was not nationalist enough because it assumed that the Aryans were not the first inhabitants of India. Obviously, Hindu nationalist leaders could not appreciate the writings of Aryanists in which it was said that the Hindus were 'like their English masters, foreigners who entered the country at an earlier date'.[58] This was another motive for rejection related to the

[56] Leopold, 'The Aryan theory of race', p.281.

[57] Sarvarkar, *Hindutva*, p.121.

[58] J. Leopold, 'British applications of the Aryan theory of race to India, 1850-

importance of territory. Refusing the idea of an Aryan invasion, Golwalkar maintains that the 'Hindus come into this land from nowhere, but are indigenous children of the soil always, from time immemorial and are natural masters of the country'. In order to make this point without contradicting prestigious predecessors such as Tilak, Golwalkar concedes that the 'Aryans, i.e., the Hindus, lived in the region of the North Pole'. But he argues that modern palæontological researches demonstrate that the North Pole is not stationary, and that 'quite long ago it was in that part of the world, we find, is called Bihar and Orissa at the present'.[59]

Its transnational connotations are the third motive for the resistance shown towards the Aryan theory by Hindu nationalist ideologues, especially because some Orientalists and Theosophists used it precisely as a lever for their universalism: the idea that the dominant European and the Indians belong to the same racial family, which used to be appreciated as a means to recover one's self-esteem, is now dismissed because it might inhibit nationalism.

Savarkar's emphasis on the territory opportunately reduced the transnational connotations of Aryanism: this concept does not refer any longer to the 'racial links' with the dominant white power, but only to the Hindus of India in a purely nationalistic perspective. This aspect of Savarkar's thought was probably due to his reading of Arya Samajist ideologues such as Guru Datt Vidyarthi who wrote for instance: 'I do not use the word Arya in the sense in which it is taken by the modern Europeans: on the other hand, I mean by it the inhabitants of Aryavarta and Aryavarta only'.[60]

Finally, the racial criterion is not the most relevant one to distinguish the Hindus from the community perceived as their main aggressor, the Muslims, many of whom were converts. Taking the case

---

1870', *English Historical Review* LXXXIX, 352 (July 1974), p.589.

[59] Golwalkar, *We, or our nationhood defined* , p.13. Interestingly, this theory has been introduced in the history textbooks in the States controlled between 1990 and 1992 by the Bharatiya Janata Party, the political front of the R.S.S.

[60] Cited in Leopold, 'The Aryan theory of race', p.293. For a biographical sketch of Vidyarthi, see Swami Vedananda Tirtha (ed.), *Wisdom of the Rishis or complete works of Pandita Guru Datta Bidyarthi* (Lahore, n.d.), pp.i-iv.

of a Bohra or a Khoja, Savarkar explains that: 'He possesses—in certain cases they do—pure Hindu blood; especially if he is the first convert to Mohammedanism he must be allowed to claim to inherit the blood of Hindu parents'.[61] In this case, Savarkar admits that the division is not a racial but a cultural one:

> It is clear that though their original blood is thus almost unaffected by an alien adulteration, yet they cannot be called Hindus in the sense in which that term is actually understood, because we Hindus are bound together not only by the tie of the love we bear to a common fatherland and by the common blood that courses through our veins and keeps our heart throbbing and our affections warm, but also by the tie of the common homage we pay to our great civilisation—our Hindu culture, which could not be better rendered than by the word Sanskriti.[62]

This reference to the major role of culture in the definition of a nation leads us to the main point: race cannot be over emphasised by Savarkar because he has inherited a 'xenology' where the racial criterion was downgraded vis-à-vis the cultural attitude.

(2) *Hierarchical integration versus racism.* As we have seen with W. Halbfass and R. Thapar, traditionally culture not race was *the* factor of exclusion in India; therefore, this exclusion was not insuperable. The Hindu nationalist leaders maintain this tradition. For Savarkar, Sister Nivedita (the Irish disciple of Vivekananda) was a true Hindu: 'For she had adopted our culture and come to adore our land as her Holyland. She *felt* she was a Hindu and that is, apart from all technicalities, the real and the most important test.'[63] Therefore, the preponderance of the relation with the land and the culture allows a sort of subjective 'raciality'—the contradiction in terms already noticed above.

Interestingly, Golwalkar himself defined race in cultural terms:

> Race is a hereditary Society having common customs, common language, common memories of glory or disaster; in short, it is a population with a common origin under one culture. Such a race is by far the most important ingredient of a Nation.[64]

[61] Sarvarkar, *Hindutva*, p.101.
[62] Ibid., p.92.
[63] Ibid., p.130.
[64] Golwalkar, *We, or our nationhood defined* , p.26.

Race is not a primary identity to which people would belong—or be excluded from—because of their genes; it is a society whose culture is shaped by history. Further, some passages of Golwalkar's book suggest that the race spirit itself can be shaped by traditions of the people:

The aspirations of the individual, as also of the Race are conditioned by its mental frame. As is the mould in which the Racial mind is thrown—of course by its agelong traditions—so are its desires, its aspirations. It is the Race Consciousness awakening to march further on, but it must tread the road into which its past traditional way has led it.[65]

This subordination of the genetic heredity to the work of culture in the long term is incompatible with biological racism. Interestingly, Golwalkar can only enjoin the Muslims to integrate to the Hindu nation by renouncing their culture:

Culturally, linguistically, they must become one with the National race; they must adopt the past and entertain the aspirations for the future, of the National race; in short, they must be 'Naturalised' in the country by being assimilated in the Nation wholly.[66]

The term 'race', if we define it on the basis of biological criteria, becomes more and more inadequate here since the Muslims are supposed to be able to change their race even when they are not converts but descend from the stock of invaders of the Arab or Turanian races (a notion much in vogue at the beginning of the century). In fact, the use of the concept of race is here close to that of 'ethnic nation' since the Other is required to adopt the culture, the language, the historical legacy and the aspirations of the Hindus.If he does not, he will not be eliminated but will be treated statutorily as an inferior. P.-A. Taguieff's typology, contrasting the racisms of domination and extermination, is useful at that stage. In the latter case, the obsession with racial purity makes the elimination of the Other, who *cannot* be integrated, a necessity; whereas, in the former case, ethnic groups are ordered hierarchically but they can entertain relationships: the Other is thinkable, at a subordinate rank.[67] The following quote

[65] Ibid., p. 39.
[66] Ibid., p. 54.
[67] Taguieff, *La force du préjugé*, p.174.

from Golwalkar illustrates this racism of domination because in it non-Hindus are enjoined to become Hindus—which marks the rejection of the biological logic—but if they chose to remain 'aliens', they can only occupy a position of inferiority. He writes:

> the non-Hindu people in Hindusthan must either adopt the Hindu culture and language, must learn to respect and hold in reverence Hindu religion, must entertain no idea but those of glorification of the Hindu race and culture, i.e. they must not only give up their attitude of intolerance and ungratefulness towards this land and its agelong traditions but must also cultivate the positive attitude of love and devotion instead—in one word they must cease to the foreigners, or may stay in the country, wholly subordinated to the Hindu nation, claiming nothing, deserving no privileges, far less any preferential treatment—not even citizen's rights.[68]

This alternative is consistent with the core of the 'traditional xenology', according to which alien groups were required to integrate the autochthonous society of the varnas at a rank necessarily inferior to the Brahmans who were the custodians of the social as well as ritual order. Moreover, Golwalkar considered as *mlecchas* 'those who do not subscribe to the social laws dictated by the Hindu Religion and Culture'.[69] Simultaneously, he praised the *varna vyavastha* as the best social system.[70]

This cultural inheritance is however blended with foreign influences. Golwalkar obviously borrows his distinction between 'citizens' and the other nationals from Bluntschli, who considered that the former were entitled to exert political rights forbidden to the latter.[71] He was also probably impressed by the book of J. Burgess from which he borrowed one of its definitions of nationalism, and in which one finds a strong plea in favour of homogeneous ethnic nations. Referring to

[68] Golwalkar, *We, or our nationhood defined* , pp.55-56.

[69] Cited in Pandey, 'Which of us are Hindus?', p.258. (The quotation probably comes from *Bunch of Thoughts* rather than from *We, or our nationhood defined*).

[70] We can read, in a compilation of Golwalkar's speeches and writings: 'The Hindu people, they ['our forefathers'] said, is the Virat Purusha, the Almighty manifesting Himself...this means that the people who have this fourfold arrangement [the varna system], i.e., the Hindu people, is our God'; *Bunch of Thoughts* (Bangalore, 1966), p.49.

[71] M. Bluntschli, *Théorie générale de l'état* (Paris, 1881), p.197.

Bluntschli, Burgess writes:

The reigning nationality is in perfect right and pursues, from a scientific point of view, an unassailable policy when it insists, with unflinching determination, upon ethnical homogeneity here. It should realise this, of course, through the peaceable means of influence and education, if possible. When however, these shall have been exhausted in vain, then force is justifiable. It may righteously deport the ethnically hostile element in order to shield the vitals of the state from the forces of dissolution, and in order to create the necessary room for a population sufficient in numbers, in loyalty and capacity to administer the empire and protect it against foreign powers.[72]

Such ideas foreshadowed developments which took place in Europe a few decades after their formulation. They undoubtedly influenced Golwalkar in the way he dealt with Muslims. However, he did not follow Burgess on deportation: physical elimination was not explicitly part of his programme in 1938, and he still favoured a form of integration of the minorities in a hierarchical framework.

We can see this approach at work more obviously in an anonymous pamphlet, *Great Danger to the Hindus*, written by a Savarkarite.[73] Here, the author invites the Muslims to join the Hindu mainstream at a subordinate but quite high level:

You behave as if you are living in a country with which you have no concern, just as travellers live in a way side inn for a few days and go away.... Once you begin to have that natural feeling of human beings, that love of the dear Motherland, that moment we will take you into our fold and christen you Kshatriyas! Then within a generation you will all become Muslim-Hindu-Kshatriyas, without, in any way going against the important teaching of the Holy Prophet.... After all Religion is a personal one and a man who wears a dress and calls himself a Muslim does not become one if he does not behave according to the broad tenets of Islam. Hence dear Brethren—most of you were Hindus once and just because you have changed your religion you cannot become foreigners—call yourself proudly Kshatriyas and begin to act like Kshatriyas.... I tell you that once you call yourself Kshatriyas, that moment the Hindu-Moslems problem will vanish like mists before the powerful sun. Come on brothers, become Kshatriyas.[74]

[72] J.W. Burgess, *Political Science and Comparative Constitutional Law*, vol. 1 (Boston, 1890), p.42.

[73] The author of this text is S.R. Narayana Ayyar, a *vakil* from Coonoor who announced to Savarkar that he wanted to write a pamphlet with the same title in 1938 (Savarkar Papers, NMML, reel no 1, File no.5, letter dated 16 May 1938).

[74] An Obscure Hindu, *Grave Danger to the Hindus* (Puthujara, 1940), pp. 75-

This kind of discourse conforms with the 'traditional xenology': the Hindu elite is willing to integrate any community to the extent that it respects an orthopraxy fixed by the Brahmanical order, irrespective of racial origin. True, the author emphasises that most of the Indian Muslims are of Hindu or Aryan descent, but it does not make any difference for the others. Some Indian Muslims are not Aryans in any—necessarily subjective—taxonomy: there are people of Mongol, Touranian and Arab origins among them, for instance. But the urging to integrate applies to them too.

Such a text testifies how hollow must have been the influence of the biological racial theories, especially among the second-rank leaders from which it emanates. The eugenic logic is obviously incompatible with the 'traditional xenology' in which the caste system is the regulating agency. Moreover, Bhai Parmanand, who succeeded to Moonje as President of the Hindu Mahasabha in 1933, cannot see in Hitler's 'lesson for India', anything other than the primitive caste system:

> The message that he sent on the Annexation [of Austria] in which he described himself as a tool in the hands of the Lord of Destiny for the unification of Germany reminded me of the assurance of Lord Krishna that whenever the world has need of him, He manifests Himself. Is the unity of India complete? I submit not. British India and Indian India to use the common parlance, are divided from each other. They are one and indivisible in every respect except politically. Where is the Hitler who will bring about their unification? ...Hitler's theory is National Socialism.... I find a great affinity between Hitler's National Socialism and the Varnashrama of the Hindus.[75]

This analysis is indicative of the partiality of the Hindu nationalists' understanding of fascism: they play down its eugenic content and focus on its authoritarian and hierarchical corporatist organisation of society, which they assimilate to the most familiar, organic varna system of the 'traditional xenology'. In this perspective, when G. Pandey characterised Golwalkar's praise of the *varna vyavastha* as 'an upper-caste racism',[76] he summarised the ambivalence of Hindu nationalism.

6.

[75] *Hindu Outlook*, 12 October 1938.

[76] Pandey, 'Which of us are Hindus?', p.252.

Savarkar and Golwalkar were probably as much influenced by the Brahmanical *Weltanschauung* of the 'Indian traditional xenology' as by the European notion of biological racism. Hindu nationalist ideologues, in my interpretation, did not look beyond the evolutionist authors and become acquainted with eugenic, fascist writers; this was because they felt profound affinities with the outlook of the former: an organicist theory based on concepts of physics and zoology. Haeckel and Huxley were zoologists; Darwin was a naturalist and Tyndall a physicist; and Herbert Spencer applied the latters' evolutionist and organicist ideas to society (for instance in *Social Statics*, 1851). Interestingly, students of natural science were always strongly represented in the R.S.S. Hedgewar was a doctor; Golwalkar studied and taught zoology; Rajendra Singh, who took over the organisation in 1994, graduated in physics and taught that subject; and H.V. Seshadri, the movement's general secretary, graduated in chemistry.

The affinities between Hindu nationalism and some Western applications of natural science to society, hark back to the Hindu view of the world. In a way it is zoological since the universe is described as being formed of *jatis*. In itself, this vision inhibits the development of a eugenic form of racism. Savarkar as well as Golwalkar translates race by *jati* or vice versa;[77] this terminology must be taken literally. As Olivier Herrenschmidt suggests, the true meaning of *jati* is species,[78] a definition Monier-Williams had already given in his Sanskrit dictionary. There are animal as well as human jatis along a continuum, each with a special *dharma*. Therefore, there cannot be one Hindu race opposed to other races. There can exist only one Hindu culture defining the social rules implemented by a certain human community in which different species co-exist in a hierarchical relationship. This society cannot but be open to the other species who adopt these rules. And the ones who do not are necessarily the lowest groups. In practice, Muslims are considered as untouchables in many Indian localities. The hierarchical view of the caste system is thus extended to the other

[77] See for instance the Hindi version of Savarkar, *Hindutva* (New Delhi, n.d.), p.30.

[78] O. Herrenschmidt, *Les meilleurs dieux sont hindous* (Paris, 1989), p.252.

species: hierarchical principles regulate not only the Hindu social system, but also of course the whole society and even the universe—and upper castes, primarily Brahmans, occupy a prominent position in this schema. The fact that the Hindu nationalist ideologues remained more interested in social, hierarchical unity than in racial purity is confirmed by their interpretation of the Hindu decline.

The cause of the Hindu decline is not racial but social

In the late nineteenth and early twentieth century, many of the European theoreticians of decline explained this phenomenon as a racial degeneration caused by interbreeding.[79] Even though one of the first exponents of this theory, Gobineau, was a Frenchman,[80] his ideas reached England, along with those expressed in a very similar vein in the United States by Samuel G. Morton.[81] But none of the Hindu nationalist ideologues cites him or other English writers who developed similar theses, such as Charles B. Davenport, Madison Grant, Louis Agassiz and of course Houston Stewart Chamberlain.

The idea of decline has been very prominent in the discourse of the Hindu intelligentsia from an early stage. M.G. Ranade (1842-1901) stated: 'All admit that we have been deformed'.[82] But during the nineteenth century the Hindu socio-religious reform movements attributed this decline to social causes more than to any racial degeneration.

[79] This school of thought, though not prominent, was represented in India (Leopold, 'British applications', p.593).

[80] For a superb though concise analysis of Gobineau's theory, see J.E. Schlanger, *Les métaphores de l'organisme* (Paris, 1971), p.184.

[81] In 1911, Earl Finch opened his lecture at the first Universal Congress of Races in London with these words: 'The disciples of Gobineau in France and the ones of Morton in America have stressed that interbreeding has had and can only have disastrous consequences' (cited in Taguieff, *La force du préjugé*, p.338).

[82] 'Revivalism versus reform' in W.T. De Bary (ed). *Sources of Indian Tradition* (New York, 1964), vol.2, p.135. In the address he delivered at the Indian National Social Conference of 1897, Ranade declared: 'In the case of our society especially, the usages which at present prevail among us were admittedly not those which obtained in the most glorious periods of our history. On most of the points which are included in our programme, our own records of the past show that there has been a decided change for the worse...'. 'Revival and reform', in M.G. Ranade, *Religious and Social Reform* (Bombay, 1902), p.168.

Rammohan Roy, as early as 1821, blamed the 'division into castes, which has been the source of want of unity…'.[83] The physical defects of the Hindu population were certainly emphasised, echoing the criticism of effeteness expressed by the British, especially with regard to Bengal.[84] But the racial weakness of the Hindu was not considered as such. The emphasis, as in the Arya Samajist ideology, remained on the sociological origins of Hindu decline.

Dayananda ascribed it to the gradual deterioration that followed the Golden Age of Indian domination. It occurred in spiritual practices (polytheism replacing monotheism; idol worship; and so on) and in social institutions—child marriage, forbidding remarriage of widows, multiplication and insulation of castes whose system becomes hereditary, introduction of untouchability, lowering of the position of women. Dayananda's goal was to re-establish the so-called original vedic social system based on *varna*, because of its organic unity and flexibility. Dayananda described these four vedic 'classes' as merely born out of the collectivity's needs in terms of socio-economic complementarity, claiming further that status distinctions came at a later stage. Originally, therefore, contended Dayananda, children were placed in each *varna* according to their individual qualities:

> The fixture of the varna according to merits and actions should take place at the 16th year of girls and 25th year of boys. Marriages also should take place in their own varna, that is, a Brahman man should be married to a Brahman woman; a Kshatriya to a Kshatriya, a Vaishya to a Vaishya, and a Shudra to a Shudra. This will maintain the integrity of each varna as well as good relations.[85]

It was in order to return to this ideal *varna* system, that the Arya Samaj promoted marriages of adolescents and inter-caste marriages. (Munshi

[83] 'The Brahmunical magazine or the missionary and the Brahmun being a vindication of the Hindoo religion against the attacks of Christian missionaries', in *English Works of Raja Rammohun Roy*, vol.1 (Calcutta, 1928), p.160.

[84] The development of gymnasia was part of the socio-religious reform programme; J. Rosselli, 'The self-image of effeteness: physical education and nationalism in nineteenth-century Bengal', *Past and Present* 86 (1980), pp.121-48.

[85] Swami Dayananda, *The Light of Truth*, p.115.

Ram thus had his daughter—Khatri by caste—married to an Arora.)[86] In the 1920s and 1930s, the way Munshi Ram—renamed Shraddhananda after his vows of renunciation in 1917—addressed the question of Hindu decline is quite revealing. He strongly adhered to the myth of a primordial vedic race but attributed its decline to social defects.

Shraddhananda contributed towards institutionalising a Hindu nationalistic vulgate of capital importance for the consolidation and the propagation of this identity, insofar as it implanted the myth of a primordial, sovereign and chosen people:

> the Veda was revealed in the beginning of creation for all races. It contains germs of all sciences—physical, mental and psychical. But it cannot be denied that the glorious period of the supreme achievements of the vedic Church was the bright period of Indian History. When India was the center of vedic propaganda and missionaries were sent from it to different parts of the world, it was also the seat of a world-wide empire, and Indian kings exercised direct sovereignty over Afghanistan, Baluchistan, Tibet, etc. and Indian colonists colonised Egypt, Rome, Greece, Peru and Mexico.[87]

This assertion of the primary role of India as the centre of a universal vedic civilisation in the beginning of time is an unchanging element of the Arya Samaj. In 1926, Munshi Ram justifies this antecedence by the fact that:

> the plateau of Tibet was the first to come out of water and therefore the revelation of the Vedas was imparted to early humanity at the sacred soil. Mankind was then divided into the good or virtuous and the bad or vicious. The first were named 'Aryas' and the latter 'Dasyus' in the Veda itself.[88]

Notwithstanding this emphasis on the ancient value of the Aryas, the Hindus have become a 'dying race' because of social defects. The date of the decline is fixed, as in Dayananda's book, after the *Mahabharata* war, but Shraddhananda elaborates this point in referring to the disintegration of the *varna* system: 'in the plains of Kurukshetra the spirit

[86] R.S. Pareek, *Contributions of Arya Samaj in the Making of Modern India 1875-1947* (New Delhi, 1973), p.132.

[87] M.R. Jambunathan (ed.), *Swami Shraddhananda* [Autobiography] (Bombay, 1961), pp.155-6.

[88] Shraddhananda, *Hindu Sangathan—saviour of the dying race* (Delhi, 1926), p.71.

of Indian bravery was crushed and Brahman domination was unleashed reducing the other Varnas to servitude'.[89]

The way was thus opened up for all the social ills that were to bring about a degeneration from which India had not yet recovered; yet, in the same work, the author does not detect any of these ills until the time of Harsha, at the head of the last Indian Empire in the eighth century, and therefore undeniably long after the *Mahabharata* war: true, the castes were tending to become hereditary but they were not yet too fragmented, child marriages were only just starting to develop and more than anything else—a finally decisive criterion for Shraddhananda—till the time of Harsha, 'no non-Aryan community lived in India, and if some non-Aryans did come and settle down there, they were absorbed in the Hindu community...'.[90] It was after the Muslim invasions that the decline was hastened because they did not assimilate into the social system.

The fragmentation of an organic social system is thus perceived as the root cause of the decline, while the idea of a racial degeneration is simply omitted. The same phenomenon is obvious in the writings by Savarkar, Golwalkar and Bhai Parmanand in the 1920s and 1930s. These three authors consider the development of Buddhism as the first cause of decline, because of its sociological implications. Savarkar, in *Hindutva*, considers the promotion of 'ahimsa and spiritual brotherhood'[91] as a major factor of the invasion by the Huns and the Shakas, not only because the Hindus had lost their martial values, but also because they had been taught to consider their enemies as part of the same humanity from a universalistic point of view.[92]

Golwalkar's and Parmanand's analysis is more sociological. The former explains that the introduction of renunciation as the ultimate goal of religious life led to a new individualistic spirituality, something the ritualistic vedism did not know:

Over-individualisation in the field of religion followed and the consequence

[89] Ibid., p.79.
[90] Ibid., pp.5-6.
[91] Savarkar, *Hindutva*, p.20.
[92] Ibid., p.21.

was that the individual became more prominent than the society, the nation. For those whom the spirit of true religion did not touch intensely, this was another name for self-seeking, even at the cost of the welfare of the whole.[93]

The interchangeability of the words society and nation deserves to be noticed here because it is the key to Golwalkar's argument: the Hindu national decline began when the social corporate structure of the original *varna* system desintegrated under the impact of Buddhist principles.

This argument is formulated in a more explicit manner by Bhai Parmanand. In his book *Hindu Sangathan*, the rise of Buddhism is again described as the origin of the Hun invasion because 'the rosary could not be a match for the sword'.[94] Besides, its sociological implications were utterly destructive:

The ideal of personal salvation is the root-cause of our selfishness and this alone has been responsible for the downfall of our nation. It is diametrically opposed to the idea of social duties.... Instead of drawing the people's attention to their real duties under the caste and ashrama system [the *varnashrama vyavastha*] and trying to remove their defects [Buddha] wrongly concluded that these systems alone were responsible for all social evils.... The abolition of castes and ashramas cut at the very root of social duties. How could a nation hope to live after having lost sight of this aspect of Dharma? 'Equality for all' is an appealing abstraction; but the nation could not long survive the rejection or destruction of Dharma.[95]

Hindu degeneration is thus constantly interpreted as resulting primarily from the decline of a so-called vedic social order characterised by the organic solidarity and complementarity of hierarchised *varna*. In this process, the quest for individual salvation, initiated by Buddhism and the development of hereditary *jatis*, invented by the Brahmans, are seen as the main factor of the degradation. In this perspective, the aim of the Hindu nationalist movement is to remedy this situation by restoring the so-called original society whose organic unity designated it as a perfect nation model. The appeal to 'Hindu Sangathan', the organisation and unity of the Hindus, largely stemmed from this approach.

[93] Golwalkar, *We, or our nationhood defined*, p.14.
[94] Parmanand, *Hindu Sangathan* (Lahore, 1936), p.21.
[95] Ibid., pp.126-7.

Thus, in the Hindu nationalist ideology, the idea of decline is not related to the loss of racial purity. And the quest for revival does not imply any racial purification. On the contrary, the consolidation of Hindu society is presented as a preliminary stage likely to enable the Hindus to absorb the Muslims (descendents of non-Aryan invaders as well as 'natives').[96] The conception of decline expressed by the Hindu nationalist leaders of the 1920s and 1930s confirms a certain indifference towards racial purity compared to social unity.

The main conclusion of this enquiry seems to lie in the ambivalent response of the Hindu nationalist ideologues of the 1920s and 1930s to the European biological theories. These ideologues had inherited a 'traditional xenology' where the racial criterion was minimised compared to the degree of orthopraxy: the caste system reveals here its integrative capacity inasmuch as everybody can find a place in it according to one's rank. All in all, the hierarchical principle of the caste system makes the eugenic criterion of elimination difficult to apply: the exclusion can only be partial; it takes the form of a rejection at the periphery but not outside the whole of the society.

This does not mean that the Hindu nationalist ideologues did not expound a racial theory. They did so but it was more a racism of domination than a racism of extermination. This specificity was again in accordance with the 'traditional xenology': the Other is not excluded but he can be only integrated at a subordinate rank. The members of minorities who refuse to become Hinduised are bound to remain statutory second-rate citizens from the Hindu nationalist point of view. This kind of discrimination is, indeed, nothing but a form of 'upper caste racism'.

[96] In this respect the view of Bhai Parmanand is similar to the one of Savarkar and Golwalkar which we studied in the second section (ibid., p.188).